Comparative Insolvency Law

Comparative Insolvency Law

The Pre-pack Approach in Corporate Rescue

Bo Xie

Lecturer in Law, University of Dundee, UK

Edward Elgar
PUBLISHING

Cheltenham, UK • Northampton, MA, USA

Published by
Edward Elgar Publishing Limited
The Lypiatts
15 Lansdown Road
Cheltenham
Glos GL50 2JA
UK

Edward Elgar Publishing, Inc.
William Pratt House
9 Dewey Court
Northampton
Massachusetts 01060
USA

A catalogue record for this book
is available from the British Library

Library of Congress Control Number: 2016944273

This book is available electronically in the **Elgar**online
Law subject collection
DOI 10.4337/9781781007389

Printed on elemental chlorine free (ECF)
recycled paper containing 30% Post-Consumer Waste

ISBN 978 1 78100 737 2 (cased)
ISBN 978 1 78100 738 9 (eBook)

Typeset by Columns Design XML Ltd, Reading
Printed and bound in the USA

Contents

Preface

Corporate rescue, as an alternative to liquidation, has gained considerable popularity in insolvency practice on both sides of the Atlantic during the last three decades and in continental Europe in recent years. The pre-pack approach, in particular, has emerged as an innovative corporate rescue method that incorporates the virtues of both informal (out-of-court) and formal (judicial) insolvency proceedings. At the same time, an expedited and transaction cost-oriented approach to insolvency might prejudice the interests of certain classes of creditors negating, to an extent, time-honoured essential features of insolvency law like creditor participation as it is their interests that are at stake.

This book provides a critical analysis of corporate rescue, drawing on a variety of legal and policy-making sources both at the national and the international level. It examines the pre-pack approach to corporate rescue using a comparative angle and offers a discussion and evaluation of mechanisms that facilitate corporate rescue in comparing those of the UK (in terms of economic importance), EU jurisdictions and the USA. The book goes beyond the well-known advantages of the pre-pack approach to examine the undesirable effects it may have as it gives rise to the risk that corporate rescue practice might develop under the shadow of the law and give rise to a far greater potential for self-serving behaviour that existing law could otherwise tightly curtail. Clearly, conflict of interests and even the likelihood of self-dealing by management are less well regulated in the context of pre-pack proceedings than under formal insolvency law and this intensifies the concerns over potential abuses or just opportunistic behaviour by insiders who might attempt to game the system to benefit themselves at the expense of others. To properly and thoroughly discuss these issues, the book is structured around the examination of eight questions, which are each the subject of study of a specific chapter.

To this effect, the first chapter deals with the concept of 'corporate rescue': the challenges corporate rescue efforts may face, and how the pre-pack approach, as a hybrid of out-of-court (informal) and formal ways of rescue, copes with those challenges. Is this pragmatic approach capable of accommodating different goals in corporate rescue? Chapter 2 considers how pre-pack administrations fit into the development of the English corporate rescue system, and why they are developed so rapidly in practice, despite their controversial reputation. What are the practical effects of the pre-determination feature of pre-packs on the conventional role of administrators? In Chapters 3 and 4, the book examines what contributes to the particular risks of the opportunistic use of pre-pack sales to connected parties. What are the possible solutions to address the concerns that have been raised? Would heightened standards of disclosure and newly fashioned professional regulations be sufficient to achieve their set goals, namely, protection of general creditors from management's opportunistic behaviour?

After this general discussion and examination of pre-packs in the UK law context, the book proceeds, in Chapters 5 and 6, to examine how the pre-pack approaches have changed the insolvency landscape in the USA. Two increasingly popular US practices possess 'pre-pack' characteristics by fast-tracking the US Chapter 11 reorganisation procedure: pre-packaged bankruptcy filings and section 363(b) pre-plan sales. They are both examined in Chapters 5 and 6 respectively.

The key inquiry as regards pre-packaged bankruptcy filings relates to the requirement of pre-petition solicitation of votes and their implications on creditor protection. Moreover, s 363(b) pre-plan sales as a substitute for true reorganisation may be the closest to UK pre-pack sales in the sense that both processes aim at value realisation through expedited going-concern sales coupled with a denial of creditor participation in the process. In this context the following issues are examined in depth in Chapter 6: What are the standards the US bankruptcy courts apply when permitting a particular s 363 pre-plan sale? Is the judicial scrutiny adequate and effective in distinguishing expedited sales in which speed is essential and those in which it is merely tactical? How does the US approach in ameliorating the concerns of abuse raised in the accelerated sale process in insolvency differ with that of the UK?

In recent years and in part as a response to forum shopping by continental European companies nearing bankruptcy, many European countries have enacted reforms to their insolvency framework in order to meet the challenges of the changing economic environment. Accordingly, Chapter 7 examines the pre-pack or equivalent mechanisms that have been implemented or are under consideration in select European jurisdictions, namely, France, Germany and the Netherlands. What are the strengths and weaknesses of each system in utilising the pre-pack and similar approaches in corporate rescue while limiting the negative impact that the speed through which proceedings are concluded has on accountability to and adequacy of safeguards for creditors?

Chapter 8 examines the implications of the UK pre-pack proceedings on insolvency forum shopping for companies that are mindful to effectuate a quick pre-packed business sale through the administration procedure. What are the challenges this phenomenon poses amid recent changes that the EU policy-makers are contemplating in order to provide a common set of rules to first regulate conflict-of-law issues at the European level and, then, to act as a driver for domestic legislative changes that are intended to address the challenge of forum shopping in Europe?

Finally, Chapter 9 provides the conclusion. It consolidates the findings of analysis undertaken in the preceding chapters, including comparative analysis. On that basis this chapter makes a number of proposals to augment control mechanisms in order to limit the controversy surrounding the pre-pack business sales to connected parties in the UK, and improve the levels of scrutiny and transparency in the key decision-making process.

Table of cases

Table of legislation

PART I

Introduction

1. Corporate rescue – the new orientation of insolvency law

INTRODUCTION

In the modern legal regime for corporate insolvency there are two basic routes which can be followed in dealing with a company that is failing: liquidation and corporate rescue. Both provide a collective way of settling the fate of the company when the claimants cannot resolve the company's financial troubles through private negotiations. Yet they provide two distinct paths to address the financial difficulties of a business. Liquidation serves the basic purpose of winding up an ailing company through an orderly collection and realisation of assets for the benefit of the claimants. The net value that is gathered through this collective debt collection process is then distributed among claimants according to a statutory system of priorities. On the other hand, corporate rescue procedures provide an alternative to the immediate liquidation of the ailing company, seeking to provide companies in financial difficulty with a period of respite in which compromises and rescue arrangements can be made. But, what exactly do we mean when we use the term 'corporate rescue'? What values and purposes does it serve? How can a rescue be achieved? What conceptual, legal and practical problems arise in relation to corporate rescue?

This introductory chapter will offer a brief overview of the above issues in order to provide the contextual background to the use of 'pre-packs' as a corporate rescue strategy. This chapter is divided into six sections. After these introductory remarks, sections 2 and 3 provide essential definitions for the purposes of this book. Section 4 reviews theories underpinning the goals of insolvency law and corporate rescue, examining how the various and competing goals that underlie the insolvency system could be effectively served. Section 5 considers different approaches to retaining the going-concern value in businesses that are in financial distress and the unique features of pre-pack restructuring. The last section reflects on the challenges in corporate rescue, and points out what causes controversy comes from in the case of the pre-pack rescue approach.

THE CONCEPT OF CORPORATE RESCUE

The term 'corporate rescue' is understood in very different ways by policy-makers, judges and scholars. These differences often stem from the divergent standpoints regarding the approaches and purposes of rescue actions in response to companies' financial troubles. First, corporate rescue can be premised on (contractually agreed) informal mechanisms as well as on formal collective legal proceedings. Professor Belcher defined the term 'corporate rescue' as 'a major intervention necessary to avert eventual failure of the company'.[1] Such a broad definition encompasses any drastic remedial action to a company at a time of corporate crisis, including both the informal and formal strategic rescue responses.[2] In contrast, a narrow definition of the term uses it to cover only the operation of legal proceedings, which offer facilitating mechanisms for rescuing financially distressed companies. Furthermore, the term may be defined differently as a way to reflect the various outcomes of rescue activities. Corporate rescue, or 'corporate reorganisation' in North American terminology, may be regarded as an alternative to immediate liquidation of the company, with the aim to prevent the death of the company. In the UK, the scope of rescue is wider, including both a turnaround of the company and alternatively preserving the core of a company's business. Underlining such differences is the distinction between 'company rescue' and 'business rescue'.

Company rescue works towards the restoration of a company in difficulty, which leads to the preservation of the legal entity itself so that the company can continue operations after reorganisation. In contrast, business rescue implies the termination of the old company, but the actual business and its activities will remain as a cohesive, productive unit under new ownership. This happens where a company is insolvent but successful steps are taken to retain the business as an operational enterprise, to sustain the employment of groups of workers and to ensure the survival of some economic activity.[3] Company rescue often involves changes in the management of the company and is usually achieved through

---

1 A Belcher, *Corporate Rescue* (Sweet and Maxwell, London 1997), 12.

2 *Ibid.*, 12.

3 V Finch, *Corporate Insolvency Law: Perspectives and Principles* (2nd edn, CUP, Cambridge 2009), 188.

reorganising methods such as refinancing, debt composition or rescheduling, downsizing activities, and making redundant part of the workforce to offer temporary relief.[4] Business rescue is commonly achieved through the sale of the company's assets and business as a going concern, which, as commonly believed, could generate more value than assets being sold in a piecemeal fashion.

For the purposes of this book, the term 'corporate rescue' will refer to collective strategic rescue proceedings under a legal framework designed to facilitate either the preservation of the distressed company itself or the rescue of its underlying business by transferring it to a new owner. It should be clarified that rescue outcomes can be achieved not only through rescue-oriented proceedings but also through a liquidation procedure. As mentioned earlier, the liquidation procedure is oriented to the winding-up of the company by ceasing its operations, realising its assets and paying off its debts and liabilities.[5] In the process of realising its assets, a result that amounts to a rescue may be achieved where the company's assets are sold in the form of a complete takeover or a bulk sale of the assets, which involves the sale of the entire business, including goodwill and other intangibles.[6] Nevertheless, despite the rescue outcomes, the liquidation procedure is not recognised as part of corporate rescue proceedings in the sense used here since its goal is different. The distinctive feature of a rescue procedure is that it is designed to capture the going-concern surplus in corporate restructurings and insolvency, in general. The going-concern surplus can be obtained if the business and assets are preserved as an operating unit, surviving either through a successful company turnaround or reorganisation, or through a going-concern sale, where the whole or substantial business and assets of the ailing company are preserved.

---

[4] J Armour, A Hsu, and A Walters, *The Impact of the Enterprise Act 2002 on Realisations and Costs in Corporate Rescue Proceedings* (2006) Report to The Insolvency Service <http://citeseerx.ist.psu.edu/viewdoc/download?doi=10.1.1.96.6853&rep=rep1&type=pdf> accessed 30 July 2015, 2.

[5] G McCormack, *Corporate Rescue Law: An Anglo-American Perspective* (Edward Elgar, Cheltenham 2008), 3.

[6] J Armour, 'The Law and Economics of Corporate Insolvency: A Review' (2001) ESRC Centre for Business Research, University of Cambridge, Working Paper No. 197 <http://www.econ.jku.at/members/Buchegger/files/Juristen/armour_2001_corporate%20insolvency.pdf> accessed 30 July 2015, 4.

THE SURPLUS OF GOING-CONCERN VALUE

It is commonly acknowledged that the rationale of corporate rescue is to capture the surplus of going-concern value of the assets of the ailing company, in that the value of a company's business operations is likely to be far greater than the scrap value of its assets.[7] As has been noted: '[w]e have a going-concern surplus (the thing the law of corporate reorganisations exists to preserve) only to the extent that there are assets that are worth more if located within an existing firm. If all the assets can be used as well elsewhere, the firm has no value as a going concern.'[8] The expression 'going-concern value' is contrasted with piecemeal liquidation value, which is referred to as the value realised when the parts of the business and assets are broken up and sold off separately. The going-concern value could be measured by estimating the income stream that the assets would generate if they were kept together, taking into account the risk of reorganisation failure and comparing it to the amount that the assets would realise if they were sold off separately.[9]

But what are the sources of going-concern surplus that exceed their piecemeal liquidation value? In other words, where does the additional value come from? Traditional thinking places the source of going-concern surplus in the intangibles associated with the running of the business, such as goodwill and intellectual property. It follows that salvaging a company's going-concern value can be achieved by holding together a 'bundle' of intangible assets (patents, accounts receivable, customer lists and orders, etc.) and employees, and outsourcing most manufacturing activities. Nevertheless, this assertion has been challenged in the wake of the tremendous change in fundamental forces at work in the economy, brought on especially by the decline of heavy industry, technological advances, easier access to capital and credit markets, globalisation and the birth of a service-based economy. The premise of the going-concern value in the traditional sense has also been questioned by the argument that if the intangible assets are the only source of the going-concern surplus, most failed companies may be said to have no

---

[7] McCormack, *Corporate Rescue Law: An Anglo-American Perspective*, 3.

[8] DG Baird and RK Rasmussen, 'The End of Bankruptcy' (2002) 55 *Stanford Law Review* 751, 758.

[9] See DG Baird and TH Jackson, 'Corporate Reorganisation and the Treatment of Diverse Ownership Interests: A Comment of Adequate Protection of Secured Creditors in Bankruptcy' (1984) 51 *University of Chicago Law Review* 97, 109. See also TH Jackson, *The Logic and Limits of Bankruptcy Law* (Harvard University Press, Harvard 1986), 184.

going-concern surplus, as their failure is usually due to their lack of valuable intangible assets, having neither a sound business strategy nor a good reputation.[10]

The basis of the modern economy has transformed from the traditional manufacturing activity to the information-based economy, in which the most valuable resource may be human capital and relationship networks.[11] It is argued that going-concern value resides principally in various relationships 'among people, among assets, and between peoples[sic] and assets'.[12] Costs incurred in creating most of these necessary relationships will inevitably be lost if the business is scattered to the wind through a piecemeal sale of assets,[13] and starting a business from scratch is expensive and time consuming and entails a large degree of entrepreneurial risk.[14] These points have been well made by the legal department of the International Monetary Fund:

> in the modern economy, the degree to which an enterprise's value can be maximised through liquidation of its assets has been significantly reduced. In circumstances where the value of a company is increasingly based on technical know-how and goodwill rather than on its physical assets, preservation of the enterprise's human resources and business relations may be critical for creditors wishing to maximise the value of their claims.[15]

DIVERSE THEORIES OF INSOLVENCY LAW AND THE GOALS OF CORPORATE RESCUE

Although it has been commonly recognised that corporate rescue is concerned with how to capture and maximise the going-concern surplus of distressed companies and how to distribute it among corporate

---

[10] See DG Baird and RK Rasmussen, 'Chapter 11 at Twilight' (2003) 56 *Stanford Law Review* 673, and Baird and Rasmussen, 'The End of Bankruptcy', 751.

[11] McCormack, *Corporate Rescue Law: An Anglo-American Perspective*, 7.

[12] L Lopucki, 'The Nature of the Bankrupt Firm: A Reply to Baird and Rasmussen's The End of Bankruptcy' (2003) 56 *Stanford Law Review* 645, 652.

[13] McCormack, *Corporate Rescue Law: An Anglo-American Perspective*, 4–5.

[14] H Miller and S Waisman, 'Does Chapter 11 Reorganisation Remain a Viable Option for Distressed Businesses for the Twenty-First Century?' (2004) 78 *American Bankruptcy Law Journal* 153, 192–3.

[15] Legal Department of International Monetary Fund, *Orderly & Effective Insolvency Procedures: Key Issues* (1999) <http://www.imf.org/external/pubs/ft/orderly/> accessed 30 July 2015.

constituents, different standpoints have been taken on the ways and means of realising this maximisation and whose interests should be protected. In order to reflect these different points of view, it is important to understand the diverse normative theories and hypotheses about the appropriate objectives and purposes of corporate insolvency law.

The modern debate began in the US during the 1980s over the question whether insolvency law does – or should – seek only to maximise the returns to pay creditors of an insolvent company, or whether other goals do or should matter; such as preserving jobs, rehabilitating troubled companies and protecting the interests of local communities.[16] Among the competing views on the goals or values that insolvency law should reflect, on one side, there is a 'market and assets' camp focusing on the assets of the debtor and value maximisation for creditors. On the opposite side is the 'enterprise and forum' camp, which argues that preserving an enterprise is to the benefit of many more interests than merely those of the owners and creditors, and the function of bankruptcy procedures is to establish a forum where all the interests which may be affected by the business failure can be heard.[17]

The Creditors' Bargain Theory

The creditors' bargain theory was advanced and developed by Professor Thomas Jackson with Douglas Baird and Robert Scott.[18] The classical argument it propounded is that corporate insolvency law, at its core a collective debt collection mechanism, should be concerned only with the maximisation of creditors' returns and creditors' distribution questions.[19]

---

[16] Armour, *The Law and Economics of Corporate Insolvency: A Review*, 8.

[17] A Flessner, 'Philosophies of Business Bankruptcy Law: An International Overview' in JS Ziegel (ed) *Current Developments in International and Comparative Corporate Insolvency Law* (OUP, Oxford 1994), 13–24.

[18] See TH Jackson, 'Bankruptcy, Non-Bankruptcy Entitlements, and the Creditors' Bargain' (1982) 91 *Yale Law Journal* 857; also Jackson, *The Logic and Limits of Bankruptcy Law*; DG Baird and TH Jackson, 'Bargaining After the Fall and the Contours of the Absolute Priority Rule' (1988) 55 *University of Chicago Law Review* 738; Baird and Jackson, 'Corporate Reorganizations and the Treatment of Diverse Ownership Interests: A Comment on Adequate Protection of Secured Creditors in Bankruptcy'; T Jackson and R Scott, 'An Essay on Bankruptcy Sharing and the Creditors' Bargain' (1989) 75 *Virginia Law Review* 155.

[19] For the description of the common pool problem, see Jackson, *The Logic and Limits of Bankruptcy Law*, 11–12; and Baird and Jackson, 'Corporate

First, it views insolvency law as a collectivised debt collection mechanism and as a response to the 'common pool' problem.[20] To prevent the destruction of value caused by individual creditor actions against assets, interested persons need to act collectively.[21] The collectivist compulsory system of insolvency law is justified on the grounds of a hypothetical bargain assumption that were company creditors free to agree on forms of enforcement of their claims on insolvency, they would agree to collectivist arrangements rather than procedures of individual action or partial collectivism.[22]

Second, the cornerstone of the creditors' bargain theory is the normative claim that pre-insolvent entitlements should not be impaired in the collective insolvency process.[23] Through a hypothetical bargain that focuses on the key bankruptcy objective of maximising the welfare of the group through collectivisation, the creditors agree to act as a group under a regime replicating their non-bankruptcy collection rights.[24] Bankruptcy law should change a substantive non-bankruptcy rule only when doing so preserves the value of assets for the group of investors holding rights in them.[25] Third, the broad concerns regarding business failures and social welfare are not bankruptcy problems at all but 'that of the bulk of laws outside of bankruptcy'.[26] As it is accepted here that bankruptcy law is primarily concerned with recognising non-bankruptcy entitlements and ensuring a deployment of assets that is in the interests of all those with rights to the assets under state law, it follows that the problems brought

---

Reorganizations and the Treatment of Diverse Ownership Interests: A Comment on Adequate Protection of Secured Creditors in Bankruptcy', 103–5.

20 Jackson, *The Logic and Limits of Bankruptcy Law*, 9–11.

21 Baird and Jackson, 'Corporate Reorganizations and the Treatment of Diverse Ownership Interests: A Comment on Adequate Protection of Secured Creditors in Bankruptcy', 106.

22 Jackson sees bankruptcy as 'a system designed to mirror the agreement one would expect the creditors to form among themselves were they to negotiate such an agreement from an *ex ante* position'. See T Jackson, 'Bankruptcy, Non-Bankruptcy Entitlements, and the Creditors' Bargain' (1982) 91 *Yale Law Journal* 857, 860.

23 Jackson and Scott, 'An Essay on Bankruptcy Sharing and the Creditors' Bargain', 159.

24 'A central premise underlying the creditors' bargain theory is that a system of state law entitlements (including priorities among secured and unsecured creditors) is already in place.' *Ibid.*, 159.

25 Baird and Jackson, 'Corporate Reorganizations and the Treatment of Diverse Ownership Interests: A Comment on Adequate Protection of Secured Creditors in Bankruptcy', 100.

26 *Ibid.*, 103.

by business failures are not bankruptcy problems. Bankruptcy proceedings should not be the place to implement a policy that society does not enforce outside of bankruptcy and that is unrelated to the preservation of assets for the firm's investor group.[27] It follows from the above arguments under this theory that the protection of the non-creditor interests of other victims of corporate misfortune, such as employees, managers, suppliers and the community at large ought not to be a concern of insolvency law.[28]

The creditor wealth maximisation argument has been highly influential and has been put into legislative effect in many jurisdictions.[29] However, this normative theory has been subject to extensive criticism by a number of schools of thought. Major concerns have focused on challenging the claim that insolvency is simply a debt collection process for the benefit of creditors and that the only legitimate goal of insolvency law is creditor wealth maximisation. The creditor wealth approach considers only hypothetical contract creditors, which is only one group of victims suffering from the company's financial distress, and this, it has been said, fails to take account of the wide range of other stakeholders (for instance, employees, dependent suppliers, regular customers and the local community at large) that the corporate insolvency may have an impact on.[30] It is criticised that the creditor wealth maximisation view focuses only on

---

[27] *Ibid.*, 102.

[28] Jackson, *The Logic and Limits of Bankruptcy Law*, 25. See also Baird and Jackson, 'Corporate Reorganizations and the Treatment of Diverse Ownership Interests: A Comment on Adequate Protection of Secured Creditors in Bankruptcy', 103. It recognises these problems as general problems, not as bankruptcy problems. Therefore: 'Social reform should be brought about through a broad changes in the substantive law rather than through ad hoc modifications of rights in bankruptcy.'

[29] Such as the German Insolvency Code of 1994. The English insolvency law also provides some support for this argument. The interests of creditors take primacy over the interests of all other groups when the company seems to be in financial distress. It can also be seen from the shift of the directors' fiduciary duty of loyalty to the creditors of the company in the 'twilight' period and the administrator's duty to act in the interests of creditors as a whole. See Finch, *Corporate Insolvency Law: Perspectives and Principles*, 29 and Armour, 'The Law and Economics of Corporate Insolvency: A Review'.

[30] DR Korobkin, 'Contractarianism and the Normative Foundations of Bankruptcy Law' (1993) 71 *Texas Law Review* 541, 555. See also E Warren, 'Bankruptcy Policy' (1987) 54 *University of Chicago Law Review* 775, 787–8.

economic value and is incapable of recognising non-economic value aspects, such as moral, political, social and personal considerations.[31]

Rejecting the view that bankruptcy law is merely a response to the problem of collecting debt, Professor Korobkin presents a value-based account which views bankruptcy law as 'a response to the many aspects of financial distress – moral, political, personal, social, and economic – and, in particular, to the grievances of those who are affected by financial distress'.[32] Because the participants' varied grievances typically reflect conflicting and fundamentally incommensurable values, bankruptcy law has a distinct function to provide a forum for an ongoing debate in which these diverse values can be expressed and sometimes recognised.[33] Moreover, the idea that a troubled company constitutes a mere pool of assets is also challenged. It is claimed that the company is not purely a lifeless pool of assets but an enterprise with personality:

> Unlike mere property, a corporation, whether in or out of bankruptcy, has potential. A corporation can continue as an enterprise: as an enterprise, it can change its personality and, perhaps more importantly, whether the corporation continues and how it changes its personality affects people in ways that are not only economic.[34]

Professor Elizabeth Warren has criticised the creditors' bargain theory for facilitating the externalisation of costs. She noted that many of the social costs incurred in the creation of a firm were borne by those parties who are not creditors and who have no formal rights to the assets of the business, such as employees, communities, suppliers, customers and others. When the firm failed, those parties were left with the costs as the parties with formal legal rights against the debtor never completely internalise the full costs of a business failure.[35] Therefore it is argued that insolvency law should look beyond pre-insolvency rights and recognise the interests of parties who lack formal legal rights in the pre-insolvency

---

[31] See DR Korobkin, 'Rehabilitating Values: A Jurisprudence of Bankruptcy' (1991) 91 *Columbia Law Review* 717, 762. Korobkin, 'Contractarianism and the Normative Foundations of Bankruptcy Law', 581. Korobkin pointed out that 'the problem of collecting debt is a complex one, implicating moral, political, personal, social, as well as economic values'.

[32] See Korobkin, 'Rehabilitating Values: A Jurisprudence of Bankruptcy', 721.

[33] *Ibid.*, 721–2.

[34] *Ibid.*, 745.

[35] E Warren, 'Bankruptcy Policy Making in an Imperfect World' (1993) 92 *Michigan Law Review* 336, 356.

scenarios as the protection insolvency law gives to these parties is derivative in nature and limited in scope.[36]

A Broad-based Contractarian Model

In his later work, Professor Donald Korobkin offered an alternative contractarian model, insisting on his proposition that the main purpose of bankruptcy law is to exist as a distinct system that deals with the general problems of financial distress, and not to specifically address the problem of recovering debt.[37] Instead of viewing insolvency law as the set of rules that contractual creditors would agree to from behind the veil of ignorance,[38] Korobkin considered bankruptcy legislation to be 'the product of social exigency, moral conflict, and political compromise'.[39] He propounded a normative framework for bankruptcy law based on a hypothetical bargain struck by the representatives of all interests that might be affected by a company's decline.[40] There should be some 'normative foundations' of bankruptcy law on which conflicting parties develop their arguments. The normative principles will prescribe limits on how bankruptcy law should alter the rights, authority and practical leverage of persons in financial distress, and offer a justified standpoint for evaluating which legal, political and personal advantages ought to be preserved and which ought to be modified.[41]

By constructing a hypothetical 'initial status quo' for the choice of the normative principles, Korobkin asserted that the parties would choose

---

[36] *Ibid.*

[37] See Korobkin, 'Contractarianism and the Normative Foundations of Bankruptcy Law'.

[38] The 'veil of ignorance' is a position in which: 'no one knows his place in society, his class position or social status; nor does he know his fortune in the distribution of natural assets and abilities, his intelligence and strength, and the like. Nor, again, does anyone know his conception of the good, the particulars of his rational plan of life, or even the special features of his psychology such as his aversion to risk or liability to optimism or pessimism.' See Korobkin *ibid.*, 564 referring to Rawls' famous concept, utilised as an important building block of his theory of justice. See further J Rawls, *A Theory of Justice* (Harvard University Press, Harvard 1971).

[39] Korobkin, 'Contractarianism and the Normative Foundations of Bankruptcy Law', 543.

[40] McCormack, *Corporate Rescue Law: An Anglo-American Perspective*, 28.

[41] Korobkin, 'Contractarianism and the Normative Foundations of Bankruptcy Law', 551.

two principles to govern insolvencies: (1) the 'principle of inclusion' and (2) the 'principle of rational planning'.[42] The principle of inclusion emphasises that all affected parties would be eligible to press their demands in the context of financial distress, although this does not speak to all parties whose particular demands should ultimately be recognised or denied.[43] The 'principle of rational planning' has two essential ingredients: (1) the insolvency law must be broadly effective, promoting as many aims as possible; (2) when it is not possible to achieve all the aims, it must work to achieve the aims that are most important.[44] On this model, the bargainers all know they may be affected by the insolvency, but no one knows if he will be: a debtor; an unsecured creditor whether contractual or involuntary; a secured creditor; an ordinary employee; a member of the community that is otherwise unconnected to the debtor company; or somebody in a different kind of relationship.[45] Therefore, the bargainers would prefer a principle that is 'somehow capable of maximising their welfare whichever positions they happened to occupy in varying contexts'.[46] But if no principle can guarantee the best outcome for all parties under all circumstances, then 'as a matter of self-interest under conditions of radical uncertainty, they would want a principle that had the effect of mitigating, at least to some degree, the hardship experienced by persons in the worst-off positions'.[47] Those in the worst-off position are 'relatively powerless in promoting their aims' and since they 'have the most to lose if their aims are frustrated', are the most vulnerable.[48] Therefore, the principle of rational planning is to maximally satisfy the aims of parties as a whole by virtue of protecting the most vulnerable parties in the context of financial distress over those who are less vulnerable.

The contractarian approach has been subjected to extensive criticism. It has been said that *ex ante* hypothetical bargain theories of insolvency law are open to the objection that they amount to little more than an argument that thoughtful, interested, objective and neutral law makers would come

---

[42] *Ibid.*, 575–89.

[43] *Ibid.*, 575.

[44] *Ibid.*, 581.

[45] McCormack, *Corporate Rescue Law: An Anglo-American Perspective*, 28.

[46] See Korobkin, 'Contractarianism and the Normative Foundations of Bankruptcy Law', 578.

[47] *Ibid.*, 579.

[48] *Ibid.*, 584.

to the proponent's conclusions about insolvency.[49] By constructing a hypothetical original position in which the various players act in an economically rational manner according to a single set of criteria, the contractarian approach is unable to recognise the complex realities of business life and the many possible considerations the decision-makers may take into account in the matrix of circumstances.[50] Furthermore, the value-based account does not in itself explain clearly important distributional issues, such as how to judge trade-offs between fairness or justice and wealth creation, and neither does it provide a working standard to measure this. It is further argued that the contractarian approach fails to explain how agreements can be reached behind the veil as to who in a potential insolvency is most vulnerable and thus should enjoy priority of protection over those occupying less threatened positions.[51]

The Team Production Theory

A team production theory of corporate reorganisation law has been recently developed by Professor Lynn LoPucki.[52] It is based on the original team production theory of the corporation introduced by Margaret Blair and Lynn Stout in 1999,[53] in which the interests of corporation are understood as 'a joint welfare function of *all* the individuals who make firm-specific investments and agree to participate in the extra-contractual, internal mediation process within the firm'.[54] The team membership may include: stockholders; company managers; other employees; suppliers; creditors; customers; local governments; regulatory agencies and others.[55] In order to share all the costs and benefits of incorporation, and because of the impossibility of reaching that effect through direct contracts in some circumstances, team members

---

[49] See McCormack, *Corporate Rescue Law: An Anglo-American Perspective*, 29–30 referring to CW Mooney 'A Normative Theory of Bankruptcy Law', whose comments were framed with particular reference to Korobkin's theory.

[50] McCormack, *Corporate Rescue Law: An Anglo-American Perspective*, 30.

[51] See Finch, *Corporate Insolvency Law: Perspectives and Principles*, 39–40.

[52] LoPucki, 'A Team Production Theory of Bankruptcy Reorganisation' (2004) 557 *Vanderbilt Law Review* 741.

[53] MM Blair and LA Stout, 'A Team Production Theory of Corporate Law' (1999) 85 *Virginia Law Review* 247.

[54] *Ibid.*, 288.

[55] LoPucki, 'A Team Production Theory of Bankruptcy Reorganisation', 749.

can delegate an independent authority group – the board of directors – to divide profit and loss among them, based on each member's contributions to the team.[56] Under the team production theory, corporate reorganisation is viewed not as a regulation imposed by government but instead as 'a contract term by which creditors and shareholders agree to subordinate their legal rights to the preservation of the going concern'.[57] The preservation of the corporate entity is an independent value that partially accounts for the choice of reorganisation over liquidation.[58]

By leaving the board of directors in full control, while at the same time limiting creditors and shareholders to their bankruptcy entitlements, the team production contract has, in effect, granted the non-legally enforceable entitlements of team member priority over the legally enforceable claims of creditors and the interests of shareholders.[59] Professor LoPucki asserts that this treatment is appropriate because honouring team production entitlements is efficient as those entitlements are payable under the team production contract and the team production contract is the bargain actually struck by team members. This is not only to reward past contributions, but also to incentivise future contribution to the team effort.[60] The calculation of the benefits of reorganisation must also take into account distributions to all team members instead of only those to creditors and shareholders.

In a nutshell, the team production theory attempts to offer a justification of corporate reorganisation by adopting the new contractarian theory of the public corporation introduced by Professors Blair and Stout in 1999 to the bankruptcy reorganisation regime. Nevertheless, critical questions remain unresolved. The theory relies on an independent board of directors, acting as fiduciaries, to divide profit and loss among them based on the team members' respective contributions to the team. But it remains debatable whether the directors will do 'the right thing', given that the theory is based on a 'wholesale grant of unfettered power to directors'.[61] It is asserted that directors would function less like disinterested trustees and more like representatives in a legislature who are expected to vigorously defend the interests of the particular constituents

---

[56] Blair and Stout, 'A Team Production Theory of Corporate Law', 749–50.

[57] LoPucki, 'A Team Production Theory of Bankruptcy Reorganisation', 743.

[58] *Ibid.*, 769.

[59] *Ibid.*, 758.

[60] *Ibid.*, 750.

[61] *Ibid.*, 778.

who elect them.[62] It is explicitly accepted that team members trust directors not because they think directors will do a good job, but because team members lack better alternatives.[63]

The Multiple Values/Eclectic Approach

Professor Elisabeth Warren considers that the creditors' bargain theory, as a single, unified theory of bankruptcy, is more of an intellectual view of bankruptcy than a complex one and runs a great risk of providing answers that, while quite sensible within confined, abstract schemes, will not work in a complex real-life corporate environment.[64] She has offered a 'dirty, complex, elastic, interconnected view of bankruptcy' from which outcomes cannot be predicted, and nor can all the factors relevant to a policy decision be fully articulated.[65] She explained what she has offered is 'a comprehensive statement about the various and competing goals that underlie the bankruptcy system' so as to provide useful assistance to the legislative and judicial decision-making.[66]

Warren describes bankruptcy as a collection system that determines: the value of a failing business; how to distribute that value among parties whom the failure affects; and the extent to which affected parties can externalise the costs of failure to others who did not deal with the debtor. This system, according to her, is aimed toward four principal goals:

> (1) to enhance the value of the failing debtor; (2) to distribute value according to multiple normative principles; (3) to internalise the costs of the business failure to the parties dealing with the debtor; and (4) to create reliance on private monitoring.[67]

---

[62] See Blair and Stout, 'A Team Production Theory of Corporate Law', footnote 136 at p 302.

[63] LoPucki, 'A Team Production Theory of Bankruptcy Reorganisation', 778.

[64] Warren, 'Bankruptcy Policy Making in an Imperfect World', 813.

[65] *Ibid.*, 811.

[66] 'I have not offered a single-rationale policy that compels solutions in a particular case. I have not given any answers to specific statutory issues. I have only identified normative considerations that may drive legislative and judicial decisions.' *Ibid.*, 795–6.

[67] Warren, 'Bankruptcy Policy Making in an Imperfect World', 343–4.

Unlike in the creditors' bargain theory where pre-insolvency entitlements should never be impaired to accomplish purely distributional goals,[68] Warren asserts bankruptcy law can alter the interested parties' non-bankruptcy rights because bankruptcy and non-bankruptcy rights laws deal with different kinds of default. Non-bankruptcy law provides a collection scheme that copes with the single default where only one creditor complains about repayment. On the other hand, the bankruptcy collection scheme concentrates on the debtor's widespread default and the collapse of every creditor's prospects for repayment.[69] The policy issues involved in the two scenarios present critical differences and thus different distributive schemes ought to be adopted.[70]

Warren listed a series of distributive rationales of bankruptcy law, such as favouring creditors but also pointed out that the distributive goals may conflict with each other. She asserted that it is difficult or even impossible to provide a consistent answer to questions such as how to reallocate the resources and how to solve the conflict between the different distributive goals.

With regard to the question of whose interests bankruptcy should serve, Professor Warren views bankruptcy as 'an attempt to reckon with a debtor's multiple defaults and to distribute the consequences among a number of different actors'.[71] Although bankruptcy encompasses a number of competing and sometimes conflicting values in this distribution, no one value, she asserted, should dominate so that bankruptcy policy can be a composite of factors that offers a better answer to the question 'how shall the losses be distributed?'[72] In her view, however, the insolvency regime only protects the interests of parties without formal legal rights in an indirect fashion, largely through provisions that permit businesses to reorganise instead of being shut down by a few anxious creditors.[73]

---

[68] Jackson and Scott, 'An Essay on Bankruptcy Sharing and the Creditors' Bargain', 159.

[69] Warren noticed that there are: 'two prototypes of default: first, the single default where only one creditor complains about repayment and the remaining creditors are evidently (even if only temporarily) content with their repayment prospects; and second, the debtor's widespread default and collapse in which every creditors' prospects for payment are sharply diminished.' See Warren, 'Bankruptcy Policy Making in an Imperfect World', 781.

[70] *Ibid.*, 782.

[71] *Ibid.*, 777.

[72] *Ibid.*

[73] Warren, 'Bankruptcy Policy Making in an Imperfect World', 355–6.

The Explicit Values Approach to Insolvency Law

The aforementioned debate is primarily American. Similar debates on the objectives of corporate insolvency and the values of corporate rescue have also taken place in the UK. UK bankruptcy legislation has been rather creditor-oriented with an unforgiving attitude toward unpaid debt and credit. A liquidation culture prevailed in England until 1986, when deep recessions caused Parliament to reassess this position.[74] In the Cork Report[75] which was published in 1982, the Review Committee suggested that the aims of a good modern insolvency law should include those that:

> (i) recognise the effects of insolvency are not limited to the private interests of the insolvent and his creditors, but that other interests of society or other groups in society are vitally affected by the insolvency and its outcome, and to ensure that these public interests are recognised and safeguarded;
>
> (j) provide means for the preservation of viable commercial enterprises capable of making a useful contribution to the economic life of the country;[76]

It emphasised the social and personal detriment caused by shutdowns and wholesale redundancy[77] and the benefits to the country's economic life of preserving viable commercial enterprises, because corporate failure was usually accompanied by wider repercussions falling not only upon intimately connected parties such as directors, shareholders and employees, but also on other interests, such as suppliers.[78]

---

74 PR Wood, *Principles of International Insolvency* (2nd edn, Sweet and Maxwell 2007), 175.

75 Kenneth Cork and Insolvency Law Review Committee, *Insolvency Law and Practice: Report of the Review Committee* (Cmnd 8558, 1982). The Cork Committee, the chairman of which was the late Sir Kenneth Cork, was appointed in 1977 with wide-ranging terms of reference covering corporate and individual insolvency. Its report led to a government White Paper in 1984 – A Revised Framework for Insolvency Law (Cmnd 9175, 1984), setting out an intention to implement the bulk, but not all, of the Committee's recommendations. This eventually led to the Insolvency Act 1986.

76 Cork and Committee, *Insolvency Law and Practice: Report of the Review Committee*, 54–5. There were (a) to (l) aspects contained in the aims of a good modern insolvency law.

77 IF Fletcher, 'UK Corporate Rescue: Recent Developments – Changes to Administrative Receivership, Administration, and Company Voluntary Arrangements – the Insolvency Act 2000, the White Paper 2001, and the Enterprise Act 2002' (2004) 5 *European Business Organization Law Review* 119, 122.

78 Cork and Committee, *Insolvency Law and Practice: Report of the Review Committee*, 56.

Professor Sir Roy Goode also suggests that corporate insolvency law should have four overriding objectives: (1) to rescue the debtor company where this is practicable; (2) to maximise the return to creditors as a whole where the company itself cannot be saved; (3) to establish a fair and equitable system for the ranking of claims and the distribution of assets among creditors, involving a limited redistribution of rights; and (4) to provide a mechanism by which the causes of failure can be identified and to disqualify those guilty of mismanagement by depriving them of their right to be involved in the management of other companies.[79] Nevertheless, given that the role of insolvency law is 'not to affect pre-bankruptcy the substance of entitlements but rather to organise a collective regime designed to ensure the preservation of those entitlements to the maximum extent possible', according to Professor Goode, it is only to this extent that the rehabilitation of an insolvent business is a legitimate function of corporate insolvency law.[80]

Professor Finch also believes that the key tasks of corporate insolvency law among other things should include: (1) facilitating the recovery of companies in times of financial crisis and stimulating the rehabilitation of insolvent companies and businesses as going concerns; (2) balancing the interests of different groupings and protecting the interests of the public and of employees in the face of financial failures or management malpractices; and (3) dissolving companies when necessary.[81] In looking for the appropriate measure of insolvency law, more specifically, with regard to the objectives and their trade-off against each other associated with the openness concerning the objectives of corporate insolvency law, Finch borrows from Gerald Frug's well-known analysis of the strategies for attempting to legitimate corporate and bureaucratic power, and offers the so-called explicit values approach to measuring insolvency law.[82] The explicit values approach 'takes on board the public and private, the procedural and substantive and the contractarian and democratic dimensions of insolvency'.[83] She advocates that the legitimacy of the processes and principles of insolvency law can be tested by reference to four benchmarks, namely efficiency, expertise, accountability and fairness: (1) 'Efficiency' looks to securing democratically mandated ends at lowest cost; (2) 'Expertise' refers to the allocation of decision and policy

---

[79] See R Goode, *Principles of Corporate Insolvency Law* (3rd edn, Sweet and Maxwell 2005), 39.

[80] *Ibid.*, 39.

[81] Finch, *Corporate Insolvency Law: Perspectives and Principles*, 27.

[82] *Ibid.*, 64.

[83] *Ibid.*

functions to properly competent persons; (3) 'Accountability' looks to the control of insolvency participants by democratic bodies or courts or through the openness of processes and their amenability to representations; and (4) 'Fairness' considers issues of justice and propensities to respect the interests of affected parties by allowing such parties access to, and respect within, decision and policy processes.[84]

Nevertheless, in cases where the four values themselves have conflicts, Professor Finch's explicit values approach did not provide any further standards for determining preferences among them in the details. There is no clear answer on whether particular trade-offs between them are desirable or not. It is suggested that the merits of particular trade-offs may only be argued for in particular contexts and cannot be preordained according to set rules.[85] Mokal has argued that Finch's understanding of the 'benchmark' concepts lacks consistency and that she is unable to provide a satisfactory account of their relationship *inter se*. According to him, 'expertise' and 'accountability' have no separate standing of their own, and should be absorbed within 'efficiency'.[86] Fairness and efficiency cannot be traded off against each other, as efficiency in itself does not provide a goal that any area of the law should aim at. The failure to distinguish between the diverse nature of her otherwise well-argued benchmarks considerably weakens Finch's approach.[87]

Summary of Findings

This section reviewed the diverse normative theories and hypotheses about the appropriate objectives and purposes of corporate insolvency law. The creditor wealth maximisation argument promoted by the classical creditors' bargain theory has been widely criticised for its failing to take account of the wide range of stakeholders beyond a company's contract creditors that the corporate insolvency may have an impact on. Different standpoints have been taken on the goals of corporate insolvency law and whose interests should be protected. However, there is no consensus as to how various and competing goals that underlie the insolvency system should be prioritised and served, nor is there a working standard to determine preferences among them. As a result,

---

84 *Ibid.*, 56.

85 *Ibid.*, 65.

86 RJ Mokal, 'On Fairness and Efficiency' (2003) 66 *Modern Law Review* 452.

87 *Ibid.*

critical questions, such as how to judge if trade-offs between different goals are desirable or not, remain unresolved.

APPROACHES TO RESCUE

With the rise in insolvency activity that was seen in the past recessions and the growing popularity of corporate rescues, a variety of rescue mechanisms have been developed within and outside insolvency law, generally falling into two categories: informal and formal rescue strategies. Informal rescues, also referred to as 'private restructurings' or 'workouts',[88] are a non-judicial process through which a distressed company and its significant creditors[89] attempt to reach an agreement to restructure and adjust the company's debt obligations without court intervention. Formal rescues, on the other hand, involve the use of legal procedures designed under insolvency legislation where the compromises and arrangements for restructuring are made under the supervision of the court or a formal legal structure.

Informal Rescues

Informal rescues are contractually based in nature and in themselves do not demand any sort of statutory intervention. A general advantage of private workouts is that they provide the debtor company and its creditors with a more flexible environment in which to negotiate the resolution of a company's financial difficulties than under insolvency procedures. Publicity concerning corporate failures is likely to be minimal, thus avoiding significant jeopardy to the goodwill and reputation of the company by the negative reactions of customers and the market. The private route allows the sale of the business to be completed in good time and with a low level of disruption from publicity, both of which are essential to preserve the value of the business. In formal insolvency procedures, the complex legal institutional constraints are likely to

---

[88] Workout was defined as 'borrower's efforts to negotiate with its lenders for a restructuring of its debts outside of bankruptcy or other court proceedings'. MS Kirschner *et al.*, 'Prepackaged Bankruptcy Plans: The Deleveraging Tool of the '90s in the Wake of Old and Tax Concerns' (1991) 21 *Seton Hall Law Review* 643, at note 7.

[89] For instance, financial creditors such as banks, or major trade creditors and bondholders.

produce more prolonged and often hostile litigation, which can have a significantly negative impact on the realisable value of the company's business.

Furthermore, the contractual basis of informal rescue action also means that the terms of restructuring can be easily altered and adjusted during negotiations in a way that formal procedures do not allow without a valid approval mechanism.[90] Private workouts are commonly negotiated between a small group of leaders and the debtor out of the public eye. In addition, cooperation among a number of major creditors involved in a negotiation can be more readily achieved than aligning the diverse incentives of all conflicting claimholder classes as attempted under the insolvency procedures.

While noting the merits, the demerits of informal rescues are also obvious. A fundamental difficulty for the contract-based mechanism is the need to secure a consensus; usually the agreement of all parties whose rights are affected. Informal rescues are based on the contractual variation of existing rights by way of compromise, waiver or deferment of debts or alteration of priorities. They can only bind parties to the contract, therefore any dissenting creditors have the power to halt informal rescues by triggering formal insolvency procedures. This renders the informal rescue a fragile device which is dependent on a high degree of cooperation among a disparate range of parties.[91] Another concern with the informal approach is its potential to prejudice the interests of less well-placed creditors, for there may be an absence of investigative powers and a lack of inquiry into the role the directors played in bringing a company to the brink of disaster.[92]

The 'London Approach', developed in the 1970s and designed to secure the cooperation of financial support for companies with liquidity problems,[93] has been successful in resolving financial distress with large UK companies, especially for the large multi-bank financed companies.[94] The British Bankers Association defined the 'London Approach' as 'a non statutory and informal framework introduced with the support of the Bank of England for dealing with temporary support operations mounted

---

[90] Finch, *Corporate Insolvency Law: Perspectives and Principles*, 208.

[91] D Brown, *Corporate Rescue: Insolvency Law in Practice* (Wiley Series in Commercial Law, J Wiley, New York 1996), 10. Finch, *Corporate Insolvency Law: Perspectives and Principles*, 209–10.

[92] Finch, *Corporate Insolvency Law: Perspectives and Principles*, 209.

[93] Goode, *Principles of Corporate Insolvency Law*, para.10-04.

[94] *Ibid.*, para.10-135.

by banks and other lenders to a company or group in financial difficulties, pending a possible restructuring'.[95] The rescue work is organised on a contractual basis, through which the potentially conflicting problems of company creditors are resolved through voluntary cooperation and coordination between the participating parties[96] without having to resort to statutory backing.[97]

The process generally involves four phases. At the initial stage of the process, the participating parties should agree among themselves to an informal 'standstill', which typically last for several months and is sufficient to prevent all relevant creditors from taking any steps to enforce their claims against the debtor company. Secondly, a team of accountants appointed by the banks will investigate the company's financial condition and produce an independent review of the company's economic viability and long-term prospects.[98] Their conclusion will be acted on by a collective decision-making process in which the main creditors work together to reach a joint view on what should be done with the company.[99] Thirdly, to promote cooperation among the relevant creditors, a lead bank, typically the bank with a floating charge over the company's assets, is normally designated to organise the gathering and distribution of the information relevant to the rescue, negotiate with the other banks and coordinate their dealings with the distressed company.[100] And finally, where negotiations are successful, an agreed business plan for the company is put into effect and is monitored.[101] One or more committees representative of the main creditor classes will normally be

---

[95] British Bankers' Association, 'London Approach' (16/02/2004) previously available at <http://www.bba.org.uk/bba/jsp/polopoly.jsp?d=130&a=2281> accessed 9 November 2007.

[96] Particularly the banks and other financial institution creditors.

[97] Goode, *Principles of Corporate Insolvency Law*, para.10-135.

[98] INSOL International, 'Statement of Principles for a Global Approach to Multi-Creditor Workouts' (Report) (2000), 2–3. And Goode, *Principles of Corporate Insolvency Law*, para.10-135.

[99] One of the crucial tasks is to safeguard a sound information flow, including information-gathering and dissemination, among the participating parties so that the action taken is coordinated in a cooperative manner.

[100] Creditor committees reduce information asymmetries that would endanger trust and cooperation between creditors and the debtor. See also P Brierley and G Vilieghe, 'Corporate Workouts, the London Approach and Financial Stability' (1999) 7 *Financial Stability Review* 168, 174; Finch, *Corporate Insolvency Law: Perspectives and Principles*, 221.

[101] Finch, *Corporate Insolvency Law: Perspectives and Principles*, 220.

established to assist the lead bank's coordination work and more importantly, to act as a provisional sounding board towards the evaluation of proposals for corporate debt restructuring and then the negotiation and implementation of the restructuring plan.[102]

The relative informality provided by the London Approach allows security interests to be adjusted, a process that may prove far less complex and expensive than receivership where a number of banks are involved.[103] The approach relies on consensus, persuasion and banking collegiality in order to reconcile the interests of different creditors to a company in difficulty.[104] Like general private restructuring agreements, rescue attempts in the London Approach typically involve creditors compromising existing rights and priority through debt-equity swaps; and postponing the date for repayments or reducing the interest rate on corporate debt, or parts of it, often accompanied by management changes, asset sales and securing new finance and new or increased director guarantees. In this context, the banks may agree to provide new funding, especially where fresh loans and attendant liquidity are necessary for the debtor's continued survival. Such additional funding is normally accorded priority over existing loans requisite creditors.[105]

It has been questioned how far the lead bank can, or has the standing to, intervene in the absence of regulatory powers.[106] The operation of such voluntary collective action depends heavily on the lead lender discharging their coordination role effectively, as well as intensive

---

[102] J Armour and SF Deakin, 'Norms in Private Insolvency Procedures: The 'London Approach' to the Resolution of Financial Distress' (2000) ESRC Centre for Business Research, University of Cambridge, Working Paper No. 173 <http://core.ac.uk/download/pdf/7151360.pdf> accessed 30 July 2015, 38–9. Such committees are often advised and assisted by professional advisers for better commercial decision-making.

[103] Finch, *Corporate Insolvency Law: Perspectives and Principles*, 219.

[104] *Ibid.*, 219–20.

[105] The traditional domination of bank debt in financing large UK debtors is identified as one of the fundamental backgrounds of the prevalence of the London Approach. See further Armour and Deakin, 'Norms in Private Insolvency Procedures: The 'London Approach' to the Resolution of Financial Distress', 38.

[106] Brown, *Corporate Rescue: Insolvency Law in Practice*, para.1.31. It becomes even more difficult for banks to coordinate given the increasing complexity of financial structures where hedge funds and private equity groups grew explosively in power and influence in recent years. This dramatically reduces the ability of the banks to pressure such parties into agreeing a rescue plan. See further V Finch, 'The Dynamics of Insolvency Law: Three Models of Reform', (2009) 3 *Law and Financial Markets Review*, 438.

cooperation among the disparate range of interested parties. It has been argued that the main difficulty of the London Approach is the lack of any formal moratorium and the need for unanimity of support from relevant creditors.[107] In addition, it is pointed out that, while this framework seems successful in large multi-bank corporate rescues, it might be less appropriate for the bulk of companies in distress where there may be only one bank and many non-financial institution creditors.[108] Moreover, corporate financing practice has developed dramatically and therefore the marketplace in which the London Approach was developed has changed dramatically.[109] Professor Finch has summarised the difficulties facing the London Approach as follows:

> [m]odes of financing are becoming more fragmented and creditors' co-ordination is proving more difficult as bank creditors are joined by bond holders, secondary debt traders, joint venture partners, special creditor and supplier groups and intermediate investors. The globalisation of financial markets and the emergence of markets for distressed corporate debt also put strains on the London Approach.[110]

Formal Rescues

The statutory rescue procedures respond to the inherent and severe coordination problems and the holdout risks associated with the informal route. Essentially they offer a collective way in which all the affected parties are participating equally and treated according to the size and seniority of their credits. A formal procedure, such as Chapter 11 of the US Bankruptcy Code or the UK Administration, normally involve a moratorium on the enforcement of a wide range of creditors' rights and so creates a more sustainable space within which a rescue can be organised.[111] Insolvency legislation also provides various mechanisms

---

[107] Finch, *Corporate Insolvency Law: Perspectives and Principles*, 223.

[108] Brown, *Corporate Rescue: Insolvency Law in Practice*, para.1.31. The complexity of the company's capital structure and the heterogeneity of the financial claims could generate severe holdout problems.

[109] Armour and Deakin, 'Norms in Private Insolvency Procedures: The 'London Approach' to the Resolution of Financial Distress', 31–3.

[110] V Finch, 'The Recasting of Insolvency Law' (2005) 68 *Modern Law Review* 713, 727. The sheer involvement of a greater number and diversity of players is likely to mitigate against the rapid, informed and cheap negotiation of rescues by a stable group of parties. See further Finch, *Corporate Insolvency Law: Perspectives and Principles*, 225.

[111] *Ibid.*, 210.

whereby compromises and arrangements can be made under the supervision of the court or a formal legal structure, one objective of which is to ensure that minority dissenters are eventually bound.[112]

In the UK, corporate rescue procedures were first introduced through the administration order procedure and company voluntary arrangements (CVA) in the Insolvency Act 1985 and were re-enacted in the Insolvency Act 1986 (IA 1986), as recommended by the Cork Committee Report on Insolvency Law and Practice. The original administration model was not a complete rescue procedure, and its main effect was to impose a moratorium on the enforcement of creditors' claims. The Enterprise Act 2002 (EA 2002) introduced a streamlined administration model to replace the original procedure. Under the new regime, the administration may function either as a gateway to winding up, a CVA or a scheme of arrangements, or as a stand-alone procedure, which may lead directly to dissolution. The administrator is required to first consider rescuing the company as a going concern, unless in the administrator's view, that is not reasonably practical and/or it is not in the interests of creditors as a whole.

American Chapter 11, commonly referred to as 'reorganisation', aims at promoting the economically viable company to recovery and maintaining the business as a going concern.[113] By granting an automatic stay to prevent creditors from collecting their claims or enforcing their liens, incumbent management is allowed to retain control of the company and is granted the exclusive right to propose a plan of reorganisation within 120 days after the Chapter 11 filing date.[114]

---

[112] For instance, a creditors' meeting will be convened within a practically reasonable period; the reorganisation plan needs to be accepted by the majority of the allowed claims. Under English administration procedure, the administrator's proposals are passed when support is obtained from a majority in value of those present and voting creditors, either in person or by proxy. In the US, claims and interests are dealt with by classes, specifying unimpaired and impaired classes. A plan is deemed to be accepted when at least two-thirds of votes and more than one-half in number of allowed claims of each voting class of creditors, and two-thirds in amount of the shares for a class of equity interests, have accepted it.

[113] It is said that the motive for introducing the Chapter 11 procedure was to increase the possibility that the company would emerge as a going concern from the reorganisation process. See J Franks and W Torous, 'Lessons from a Comparison of US and UK Insolvency Codes' (1992) 8 *Oxford Review of Economic Policy* 70, 75.

[114] The court may grant extension of this exclusive period up to 18 months after the petition date. Plan negotiations typically are conducted primarily

Both countries take a view that corporate rescues can be justified by the fact that assets used by a going concern company are more valuable than if the company was liquidated piecemeal, but the legal rescue procedures in the two jurisdictions are very different in terms of orientation and institutional arrangements. For an administration procedure, the rescue of the ailing company or the whole or part of its undertaking as a going concern is preferred, but it is not an overriding objective. The decision on which statutory purpose should be pursued is made by an outside insolvency practitioner who acts as the administrator. In contrast, the overriding objective of a Chapter 11 case, at least in theory, is the formulation and confirmation of a reorganisation plan agreed between creditors and shareholders. As already mentioned, incumbent management may remain in office and run the business as usual during the reorganisation process and are in charge of proposing a reorganisation plan.[115]

Accordingly, statutory rescue procedures are designed as a collective and inclusive rescue process under which all the parties-in-interests are equally participating and treated according to the size and seniority of their credits. In order to provide adequate protection for various groups of creditors, as well as checks and balances on the conflicting incentives among different stakeholders, the legal proceedings often involve complicated documentary accountability requirements and rounds of negotiations to conclude the approval of the rescue plan. This renders the formal approach a complex proceeding that is lengthy and costly, often eventually leading to unnecessary or premature corporate liquidations. The wider economic disruption generated gives claimholders the incentive to look for alternative restructuring strategies.

---

between the debtor and one or more official committees appointed shortly after the filing of debtor's bankruptcy petition, although any party in interest may seek to participate in negotiations. Once the debtor reaches agreement with its major constituencies on a plan that appears to have the necessary support to be confirmed, the plan will be filed with the bankruptcy court. See MD Plevin *et al.*, 'Pre-Packaged Asbestos Bankruptcies: A Flawed Solution' (2008) 44 *South Texas Law Review* 883, 886.

[115] Though the existing management can run the business in the ordinary way, court approval will be required for substantial asset sales, section 361 of the US Bankruptcy Code. For the relative merits of the US DIP model and the British PIP model, see D Hahn, 'Concentrated Ownership and Control of Corporate Reorganisations' (2004) 4 *Journal of Corporate Law Studies* 117; V Finch, 'Control and Co-ordination in Corporate Rescue' (2005) 25 *Legal Studies* 374.

Pre-pack: A Combined Form of Rescue Strategy

The 'pre-pack' process is commonly seen as a hybrid form of corporate rescue combining the advantages of private restructuring with some of the properties of the formal procedure. Pre-packaged bankruptcies were first introduced in US insolvency practice. They provided a feasible option for financially distressed companies, which allowed them to avoid the significant expense and relatively complicated negotiation process under traditional US Chapter 11 proceedings. A 'pre-packaged' Chapter 11 describes the procedure of devising a plan of reorganisation and soliciting acceptance of such a plan prior to the commencement of a bankruptcy case.[116] By doing so, an agreement is often drawn up as means of finding a compromise solution to satisfy the claims of large financial creditors. The claims of other creditors (particularly ordinary employees and trade creditors) may be left unimpaired to be paid in full under the restructuring plan.[117] By leaving them unimpaired, the company avoids negotiating with a diverse and potentially most fractious creditor group thereby avoiding a serious holdout problem.

The holdout problem can be further minimised by filing for protection under a formal procedure,[118] which has the legal power to bind dissenting creditors to the restructuring terms accepted by the majority of voting creditors,[119] that is, two-thirds in amount and more than one-half in number of those voting. This can greatly reduce the time spent in bankruptcy, because the principal remaining tasks are the approval of the disclosure statement and confirmation of the plan by the court.[120]

---

[116] Kirschner *et al.*, 'Prepackaged Bankruptcy Plans: The Deleveraging Tool of the '90s in the Wake of Old and Tax Concerns', footnote 8 at p 644. In contrast to pre-packaged cases, there are also pre-negotiated cases, where some debtors negotiated the terms of their representatives prior to bankruptcy, but did not solicit usable votes prior to filing or did not solicit them from all impaired creditor classes. See T Eisenberg and LM LoPucki, 'Shopping for Judges: An Empirical Analysis of Venue Choice in Large Chapter 11 Reorganizations' (1999) 84 *Cornell Law Review* 967, 976.

[117] TJ Salerno and CD Hansen, 'A Prepackaged Bankruptcy Strategy' (1991) 12 *Journal of Business Strategy* 36.

[118] Such as the UK administration procedure or the US Chapter 11 reorganisation.

[119] KA Mayr, 'Enforcing Prepackaged Restructurings of Foreign Debtors under the U.S. Bankruptcy Code' (2006) 14 *American Bankruptcy Institute Law Review* 469, 497.

[120] E Tashjian *et al.*, 'Prepacks: An Empirical Analysis of Prepackaged Bankruptcies' (1996) 40 *Journal of Financial Economics* 135, 138.

Similarly on the UK insolvency scene, there has been a considerable increase in the number of pre-packs in recent years.[121] The percentage of administrations going through a pre-pack procedure has increased from approximately 25 per cent in 2011 to 29 per cent in 2012.[122] Although the pre-pack strategy can be traced to other forms of insolvency proceedings such as liquidation and administrative receivership, there is a growing trend of utilising the administration procedure to implement a pre-agreed arrangement, especially after the increase in the use of administration by the EA 2002. A pre-pack administration therefore refers to the situation where arrangements for the sale of an insolvent business have been negotiated with prospective purchasers and agreed by the major creditors[123] prior to the commencement of the administration procedure, with the sale being completed almost immediately after the appointment of an administrator.

The popularity of pre-pack restructuring in the UK and the US has been recognised by other jurisdictions in Europe and these are countries starting to introduce their own versions of pre-pack procedures, such as the Accelerated Financial Safeguard procedure (*Procédure de Sauvegarde Financière Accélérée)* in France[124] and the new Protective Shield Proceedings (*Schutzschirmverfahren*) in Germany.[125] Despite the gradual

---

[121] Frisby's research samples of administration and receivership cases between September 2001 and September 2004 showed that there were 222 administration cases and 118 pre-packaged administration samples. Of the 118 administration pre-packs, 40 cases (33.9 per cent) were pre-Enterprise Act 2002 and 78 (66.1 per cent) were post-Enterprise Act 2002 cases. S Frisby, 'A Preliminary Analysis of Pre-Packaged Administrations' (Report) (R3: The Association of Business Recovery Professionals 2007), 15.

[122] The Insolvency Service, *2012 Annual Review of Insolvency Practitioner Regulation* (June 2013), 4.

[123] This study uses the expression 'major creditors' as shorthand for the parties that could exert some degree of influence on the disposal process, including the senior secured bank creditors, significant trade creditors or bondholders.

[124] The 'accelerated financial safeguard procedure' was created by the Banking and financial regulation law as of 22 October 2010, *Loi de Régulation Bancaire et Financière*, No. 2010-1249, JORF No. 0247, 23 October 2010 (Articles 57 and 58) and was codified in Article L.628-1 and L.628-7 of French Commercial Code.

[125] The 'Protective Shield Proceedings' was introduced by the 'Act for the Further Facilitation of the Reorganization of Companies' (*Gesetz zur weiteren Erleichterung der Sanierung von Unternehmen*) enacted on 7 December 2011 and now is contained in Section 270b of the German Insolvency Code.

recognition of the efficacy and efficiency of pre-pack practice in maximising the going-concern value of distressed businesses, the rescue-oriented rules offered in different jurisdictions differ as to how far they can go in seeking to promote a more cooperative and risk-taking attitude among different parties from their respective standpoints. The differences in their institutional arrangements governing insolvency and corporate rescue reflect the differences in their culture, economic environment and political constraints.

MODERN CORPORATE RESCUE CHALLENGES

As explained earlier, corporate rescues are very different in orientation from many aspects of the liquidation process. Liquidation is commonly viewed as essentially involving foreclosure and a piecemeal sale of the business's assets, while the heart of a rescue process is seen as involving the continuation of the business. Rather than relatively static distribution proceedings in a strict order of priority, corporate rescues are more of a negotiating and thus bargaining proceedings focusing on ongoing commercial viability. They are accompanied by the uncertainty of the valuation on the financially distressed company.[126]

Theoretically, the rescue process is all about preserving the so-called going concern surplus in those businesses that are financially distressed but still economically viable, and identifying and liquidating those economically distressed ones in a timely manner. However, it is empirically difficult to distinguish between financial and economic distress. It is often not obvious whether a troubled company with financial difficulty is still economically viable or not and the judgement varies with different parties due to their possession of information about the company and their private interests. Furthermore, the process is accompanied by significant uncertainty with regard to what the value of the company turns out to be.

The future prospects for the turnaround of the company may well depend on: the severity of its liquidity crisis; the outcome of negotiations for support from its senior financial creditors; the economic viability of the business; and the reaction of the market to the company's financial trouble. Therefore, the key concerns in the furtherance of the rescue process in a world of uncertainty refer to the true value of the business, and the likelihood of the successful recovery 'turn[s] importantly upon

---

[126] DG Baird and DS Bernstein, 'Absolute Priority, Valuation Uncertainty, and the Reorganization Bargain' (2006) 115 *Yale Law Journal* 1930.

evaluation of risk and a willingness to accept risk'.[127] This dynamic nature makes the corporate rescue process even more complex and demanding. On the one hand, it needs to accommodate different stakeholders with dispersed interests bargaining with each other; on the other hand, it calls for trust among those participants as well as compromise, and possibly even necessary sacrifice from some stakeholders, in order to reach the successful rescue outcomes.

As we have seen, corporate rescue includes formal activities provided by legislation and informal activities. The key challenge to efficient negotiation in the informal rescue process is the creditor coordination problem, especially for companies with a large number of creditors and complex debt structures (often a mix of public, private and bank debt). These companies are likely to suffer from creditor holdout problems, in which a minority of claimholders refuse to accept a restructuring plan, and are better off restructuring under the less stringent voting requirements of statutory procedure. Formal rules for a collective rescue procedure, on the other hand, are designed to reduce information asymmetries and wasteful strategic behaviour and to promote cooperation in order to facilitate the achievement of the most efficient outcome. For this reason the automatic stay provision and the voting rules under a statutory rescue procedure are devised to overcome the holdout problems.

Formal rescue-oriented proceedings have their advantages in providing a forum for structured negotiations among competing and diverse interests to avoid the unnecessary collapse of businesses in the chaos of financial distress. Nevertheless, the role of insolvency law is primarily, although not merely, a response to the problem of collecting debts. The formal rules in this context impose considerable limits on departing from the pre-insolvency entitlements of claimholders and on how far they can go in response to the substantial obstacles caused by the inherent uncertainty in the progression of rescue work.

Pre-pack restructuring is a hybrid form of corporate rescue and it does present an innovative approach to overcome the holdout problem in informal workouts by providing a formal procedure to solidify the outcome of private negotiations. Yet pre-pack rescue also face challenges in capturing the going concern surplus in an uncertain state of corporate distress. In particular, how should the competing interests and various goals that underlie the insolvency system (e.g. fairness or justice and wealth creation) be prioritised when a trade-off is inevitable? This

---

[127] JL Westbrook, 'The Control of Wealth in Bankruptcy' (2004) 82 *Texas Law Review* 795, 805.

problem could be more acute in a pre-pack restructuring, where trade-offs are often pre-determined and market-led, but not always in line with the statutory objectives of a particular insolvency law. These challenges are key to the successful use and completion of pre-pack arrangements and they are extensively discussed in subsequent chapters.

PART II

Pre-packs in the UK

2. A critical appraisal of the rise of pre-pack administrations

INTRODUCTION

This chapter will address the question of how pre-pack administration fits into the development of the English corporate rescue system to give a clear contextual account of the rise of pre-pack administrations. The discussion begins with the Cork Report in 1982 and the ensuing evolution of English insolvency legal frameworks towards a more consistent and purposeful system. This was the watershed moment in terms of shifting UK attitudes to corporate rescues. Then, the chapter proceeds with an analytical overview of contemporary types of rescue-oriented insolvency procedures and examines their effectiveness in facilitating corporate rescue. The last part of this chapter discusses the use of pre-pack administration and explores the reasons behind its popularity. It offers a critical appraisal of the key advantages of pre-packs in handling financially distressed businesses as compared to UK's formal rescue proceedings.

Arguably, pre-packaged arrangements have considerable merits, especially when it comes to economising in transaction costs and effecting a speedy resolution of a company failure, which otherwise may be dragged into expensive negotiations between the debtor and its creditors and drawn-out judicial proceedings. Essentially, pre-packs allow necessary preparatory work to be carried out at an early stage and without pressure from the public, and ensure a timely disposal of the business as a going concern. Furthermore, its pre-determined nature offers a high level of certainty and control to key participants in the rescue process and therefore attracts the essential support from company's main creditors. On the other hand, its striking pre-determined nature presents new challenges to the contemplated legal framework of the administration procedure. In particular, it is likely to reduce the role of the administrator who is supposed to play a key role in evaluating all possible options, as the pre-formal negotiation stage has become the focus of the insolvency decision-making but the insolvency practitioners' role at this stage could be considerably constrained by the timing of their involvement and the role they played in the pre-formal stage. Also, the majority of ordinary creditors will not be approached at the pre-pack stage and will often be presented with the 'fait accompli' outcome without being heard. This may prove prejudicial to those excluded unsecured creditors as certain important decisions affecting their interests have probably been made in the absence of the administrator and without any formal approval by all interested parties.

THE DEVELOPMENT OF UK'S RESCUE CULTURE

English insolvency law has traditionally functioned for the benefit of creditors. Its primary objective has been the repayment of the claimants. It is therefore marked as an ideologically creditor-oriented system.[1] This can be illustrated by the domination of the winding up procedures in the older corporate insolvency law system.[2] Over the last two decades, however, English insolvency law has experienced a substantial shift towards a rescue culture. This section will examine the emergence of the rescue idea and mark some notable legislative initiatives in promoting the embedded rescue culture.

The *Cork Report*

To discuss the evolution of a rescue culture in the UK, the appropriate starting point is the Review Report of the Cork Committee (the '*Cork Report*'), which was the most significant milestone in English insolvency law reforms. The publication of the *Cork Report* followed a five-year review of the law and practice relating to insolvency, bankruptcy, liquidation and receivership at the time,[3] and highlighted some serious problems with the then existing procedures. It especially criticised the focus of insolvency law on the distribution of the proceeds of the insolvent's assets among its creditors and acknowledged the benefits of

---

[1] See Belcher, *Corporate Rescue*, 13–14.

[2] Cork and Committee, *Insolvency Law and Practice: Report of the Review Committee*, 24.

[3] *Ibid.*, 36. Bankruptcy applied only to individuals and partners; it did not apply to companies incorporated under the Companies Act 1948, which were subject to the winding up provisions of the Companies Acts.

having insolvency proceedings designed specifically for corporate rescue rather than mere asset realisation.[4]

Based on a detailed and critical examination of the existing insolvency law, the *Cork Report*, among its wide terms of reference, had 'to suggest possible less formal procedures as alternatives to bankruptcy and company winding-up proceedings in appropriate circumstances'.[5] Thus, it is rightly deemed as the first official signpost to point in the direction of the rescue culture.[6] Although not all the ideas and recommendations in the *Cork Report* were enacted into legislation, or absorbed with crucial alteration, in the consequent insolvency reforms, in particular, it is not too immodest to claim that the *Cork Report* served as a significant boost for the development of a range of complementary procedures to facilitate the rescue and rehabilitation of ailing businesses.[7]

The Introduction of the Administration Order and the Company Voluntary Arrangement Procedure

The UK did not have any statutory procedures particularly designed to facilitate the attempts of corporate rescue prior to the *Cork Report*. Recommended by the *Report*, the Administration Order procedure and the Company Voluntary Arrangement procedure ('CVA') were introduced, initially in the Insolvency Act 1985 but fully adopted by the Insolvency Act 1986.[8] Both regimes were designed and meant to promote rescue attempts before eventually proceeding to asset sales and closing or breaking up the company.

---

[4] D Milman and C Durrant, *Corporate Insolvency: Law and Practice* (3rd edn, Sweet & Maxwell, London 1999), para.3-01.

[5] Cork and Committee, *Insolvency Law and Practice: Report of the Review Committee*, Part 2, 173.

[6] M Hunter, 'The Nature and Functions of a Rescue Culture' (1999) *Journal of Business Law* 941.

[7] Fletcher, 'UK Corporate Rescue: Recent Developments', 121.

[8] A bill substantially incorporating the recommendations from the *Cork Report* had a stormy passage through Parliament and become a new *Insolvency Act* 1985. However the Act was left largely unimplemented until the consolidation exercise had been completed. Two consolidating Bills were introduced into Parliament in 1986, and these in due course became the *Insolvency Act* 1986 and the *Company Directors Disqualification Act* 1986. The bulk of the *Insolvency Act* 1985 was merged with some 200 sections of the *Companies Act* 1985 to create the *Insolvency Act* 1986. On the background to the *Insolvency Act* 1985/1986, see further L Sealy, *Disqualification and Personal Liability of Directors* (5th edn, CCH Group Ltd., Kingston 2000), 103.

The administration procedure was designed to provide companies in financial difficulty with a period of respite in which to put together a rescue package or alternatively to achieve a more effective realisation of the company's assets than would be possible in a liquidation.[9] For an administration order, there were four statutory purposes, namely: (1) the survival of the company, and the whole or any part of its business undertakings, as a going concern; (2) the approval of a voluntary arrangement under Part I; (3) the sanctioning under section 425 of the Companies Act 1985 of a compromise or arrangement between the company and any such persons as are mentioned in that section; and (4) a more advantageous realisation of the company's assets than would be effected on a winding up.[10] The court could make an order providing for any one or all of the four purposes.

Complementary to the administration procedure, the CVA was a device whereby a company could reach a formal and binding arrangement with its creditors through negotiation.[11] It allowed the directors of a company to 'make a proposal to the company and to its creditors for composition in satisfaction of its debts or a scheme of arrangement of its affairs'.[12] There was no prerequisite to trigger the device that the company was in actual or impending insolvency.[13] A CVA may be concluded without any prior or subsequent insolvency proceedings or it may precede or follow a winding up or administration order, or run in parallel with a winding up and administration procedure for the benefit of the attached statutory moratorium.[14]

The significance of the two procedures in raising the profile of corporate rescue as a legitimate aim of corporate insolvency law is beyond doubt.[15] Nevertheless, in practice, neither of the procedures

---

[9] The Insolvency Service, *Productivity and Enterprise – Insolvency: A Second Chance* (Consultative document, 2001).

[10] Section 8(3) of the original IA 1986. See also Goode, *Principles of Corporate Insolvency Law*, para.10-05.

[11] L Hiestand and CK Pikington, 'CVAs – a Restructuring Tool for the Future?' (Autumn 2006) *Recovery*, 38.

[12] S 1(1) to the IA 1986. Such a proposal may also be made by administrator or liquidator when the company is in administration or being wound up. S 1(3) of the IA 1986.

[13] Goode, *Principles of Corporate Insolvency Law*, para.10-35.

[14] S 1(3) IA 1986.

[15] Milman and Durrant, *Corporate Insolvency: Law and Practice*, para.3-78.

attracted wide popularity, although there was a gradual increase of their usage over the following years (see Table 2.1).[16]

Table 2.1 The use of administration and CVA compared with liquidation and administrative receivership in 1991–1999[1]

Procedure	Liquidation[2]	Receivership	Administration	CVA
1991	21,827	7,815	206	137
1992	24,425	8,523	179	76
1993	20,708	5,362	112	134
1994	16,728	3,877	159	264
1995	14,536	3,226	163	372
1996	13,461	2,701	210	459
1997	12,610	1,837	196	629
1998	13,203	1,713	338	470
1999	14,280	1,618	440	475

Notes:
1. The figures were obtained from Historic Insolvency Statistics in the Insolvency Service http://www.insolvency.gov.uk/otherinformation/statistics/historicdata/HDmenu.htm.
2. Including compulsory liquidations and creditors voluntary liquidations.

Quite clearly, some aspects of the original formulations of the two regimes suffered serious inherent weaknesses, which could considerably reduce their robustness in facilitating corporate rescue. Most notably, the entry to the old administration procedure required first obtaining an order from the court. This entailed a strict burden of proof and a costly procedure at the preliminary stage, as the court had to be persuaded that one or more of the four authorised purposes outlined in the statute were likely to be achieved.[17] In doing so, a report from an independent expert commending the administration option (known as the 'rule 2.2 report') was inevitably indispensable, although not mandatory. This tended to generate considerable delay and expense, which was deemed to be a major impediment to this statutory device.[18] Furthermore, the court had extensive power over the procedure, and the administrator generally

[16] The insolvency statistics during 1991 to 1999 demonstrated that, taken together, the use of the two mechanisms still comprised a small proportion of all corporate insolvencies.

[17] Milman and Durrant, *Corporate Insolvency: Law and Practice*, para.3-10.

[18] Goode, *Principles of Corporate Insolvency Law*, para.10-07.

could not make distributions even to preferential creditors. More critically, the petition for an administration order could be readily blocked by the use of the effective *de facto* power of veto by qualifying floating charge ('QFC') holders[19] (generally banks or institutional lenders) through appointing an administrative receiver.[20]

With regard to the CVA procedure, the most crucial impediment appeared to be the absence of any moratorium during the crucial period between the company embarking on the process of seeking to conclude an arrangement with its creditors, and the conclusion of the process through a favourable vote to adopt the proposals.[21] As a voluntary arrangement is essentially an agreement between the company and its creditors in the form of a contract,[22] it is very much dependent on cooperation from all creditors,[23] and the proceeding could be easily frustrated by any obstructive creditor presenting a winding up petition.[24]

---

[19] A QFC holder, according to para.14 of Sch. B1 to the IA 1986, refers to a person who is the holder of a qualifying floating charge in respect of a company's property if he holds one or more debentures of the company secured:

(a) by a qualifying floating charge which relates to the whole or substantially the whole of the company's property,
(b) by a number of qualifying floating charges which together relate to the whole or substantially the whole of the company's property, or
(c) by charges and other forms of security which together relate to the whole or substantially the whole of the company's property and at least one of which is a qualifying floating charge.

[20] The Insolvency Service, 'Productivity and Enterprise – Insolvency: A Second Chance', para.2.15. Milman and Durrant, *Corporate Insolvency: Law and Practice*, para.3-15. As originally enacted, such petition was to be presented and given notice to any person having the right to appoint an administrative receiver; it would take effect only when such debenture holder did not intervene and make an appointment of an administrative receiver. Section 9(3) of the IA 1986 provided: 'where the court is satisfied that there is an administrative receiver of the company, the court shall dismiss the petition (of administration order) unless it is also satisfied that the person by whom or on whose behalf the receiver was appointed has consented to the making of the order.'

[21] Fletcher, 'UK Corporate Rescue: Recent Developments', 127.

[22] The nature of insolvency arrangements was considered by Michael Rutstein as a contract and he concluded that the principles of contract law should apply to voluntary arrangements where statute does not govern this issue in question. See further M Rustein, 'Voluntary Arrangements: Contracts or Not?' Part 1 and Part 2 (2000) 13(1) and 13(2) *Insolvency Intelligence*.

[23] Including the company management, shareholders, employees and secured, unsecured and preferential creditors.

[24] Milman and Durrant, *Corporate Insolvency: Law and Practice*, para.3-01.

This shortcoming may be overcome in practice by initiating a CVA within the framework of an administration to enjoy the advantage of the statutory moratorium. Such a combination, however, was likely to increase the cost of the exercise considerably due to the time and expense of applying for an Administration Order, as the potentially cheaper and quicker out-of-court rout introduced by the EA 2002 was not then available.[25] Furthermore, for a successful CVA, the arrangement proposal must be attractive enough so that it could obtain the required three-quarters majority approval of the voting creditors, by reference to the value of their claims, and the approval of 50 per cent of the shareholders present at a separate meeting of members.[26] So its efficacy has hinged on its implementation only in connection with viable companies with strong creditors' support and rescue prospects.

The Two Stages of Reform

The recasting of CVA by the Insolvency Act 2000

To address the inherent instability of the original CVA procedure, in April 1995 the Insolvency Service issued a consultation paper[27] which suggested reforming the original 1986 CVA procedure by introducing a moratorium mechanism to the CVA procedure. In 1999 a review group was formed to consider the further development of the rescue approach and issued a Review of Company Rescue and Business Reconstruction Mechanisms. The latter paved the way for the Insolvency Act 2000 ('IA 2000'),[28] which introduced a number of substantial reforms to the original CVA procedure. The provisions of the 2000 Act were incorporated into the IA 1986 as s 1A and Schedule A1.[29]

---

[25] *Ibid.*

[26] R. 1.19 and r. 1.20 Insolvency Rules 1986, It should be noted that under the original 1986 CVA, an approved arrangement is binding only to those creditors who were to be notified and were entitled to vote at the relevant meeting.

[27] The Insolvency Service, *Proposals for a New Company Voluntary Arrangement Procedure* (Consultative Document, 2001). Prior to this a constructive document entitled 'Company Voluntary Arrangements and Administration Orders' was published in October 1993.

[28] The IA 2000 received Royal Assent on 30 November 2000, but was not brought into force until January 2003. In substance, the 2000 Act is an amendment Act to the IA 1986.

[29] The IA 2000 is limited to 18 sections and most of the detail is set out in Schedules and supporting rules. The main rules are the Insolvency (Amendment) (No. 2) Rules 2002.

The IA 2000, first, granted a protective moratorium to eligible companies to provide a necessary breathing space for the management to assess the prospects of the company and formulate a feasible reorganisation plan. Its availability is subject to several criteria[30] and is primarily based on the size of the company, requiring that the application for a moratorium must satisfy two or more of the qualifying conditions for being a 'small company'.[31]

The moratorium comes into force as soon as certain documents are filed in court, including the proposed voluntary arrangement and a statement from the nominee, and stops at the end of the day on which the meetings (a meeting of the company and a meeting of the creditors) summoned under para. 29(1) are first held (or, if the meetings are held on different days, the latter of those days), normally within 28 days.[32] The moratorium can be extended up to a further two months beyond the initial 28 days, with the creditors' consent.[33] During the moratorium, no petition may be presented for the winding up of the company, administration, administrative receivership or any steps to enforce security over the company's property.[34]

Furthermore, this reform enhanced the ability and effects of the voluntary agreed arrangement. As originally enacted, a CVA only bound creditors who had notice of, and were entitled to vote at the creditors' meeting.[35] The amended CVA rules extended the effects of an approved CVA to any creditor who was entitled to vote at the meeting of creditors,

---

30 For the criteria, see para.3 of Sch. A1 to the IA 1986.

31 Para.3(2) of Sch. A1 to the IA 1986. Section 382 of the CA 2006 set up the qualifying conditions as the 'small company', which requires the company, in a year, to satisfy two or more of the following requirements:

1. Turnover – not more than £6.5 million;
2. Balance sheet total – not more than £3.26 million;
3. Number of employees – not more than 50.

32 Para.8(1) of Sch. A1 to the IA 1986. The documents are referred to in para.7(1) of Sch. A1.

33 Para.3.2 of Sch. A1 to the IA 1986.

34 Para.12-14 of Sch. A1 to the IA 1986. Assets subject to a fixed charge or a crystallised floating charge can only be disposed of either with the consent of charge-holder or that of the court.

35 S 5(2)(b) IA 1986: the voluntary arrangement binds every person in accordance with the rules:

(i) was entitled to vote at that meeting (whether or not he was present or represented at it), or
(i) would have been so entitled if he had had notice of it, as if he were a party to the voluntary arrangement.

including those who would have been entitled to vote but failed to receive notice of the meeting.[36] Thus, if the creditors' meeting approved the proposal, any unknown creditors will be bound unless it can be shown that the company's directors had deliberately concealed their existence.

The reform of the Enterprise Act 2002

The Insolvency Act 2000 is one of the two stages of legislative reform to the Insolvency Act 1986. Seven months after the Act of 2000 received Royal Assent, a White Paper titled *Productivity and Enterprise: Insolvency – A Second Chance*[37] was published, which articulated the principles on which the insolvency provisions in the EA 2002 were based. Part 10 of the 2002 Act introduced provisions that deal with personal and corporate insolvency, which represent the most significant changes to insolvency law since the enactment of the IA 1986.[38] The main aim of the legislation, as far as corporate insolvency goes, is to provide the legal milieu for the fostering of a rescue culture.[39] This is to be done by focusing on the administration process and making it more

---

[36] Para.37(2) of Sch. A1 to the IA 1986 provides that the approved voluntary arrangement:

'(b) binds every person who in accordance with the rules:
(i) was entitled to vote at that meeting (whether or not he was present or represented at it), or
(ii) would have been so entitled if he had had notice of it, as if he were a party to the voluntary arrangement.'

[37] The Insolvency Service, *Productivity and Enterprise – Insolvency: A Second Chance* (Cm. 5234, July 2001). Following the speech of the then Secretary of State for Trade and Industry in 1999, the Honourable Stephen Byers, the Minister, and the Chancellor of the Exchequer established a Government review of corporate rescue and business reconstruction mechanisms, and in September 1999 a consultation document was produced by a review group. The review group then produced 'A review of Company Rescue and Business Reconstruction mechanisms' in 2000. In the spring of 2001 the Government gave a commitment that it would reform the bankruptcy laws to ensure that people obtained a second chance where they became bankrupt as a result of no fault of their own. Following re-election in 2001, the Government published the White Paper. On the policy background of EA 2002, see generally L Doyle and A Keay, *Insolvency Legislation: Annotations and Commentary* (Jordan Publishing, Bristol 2007), 1433–4.

[38] The corporate insolvency provisions became operative on 15 September 2003 and the personal insolvency provisions became operative on 1 April 2004.

[39] Doyle and Keay, *Insolvency Legislation: Annotations and Commentary*, 1434.

efficient and less costly. Allied to this is the restriction on QFC holders appointing administrative receivers.

Restriction on the use of administrative receivership Prior to the EA 2002, administrative receivership and liquidation were the most popular methods of dealing with corporate distress.[40] By section 250 of the EA 2002 a new Chapter IV[41] is inserted into Part 3 of the IA 1986, under which a holder of a floating charge created on or after 15 September 2003 may no longer appoint an administrative receiver save for some exceptional cases.[42] Instead, the charge holders are to secure their protection by using the administration process and will enjoy accorded enhanced rights of appointment and intervention under the new administration procedure.[43]

Historically speaking, administrative receivership was merely an individual debt enforcement method devised for a debenture holder with a floating charge to recover his security.[44] The administrative receiver, a qualified insolvency practitioner, is appointed by such security holders and is required to act primarily for the interests of the appointing debenture holder. The receiver owes only a limited duty of care to the company as the primary duty of care is to the appointor[45] and his

---

[40] This can be seen from the statistics about the use of Administrations and CVAs during 1991–1999 presented in Table 2.1 (p. 39).

[41] It is entitled *Prohibition of Appointment of Administrative Receiver.*

[42] Section 72A(4) of the IA 1986 imposes such time limitation on the application of the prohibition of appointment of administrative receiver. The exceptions, identified in Sections 72B to 72GA, are designed for some situations related to the capital market, public-private partnership, utility project, urban regeneration projects, financial market transactions and registered social landlords respectively.

[43] See especially paras.14 and 36 of Sch. B1 to the IA 1986. In cases of an out-of-court appointment by a QFC holder there is no requirement that the company is or is likely to become unable to pay its debts as there is where the court makes an administration order or where an out-of-court appointment is effected by a company or its directors. Para.36 of Sch. B1 confers a level of priority on the holder of a QFC by allowing the charge holder to nominate its own administrator on the hearing of an administration application.

[44] Goode, *Principles of Corporate Insolvency Law*, para.9-01.

[45] Goode, *Principles of Corporate Insolvency Law*, para.9-23. J Armour and S Frisby, 'Rethinking Receivership' (2001) 21 *Oxford Journal of Legal Studies* 73, 76–7. J Armour *et al.*, *The Impact of the Enterprise Act 2002 on Realisations and Costs in Corporate Rescue Proceedings* (Report to the Insolvency Service, 2006) <http://citeseerx.ist.psu.edu/viewdoc/download?doi=10.1.1.96.6853&rep=rep1&type=pdf> accessed 30 July 2015, 2–3. The receiver's position is dual-faceted in terms of the duties owed contemporaneously by him to the company

obligations to the company were subordinated to the duties owed to the debenture holder who appointed him.[46] Yet once in office, the receiver was granted a broad package of rights to manage the whole or a substantial part of the whole of the debtor company's property and the receiver was statutorily deemed to be the company's agent unless and until it goes into liquidation.[47]

The receivership procedure raised a fierce debate about its merits and demerits. Its opponents claimed that the wide-ranging powers held by the receivers and actually by the appointer could provide them with perverse incentives to close down a distressed business 'too quickly'.[48] The fact that this statutory process was primarily designed to generate cash to repay debenture holders provoked serious doubt as to its ability to facilitate corporate rescue and safeguard the interests of other corporate stakeholders, especially those of general unsecured creditors and employees.[49] It was widely held that the receivership device had led to excessive premature liquidations with quick assets sales on a break-up basis, as the administrative receiver may have inadequate incentives to stray far from the 'bottom line'[50] to maximise the available value of the company, especially when the appointing debenture holder is over-secured, that is, the value of the assets subject to its charge is greater than the amount of secured debt owed.[51]

---

and to his appointing debenture-holder. It is commented that the deeming of an administrative receiver as agent of a company until liquidation is unusual in nature since it does not operate for the benefit of the company – which itself has no power to determine the agency relationship or to control the function of the administrative receiver – but rather, serves to protect the appointing debenture-holder's security. See further Doyle and Keay, *Insolvency Legislation: Annotations and Commentary*, 79.

[46] Goode, *Principles of Corporate Insolvency Law*, para.9-23. In the case *Downsview Nominees Let v First City Corp Ltd* [1993] AC 295, Lord Templeman recognised that the receiver's duties to the company over the assets of which he is appointed are subordinate to the receiver's primary duties owed to his appointing debenture-holder.

[47] S 29(2) IA 1986. The power of the administrative receiver is specified under section 44(1) of the IA 1986.

[48] Mokal, *Corporate Insolvency Law: Theory and Application*, 212.

[49] S Frisby, 'In Search of a Rescue Regime: The Enterprise Act 2002' (2004) 67 *MLR* 247, 251.

[50] This is to satisfy the recovery of debt owed to the appointing-creditor.

[51] Frisby, 'In Search of a Rescue Regime: The Enterprise Act 2002', 251–2. Armour *et al.*, *The Costs and Benefits of Secured Creditor Control in Bankruptcy: Evidence from the UK*, 1.

The supporting arguments centred on the fact that although the broad package of rights granted to the receiver, who acted primarily for the interests of the appointing debenture holder, was structurally imbalanced for a legal institution, this kind of allocation of controlling rights was likely to be more efficient; giving control over enforcement to the main creditor could reduce the total monitoring and decision-making costs. This privilege, as it was argued, allowed the major creditor to make good use of its investment in information-gathering about the debtor, thus generating more savings for parties, who otherwise could suffer more loss from their likely inappropriate enforcement decision particularly when information is costly to them.[52]

Nevertheless, in the White Paper, the Government upheld the opposite view:

> An administrative receiver is entitled to solely consider the interests of his or her appointor when determining the timing of a sale of a business. Where an offer is made which is sufficient to satisfy the secured creditor's claim and the administrative receiver's costs, there would appear to be little incentive for the receiver to delay the sale with a view to obtaining a better offer which might provide some return for unsecured creditors.[53]

Based on the perceived prejudice to the interests of other stakeholders in receivership[54] and the desire for more collective, accountable and fair proceedings, where the insolvency practitioner could make decisions to ensure value-maximising disposals of a distressed business for the benefits of different groups of stakeholders,[55] the EA 2002 substantially abated the right of the QFC holder to appoint an administrative receiver.

Redesigning the administration procedure

Having significantly enlarged the channel that led to administration through the abrogation of the right of initiating an administrative

---

52 Armour and Frisby, 'Rethinking Receivership', 81–5.

53 The Insolvency Service, 'Productivity and Enterprise – Insolvency: A Second Chance', para.2.3.

54 Mokal, *Corporate Insolvency Law: Theory and Application*, 212. S Frisby, *Report on Insolvency Outcomes* (Report to the Insolvency Service, 2006), previously available at <http://www.insolvency.gov.uk/insolvencyprofessionandlegislation/research/corpdocs/InsolvencyOutcomes.pdf> accessed 15 January 2012, 65.

55 R Mokal, *Administrative Receivership and Administration – an Analysis* (2004) <http://papers.ssrn.com/sol3/papers.cfm?abstract_id=466701> accessed 30 July 2015, 14–15.

receivership, the EA 2002 replaced the old administration with a new streamlined administration procedure and overhauled the whole process in an effort to make it more efficient and attractive.[56]

Streamlining the procedure and three routes to initiate an administration procedure To address the delay and expense involved in the operation of the statuary procedure, the EA 2002 introduced a new out-of-court entry route and made the selection of routes into the new administration much more flexible. Traditionally, an administration could only be initiated by a petition for a court order. In contrast, there were three routes to initiate the administration procedure under the reformulated regime.

The court may issue an administration order on a petition for such order only if the applicant[57] gives evidence (1) of the insolvency or likely insolvency of the company, and (2) that the administration order is reasonably likely to achieve the purpose of administration.[58]

Furthermore, an administrator may be appointed out-of-court by a QFC holder.[59] The QFC holder must file a notice of appointment with the court, including a statutory declaration that the qualified floating charge is enforceable and a statement by the administrator that in his opinion the purpose of administration is reasonably likely to be achieved.[60] It should be noted that there is no requirement that the company is or is likely to become unable to pay its debts. This out-of-court appointment route is commonly regarded as compensation to the QFC holder for blocking his right to initiate administrative receivership.[61]

Furthermore, the out-of-court appointment of an administrator can be made by the company or its directors provided there is no objection from a person who is or may be entitled to appoint an administrative receiver or administrator of the company.[62] The company or the directors must file a statutory declaration that the company is or is likely to become

---

[56] Doyle and Keay, *Insolvency Legislation: Annotations and Commentary*, 1434.

[57] An application to the court for an administration order may be made only by the company, the directors of the company, one or more creditors of the company, or the justices' chief executive for a magistrates' court, as well as a liquidator and a supervisor of a CVA. Para.12 of Sch. B1 to the IA 1986.

[58] Para.12 of Sch. B1 to the IA 1986.

[59] Para.14(1) of Sch. B1 to the IA 1986.

[60] Para.18 of Sch. B1 to the IA 1986.

[61] Armour *et al.*, *The Costs and Benefits of Secured Creditor Control in Bankruptcy: Evidence from the UK*, 5.

[62] Para.28 of Sch. B1 to the IA 1986.

unable to pay its debts, and a statement by the administrator that, in his opinion, the purpose of administration is reasonably likely to be achieved.[63] The company or the directors cannot appoint an administrator within 12 months of a moratorium of a failed CVA or if there is an extant winding up or administration petition, or if there is an administrative receiver in post.[64] The rationale behind these provisions is to require the directors of the company, or bank creditors when the company is in a state of insolvency, to put it into some type of formal insolvency proceedings with reasonable promptness.

In addition, a clear exit from administration is also emphasised by setting a time constraint requiring that the appointment of an administrator will cease automatically at the end of the period of one year after the appointment takes effect. The term of office could be extended by a maximum of six months with the consent of the creditors,[65] or by the court on the administrator's application with no stated limits to the extension.[66]

Another change is that the Act by means of s 248 enables an administrator to make a distribution to secured or preferential creditors without the consent of the court and to other creditors with the consent of the court.[67] Previously, under the old regime, the administrator was granted permission to make distributions to preferential creditors only if such a power could be properly regarded as necessary or incidental to achieve the purpose of the administration order. This extension of power removes this constraint and therefore gives administrators greater flexibility.[68]

Reformulating the purposes of the administration process The EA 2002 imposes a clear rescue-oriented objective on the revised administration procedure to facilitate the survival of the company or its business if possible. The original administration model was not a complete rescue procedure. Its main effect was to impose a moratorium on the enforcement of creditors' claims, and restructuring was carried out through an associated CVA or a compromise of arrangements under s 425 of the CA

---

63 Paras.27(2)(a) and 29(3) of Sch. B1 to the IA 1986.

64 Paras.24 and 25 of Sch. B1 to the IA 1986.

65 This requires the unanimous approval of secured creditors, plus 50 per cent by value of the unsecured claims with a tangible interest. Para.78 of Sch. B1 to the IA 1986.

66 Paras.76-8 of Sch. B1 to the IA 1986.

67 Para.65 of Sch. BI to the IA 1986.

68 See *Re The Designer Room Ltd* [2004] EWHC 720 (Ch).

1985.[69] The court could make an order providing for any one or more of four purposes specified by the formerly operative s 8(3) of the IA 1986. The revised scheme requires the administrator to carry out his duties following a priority hierarchy of the purposes of the administration procedure under paragraph 3(1) of the Schedule B1 to the IA 1986, on top of which he is to rescue the company as a going concern.

Paragraph 3 of Schedule B1 to the IA 1986 lists three statutory objectives in a hierarchical form for the administrator to pursue, namely:

(a) rescuing the company as a going concern, or
(b) achieving a better result for the company's creditors as a whole than would be likely if the company were wound up (without first being in administration), or
(c) realising property in order to make a distribution to one or more secured or preferential creditors.

It should be noted that the original first objective in the Enterprise Bill referred only to 'rescuing the company'.[70] It was later amended by adding 'as a going concern' in order to make it clear that this objective is 'not to preserve an empty shell of a company but rather to rescue the company with the whole or a substantial part of its business intact'.[71] According to this understanding, it can be claimed that objective (a) i.e. rescuing the company as a going concern, can be achieved either by turning the company around and restoring it to profitable trading,[72] or by

---

[69] Goode, *Principles of Corporate Insolvency Law*, 327.

[70] The first two purposes of administration listed in the Enterprise Bill were: (a) with the objective of rescuing the company, or (b) where it is not reasonably practicable to rescue the company, with the objective of achieving a better result for the company's creditors as a whole than would be likely if the company were wound up (without first being in administration).

During the passage of the Enterprise Act, in giving evidence at the Standing Committee stage, Mr Douglas Alexander, Minister of E-Commerce and Competitiveness stated that: '[t]he purpose 'to rescue the company' evidently means to rescue the company as a going concern, with the whole or much of its business intact. We are confident that the courts would interpret the purpose in exactly that way. If the objective of administration were to rescue the company's businesses rather than the company itself, frankly there would be little incentive for directors of the company to enter into administration, which is one of the intentions of the Bill.'

[71] Goode, *Principles of Corporate Insolvency Law*, para.10-29.

[72] This can be done by facilitating a reorganisation of its capital structure through a CVA or a Scheme of Arrangement.

preserving a substantial part of the company's business, which encompasses proposals to sell the company's business as a going concern.

In contrast, objective (b) achieving a better result for the company's creditors as a whole than would be likely if the company were wound up, is normally the result where the company or its substantial businesses and assets are sold as a going concern.[73] 'Better result' here refers to a better financial result and implies a comparison of returns to creditors in administration with their likely dividend in liquidation.[74] It does not appear mutually exclusive with objective (a), since both objectives will be achieved if a company's substantial business is rescued through a sale, which would be expected to yield more money for creditors than they might expect in liquidation.[75]

Nevertheless, the overlap is largely academic.[76] The practical viewpoint often regards objective (a) as achieving a turnaround of the company with the whole or substantial part of the business preserved, and objective (b) is one that is achieved by selling the company's business and assets as a going concern.[77] The Explanatory Notes to the EA 2002 also consider objective (a) as company rescue by suggesting that 'if the administrator thinks that a company rescue is not reasonably practical, or would not achieve the best result for the creditors as a whole, he or she will seek a better result for the creditors than on a winding-up'.[78]

It should be clear that the desire for company rescue shall not be pursued at the expense of the company's creditors. Para. 3(2) requires the

---

[73] In some situations, it might be achieved by continuing the 'trading out' of existing contracts where the business has no long-term viability or processing an assets sale in administration without any 'trading on' if the costs of conducting a liquidation are anticipated to be greater than those of an administration. See J Amour and RJ Mokal, *Reforming the Governance of Corporate Rescue: The Enterprise Act 2002* (ESRC Centre for Business Research, University of Cambridge, Working Paper No. 289) <http://citeseerx.ist.psu.edu/viewdoc/download?doi=10.1.1.167.5939&rep=rep1&type=pdf> accessed 30 July 2015.

[74] *Ibid.*

[75] Such a situation will be judged according to para.3(2) and para.3(3) – whether para.(1)(b) would achieve a better result for the company's creditors as a whole.

[76] Amour and Mokal, *Reforming the Governance of Corporate Rescue: The Enterprise Act 2002*, footnote 100.

[77] This can be detected in many administrator's proposals and reports.

[78] The Explanatory Notes to the Enterprise Act 2002 <http://www.legislation.gov.uk/ukpga/2002/40/notes/division/4/10/2> accessed 30 July 2015, para.650.

administrator to perform his functions in the interests of the company's creditors as a whole in selecting objectives between (a) and (b). It is suggested that the duty to serve the interests of the company's creditors as a whole would compel the administrator to pursue the second objective where this would realise more for the creditors than a re-organisation achieving objective (a).[79] This is in line with the comments of Lord McIntosh of Haringey, the Minister responsible for steering the Enterprise Bill through the House of Lords, in the legislative process:

> We do not want an administrator to have to pursue a company rescue that would be reasonably practicable but would result in a lower return to creditors ...[80]

Therefore, primacy is given to maximising overall returns to creditors rather than to rescue per se.

OVERVIEW OF RESCUE-ORIENTED PROCEEDINGS IN THE UK

Within the path of corporate financial decline, a range of options can be employed for the purpose of rescuing the company or the business of the entity before resorting to a piecemeal-sale liquidation. As discussed earlier, there are three statutory rescue options available under the current English insolvency system: namely, CVA, Schemes of Arrangement under Section 895 of the CA 2006[81] and the administration procedure.[82] I will now discuss each of them in turn, providing also a concise appraisal of the merits and demerits of each route.

Company Voluntary Arrangements

A CVA is a mechanism for a company to come to a legally binding agreement with its creditors in satisfaction of their claims. It typically

---

[79] *Ibid.*

[80] Hansard HL vol 639 col 1101 (21 October 2002).

[81] This section is from Section 425 of the old Companies Act 1985 without significant amendment. It came into effect on 6 April 2008.

[82] The receiver would also attempt some form of rescue in a proper situation. However, as in receivership the secured creditors enjoy an overriding priority and control during the proceedings. There is concern that this characteristic is likely to produce a 'perverse incentive' to the rescue endeavour, especially when the appointing debenture holder is over-secured.

involves the continuation of trading under which the company makes periodic payments from its trading income to the supervisor of the CVA for distribution in accordance with its terms, a process which may continue for a considerable time.[83] A CVA may be made whether or not the company is insolvent or likely to become insolvent[84] and it was designed to encourage the directors of viable companies to instigate change before encountering severe financial difficulty.

The CVA procedure

A CVA may either precede, follow, or run in parallel with an administration or winding-up or be pursued on its own, without any prior or subsequent insolvency proceedings. A distinctive feature of the CVA is that it allows the directors to retain the managerial control while its debts are being re-scheduled, although a qualified insolvency practitioner will be appointed as a nominee to scrutinise the arrangement proposed by the company directors.[85] The directors of the company may, however, only propose a CVA where the company is not in administration or liquidation.[86] If the company is in administration or liquidation, only the administrator or the liquidator may make the relevant proposal, and will usually be the nominee, otherwise it can be any qualified insolvency practitioner.[87]

The nominee has to monitor the company's affairs for the purpose of forming a professional judgement on whether the proposal has a reasonable prospect of being approved and implemented and whether the company is likely to have sufficient funds to enable it to continue to carry on its business during the moratorium.[88] The IA 2000 introduced the new CVA moratorium procedure for 'small eligible' companies, which will be granted with the professional validation by the nominee. Yet for the cases beyond small eligible companies, there is still no such moratorium on the

---

[83] R Goode, *Principles of Corporate Insolvency Law* (4th edn, Sweet and Maxwell, London 2011), para.12-26.

[84] S 1 IA 1986.

[85] A proposal is formulated by the directors if the company is not in administration or liquidation or by the administrator or liquidator if it is.

[86] Rules 1.2 and 1.3 IR 1986. According to ss 1(1) and (3) of the IA 1986, where the company is in administration only the administrator may make the proposal and where it is in liquidation, only the liquidator is entitled to do so.

[87] S 1(1) and 1(3) IA 1986.

[88] Para.24 of Sch. A1 to the IA 1986. Finch, 'The Recasting of Insolvency Law', 727.

enforcement of creditors' rights unless a CVA is initiated within an Administration procedure.

A meeting of the company and its creditors will be convened to vote upon the proposed arrangement with or without modifications. The proposal shall not affect the right of a secured creditor of the company to enforce his security without the concurrence of the creditor concerned. As mentioned above, the proposal must be approved by a 75 per cent majority of the creditors. This is measured in terms of the value of the unsecured portion of their debts and a simple majority of the shareholders present at a separate meeting of members, the value being determined by the number of votes conferred by the company's articles.[89] Once the decision to approve the CVA has become effective, the CVA becomes legally binding on all parties who had notice of the meeting and were entitled to vote at it, whether or not they were actually present or were represented.[90] The nominee becomes the supervisor of the CVA upon acceptance of said arrangements.[91]

In certain situations, CVAs could offer distinct flexibility for company directors to propose any sort of composition they think may be acceptable to creditors before the company becomes seriously insolvent. Another advantage of using a CVA is confidentiality. There is no statutory requirement for a public announcement, official records or any other sort of statement, therefore this rescue device is particularly appropriate for those companies whose business is reputation-based.[92] Fletcher argued that the procedure has proved to be a remarkably cost-effective way of resolving the problems of some financially troubled companies, especially in those cases where the significant creditors of the company are not excessively numerous and are known to be supportive, and the terms of a prospective arrangement may be concluded by a consultative process so that a sufficient majority of votes may be accrued to secure the expeditious adoption of the proposal, and therefore the possibility for disruptive tactics on the part of dissenting creditors can be kept to a minimum.[93]

A successful CVA contains some fundamental ingredients. First, the arrangement plan needs to be realistic and viable, that is, acceptable to

---

89 R 1.19 and r 1.20 IR 1986.

90 S 5(2) IA 1986.

91 S 7 IA 1986.

92 D Milman and F Chittenden, *Corporate Recue: CVAs and the Challenge of Small Companies* (Chartered Association of Certified Accountants, London 1995), 31.

93 Fletcher, 'UK Corporate Rescue: Recent Developments', 133.

the different groups of creditors.[94] This requires the incumbent management to be capable of expending the resources necessary to effectuate a comprehensive solution and to modify the reorganisation process. Secondly, creditors' support for the plan and willingness to negotiate the arrangement is vital for the success of the arrangement.[95] The difficulty here is that while the survival of the company as a going concern is likely to generate more benefits than the liquidation alternative, the creditors' decision mainly depends on balancing the costs of negotiation against the prospects of disruption and unproductive outcomes. Given the long duration and unpredictability involved, there are always cases where some creditors, especially secured creditors, may insist on a simpler and more direct way to gain the proceeds of the ailing business so as to receive the repayment of their money as quickly as possible. This is especially the case when there is no automatic stay on enforcement by the creditors of large companies or no extension after the initial moratorium for small eligible ones. Larger companies may enter administration to secure the moratorium they need while negotiating a CVA, but administrations are more costly than CVAs. Furthermore, securing new funds in order to finance continuing activities while negotiating is also a fundamental challenge for CVAs. The availability of longer-term financing will crucially affect the success or failure of a CVA since creditors are unlikely to agree to the company's proposals without the prospect of secure funding.[96]

As a pioneering rescue procedure in the UK insolvency system, the overall policy objective behind the process is to ensure the continuation of the company as a going concern wherever possible.[97] Nevertheless, due to the aforementioned reasons, most CVAs do not in fact involve reorganisation of the company; rather, they focus on preservation of the business with a view to its sale as a going concern and/or disposal of particular assets, followed by a distribution of realisations by way of dividend, after which the company is usually wound up.[98]

---

[94] Frisby, 'Report on Insolvency Outcomes', 63.

[95] *Ibid.*

[96] See Finch, *Corporate Insolvency Law: Perspectives and Principles*, 345, and Finch, 'The Dynamics of Insolvency Law: Three Models of Reform', 441.

[97] The Insolvency Service, *Encouraging Company Rescue – A Consultation* (June 2009), 12.

[98] Goode, *Principles of Corporate Insolvency Law* (4th edn 2011), para.12-43.

Proposals for reforming CVAs

A consultation document,[99] issued in June 2009 by the UK's Insolvency Service, invited views on a number of possible measures to further enhance the existing corporate insolvency regime in enabling viable businesses facing temporary difficulties to turn themselves round. The consultation focused on four main proposals to promote greater use of CVAs as a route for the restructuring of a company's affairs by providing an effective moratorium and facilitating access to CVA financing by increasing the company's ability to offer new security.[100]

There are two mutually exclusive proposals for moratorium provisions. One proposal is to extend to medium and large companies the option of a protective moratorium against creditor action for up to 28 days – currently only available to small companies – so the larger companies too can benefit from a 'breathing space' in which they can seek agreement with their creditors to deal with their debts.[101] The other proposal is to create a new, court-sanctioned CVA moratorium, which allows directors of a company to apply to the court for an initial private hearing at which the court could grant a moratorium of 42 days with the possibility of a further extension. Under this proposal the court needs to satisfy itself that: (1) the company is unable to pay its debts, or is likely to become unable to pay its debts within three months of the hearing date; (2) there is a reasonable prospect of a CVA being approved by the creditors; and (3) in the circumstances, sanctioning a moratorium would be in the interests of creditors as a whole.[102] A qualified insolvency practitioner would also be involved at certain key stages of the application process and would help to safeguard the interests of creditors while the moratorium was in force.

There are also proposals for greater room to create new secured charges within CVAs to enable a company that is considering a CVA to

---

[99] It was entitled 'Encouraging Company Rescue – A Consultation'.

[100] Proposals in this consultation document included: a) an extension of small company moratorium provisions to larger companies; b) the proposal of court-sanctioned moratorium; c) a super-priority of rescue finance in administration expenses; d) a greater ability to create new secured charges in an administration; and e) a greater ability to create new secured charges in a CVA.

[101] This proposal allows the directors of the company to obtain a moratorium by filing documents with the court preventing creditors from taking action against the company or its property for an initial period of 28 days where the nominee considers that the directors' CVA proposal has a reasonable prospect of success and of being approved by at least 75 per cent of creditors. See *Encouraging Company Rescue – A Consultation*, 14–15.

[102] See *Encouraging Company Rescue – A Consultation*, 16–17.

secure new finance, conditional upon the CVA proposal being agreed by creditors. Under these proposals, the new finance could be secured against any property that is not already encumbered by fixed security; or as a subordinate fixed charge on any property; or as a first charge ahead of other fixed charges or an equal first charge on property already subject to a fixed charge, subjected to the agreement of the existing fixed charge holder(s) or the court and only where there is no scope for new or subordinate fixed charges.[103] A company proposing a CVA would thus be able to offer a rescue finance provider security over unencumbered property, or a second charge on secured property, or a first charge on any of the company's property ranking either ahead of or equal to an existing first charge. In each case the rescue finance provider would get priority over an existing floating charge holder and ahead of unsecured creditors.[104]

In circumstances where the rescue finance is to be secured by a priority or equal first charge, either the existing fixed charge holder(s) should consent to this or, if such consent is not provided, the court should decide whether the following three requisite conditions would be met: (1) the granting of such security for this rescue finance is necessary in order to obtain that finance; (2) the interests of existing fixed charge holders are adequately protected; and (3) obtaining the rescue finance is in the best interests of creditors as a whole.[105]

Feedback received on the 2009 consultation suggested that the moratoria proposals were broadly welcome but responses on the finance-related proposals were divided. There was a broad consensus in favour of a court-sanctioned moratorium when proposing a CVA over the extension of small company moratorium provisions to larger companies.[106] A further consultation exercise, *Proposals for a Restructuring Moratorium – a*

[103] *Ibid.*, 22–3.

[104] *Ibid.*, 23.

[105] *Ibid.* The burden of proof would be on the company to show that they are met. The fixed charge holder would receive notice of this court hearing and would have the opportunity to make representations to the court to reach its decision.

[106] Summary of Responses on the consolation paper and the accompanying Ministerial Statement suggested the extension of small company moratorium provisions to larger companies would have limited benefits both as CVAs cannot be used to restructure secured debt and as an extended CVA moratorium would not cover the period prior to the launch of the CVA during which the terms of the financial restructuring were negotiated.

Consultation,[107] was launched in July 2010 proposing a far wider restructuring moratorium, which would be available to the company which is either seeking a contractual compromise with its creditors or proposing a statutory compromise by way of a CVA or Scheme of Arrangement.[108] Therefore it would not only apply to any company that could be subject to a CVA or to a Scheme of Arrangement under Part 26 of CA 2006 but available to all companies restructuring their debts.

The Government in the 2010 Consultation set out further proposals for a new three-month court-sanctioned moratorium for companies seeking to restructure their debt. In order to obtain a moratorium, the company must satisfy the eligibility test[109] and certain qualifying conditions, which require the directors to demonstrate that: (1) there is a reasonable prospect that a compromise or arrangement can be agreed with its creditors and (2) the company must be able to show that it is likely to have sufficient funds to carry on its business during the moratorium.[110] Directors' views would require confirmation by an insolvency practitioner. If a moratorium was sanctioned, the court would confirm the appointment of an independent insolvency practitioner to act as 'the monitor' to safeguard creditors' interests during the moratorium period.[111] The moratorium would only remain in force while the qualifying conditions were met.[112] The company would remain under the control of its directors during the moratorium subject to certain constraints[113] and sanctions in addition to ongoing checks by the monitor.

---

107 The Insolvency Service, *Proposals for a Restructuring Moratorium* (Consultation, July 2010).

108 It is proposed that the restructuring moratorium will be capable of covering, if required, both initial negotiations aimed at developing a compromise proposal, and the time required for creditor approval of a statutory proposal.

109 Certain types of companies will be excluded. In addition to those insurance companies, banks and companies involved in specific financial market transactions – any subsidiary of a company (a) whose centre of main interests is in another EU Member State and (b) which is being wound-up will also be excluded. For more details on the eligibility tests, see *Proposals for a Restructuring Moratorium*, 13 and Annex B.

110 *Ibid.*, 13.

111 The monitor would act on behalf of the court, and would be independent of the interests of any creditor or creditors. *Ibid.*

112 Proposals for safeguarding the interests of creditors and deterring abuse by companies or their directors during the moratorium period are provided in part 4 of the Consultation paper at 16–21.

113 A range of provisions is provided to deter any misconduct or abuse by directors. See *Proposals for a Restructuring Moratorium*, para.4.20.

An important feature associated with the proposed moratorium was that a CVA prepared while a moratorium was in force should not be capable of compromising debts arising during the moratorium. Any such debts must be paid in full, and the relevant creditors should not be prevented from enforcing their debts while the CVA was in place regardless of the expiration of the moratorium.[114] Also, moratorium debts would have a 'super-priority' status in any subsequent insolvency process, provided that the procedure is entered into immediately after the moratorium.[115] Such a provision would provide greater financial security for those trading with the company during the moratorium, and help the company secure funding that may be required to support its business in moratorium.

The proposals embrace key features of the US Chapter 11 process, in particular the fact that the directors remain in place during the moratorium (akin to the 'debtor in possession' concept) and the super-priority status of any funding during the moratorium. According to the Summary of Responses published in May 2011,[116] stakeholders suggested that the basic proposal was welcome, but more specific detail was needed on the workings of the proposed restructuring moratorium and how such legislation might be framed. More detail was required in relation to both qualifying conditions and more clarity was required about the role of the monitor. Also, as currently drafted, the moratorium does not prevent the exercise of ipso facto clauses, which allow a counterparty to exercise contractual termination rights upon the insolvency of the company. This is a key concern of secured lenders as the right of suppliers to invoke contract termination clauses on the onset of insolvency is presented as one of the biggest obstacles to a successful restructuring.[117] As this stage,

---

[114] *Proposals for a Restructuring Moratorium*, para.4.24.

[115] *Ibid.*, para.4.25.

[116] The Insolvency Service, *Proposals for Restructuring Moratorium – Summary of Responses* (May 2011) previously available at <http://webarchive.nationalarchives.gov.uk/+/http://www.insolvency.gov.uk/insolvencyprofessionandlegislation/con_doc_register/Moratorium/SummaryOfResponses.pdf> accessed 15 March 2014.

[117] Most of the respondents believe there should be certain restriction to stop some suppliers demanding 'ransom' terms for continuing supply if the company has continued to meet all its obligation in terms of payment and other contractual obligations. However, a counter argument made by some respondents is that this would go against contracts which have been freely entered into by both parties.

the Government is working with stakeholders both to refine the moratorium proposals and to consider in more detail the additional concerns that have been raised during consultation.[118]

Schemes of Arrangement[119]

This long-established statutory device applies where a company may wish to form a compromise arrangement with its creditors, or any class of them, or its members, or any class of them. Therefore schemes of arrangement may be regarded as a limited form of statutory corporate rescue mechanism.[120] Unlike a CVA, a scheme requires court approval. The creditors, the company itself or its members, or the liquidator/administrator, where the company is being wound up or has entered an administration procedure, can initiate a scheme through a petition to the court.[121] As with the CVAs, schemes of arrangement can be entered into by companies that are still solvent, and no statutory moratorium is imposed to protect the debtor until the court has sanctioned the scheme. In a stand-alone scheme of arrangement, the directors of the company could continue to absolutely control its affairs during the scheme, subject to no supervision from an outside insolvency practitioner.

The court is involved in the procedure in at least two stages: (1) on convening the necessary meetings of creditors and members and (2) on the petition to sanction the scheme as approved by the appropriate majorities of the meetings.[122] Due to the complexity of the approval arrangements, meetings of affected classes of creditors or members of the company are convened separately.[123] For the approval of the scheme, the

---

118 The Parliamentary Under-Secretary of State for Business, Innovation and Skills (Mr Edward Davey): *Written Ministerial Statement on Government Policy following the Restructuring Moratorium Consultation* (11 May 2011) <http://www.publications.parliament.uk/pa/cm201011/cmhansrd/cm110511/wmstext/110511m0001.htm> accessed 30 July 2015.

119 This regime was previous prescribed in ss 425–7 of Companies Act 1985. The provisions of Part 26 of CA 2006 restate ss 425–7 of the 1985 Act.

120 S 895(1) CA 2006.

121 S 896 of CA 2006.

122 Finch, *Corporate Insolvency Law: Perspectives and Principles*, 328.

123 In practice, schemes have not been approved unless they have satisfied the interests of all parties affected. Furthermore, if the meetings are not divided properly or do not reflect all interests of the different classes, the court may refuse to sanction the scheme. It is often difficult, however, to know what constitutes a class for the right purposes. The Company Law Review Steering Group is in favour of the court having the discretion to decide class issues at the

compromise or arrangement proposal shall be agreed by a majority in number representing 75 per cent in value of the creditors or class of creditors or members or class of members who are present and vote at the convened meeting.[124] On such approval being obtained, the scheme must be approved by the court, which will consider issues of procedural fairness, hear objections from dissenters and decide whether the scheme is 'fair and reasonable'.[125] Once sanctioned by the court, the scheme will bind all creditors or the class of creditors or the members or class of members, and the company.[126] This procedure has several advantages that other rescue proceedings may not enjoy. Schemes may be tailored to corporate needs and there are no statutory prescribed contents for such schemes, therefore they are very flexible and can be used in conjunction with liquidation or administration or as an alternative to liquidation.[127] Furthermore, it allows the existing directors to stay in control of the company and the schemes may be formulated and approved without any requirement. This could encourage early attention to corporate difficulties and timely responses to the problems.

Yet schemes of arrangement also present several disadvantages. For example, a major constraint is that no moratorium is involved, and thus in the period between the initial formulation of a scheme and its becoming effective via court order, each individual creditor is able to exercise all the rights and remedies that he possesses against the company debtor. Furthermore, schemes may have to be coupled with administration if any protection is to be secured. As a result, in practice, schemes can prove slow and complicated and likely to attract high legal costs. Therefore this device remains under-utilised and generally employed in the preservation of larger companies.[128] Their usefulness is mainly limited to larger

---

application stage. It is also suggested that the courts should be able to sanction a scheme even if classes had been wrongly constituted or, in appropriate circumstances, where separate meetings had not been held. See further Finch, *Corporate Insolvency Law: Perspectives and Principles*, 327–8. See further the Company Law Review Steering Group, *Modern Company Law for a Competitive Economy: Final Report* (2001), paras.13.7 and 13.8.

124 S 899(1) CA 2006.

125 Finch, *Corporate Insolvency Law: Perspectives and Principles*, 325.

126 S 899(3) CA 2006.

127 Finch, *Corporate Insolvency Law: Perspectives and Principles*, 325–6.

128 JR Lingard, *Corporate Rescues and Insolvencies* (Butterworths, London 1989), 49.

enterprises with complex corporate financing structures, where these enterprises require a long-term settlement.[129]

The Administration Procedure

Where the administration procedure is used, an interim moratorium protection is obtained automatically with the presentation of application for an administration order or a court filing of a notice of intention to appoint an administrator.[130] The moratorium freezes enforcement of the rights of secured and unsecured creditors which, then, may only be exercised with the permission of the court or the consent of the administrator, preventing the company from going into voluntary or compulsory winding up.[131] Once the process of administration begins, the coordination and control of the company's affairs are concentrated in the hands of the administrator, who is vested with legal obligations to act fairly and to pursue his powers in the interests of the creditors as a whole.[132]

Upon his appointment, the administrator becomes an officer of the court whether appointed by court process or not and will act as an agent of the company.[133] The administrator has extensive powers to do anything necessary for the management of the affairs, business and property of the company.[134] The appointment of an administrator does not in itself affect the status of a director as such. The powers of the directors, however, are curtailed on the administrator's appointment. They cannot exercise management powers which could interfere with the exercise of the administrator's duties and competences.[135] Furthermore, the directors have a duty to cooperate with the administrator;[136] breach of this duty by company

---

129 D Milman, 'Reforming Corporate Rescue Mechanisms' in J Lacy (ed) *Reform of United Kingdom Company Law* (Cavendish, London 2002), 415.

130 Para.44 of Sch. B1 to the IA 1986. In the case of an out-of-court appointment, an interim moratorium arises immediately upon the filing with the court of notice of intention to appoint. A further moratorium arises upon the filing of the appointment. In the case of a court appointment, an interim moratorium arises as soon as the application is lodged with the court. A further moratorium arises upon the making of the administration order.

131 Paras.23(1) and 43(2) of Sch. B1 to the IA 1986.

132 Para.3(2) of Sch. B1 to the IA 1986.

133 Paras.5 and 69 of Sch. B1 to the IA 1986.

134 Para.59(1) of Sch. B1 to the IA 1986.

135 Para.64 of Sch. B1 to the IA 1986.

136 S 235 IA 1986. The provision is an investigative power providing for an informal procedure for all office-holders to obtain information.

directors may lead to their disqualification.[137] Generally, the administrator has the power to remove and appoint any directors of the company.[138]

The administrator must prepare a statement setting out proposals for achieving the purpose of the administration,[139] and initiate a creditors' meeting to allow those who will be principally affected by the implementation of the plan to vote on the proposals.[140] However, such meetings need not to be convened where the statement of proposals states that the administrator thinks that the company has sufficient property to enable each creditor to be paid in full or has insufficient property to enable a distribution to be made to unsecured creditors other than by virtue of s 176A(2)(a),[141] or where neither of the first two objectives of para.3 of the Sch. B1 can be achieved.[142]

At the creditors' meeting, the class of creditors which will be principally affected by the implementation of the proposal votes.[143] The law provides that the administrator's proposals cannot affect the rights of a secured creditor to enforce its security.[144] Therefore, normally, only unsecured creditors are entitled to vote on the proposals. Secured creditors are only entitled to vote where their claim exceeds the value of their security.[145] The proposal may be approved without modification or

137 Ss 6 and 9 of the Company Directors Disqualification Act 1986.

138 Para.61 of Sch. B1 to the IA 1986.

139 A copy of the plan must be sent to the company's creditors as soon as is reasonably practicable after the company has entered administration, within a maximum of eight weeks, subject to extension. Para.49 of Sch. B1 to the IA 1986.

140 The administrator shall initiate a creditors' meeting as soon as reasonably practicable but in any event within the period of ten weeks beginning with the date on which the company enters administration. See para.51(2) of Sch. B1 to the IA 1986.

141 This relates to the prescribed part. Under the new s 176A of the IA 1986 where assets are subject to a floating charge created on or after 15 September 2003, the administrators (or liquidators or receivers) must make a prescribed part of the company's net property available for the satisfaction of unsecured debts and must not distribute that part to the proprietor of a floating charge except in so far as it exceeds the amount required for the satisfaction of unsecured debts.

142 Nevertheless, the law allows creditors of the company whose debts amount to at least 10 per cent of the total to require the administrator to summon an initial creditors' meeting. Para.52 of Sch. B1 to the IA 1986.

143 Mokal, *Corporate Insolvency Law: Theory and Application*, 252.

144 Para.73(1)(a) of Sch. B1 to the IA 1986.

145 R.2.40(1) IR 1986. They are, however, entitled to vote in respect of the full value of their claims if the meeting is required under para.52(2) of Sch. B1.

approved with modifications to which the administrator consents.[146] A resolution on the administrator's proposal requires only overall majority in the value of the debts owed to those present or voting.[147] Should the administrator put forward a proposal for a CVA, voting to approve it would be necessary, which requires a majority in excess of three-quarters in value of the creditors present and voting on the resolution.

The administrator is required to manage the company's affairs in accordance with the proposals that have been approved by the creditors, save in exceptional circumstances.[148] If the meeting fails to obtain approval of the administrator's proposals even as revised, the court may terminate the administration, put the company into winding up, or make another order as it thinks appropriate.[149]

Duties of the administrator

The duties and liabilities of the administrator derive from the fact that he occupies three overlapping but distinct positions, namely, the officer of court;[150] the officer and agent of company;[151] and the statutory office-holder.[152] As said earlier, the administrator is an officer of the court whether or not he is appointed by the court.[153] This status entitles him to a right of access to the court for the provision of directions and protection from the law of contempt against interference with his management of the company's affairs and the performance of his duties.[154] In terms of duties, the consequence of being an officer of the

---

146 Para.53(1) of Sch. B1 to IA 1986.

147 R 2.42(1), (2) IR 1986.

148 Paras.68(1) and (2) of Sch. B1 to IA 1986.

149 Para.55 of Sch. B1 to the IA 1986.

150 Para.5 of Sch. B1 to IA 1986.

151 Para.69 of Sch. B1 to IA 1986.

152 The administrator is an office-holder within the meaning of s 233(1) of IA 1986, entitled to exercise the powers as office-holders under Pt VI of the 1986 Act ('Miscellaneous Provisions applying to Companies which are Insolvent or in Liquidation'). See G Lightman, *et al.*, *The Law of Administrators and Receivers of Companies* (Sweet and Maxwell, London 2007).

153 Para.5 of Sch. B1 to IA 1986.

154 Para.64(1) of Sch. B1 to IA 1986. Any power conferred on the company or its officers, whether by this Act, or the Companies Act or by the memorandum or articles of association, which could be exercised in such a way as to interfere with the exercise by the administrator of his powers is not exercisable except with the consent of the administrator, which may be given either generally or in relation to particular cases. Para.63 of Sch.B1. See further Doyle and Keay, *Insolvency Legislation: Annotations and Commentary*, 627–8, Lightman *et al.*,

court is that the administrator is obliged to act fairly and honourably,[155] and is required to act independently and impartially and to be seen to be doing so, in his management of the company its property and its affairs.[156]

Furthermore, the administrator is the company's agent in exercising his right to take custody or control of all of the property to which he thinks the company is entitled, and managing the company's affairs.[157] Therefore, the administrator will owe the usual fiduciary duties to the company.[158] In *Oldham v Kyrris*,[159] which concerned the question of whether an administrator owes unsecured creditors a common law duty of care to take reasonable care in the conduct of the administration, Parker LJ recognised that 'the position of an administrator appointed under the 1986 Act vis-à-vis creditors is directly analogous to that of a director vis-à-vis shareholders'.[160] As to whom the general fiduciary duty

---

The Law of Administrators and Receivers of Companies, 234–5, and Sealy and Milman, *Sealy & Milman's Annotated Guide to the Insolvency Legislation*, 58.

155 Finch, *Corporate Insolvency Law: Perspectives and Principles*, 278.

156 Lightman *et al.*, *The Law of Administrators and Receivers of Companies*, 245. Sir WM James held that: 'it is of the utmost importance that the liquidator, as the officer of the Court, maintains an even and impartial hand between all the individuals whose interests are involved in the winding-up.' *Re Contract Corporation. Gooch's case*, (1871) L.R. 7 Ch App.207 at 211. Although this case concerned the position of official liquidator, an administrator, who is in the same position, should also be placed under such obligation.

157 Paras.69 and 64(1) of Sch. B1 to IA 1986. He is not, however, like a normal agent, subject to control and direction by his principal – the company, as the Act provides that 'a company in administration or an officer of a company in administration may not exercise a management power without the consent of the administrator'. It has been suggested that the main object of this statutory position is to try to ensure that the administrator, at least in the normal case, incurs no personal liability on any contract or other obligation that he may enter into on the company's behalf. Sealy and Milman, *Sealy & Milman's Annotated Guide to the Insolvency Legislation*, 58–9.

158 *Ibid.*, 59. Lightman *et al.*, *The Law of Administrators and Receivers of Companies*, 235. Indeed, it has been pointed out that the legislation clearly assumes that the administrator owes fiduciary duties to the company. And it can be seen from the expression of the misfeasance provision, where a misfeasance claim against the administrator can be based on the allegation that he 'has breached a fiduciary or other duty in relation to the company'. Para.75(3)(c) of Sch. B1 to IA 1986.

159 *Oldham & Ors v Kyrris and Anor* [2003] EWCA Civ 1506.

160 [2003] EWCA Civ 1506, para.143. Although this case was decided under the old law, its reasoning applies equally to the reformed new administration procedure under the EA 2002.

is owed, the company or the creditors, in this case, it was held that '[a]bsent some special relationship,[161] an administrator appointed under the 1986 Act owes no general common law duty of care to unsecured creditors in relation to his conduct of the administration'.[162]

To ensure that the administrator is kept accountable, nevertheless, the amended Insolvency Act imposes on administrators a comprehensive code of duties which are owed to the company. The administrator is under an overriding duty to perform his functions in the interests of the creditors as a whole when acting as the agent of the company.[163] There is a further statutory duty requiring that administrators perform their functions as quickly and efficiently as is reasonably practicable.[164]

Duty to select a purpose of administration For an administrator, the most significant obligation is to select and settle upon a purpose for the administration procedure by referring to a hierarchical list of possible objectives arranged in descending order and a set of instructions about how he should decide which objective to pursue. Only if he thinks that particular circumstances defined in the statutes[165] are present, can he

---

161 By analogy of the fiduciary duties by directors to shareholders, the events described by Mummery LJ in *Peskin & Anor v Anderson & Ors* [2001] 1 BCLC 372 that are capable of constituting special circumstances and of generating fiduciary obligations may take place when, for instance, there is a duty of disclosure of material facts to shareholders, or an obligation to use confidential information and valuable commercial and financial opportunities, which have been acquired by directors in that office, for the benefit of the shareholders, and not to prefer their own interests at the expense of the shareholders. [2001] 1 BCLC 372, at para.33. The *Peskin* case concerned the issue of whether the directors of a company owed fiduciary duties to the shareholders. In the course of his judgment in this case, the judge distinguished between fiduciary duties owed by directors to the company and fiduciary duties owed by directors to shareholders.

162 [2003] EWCA Civ 1506, para.141.

163 Para.3(2) of Sch. B1 to IA 1986. However, according to para.3(4), if the last purpose of administration (realising property in order to make a distribution to one or more secured or preferential creditors) is achieved, the administrator has a statutory mandate to ensure to 'not unnecessarily harm the interests of the creditors of the company as a whole'.

164 Para.4 of Sch. B1 to IA 1986. It is suggested that this duty overlaps with but gives further precision to the common law duty to exercise reasonable skill and care. See Lightman *et al.*, *The Law of Administrators and Receivers of Companies*, 244.

165 Particularly by para.3(3)(a) or (b), or para.3(4)(a) and (b) of Sch. B1 to IA 1986.

descend a step through the statutory hierarchy and consider the next possible objective.

The statute further provides some criteria for selecting from the three objectives. The selection of objective (a) and objective (b) is subject to para.3(3), which states:

> The administrator must perform his functions with the objective specified in sub-paragraph (1)(a) unless he thinks either-
>
> (a) that it is not reasonably practicable to achieve that objective, or
> (b) that the objective specified in sub-paragraph (1)(b) would achieve a better result for the company's creditors as a whole.

This selection criterion must be read together with para.3(2):

> Subject to sub-paragraph (4), the administrator of a company must perform his functions in the interests of the company's creditors as a whole.

In ascertaining the statutorily defined circumstances that make one or other of the objectives the appropriate one to pursue, the statute explains that the administrator should consider the collective interest of creditors and also whether a particular course of action would be reasonably practicable. Nevertheless, it has been argued that the use of the verb 'think' does not mean that the administrator's duty to settle upon a purpose for the administration is of a subjective nature.[166] The duty by which he is bound is indeed independent of his 'thinking', because lower priority objectives are available to the administrator only if the instruction of how to decide which objective to pursue is satisfied. Namely, the administrator may select either of the first two objectives only while complying with his duty to act in the interests of creditors as a whole; likewise, he may only choose the third objective while complying with his duty not to inflict unnecessary harm to creditor interests. In both situations, discharging his duties is independent of his 'thinking'.[167]

When considering the use of the word 'thinks' in the context of the administrator's duty to select the objective of administration, Parliament has explicitly spelt out that the administrator's most fundamental decision has been designed to be subject to the rationality test:[168]

---

166 Mokal, 'Administrative Receivership and Administration – an Analysis', 17.

167 *Ibid.*

168 See Mokal, *Corporate Insolvency Law: Theory and Application*, 237.

> The word 'thinks' in those paragraphs means that the administrator will have to reach a considered view [about which objective to pursue]. In such situations, the administrator's decision would be subject to a rationality test by which it would be challenged if it could be shown that no reasonable administrator would have acted in such a way in those circumstances.[169]
>
> If necessary, we would expect the courts to assess whether the office-holder, in this case the administrator, has been rational in his decision. We are not seeking to apply any other test.[170]

It is clear that the administrator must choose which objective to pursue rationally. The following section considers in more detail the standard of rationality to be applied to the decisions and actions of the administrator.

Duty to act rationally The duty to act rationally has deep roots in the law governing fiduciaries.[171] But which standard of rationality should apply to the administrator is the question we should ask when considering the degree to which courts are willing to interfere with the decision-making of a fiduciary. Given that the context in which the exercise of the administrator's discretionary powers may be materially different, it is necessary to first understand the various categories of fiduciary obligations and to which class the administrator's obligations might fall into, and then to examine the substance of the standard by which the administrator's decision-making is to be judged.

A fourfold classification of fiduciary power has been identified by Walton J in *Mettoy Pension Trustees Ltd v Evans*:[172] Category 1 comprises any power given to a person to determine the destination of trust property without that person being under any obligation to exercise the power or to preserve it. Category 2 comprises any power conferred on the trustees of the property or on any other person as a trustee of the power itself. A power in this category is called 'a fiduciary power in the full sense'. Category 3 comprises any discretion which is really a duty to form a judgment as to the existence or otherwise of particular circumstances giving rise to particular consequences. Category 4 comprises discretionary trusts that is to say cases where someone, usually but not necessarily the trustees, is under a duty to select from among a class of

169 Hansard HL vol 633 cols 569-70 (10 April 2002).

170 Hansard HL vol 639 col 1105 (21 October 2002). See Lightman *et al.*, *The Law of Administrators and Receivers of Companies*, 247.

171 *Ibid.*, 246.

172 *Mettoy Pension Trustees Ltd v Evans and others* [1991] 2 All ER 513.

beneficiaries those who are to receive income or capital of the trust property, and the portions they are to receive.[173]

It seems clear that the most fundamental of the administrator's duties, settling upon the appropriate objective of the administration, falls squarely within category 3, where the fiduciary is required firstly, to ascertain whether certain facts do or do not exist, and secondly, to embark upon the course laid down as following from the existence of those facts, or from their absence, or from the satisfaction of certain conditions, as appropriate. It follows that the discretion to choose the objective of the administration is subject to the fiduciary duty to ascertain the statutorily defined circumstances, which make one or other of the objectives appropriate to pursue.[174] Therefore, the discretion to settle upon the objectives is really a duty of the administrator to form a judgment as to the existence or otherwise of particular circumstances giving rise to particular consequences.[175]

Having clarified the classification of the administrator's fiduciary discretion in choosing a proper procedure objective, the chapter comes to consider the question of what standard of rationality is to be used to judge the administrator's decision-making. To flesh out the standard for the administrator, the court will draw on the case law providing substance to the rationality test in the context of other fiduciary relationships.[176] The basic formulation of the rationality requirement is that the administrator must not act in a way in which no reasonable administrator would act in the particular circumstances of a case.[177]

---

[173] [1991] 2 All ER 513, 545–6.

[174] Mokal, *Corporate Insolvency Law: Theory and Application*, 236.

[175] Lightman *et al.*, *The Law of Administrators and Receivers of Companies*, 255.

[176] *Ibid.*, 237–8.

[177] *Ibid.*, 246. The basic formulation of the rationality requirement is that the administrator must not act in a way in which no reasonable administrator would act in the particular circumstances of a case. See related cases *Re Edennote Ltd, Tottenham Hotspur plc and others v Ryman and another* [1996] 2 BCLC 239; *Edge v Pensions Ombudsman* [2000] Ch 602. In *Re Edennote Ltd* [1996] 2 BCLC 239, it was held that 'an exercise by a liquidator of powers conferred on him by statute must be judged by reference to what is commonly referred to as the *Wednesbury* test, that is that an exercise of a statutory power or discretion may be called in question, not only if it can be shown that the exercise of the power is utterly unreasonable – that it went beyond what any reasonable person properly instructed could have considered proper – but also if it is shown that the person exercising the power, though acting in good faith, took into account considerations which he ought not to have taken into account or failed to take

The *Re Hastings-Bass*[178] case was decided by the Court of Appeal in the context of trusts with respect to the exercise of Category 3 discretion. In this leading case, the Court of Appeal upheld the validity of an exercise by trustees of the statutory power of advancement, save to the extent that it was necessarily void for perpetuity, on the basis that:

> a trustee is given a discretion as to some matter under which he acts in good faith, the court should not interfere with his action notwithstanding that it does not have the full effect which he intended, unless (1) what he has achieved is unauthorised by the power conferred upon him, or (2) it is clear that he would not have acted as he did (a) had he not taken into account consideration which he should not have taken into account, or (b) had he not failed to take into account considerations which he ought to have taken into account.[179]

Evaluation of the revised administration procedure as a corporate rescue vehicle

Quite obviously, the EA 2002 intends to impose on the administration procedure a rescue-oriented mission to facilitate the survival of a financially distressed company or its business where possible. Nevertheless, it has been observed that the procedure has been increasingly used as a substitute for liquidation. The EA 2002 reform provides the new procedure with a seamless exit route either via CVL by filing certain documents at Companies House when the administrator thinks there will be a distribution to unsecured creditors,[180] or continuing directly to dissolution if there are no assets left to be distributed.[181]

Regarding the outcomes of administration cases, it has been shown that only a small minority of administration cases lead to genuine company rescue outcomes, as distinct from business rescue results, while the majority of administration cases lead to asset sales, whereby a company's assets are sold on a break-up basis.[182] A practical obstacle that may

---

into account considerations which he ought to have taken into account.' [1996] 2 BCLC 239, 394.

178 *Re Hastings-Bass* [1975] Ch 25.

179 *Ibid.*, 41.

180 Para.83 of Sch. B1 to the IA 1986.

181 Para.84 of Sch. B1 to the IA 1986.

182 According to Frisby's *Report on Insolvency Outcomes*, 32 per cent of the post-EA 2002 administration cases sample are going concern sales of the company's business, while 56 per cent go for asset sale where a company's assets were sold on a break-up basis. Whole or part company rescues among the post-EA administration case sample are 2.4 per cent and in the pre-EA sample 4.7 per cent. See Frisby, *Report on Insolvency Outcomes*, 61. See also The

undermine the ability of the administration to function as a timely and efficient corporate rescue vehicle is the limited or non-existing recourse to fresh capital support. Additional funding is often crucial for any attempt at rescue work to enable the company to continue trading and operating during the course of the administration. Nevertheless, the new administration regime does not give fresh consideration as a super-priority for such funding. Moreover, the modern administration procedure has been criticised because, although the government's objective is to enhance the prospects of a successful rescue, 'it simply directs administrators towards a certain end without providing them with any new apparatus to achieve it'.[183]

The reason for low company rescue rates in administration cases should not just be attributed to the difficulties of achieving a company rescue once the troubled company enters into a formal insolvency procedure. Indeed, it has been suggested that some elaborate rescue operations take place as informal, or 'behind-the-scenes' rescues in the pre-insolvency stage.[184]

What happens frequently in practice is that when there is a concern for the economic plight of the company, the bank, which typically enjoys comprehensive security over the company's assets in the form of a fixed or floating charge, will institute an independent review of the business to assess the company's financial health.[185] This is normally started with a specialised service within the bank's central rescue unit, which is set up to intervene early with the problem loans and provide a greater opportunity for rescue and recovery, without necessarily resorting to formal

---

Insolvency Service, *Enterprise Act 2002 – Corporate Insolvency Provisions: Evaluation Report* (January 2008). Rescue of part of the company is defined as where the company emerges from the procedure under the same ownership but conducting a reduced activity or set of activities. It has been pointed out that once insolvency intervenes, the general view was that in the majority of cases the most positive outcome would be a rescue of the business rather than of the corporate entity itself. See S Frisby, 'Not Quite Warp Factor 2 yet? The Enterprise Act and Corporate Insolvency (Pt 2)' (2007) 7 *Journal of International Banking and Financial Law* 398.

[183] Frisby, 'In Search of a Rescue Regime: The Enterprise Act 2002', 262.

[184] See J Franks and O Sussman, *The Cycle of Corporate Distress, Rescue and Dissolution: A Study of Small and Medium Size UK Companies* (2000) <http://facultyresearch.london.edu/docs/306.pdf> accessed 30 July 2015.

[185] Due to the concentrated nature of UK corporate debt, the banks monitor the performance of their debtors' accounts closely.

procedures.[186] In particular, there are three possible outcomes after the rescue unit: (1) the company may have been successfully turned around;[187] or (2) the company might close its account at the bank and go to another bank, termed 'rebanking';[188] (3) alternatively, companies may be regarded as failing and beyond rescue and be placed in formal insolvency.[189] An empirical study on small to medium-sized UK companies published in 2000 suggested that about 75 per cent of companies managed emerge from the rescue process outside the formal procedures. They were either turned-around or they repaid their debt by finding alternative sources of funding.[190] The remaining 25 per cent of cases entered into some form of insolvency procedure.[191]

Creditor banks' increasingly sophisticated forecasting and monitoring systems may suggest that only in exceptional circumstances will companies suddenly falter and arrive at unplanned formal insolvency.[192] The rescue units located within the banks often prescribe appropriate remedies with a range of restructuring and turnaround techniques to support the troubled companies. Where these informal rescue processes are unsuccessful, the bank creditors will be in a position to invoke administration proceedings. The statutory procedure, on the other hand, normally requires additional funding to embark on any trading activities, so without adequate financial support, a company rescue will very often be ruled out quickly and a liquidation strategy, whether through CVL or otherwise, will be the only realistic option.

---

186 On average companies remain in the central rescue unit about 7.5 months. See Franks and Sussman, *The Cycle of Corporate Distress, Rescue and Dissolution: A Study of Small and Medium Size UK Companies*.

187 Turnarounds are often accompanied by management changes, asset sales and new finance or directors' guarantees.

188 Rebanking may be either at the request of the first bank, because of a disagreement over strategy, or because the borrower is able to obtain better terms elsewhere.

189 In this case, the company will be placed in another unit usually called the Debt Recovery Unit. See Franks and Sussman, *The Cycle of Corporate Distress, Rescue and Dissolution: A Study of Small and Medium Size UK Companies*.

190 These rescue tactics include calling back some or all of the bank debt, restructuring the business including asset sales and managerial replacement. This study was based on the private records of three UK clearing banks, surveying all the companies that entered the central 'rescue unit' of these banks, within a certain 'sampling window'.

191 Usually administrative receivership or winding up. Franks and Sussman, *The Cycle of Corporate Distress, Rescue and Dissolution: A Study of Small and Medium Size UK Companies*.

192 S Harris, 'The Decision to Pre-Pack' (Winter 2004) *Recovery* 26.

Having discussed the modest emphasis placed on company rescue by the new administration regime, the next question to examine is whether the possibility of rescuing the company has been considered as exhaustively as it deserves in pre-pack processes. It is clear from the above discussion that, before immersing himself in a business sale, the insolvency practitioner has to consider the possibility of a turnaround of the company and to give that a fair chance. He may not be entitled to brush aside this option before he can show that the possibility has been seriously explored and all the efforts proved fruitless. Therefore, when objecting to the business sale in pre-packs for not being able to rescue the company, it is important to consider the stage of the rescue process, and whether any rescue activity has been taken before the company is put into administration.

A CRITICAL ANALYSIS OF THE PRE-PACKAGED ADMINISTRATION PROCESS

No formal definition of 'pre-packaged administration' or of similar strategies appears within the UK insolvency statutes. It is commonly held that a pre-pack is the sale of an insolvent business where all arrangements for the sale are agreed and put in place before the company enters formal insolvency. In practice, there are different forms of pre-packing depending on context. For instance, the structure of pre-packs used in the context of a merger and acquisition differs sharply from that used in conjunction with an administrative receivership. Pre-packs examined in this book purely refer to pre-packaged administration cases,[193] where the arrangements for the sale of an insolvent business have been negotiated with prospective purchasers and agreed by the major creditors[194] prior to the commencement of the administration procedure, with the sale being completed almost immediately with the appointment of an administrator.

The key difference between pre-packs and business sales within the boundaries of administration is that the pre-pack sale is arranged before the appointment of an administrator and outside the administration procedure. Upon the appointment of an administrator, detailed plans are

---

[193] Particularly the cases after the EA 2002 reform.

[194] This study uses the expression 'major creditors' as shorthand for the parties which could exert some degree of influence on the disposal process, including the senior secured bank creditors, significant trade creditors or bondholders.

worked out for the prompt sale of the business soon after the commencement of administration. To tease out particular problems, pitfalls and possibilities of pre-pack issues and gain a better understanding of the specification of the term 'pre-packs' used in this book, it is necessary to take a close look of the pre-formal process.

The Pre-formal Negotiation Stage

As it has been commonly observed in pre-packs, a going-concern sale is often conceived weeks or months before the appointment of an office-holder as the administrator. During the pre-administration stage, more features of out-of-court restructuring techniques may be demonstrated than those of the statutory procedure, as the bargain is carried out with very few, if any, statutory constraints, although the legislative requirements need to be re-considered so as to avoid potential future litigation.[195]

What happens frequently in practice is that insolvency professionals are called in to work alongside the management of the troubled company when there is a serious concern of the economic plight of the company. The uncertainty of financial distress requires a management strategy that involves professional advice on company contingent liabilities and litigation issues. Professional advisors will also help management to cope with pressure from company creditors. Work at this stage normally includes: seeking further funding for the company; consulting with the major creditors as regards their support to the likely options; and marketing the business and negotiating with prospective purchasers.

The position of management in the pre-formal negotiation stage

The incumbent management generally have more control in connection to the pre-packing procedure than in the administration proceedings. At the pre-administration stage, corporate management retains extensive managerial control of the company along with its capacity to issue instructions on behalf of the company through residual management powers. In contrast, in the administration procedure the appointment of administrators means that directors' control over company decision-making will be significantly restricted. When an administrator has taken up his post, he takes over the control and management of the company and its property. The directors of the company may still maintain

---

[195] Notwithstanding, the shadowy bargaining is usually fraught with numerous problems regarding transparency and accountability of the decision-making process.

day-to-day management functions but they cannot exercise any management powers without the consent of the administrator and can be removed or replaced at any time.[196]

This may be one explanation of why directors may have little incentive to initiate an administration procedure when the company shows the first strong signs of financial distress. The key insolvency decisions in a world of uncertainty 'turn importantly upon evaluation of risk and a willingness to accept risk'.[197] The degree to which the management would like to take risks may well depend on the financial condition of the company and the likelihood of preserving their jobs. When an incumbent manager expects that the law will displace him after the commencement of statutory proceedings, he is likely to delay a petition as long as possible while adopting high risk strategies to move the company out of trouble, regardless of the risk to creditors. The pre-pack strategy is attractive in the sense that it maximises the ability of incumbent management to participate in the decision-making of the ailing company.

Involvement of insolvency professionals in the pre-formal stage

Insolvency professionals are often introduced into a troubled company as soon as the worrying signs of the company's business progress arise.[198] Corporate restructuring advisors could be called in by the company's directors to provide essential input for the solution to the company's financial difficulty and further financing. They can also be the advisors from the institutional creditor's in-house advisory team to assist with the investigation of the company's financial troubles, providing independent business reviews on behalf of the institutional clients.[199] Moreover, they could also work for the individual directors or shareholders, advising in their personal capacity during the insolvency of the company, such as the preparation of the statement of affairs. Accordingly, their clients could respectively be the bank, the company and the individual directors or shareholders.[200]

---

196 Paras.61 and 64 of Sch. B1 to IA 1986.

197 Westbrook, 'The Control of Wealth in Bankruptcy', 805.

198 Finch, 'Doctoring in the Shadows of Insolvency', 692.

199 *Ibid.*, 694.

200 Normally, the engagement letter will set out the nature and scope of the advisory assignment, and the terms and conditions on which professional services are supplied. A Walters and M Seneviratne, *Complaints Handling in the UK Insolvency Practitioner Profession* (2008) <http://papers.ssrn.com/sol3/papers.cfm?abstract_id=1094757> accessed 30 July 2015, 13.

A significant part of the work of insolvency specialists in a pre-pack involves advisory work at the pre-formal stage. It can be carried out by a variety of professionals from different backgrounds, not necessarily with the same qualification. Categorised by qualification, one group of insolvency specialists is the Insolvency Practitioners, who are members of the Recognised Professional Bodies ('RPBs'). The other group is the turnaround professionals experienced at rehabilitating under-performing companies but who have not qualified as IPs. Only these who are qualified IPs are eligible to act as office-holders[201] in a designated insolvency proceeding. However those non-IP professionals are free to engage in the turnaround work prior to the commencement of a statutory procedure.

The advisory work is based on a contract relationship between the insolvency professionals and their clients. Such a relationship renders them contractual agents of their clients. Thus, insolvency specialists are subject to the general private law obligations in the form of fiduciary duties and duties of care and skill, arising from a contract where they undertake to act for clients in an advisory capacity or in equity.

It is acknowledged that by working alongside management and coordinating the process, the insolvency advisors play a significant role in reviewing the level and nature of the company's financial distress and proposing a recovery plan. In contrast to the position of an administrator or a supervisor of a CVA, the insolvency specialist involved in the pre-administration stage of a pre-pack is largely under no statutory duties to act in the best interests of those affected by his work, although the professional conduct regulations, which will be explained in detail in the next chapter, provide some restrictions on possible conflict of interests and require that in certain circumstances insolvency professionals should function as office-holders. Since those negotiating the pre-pack on behalf of the claimants do not owe fiduciary duties to all claimants, they are free to negotiate terms that primarily benefit their own clients in being paid on more favourable terms than the dissidents' claims.

The disenfranchisement of general unsecured creditors

Compared with the statutory institution of the administration procedure, pre-packs appear unable to accommodate the participation of all affected creditors in the decision-making process. There is no formal voting mechanism in pre-packs as regards business sales, although this is not just confined to pre-packs, since the majority of all administration

[201] A person who acts as a liquidator, trustee in bankruptcy, administrative receiver, administrator or supervisor under a voluntary arrangement.

business sales involve the same disenfranchisement issues.[202] Apart from the said absence of effective formal participation, certain groups of creditors who have little ability to influence the private restructuring process will also be excluded from the negotiation process and will not be informed of the pre-arranged sale before the decision to make the deal has been concluded. In the pre-formal stage, the creditors' ability to participate relies heavily on their ability to assess the business risk of the debtor company, which is directly related to their ability to gain access to information and use of information.[203] It is common practice for financial creditors use the requisite warranties and covenants in their loan agreements to be kept apprised of the debtor's financial position and managerial behaviour.[204] These contractual rights secure a steady flow of information from the company and its senior managers to requisite creditors to help determine the probability of default.[205] Furthermore, with the acquired information the banks are likely to become privy to the managerial decisions of the company, or even get represented on the board.[206] This could give the banks tremendous advantages to improve their position and bargain for a plan of action designed in their best interests during the private out-of-court process.

General unsecured creditors, on the other hand, may not have the amount of resources and commercial muscle possessed by their secured counterparts to ensure that they are kept fully informed about the debtor's financial situation.[207] In addition, general small creditors normally have limited *ex ante* contracting ability to protect their interests. The average trade creditors, for example, do not normally attempt to draft contracts on a transaction-specific basis, as normal trading arrangements may involve sums of money that are too small and time scales that are too short to justify extensive contractual stipulations.[208]

---

[202] Statistics of all administration business sales showed that in 76 per cent of cases, the formal voting mechanism on the issue of the sale itself is absent. See S Frisby, *A Preliminary Analysis of Pre-Packaged Administrations* (Report to R3, 2007) <https://www.r3.org.uk/media/documents/publications/press/preliminary_analysis_of_pre-packed_administrations.pdf> accessed 30 July 2015, 35.

[203] Finch, 'The Recasting of Insolvency Law', 722.

[204] *Ibid.* The terms of debentures may require the information, financial data and detailed figures for example, to be supplied on a periodic basis to financial creditors.

[205] *Ibid.*, 517.

[206] *Ibid.*, 84–8.

[207] Frisby, *A Preliminary Analysis of Pre-Packaged Administrations*, 28.

[208] Finch, *Corporate Insolvency Law: Perspectives and Principles*, 84.

Involuntary creditors,[209] tort creditors for instance, are in a worse position as they have no chance of contracting for their interests. Creditors may acquire information from other sources apart from through the use of such contractual rights. Information such as financial statements, annual resolutions and directors' and auditors' reports can be obtained at Companies House. When a company enters into administration, the administrator appointed will be furnished with a statement of affairs from the company management and must report in turn to all creditors. However, creditors may well gain such information only at a very late stage and this tardiness will often rule out any action to forestall directorial failures or influence the decision-making.[210]

The Pre-determined Nature of Pre-packs

A pre-pack is essentially a pre-determined arrangement.[211] The critical factor that distinguishes a pre-pack sale from a business sale within administration is that the details of the sale have been almost irrevocably pre-arranged prior to the official appointment of an administrator.[212] Non-pre-pack business sales also commonly involve a certain degree of pre-involvement with some planning activities such as information gathering. Yet the main decision (more often, to whom to sell, at what price) and proceedings are driven by consideration and assessment which may arise post-appointment of the administrator.[213] The pre-formal negotiation is likely to establish a single way forward which will exclude any consideration for other effective options for the company,[214] and the practical effect of the pre-formal negotiation is that the substantial work of how to deal with the insolvent company is carried out at the pre-formal stage, leaving little to be arranged in the context of the statutory procedure whose main purpose is to complete the pre-arranged deal.

---

209 The creditor may be involuntary, as where a party is injured by the company and is a tort claimant with an unsecured claim against the company. Such involuntary creditors cannot adjust their claims to reflect the creation of a security interest. *Ibid.*, 86.

210 *Ibid.*, 517.

211 Frisby, *A Preliminary Analysis of Pre-Packaged Administrations*, 11.

212 *Ibid.*, 9.

213 *Ibid.*

214 See Finch, 'Pre-Packaged Administrations: Bargains in the Shadow of Insolvency or Shadowy Bargains'.

The pre-pack negotiation involves two different approaches: a sale deal may have been prepared prior to the introduction of the administrator by the company's management with the assistance of the company advisor, or the administrator has been involved in the run-up to the pre-pack arrangement from the very beginning of negotiations. Either way, any action or decision being taken during the negotiations stage could produce an initial set-up, and establish a single way forward with a strong bias towards the achievement of what was agreed in the pre-pack deal. When the administrator is officially appointed, the condition facing the company may well be that, on the one hand, the deal to sell the business is well arranged and everything is in place, on the other hand, no or insufficient funding is available to keep the company trading and a rapid introduction of a purchaser may ensure continuity of the customer and supplier relationship.[215] In such a situation, it would most likely be concluded that there is no other option than a quick business sale and the pre-packaged deal would produce the best result for creditors. Even where there are other options, pursuing them instead of the agreement on the table would involve a certain degree of confusion, delay and uncertainty, running a serious risk of losing the support of the strongest players – the banks with the floating charges.

It is arguable that the framework of pre-packs is likely to reduce the role of the administrator who is supposed to play a key role in evaluating all possible options and aim to achieve an optional outcome for the creditors as a whole. The pre-formal negotiation stage has become the focus of the insolvency decision-making but the insolvency practitioners' role at this stage could be considerably constrained by the timing of their involvement and the role they played in the pre-formal stage. Traditionally, the administrator when appointed is required to review the company's business affairs before making his proposals and putting them in front of the meeting for approval. But in pre-packs, the deal is typically negotiated between the company management and the potential buyer with the assistance of the insolvency practitioner, agreed by the major creditors of the company. Certain important actions and decisions have probably been made in the absence of the administrator and without any formal approval by all interested parties. This can result in prejudice against the interests of the creditors that have not been part of the pre-pack negotiations.

---

[215] A Lockberbie and P Godfrey, 'Pre-Packaged Administration – the Legal Framework' (Summer 2006) *Recovery* 21, 22.

THE LEGALITY OF PRE-PACKS IN PURSUING A QUICK SALE

The main strategy of pre-pack arrangements is to sell the businesses of the ailing company, preferably as a going concern. The rationale behind the sale is often justified on the basis that selling a business as a going concern is likely to realise more value than on a break-up sale of assets. Therefore, the second objective of the reformulated administration procedure, achieving a better return for creditors as a whole than would be achieved in liquidation, is often pursued in most of the pre-packaged administration cases. This has brought up the question of the legitimacy of the pre-pack option for its exclusive insight towards a business sale, questioning whether the possibility of rescuing the company has been considered as properly as it deserves in pre-packs.

Justifying Business Sales

Having discussed the modest emphasis on company rescue of the revised UK administration regime, it is clear that the pursuit of a pre-pack as a strategy to sell the substantial business of the company must be justified, either because it is impossible to rescue the company or because such a sale will serve creditors better than any rescue efforts. That is to say that an administrator is obliged to pursue a going-concern sale where he thinks this is the best course for the interests of the creditors as a whole, even where it might be possible to rescue the company. But the insolvency practitioner is duty bound before becoming immersed in a business sale to consider the possibilities of the turnaround of the company. He may not be entitled to brush aside this option before he can show that the possibility has been seriously explored and all the efforts proved fruitless.

The concern is that in a pre-pack situation, where the decision to sell the business of the company is made before the administrator is in office, the administrator has no opportunity to consider thoroughly all possible ways to rescue the company, since the decision to sell the business was adopted prior to his appointment.[216] This is also true in another common scenario where the insolvency practitioner who is appointed as administrator has been engaged in the run-up to the pre-pack arrangement. Having spent weeks preparing to sell the business, it is argued that once

---

[216] P Walton, 'Pre-Packaged Administrations – Trick or Treat' (2006) 19 *Insolvency Intelligence* 113, 115–16.

formally constituted the administrator cannot sensibly claim to have ever thought about a possible rescue plan, since the administrator was appointed to his position to effect a pre-determined business sale. Therefore the statutory duty to consider rescuing the company is never properly discharged.[217]

But how could the duty to consider the alternative rescue route be carried out in the context of a pre-pack arrangement? The problem with pre-pack deals is that their expeditious and pre-determined nature means that the pre-pack deal is conceived at the beginning of the process of seeking a solution to the company's financial distress. If the pre-pack strategy is determined at the very beginning of this process, there is a danger that the pre-pack arrangement becomes self-fulfilling, limiting efforts to pursue a rescue strategy even where there is a chance for the company to return to profitability. To address some justifiable scepticism, a detailed explanation should be given to the general creditors recording how all the necessary measures to rescue the company have been taken before resorting to a business sale and how the rescue possibility has been explored and the details and results of such an exploration.

Sale before the Creditors' Meeting

As mentioned earlier, the statutory procedure is designed to be an inclusive proceeding by granting voting rights to affected creditors in the final decision of the administrator's proposals. The law, through para.53(1) of Sch. B1 to the IA 1986, subjects the proposals to unsecured creditors' approval with a specified majority unless the administrator thinks that they will receive no recoveries, in which case secured creditors have to take a vote for their affected interest. Arguably, the inclusive participation rights of all affected creditors in voting on the proposal will exert a significant influence on the course of the procedure and the decision-making.[218]

In pre-packs, however, the business sale is conducted swiftly, where the general creditors' right to participate in the process by voting on the administrator's proposals is always subjugated to commercial considerations necessitating the expeditious conclusion of the pre-arranged deal. Given that general unsecured creditors, if affected by the implementation of the administrator's proposals, have legitimate voting rights on what should be done with the company, it is reasonable to ask whether it is

[217] *Ibid.*

[218] Frisby, *Report on Insolvency Outcomes.*

appropriate for an administrator to effect a pre-packaged disposal of the business and assets of the company immediately following his appointment.

There are cases indicating that the administrator has the authority to take important decisions (e.g. to sell the assets) before the matter comes before the creditors' meeting, if commercially justified. Early in 1987, in an unreported hearing involving *Charnley Davies Ltd*, Vinelott J. confirmed the advice given to its administrator by counsel that the (then) Section 17(2)[219] of the IA 1986 was wide enough to empower an administrator to sell the *entire* undertaking of the company in advance of the creditors' meeting if he considered that such a course was in the best interests of the company and its creditors.[220] It was held that although the administrator, as an officer of the court, has the statutory right to apply to the court for directions in connection with his functions[221] or with any aspect of his management of the company's affairs business or property,[222] he does not necessarily need the sanction of the court to do so. He ruled that the words 'in accordance with any directions' in s 17(2)(a) meant 'in accordance with such directions, if any, as are given by the court' and not 'only to the extent specifically permitted by any directions given the court'. Consequently the administrators were not required to obtain the directions of the court before selling the company's assets.

Vinelott J.'s original view was accepted and confirmed by Neuberger J. in the more recent case *Re T&D Industries Plc* where he took a similar view in relation to the sale of assets prior to the creditors' meeting. He contemplated that the administrator should feel free to back their own judgment in cases of urgency and the court's power to make such an order under the original s.15 of 1986 Act should only be exercised in circumstances in which it can readily be seen that the disposals are really the only sensible course to be adopted and when unsecured creditors have

---

219 Section 17(2): the administrator shall manage the affairs, business and property of the company-

(a) at any time before proposals have been approved (with or without modifications) under section 24 below, in accordance with any directions given by the court, and

(b) at any time after proposals have been so approved, in accordance with those proposals as from time to time revised, whether by him or a predecessor of his.

220 See Sealy and Milman, *Sealy & Milman's Annotated Guide to the Insolvency Legislation*, 63–4.

221 Para.63 of Sch. B1 to the IA 1986.

222 Para.68(2) of Sch. B1 to the IA 1986.

had a chance to say what they think about the proposals in the administration.[223] In the judgment, he emphasised the fact that:

> [a] person appointed to act as an administrator may be called upon to make important and urgent decisions. He has a responsible and potentially demanding role. Commercial and administrative decisions are for him, and the court is not there to act as a sort of bomb shelter for him.[224]

Parliament seems to have favoured Neuberger J's analysis. The new wording of para.68(2)[225] under the new administration regime regulates administrators' obligation to act in accordance with directions made by the court and makes it clear that the administrator should comply with the court's directions if the court chooses to give them. This clearly implies that such directions are merely restrictive of the otherwise general nature of the administrator's powers under para.59.[226]

It has been held by Lawrence Collins J. in *Re Transbus International Ltd* that although there is a slight difference in the structure and wording between the 1986 Act and the Schedule B1 to the amended IA 1986, a similar meaning is to be given to the new wording.[227] This case considered the question of whether administrators had power under Sch. B1 to sell the assets of a company prior to approval by creditors of the administrators' proposals or whether they could do so only under the direction of the court. It was held that administrators are permitted to sell the assets of the company in advance of their proposals being approved. To support his decision, Lawrence Collins J. suggested:

> There will be many cases where the administrators are justified in not laying any proposals before a meeting of creditors. This is so where they conclude that the unsecured creditors are either likely to be paid in full, or to receive no payment, or where neither of the first two objectives for the administration can be achieved: see para.52 of the Schedule. If, in such administrations, administrators were prevented from acting without the direction of the court it

---

223 *Re T&D Industries Plc* [2000] 1 WLR 646, 654.

224 [2000] 1 WLR 646, 657.

225 'If the court gives directions to the administrator of a company in connection with any aspect of his management of the company's affairs, business or property, the administrator shall comply with the directions.'

226 Armour and Mokal, *Reforming the Governance of Corporate Rescue: The Enterprise Act 2002*, 15. Para.59 of Sch. B1 provides the general powers of administrators. Para.59(1) states that the administrator of a company may do anything necessary or expedient for the management of the affairs, business and property of the company.

227 *Re Transbus International Ltd* [2004] 2 BCLC 550, 10–12.

> would mean that they would have to seek the directions of the court before carrying out any function through the whole of the administration. The 2002 Act reflects a conscious policy to reduce the involvement of the court in administrations, where possible.[228]

It is therefore clearly suggested, both under the old law and under the reformed regime, that the administrators have the authority to sell assets of a company in advance of their proposals being approved by creditors at the statutorily required meeting without the direction of the court. Nevertheless, the courts have recognised the risk that to take such action, without giving creditors the opportunity to consider the administrator's proposals, would frustrate the ability of the meeting to take meaningful decisions about the direction of the administration and its purpose. In *Re Consumer & Industrial Press Ltd*,[229] although Peter Gibson J. refused the administrators' application for the court's approval to sell some property subject to a fixed charge primarily on the basis that he considered that the sale would have been delayed unreasonably, the judge expressed his concern that:

> The scheme of the Act requires an administrator to send a statement of his proposals to all creditors, to enable the creditors at a meeting to determine whether or not the proposals should be implemented. If an order were given under section 15 allowing the joint administrators to dispose, in effect, of all the assets of the company, there would be no point in having a meeting of creditors.

It was therefore thought prudent for the administrator to seek the leave of the court in cases of doubt.

As to this concern, Neuberger J. expressed his views in *Re T&D Industries Plc* as:

> There will be many cases where an administrator will be called upon to make urgent and important decisions and where the urgency means that there is no possibility of a section 24 creditor's meeting being called to consider the decision prior to it having to be made. However, the importance of the decision and the time involved may well be such that the administrator should have what consultation he can with the creditors. An obvious case might be where there were three days to make a decision and there were only four creditors of the company, or there were four creditors who make up 80 per cent in value of the total creditors of the company. In those circumstances, it

228 [2004] 2 BCLC 550, 14.

229 *Re Consumer & Industrial Press Ltd* (No. 2) (1988) 4 BCC 72.

> seems to me that the administrator should at least consider consulting those four creditors.

As an alternative course for the administrators, he suggested that, in appropriate cases, where the proposed course is sufficiently significant and where there is sufficient time, they may ask the court to direct the summoning of an early and urgent meeting of the creditors on short notice under s 17(3) in order to seek their approval.[230]

The above cases indicate that although the courts recognised the necessity of prompt execution of a business sale without prior approval of the creditors' meeting while noting the potential problem that the meeting would be left meaningless, as emphasised, the administrator should make attempts to discuss the sale with major creditors, not only the secured creditors but also major unsecured creditors, so that they would not be excluded completely from the decision-making. There is no requirement for the court's approval and, with no confirmation from the creditors' meeting, any problem with the administrator's decision and conclusions will be left as a challenge to be mounted by disgruntled creditors if the administrator's actions subsequently turn out to have been legally defective.[231]

The fact that the majority of ordinary creditors will not be approached at the pre-pack stage and will be presented with the 'fait accompli' outcome may be an effective strategic arrangement to frustrate the holdout capacity of general creditors, and an expeditious sale may be the most efficient in terms of economising in transaction costs, but it may prove unfair to certain unsecured creditors who are excluded from the decision-making process.[232] Presumably, if they were informed, they would pursue all possible legal routes to block a sale that could prove prejudicial to their interests, interrupting the pre-packing process.

THE POPULARITY OF PRE-PACKS

The policy-maker might not have foreseen the increasing popularity of pre-packs when introducing the reform in the EA 2002, but the strategy continues to be significant in administration activities as demonstrated by recent statistical evidence. Thus, it is important to understand the reasons

---

230 *Re T&D industries Pl* [2000] 1 WLR 646, 658.

231 Armour and Mokal, *Reforming the Governance of Corporate Rescue: The Enterprise Act 2002*, 14.

232 Finch, 'Doctoring in the Shadows of Insolvency', 701.

behind the popularity of pre-packs. This will be considered from two related perspectives: first, the impact of the intellectual and philosophical movement in favour of lowering of transaction costs, embracing a Schumpeterian approach to company life cycle,[233] that has propelled the evolution of English insolvency practice in recent decades; and secondly, the compelling advantages of pre-packs in handling companies facing financial difficulties, especially in terms of speed and procedural flexibility for business sales.

The Development of the Rescue Culture and its Impact

The promotion of the rescue culture and the legislative changes are likely to lead to increased rescue activity taking place at the pre-insolvency stage.[234] As a consequence of legislative reform, there is already a notable wresting of control from dominant creditors in favour of the many unsecured creditors.[235] Under the old insolvency regime, control in UK insolvency proceedings was placed firmly in the hands of secured creditors.[236] They had the right to appoint an administrative receiver, who had plenary powers to manage the debtor company with primary responsibility to protect the interests of his appointor. The receiver was entitled to take a series of actions for the enforcement of the appointing

---

[233] Joseph Alois Schumpeter, one of the 20th century's great economic and political thinkers, famously argued that the essence of capitalism was creative destruction, by which new economic structures are born from the rubble of older ones. According to this view, insolvency *per se* is not necessarily negative but a relocation of investments, as failing projects and the replacement of non-profitable companies can be seen as a fundamental element of economic growth. For further on Schumpeter's insight on economic development and financial markets, see JA Schumpeter, *Business Cycles: a Theoretical, Historical, and Statistical Analysis of the Capitalist Process* (McGraw-Hill, New York 1939); JA Schumpeter, *Theorie der Wirtschaftlichen Entwicklung* [The Theory of Economic Development] (Dunker and Humblot, Leipzig 1912), translated by Redvers Opie for the English edition (Harvard University Press, Cambridge, MA 1934). See also AJ Kammel, 'The Law and Economics of Corporate Insolvency – Some Thoughts' in P Omar (ed) *International Insolvency Law: Themes and Perspectives* (Ashgate, Hampshire 2008), 61–2, B Gladstone and JL Lee, 'The Operation of the Insolvency System in the UK: Some Implications for Entrepreneurialism' (1995) 7 *Small Business Economics* 55.

[234] Finch, 'The Recasting of Insolvency Law', 717.

[235] Armour *et al.*, *The Costs and Benefits of Secured Creditor Control in Bankruptcy: Evidence from the UK*, V.

[236] *Ibid.*

debenture holder's rights.[237] As mentioned earlier, the reform of the EA 2002 substantially limited the use of the administrative receivership and greatly impeded the control a QFC holder is capable of exercising by utilising the administrative receivership. Although the new administration regime, in return for the disappearance of the previous provisions, gives the QFC holder unchallengeable influence on the appointment of administrator, this privilege can hardly be equivalent to the control and certainty resulting from the traditional remedy of utilising administrative receivership, as the law makes it very clear that it is the interests of the whole group of creditors which the administrator serves, not just the appointing debenture holder.

Furthermore, the new regime is designed with certain procedural constraints to safeguard the fairness and accountability of the collective administration proceeding so that the interests of the secured creditor would not be overly favoured by, for instance, the residual claimants' voting rights on the administrator's proposals. This unavoidably leaves the major creditors in a less certain and predictable position especially as regards the development of the insolvency process. As a result, it might drive secured creditors to seek other strategies, which can enable them to maintain their control over the insolvency proceedings and secure a more favourable outcome. The pre-pack practice could meet their preferences by enabling the company first to reach an arrangement that is likely to satisfy the major creditors' interests through the pre-insolvency consultation and negotiation process, and then to trigger the statutory procedure to effectuate and implement that pre-agreed arrangement. This strategy allows the key players to gain a more controlling position and thus a secured outcome under the new insolvency climate. After all, without major creditors' consent and support on the pre-packed deal, it is hardly going to be successful.

Improved Financial Forecasting and Financial Risk Management Systems

In parallel with the philosophical shift in emphasis from orderly debt collection to promoting rescue attempts of viable businesses in financial difficulty, the practice in company risk monitoring and control has become more and more sophisticated with the modernising of corporate

[237] Such as to manage the company's business; to borrow using the company's assets as security; and to take possession of a company's assets, under ss 40-43 IA 1986.

procedures.[238] The development of corporate governance and risk monitoring practices provide stakeholders with timely information about the present and possible risks and uncertainties companies face,[239] and more significantly, keep them informed about the quality of debtor companies' managerial responses to such risks.[240] This development encourages increasing attention to be paid to the possible early solutions before forecasted risks have materialised rendering the company insolvent.

Bank lenders have also kept developing recovery techniques to respond effectively to debtors' troubles so as to gain a stronger market advantage.[241] It is now a normal practice that the bank monitors the debtor's insolvency risk and management on an ongoing basis. When there is an early sign of trouble, the bank will usually place the company in its 'intensive care' unit, where an accountant or a specialist team[242] may be employed to conduct an Independent Business Review to identify, most notably, the key business issues and risks that have to be responded to, as well as deliver recommendations for the company's difficult situation.[243]

Furthermore, the increasing amount of insolvency related work vis-à-vis companies in difficulty has turned the involvement of turnaround professionals indispensable at an earlier stage. Thus, a new cadre of turnaround profession is emerging. Indeed, when the debtor's operation becomes worrisome, seeking professional advice on how to address the difficulties faced by the company is deemed to be the minimal managerial response to the company management.[244] The banks normally have a strong desire to employ turnaround professionals, who have the competence and expertise to scrutinise the company's management on their behalf and if necessary, to work alongside the management devising a

---

238 Finch, 'The Recasting of Insolvency Law', 718.

239 *Ibid.*, 719.

240 *Ibid.*, 720–21. The trend of such a change in practice cannot be isolated from the evolution of the reporting requirements on the company financial and operating stability, remarked by the Report of the Cadbury Committee on the Financial Aspects of Corporate Governance, the Turnbull Guidance, the Companies (Audit, Investigations and Community Enterprise) Act 2004, and the requirement for a business review in the directors' report for all companies except small ones under s 417 of CA 2006.

241 Finch, 'The Recasting of Insolvency Law', 724.

242 Including the industry specialist as well as insolvency practitioners. Frisby, *Report on Insolvency Outcomes*, 21.

243 See Finch, 'The Recasting of Insolvency Law', 723–4.

244 See D Milman, 'Strategies for Regulating Managerial Performance in the 'Twilight Zone' – Familiar Dilemmas: New Considerations' (2004) 4 *Journal of Business Law* 493, 496–7.

strategy for turnaround, or set up arrangements for reorganising or implementing necessary changes.[245]

The increasing ability of bank lenders to monitor insolvency risks and company management, together with the early intervention of the turnaround specialists, is likely to encourage more anticipatory actions in the 'twilight zone'.[246] It is also claimed that the tendency of increased pre-insolvency activities is likely to be encouraged by the new streamlined administration procedure.[247] Its speedier framework suggests that the administrator will be instructed at a very short notice, ideally with some positive planning for an early response to the corporate financial difficulty. This enables possible arrangements to be crafted and negotiated before the initiation of statutory procedures. The pre-pack administration is a typical route under such trend where the potential administration procedure is to be pre-packaged with informal arrangements in a confidential manner so as to protect the company reputation and business prospects.

The Merits of Pre-packs in Business Rescue

It is often highlighted by insolvency practitioners that the necessary preparatory work has to be carried out for the benefit of all stakeholders before an administration actually commences, as without which the whole case would be poorer and far less effective.[248] Undoubtedly, a clearly prearranged exit strategy will not only minimise the time it will need to be in insolvency and increase the chance of rescuing the company or the business of the company, but is also necessary to maintain good practice in today's complex business world.

Speed and publicity for business sales in some particular circumstances could be very crucial for preserving the value of the company, especially for those heavily relying on public perception, such as people/service-focused businesses, or those that have many intangible assets like a

---

245 See Finch, 'The Recasting of Insolvency Law', 735. See also V Finch, 'Doctoring in the Shadows of Insolvency' (2005) *Journal of Business Law* 690, 691–2.

246 *Ibid.*, 717.

247 Finch, 'The Recasting of Insolvency Law', 715. Subject to some specified exceptions, the administrator must present proposals to creditors within eight weeks of his appointment and shall summon the initial creditors' meeting within ten weeks of the commencement of administration. Paras.51(2) and 52(1) of Sch. B1 to the IA 1986.

248 R Robinson, 'President's Column' (Winter 2005) *Recovery*.

strong brand or intellectual property assets.[249] Empirical evidence shows that well over a third of pre-pack businesses have a service-related characteristic.[250] These perishable parts of the business may be significantly diminished by the negative reaction from customers and the market. Furthermore, when suppliers demand 'extortionate ransom payments' by increasing their prices or ceasing to supply as a company as it moves into formal insolvency, they put a further strain on a business's already stretched resources.[251] This presents the insolvency practitioner with the tremendously difficult task of trading a business out of insolvency and in many cases the only practical options left are to sell the business as quickly as possible.

A timely disposal of the business through pre-packs is instrumental in salvaging worthwhile sections of the company that might otherwise have been jeopardised by negative publicity and lengthy proceedings.[252] Companies in administration may be losing considerable value from day to day if any arrangement is preceded by a period of trading, and it is often the case that there is a failure of any party to offer sufficient funding to enable a more sophisticated rescue option to be pursued. Pre-packs, as one of the business sale strategies, almost inevitably take the form of a going-concern sale. This would maximise realisations of the surplus which would be available to creditors and also would save some employment, supplier and customer relationships, as well as afford the business a second chance.[253]

CONCLUSION

Although it is fascinating to see the emergence of the Cork Report's ideas on corporate rescue, it was a very long journey until legislation reached the present stage where facilitation of the survival of financially distressed businesses is one of its principal objectives. Most notably, the framework of the EA 2002 embodies the main proposed rescue-oriented

---

[249] M Ellis, 'The Thin Line in the Sand – Pre-Packs and Phoenixes' (Spring 2006) *Recovery* 3.

[250] S Frisby, 'The Pre-pack Progression: Latest Empirical Findings' (2008) *Insolvency Intelligence* 154, 156.

[251] R3 launched a campaign called *Holding Rescue to Ransom* in March 2011, which called for the Insolvency Rules to be amended to prevent suppliers taking such unreasonable actions.

[252] Walton, 'Pre-Packaged Administrations – Trick or Treat', 115.

[253] A Bloom and S Harris, 'Pre-Packaged Administrations – What Should Be Done Given the Current Disquiet' (2006) 19 *Insolvency Intelligence* 122, 122.

reforms by replacing old administration and administrative receivership with a new streamlined administration, and it is moving English corporate rescue law forward as a more consistent and purposeful system.

The more rescue-friendly insolvency regime, manifested in the adoption and evolution of the rescue culture in English insolvency law and its promotion of ever more rescue-friendly statutory insolvency institutions, has boosted major lenders' willingness to prevent corporate collapse and led to improvements in their financial forecasting system and financial risk management. These changes enable insolvency strategies to be crafted and negotiated before the initiation of a statutory procedure. This arguably provides a friendly environment for the popularity of pre-packs.

Despite the government attempts to provide a seamless system with more flexible options for the financially distressed companies and their creditors, certain practical constraints in the current insolvency regimes remain and they reduce their ability to positively assist in the formulation and implementation of rescue schemes. For instance, there is no statutory moratorium for a stand-alone CVA for medium and large companies or a Scheme of Arrangement, without which the rescue operation will depend heavily on creditors' support and willingness to negotiate a possible rescue arrangement and the prospect of securing new funding. The unavailability of super-priority for new capital injections during the course of corporate rescues under the formal procedures and the inclusiveness at the expense of speed of the statutory process have complicated the formal rescue process and are likely to prove expensive.

Pre-packs, by contrast, enjoy some compelling merits in preserving the value of ailing businesses. They clearly aim at selling the distressed company's business as a going concern and thus they can be held to be the best course for the interests of the creditors as a whole. Pre-packs allow necessary preparatory work to be carried out at an early stage, without pressure from the public, and ensure a timely disposal of the business to salvage worthwhile sections of the company that might otherwise have been jeopardised by the uncertainty and costs of lengthy formal proceedings. Furthermore, its pre-determined nature offers a high level of certainty and control to participants in the rescue process and therefore attracts essential support from the company's main creditors.

On the other hand, pre-packs bring new challenges. In particular, they may reduce the role of the administrator who is supposed to play a key role in evaluating all possible rescue options. While the pre-formal negotiation stage has become the focus of insolvency decision-making, insolvency practitioners' role at this stage could be considerably constrained if the timing of their involvement diminishes their role. Furthermore, the majority of ordinary creditors will not be approached at the pre-pack stage and will often be presented with a 'fait accompli' outcome without being heard. This may be an effective strategic arrangement to frustrate the holdout capacity of general creditors and an expeditious sale may be the most efficient outcome in terms of economising on transaction costs. Yet it may prove prejudicial to the interests of unsecured creditors who are excluded from the decision-making process when certain important decisions affecting their interests are made in the absence of an appointed administrator and of any formal approval by all interested parties. A closer analysis of the issues surrounding pre-packs especially in the context of sales to connected parties, and the effectiveness of potential remedies under UK law, is offered in the next chapter.

3. Pre-pack business sales to connected parties – the uneasy case for pre-pack administrations

INTRODUCTION

As explained in the previous chapter, pre-pack rescues facilitate the pursuit of quick business sales in administration immediately after the appointment of the administrator. For certain stakeholders, this is an attractive strategy in that it can allow them to participate in the process going forward in a controlled way with an assured return. However, there is considerable concern whether the interests of general unsecured creditors, who are normally excluded from negotiations at the pre-formal stage, are fairly represented in the relevant decisions. This may be the case especially when businesses are sold to connected parties,[1] raising the possibility of some form of self-dealing or unfair prejudice to certain groups of creditors. It has already been mentioned that it remains unclear whether pre-packaged business sales provide adequate incentives for insiders to seek to maximise the economic value of the troubled business for the benefit of the full range of stakeholders.

There is of course the matter of whether the disenfranchisement of certain affected creditors is a necessary trade-off to achieve procedural efficiency, which as explained in the previous chapter, it is often justified by commercial expediencies at the strategy-formulation stage of corporate rescues. This chapter will examine in detail the important issues arising in this context and attendant trade-offs. First, it will investigate the underlying concerns justifying the fairness of achieved price in pre-pack sales, particularly as regards the sensitive issue of pre-pack sales to connected parties. Is there sufficient accountability to ensure that relevant parties will discharge their duties properly, given the secrecy of

[1] It could be an individual with control of the insolvent company exercising control over the new company (the purchaser), or a company exercising control in both the old and the new company because of its level of share capital. See s 249 and 435 of the IA 1986.

the pre-pack negotiations? What are the channels to challenge them under the current insolvency regime, if there is a concern about abuse?

This chapter is structured as follows. Section two examines the underlying concerns regarding price fairness in the case of pre-packaged sales to connected parties. Section three provides a close analysis of the transparency issue in the process, as it is the main contributing factor in the concern of abusive use of pre-packs. Section four examines the potential grounds for legal liability for those who have been assisting in the pre-packaged sales in a dishonest manner, namely the company's directors and the administrator, under the prevailing statutory and common law framework.

THE PROBLEMATIC CASE OF CONNECTED PRE-PACKS

It is very common in pre-packs for the business of the distressed company to be sold to a connected party, which may be the directors of the company, the company's major shareholder or a company that is controlled or has a certain relationship with the directors or the major creditors or shareholders of the ailing company. While this is not an exclusive phenomenon in pre-packs, such sales are far more common in pre-packaged business sales than in other contexts.[2] Insolvency Service statistics, in its reports on the operation of SIP 16, show that 73 per cent of pre-pack sales in 2013 were to parties connected with the insolvent company.[3] In 2011[4] 79 per cent of pre-pack sales were to parties connected with the insolvent company; in 2010, the figure was 72 per cent.[5]

---

[2] It was suggested that 'proportionately more pre-pack sales are to connected parties than are business sales and this trend is accelerating in post-EA pre-packs in administration cases'. Figures of sales to connected parties rose from 59 per cent across the entire research period (September 2001 – May 2005) to 71 per cent in the September 2004 – May 2005 period. The corresponding figures for business sales are 47 per cent and 43 per cent respectively. See Frisby, *Report on Insolvency Outcomes*, 80, and S Frisby, 'The Pre-Pack Progression: Latest Empirical Findings' (2008) 21 *Insolvency Intelligence* 154, 156.

[3] The Insolvency Service, *2013 Annual Review of Insolvency Practitioner Regulation* (April 2014), 10.

[4] The figure for the first 6 months of 2012 is 69 per cent of pre-packs. See The Insolvency Service, *2012 Annual Review of Insolvency Practitioner Regulation* (June 2013), 4.

[5] The Insolvency Service, *Report on the Operation of Statement of Insolvency Practice 16: 1 January to 31 December 2011*, 11. For the first six months

Selling the company's business and assets back to the existing management is not illegal per se or objectionable, despite the fact that the purchasing directors may be also largely responsible for the company's parlous financial situation. Phoenix trading via pre-packs is often accused for encouraging the directors to shed their creditors and buy back the collapsed businesses at a low price.[6] Nevertheless, such accusations often lack justification. Particularly when the distress is due to industry-wide factors, parties from the same industry who would otherwise have been the most likely purchasers, will probably have no desire to expand their capacity by acquiring new businesses.[7] In such circumstances incumbent management or a connected party normally know the business well and are more likely to offer a fair price than new investors would be. Moreover, a connected sale might indeed be the only method to ensure that the disposed business is sold as a going concern.

Nonetheless, the accusation that connected pre-pack sales allow businesses to be sold at an undervalue is fathomable. When the directors of troubled companies are interested in a management buy-out, they have a vested interest in the insolvency process with a view to paying a lower price for the business. Moreover, as insiders of the company, they are liable to take advantage of information gained through their position to further their own ends in the transaction.[8] Such morally or legally dubious activities may include withholding essential information or not making reasonable efforts to promote competing bids.[9] This complements the concern that perhaps even less marketing activity is carried out when businesses are sold to connected parties than in the case of pre-packaged sales to non-connected parties. Without the threat of competing bids that may be brought by extensive marketing, the management will not be forced to raise their offer, and this would often amount to an impenetrable defence, since they could claim that the price they offered was the

---

of 2009, the figure was 81 per cent. The Insolvency Service, *Report on the Operation of Statement of Insolvency Practice 16: July – December 2009*, 14.

[6] Finch, 'Corporate Rescue Processes: the Search for Quality and the Capacity to Resolve', 507.

[7] The relevant analysis is about the obstacles to realise going-concern surplus. See M Crystal QC and R Mokal, 'The Valuation of Distressed Companies – a Conceptual Framework' (2006) BEPRESS Legal Series Working Paper 1370 <http://law.bepress.com/expresso/eps/1370/> accessed 30 July 2015, 3.

[8] They may be aware of 'soft' information about the business's viability and future prospects, which is not yet sufficiently precise to be included in any documentation.

[9] See Katz and Mumford, 'Study of Administration Cases', 51.

best price that could be obtained. To onlookers, it often appears as a strong case of an undervalued sale to allow insiders to get an advantageous price to the detriment of creditors. As a result, in certain cases there are several factors that make it difficult to justify the price of pre-pack sales.

The Importance of Marketing of Pre-pack Sales and the Economic Ramifications of 'Lame' Marketing Efforts

Once it is concluded that rescuing the company is not practical, the next thing that should be considered is selling the business of the company, preferably as a going concern, and attracting the best possible price. The ideal way to sell a business is usually to dispose of it at market value, which can normally be identified through a lengthy and extensive process of advertising the business to the relevant markets. The administrator, who organises the procedure, will seek to identify and attract potential purchasers and make contact with interested parties to generate competing bids in order to secure the best possible price for the sale.[10]

Owing to the expeditious nature of the pre-pack process, the business is rarely marketed as broadly and for as long as it is in the normal administration cases. Empirical evidence has shown that the pre-pack business sales are marketed to a far less extent than business sales within administrations.[11] This often gives observers the impression that minimal effort has been expended to attract qualified purchasers to come forward,

---

[10] Crystal QC and Mokal, *The Valuation of Distressed Companies – a Conceptual Framework*, 2.

[11] Frisby, 'The Pre-pack Progression: Latest Empirical Findings', 156. According to Frisby's empirical study on pre-packs, based on the assumption that no marketing of the business had occurred prior to the eventual sale unless the administrator's reports expressly indicated otherwise, only 18 of the 227 businesses (7.9 per cent) on the whole pre-pack database were marketed by either a reasonably widespread marketing campaign or approaching or identifying the interested purchasers or on a much smaller scale and over a shorter time period by practitioner involvement in the marketing strategy. In contrast with the pre-pack cases, of all business sale cases, out of the 412 cases on the database, 229 (55.6 per cent) gave some account of a marketing campaign. Frisby, *A Preliminary Analysis of Pre-Packaged Administrations*, 49. More recently, in the Insolvency Service's analysis of the SIP 16 information received in relation to 375 companies entering administration during the reporting period in respect of whether the administrator undertook any marketing, it is showed that administrators undertook some marketing in 50 per cent of cases. See the Insolvency Service, *Report on the First Six Months' Operation of Statement of Insolvency Practice 16*, para.3.1.5.

questioning how the highest price for the business could ever be identified within an unreasonably short period of advertising and marketing, if, indeed, they are exposed to a market at all.[12]

Marketing activities were carried out in 62 per cent of pre-packs during 2013,[13] in 60 per cent of pre-packs during the first six months of 2012 and in 51 per cent for the whole of 2011.[14] It should be noted that the quality and accuracy of those marketing records reported by the administrators are often questionable. The relevant information is based on self-reporting by the administrators in the SIP 16 Reports, especially where marketing was carried out prior to the IPs' involvement with the company, in which case the administrators probably have to rely on the directors' word.[15] Also there appears to be a wide disparity about the level of marketing taking place, and the form it took and its duration.[16] It was noted by Walton and Umfreville that: 'marketing was often reported as occurring where in fact it was very limited, such as enquires made within the IP firm itself with no genuine external marketing occurring. Sometimes, IPs have accepted the word of the directors that there is no ready market for the business outside the management team (or other connected parties).'[17]

The reasons for limited marketing in pre-pack sales are not difficult to identify. A lack of funds for use in trading during administration is often cited as an overwhelming reason for not marketing the business.[18] The statutory institution of administration perhaps envisaged that a going-concern sale would usually be preceded by a period of trading in order to identify the highest price. In practice, however, the process is more

---

12 B Xie, 'Protecting the Interests of General Unsecured Creditors in Pre-packs: the Implication and Implementation of SIP 16' (2010) 31 *Company Lawyer* 189, 194.

13 The Insolvency Service, *2013 Annual Review of Insolvency Practitioner Regulation* (April 2014), 10.

14 The Insolvency Service, *2012 Annual Review of Insolvency Practitioner Regulation* (June 2013), 11.

15 In Walton and Umfreville's research on pre-packs, marketing began prior to the IPs' involvement in over a third of all cases where marketing was carried out. See P Walton and C Umfreville, *Pre-pack Empirical Research: Characteristic and Outcome Analysis of Pre-pack Administration* (Report to Graham Review, April 2014) <https://www.gov.uk/government/publications/graham-review-into-pre-pack-administration> accessed 30 July 2015, 21.

16 *Ibid.*, 21–2. It was said that for over a third of cases there was no clear evidence from the SIP 16 Reports as to when the marketing was carried out.

17 *Ibid.*, 84.

18 *Ibid.*, 83.

complex and influenced by many more complicated variables than in an ideal world, especially when the company is in crisis. It is often the case that there is a failure to attract any fresh funding to support a trading-out in administration. In such a situation, an open market sale would seem to be impractical for there is a risk that in seeking to market the business, news of the situation would leak out, likely causing adverse consequences in the form of loss of clientele and possible pre-emptive action by aggrieved creditors.

Furthermore, it is often unlikely that there would be a ready market, and the period for which potential buyers are willing to make good offers for the ailing business may be very short. Given that there would rarely be sufficient funding to meet the costs of continuing trading, a large scale or long period of public marketing may merely delay picking apart those valuable assets at their best time. A quick pre-pack sale may well be the only way to prevent any diminution in value (especially on the brand or portfolio of the business) resulting from negative reactions from customers and the market as well as public uncertainty.

Those justifications may go some way to explaining why an accelerated business sale through pre-packs is necessary but may not stand up to a great deal of scrutiny when it comes to justifying the poor level of marketing. It is understandable that a large-scale advertising and marketing campaign would often be ineffective for distressed businesses, but this does not mean that a pragmatic approach of extracting the best value of the ailing company's business and assets is to avoid marketing the business at all. It is important to show that sufficient effort is expended to attract offers from the largest number of potential purchasers as soon as a business sale is planned. Secondly, there appears to be a certain lack of accountability as to the level of business marketing prior to the appointment of the administrator. In many pre-packs[19] where some marketing was reported to have taken place, it was carried out by the management of the company prior to the administrator's involvement.

The Need for Independent Valuations

To address the controversy and sensitivity in pre-pack sales, independent valuation specialists could bring some degree of accountability. Independent valuations are held to be an integral part of any pre-pack

---

19 It was said that marketing began prior to the IPs' involvement with the company in over a third of all cases where marketing was carried out. *Ibid.*, 21.

process, especially when the market has not been properly tested,[20] as it 'can not only demonstrate the fairness of the process, but also can be an effective counter against any subsequent nuisance claims'.[21] For valuations obtained for a business and/or its underlying assets – this includes tangible assets (plant and machinery, property, stock) as well as intangible assets (goodwill, database, website, patents, etc). To allow creditors to form a proper understanding of the pre-pack transaction, in the valuation it is critical to explain the nature of assets involved, and such matters as the amounts attributed to the various asset categories, the basis of the valuation and terms upon which the valuer has been instructed, as well as the basis upon which substantial allocations are made to maintain goodwill.[22] It is required under Dear IP 42 issued in 2009 to provide sufficient details of any valuation activities such as the name of the valuer employed, the efforts to maintain goodwill, the basis of the valuation, etc. Nevertheless, the recent report on SIP 16 showed that in a large proportion of cases, such essential information on valuation was still missing.[23]

According to Walton and Umfreville's research, an independent valuation was conducted as part of the pre-pack process in the overwhelming majority (91 per cent) of the cases reviewed. However, these appear to be desk-top valuations only and it was common for the purchase price to exactly match the valuation figure, where there was a connected sale.[24] This often raises concerns that purchasers have set a valuation as an indicator of how much they are prepared to pay, rather than by reference to the market value of the assets in question.[25] Also, there is rarely any explanation as to the valuation methods used by the valuers, and it is

---

[20] S Mason, 'Pre-packs from the Valuer's Perspective' (Summer 2006) *Recovery* 20, 20.

[21] Harris, 'The Decision to Pre-Pack', 27.

[22] The Insolvency Service, *Report on the Operation of Statement of Insolvency Practice 16: July – December 2009* (Report 2010), 8.

[23] It was reported that 77 per cent of the SIP 16 noncompliance cases in 2011 were concerned with insufficient information on valuation. See *Report on the Operation of Statement of Insolvency Practice 16: 1 January to 31 December 2011*, 8. It is also the most common reason why SIP 16 reports were not fully compliant. See *2012 Annual Review of Insolvency Practitioner Regulation*, 7.

[24] Walton and Umfreville, *Pre-pack Empirical Research: Characteristic and Outcome Analysis of Pre-pack Administration*, 84.

[25] T Graham CBE, *Graham Review into Pre-pack Administration* (Report to the Rt Hon Vince Cable MP, June 2014), para.3.10.

often limited to certain assets, normally the chattels and property, but not the intellectual property or goodwill.[26]

As explained above, limited marketing in pre-packs highlights the importance of independent valuations. It is equally important to ensure a meaningful valuation that can serve as an effective safeguard ascertaining the appropriateness of the pre-pack transaction. The appropriate basis of the assets valuation for pre-pack purposes is likely to be market value.[27] Nevertheless, the nature of pre-pack arrangements often requires valuations to be carried out within a restricted time period, within which there might be insufficient time for normal investigations and research to be carried out.[28] Furthermore, information or data needed for a valuation is materially supplied by the company directors.[29] Where the management has a vested interest in the transaction, it is possible that they may abuse their information advantage to induce biased value estimates.[30] Moreover, although it is true that a simple asset valuation and assessment of costs is able to demonstrate whether, in each case, as a result of a pre-pack sale, creditors will receive more or less than they would get in liquidation,[31] it may provide little indication as to whether the pre-pack price is the highest possible price they could achieve under prevailing market conditions.

---

[26] Walton and Umfreville, *Pre-pack Empirical Research: Characteristic and Outcome Analysis of Pre-pack Administration*, 84.

[27] Mason, 'Pre-packs from the Valuer's Perspective', 20. Market value is defined by the International Valuation Standards as 'the estimated amount for which a property or asset should exchange on the date of valuation between a willing buyer and a willing seller in an arm's-length transaction after proper marketing wherein the parties had each acted knowledgeably, prudently and without compulsion'.

[28] Mason, 'Pre-packs from the Valuer's Perspective', 20.

[29] *Ibid.*

[30] As Armour pointed out, they may be aware of 'soft' information about the business's future prospects, which is not yet sufficiently precise to be included in any documentation, and they will likely have an advantage over outsiders in determining how to analyse documents made available. See J Armour, 'The Rise of the "Pre-pack"': Corporate Restructuring in the UK and Proposals for Reform' in RP Austin and FJG Aoun (eds) *Restructuring Companies in Troubled Times: Director and Creditor Perspectives* (Ross Parsons Centre of Commercial, Corporate and Taxation, Sydney 2012), 47.

[31] A Fanshawe, 'Letter to the Editor: The Pros and Cons of Pre-packs' (Spring 2006) *Recovery*, 2.

Connected Interests and the Integrity of the Process

One of the key risks of the pre-pack practice is that it tends to put the whole process exclusively in the hands of the insiders, precluding junior creditors from having any substantial input to the sale plan. As explained in the previous chapter, the deal is normally negotiated between the company management and the potential buyer with the assistance of insolvency professionals and approval from secured creditors of the company. There is thus a worry that 'the advisors may have been too aligned with certain interests, which may be those of well-placed creditors or involved managers'.[32] The deal therefore is often perceived as an outcome of the compromise between the wish to sell the business back to management or to a connected party at a modest price and the requirement to cover the repayment of outstanding debt owed to major creditors. Therefore, in order to evaluate the conduct of key players, such as the appointed IPs and major financial creditors, in this context it is necessary to examine the kind of incentives they possess in the course of the pre-packing process.

First, the directors' incentives will be adversely affected by imminent financial distress. At this stage, the directors probably care more about their stewardship than about negotiating the best possible price for the company assets.[33] For instance, where company directors have a chance to be employed in the business by the potential new ownership, they may take a soft stance during negotiation to please a potential employer with favourable terms. Another example is when the directors are interested in a management buyout. In such a case they have a vested interest in getting a good purchase price and they may not, in the absence of a clearly defined binding legal duty to do so, provide full information undermining the goal of realising the highest value of the business. In the pre-formal stage, the corporate management retains extensive managerial control of the company and over decision-making during the process.

Secondly, the impartiality of the IPs is subjected to question in the context of pre-pack sales to connected parties. In pre-packs, the sales are

---

[32] Finch, 'Pre-packaged Administrations: Bargains in the Shadow of Insolvency or Shadowy Bargains', 574.

[33] As pointed out by Milman: 'for some directors, the philosophy adopted in times of crisis is that trying to save the present company is not a priority, what matters is preserving the business for the future and ensuring their continued stewardship and livelihood.' Milman, 'Strategies for Regulating Managerial Performance in the "Twilight Zone" – Familiar Dilemmas: New Considerations', 507.

always arranged prior to the appointment of the administrators, and the IPs will inevitably have certain pre-appointment involvement in the pre-pack negotiations. The pre-appointment involvement is often viewed with suspicion since the administrator will be appointed with an inherent bias in favour of the pre-packed deal instead conducting of an independent review into the deal. Such a bias means that they will probably not be able to make judgements in a detached, expert manner with an eye to any other rescue options.[34]

This concern is further fuelled by the directors' ability to appoint administrators out-of-court. The EA 2002 has paved the way for a company and/or its directors to appoint an administrator without strict judicial scrutiny through the out-of-court route.[35] Research has shown the predominance of director-led appointments in pre-packs as well as administration cases in general.[36] Arguably, this raises concerns as the appointed administrators may become 'too aligned with certain interests'.[37] The alignment of interests is likely to develop through the ongoing cooperation in the rescue negotiations between the insolvency advisors and corporate insiders. In working alongside the management and reviewing options for the troubled companies, decisions are likely to be made under considerable directorial influence and undue weight is placed on directorial deliberation.

---

[34] See Finch, *Corporate Insolvency Law: Perspectives and Principles*, 471–2.

[35] Under EA 2002, the holder of a qualifying floating charge, the company and the directors may appoint an administrator out-of-court. Appointment by the company or the directors is subjected to the approval of any person entitled to appoint an administrative receiver or any person who is or may be entitled to appoint an administrator under para.14. See paras.14, 22, 25 and 26 of Sch. B1 to IA 1986.

[36] According to Walton and Umfreville, the out-of-court appointment of administrators by the directors or company was used in over 70 per cent of all cases viewed in their study. See Walton and Chris Umfreville, *Pre-pack Empirical Research: Characteristic and Outcome Analysis of Pre-pack Administration*, 17. This is also the case for administration cases in general. According to the OFT's study, 75 per cent of the 500 administration records in Companies House starting in 2006 are director-led appointments. See OFT, *The Market for Corporate Insolvency Practitioner – a Market Study* (OFT1245, June 2010), para.4.5 and footnote 35.

[37] There is a worry that 'the advisor may have been too aligned with certain interests – which may be those of well-placed creditors or involved managers'. Finch, 'Pre-packaged Administrations: Bargains in the Shadow of Insolvency or Shadowy Bargains', 574.

It is true that when IPs discharge the role of administrator, they are bound by ethical and legislative duties to protect the interests of the body of creditors as a whole. The danger is that the control and appointment power the management possesses opens the possibility for directors to choose IPs who apply a 'practical' and 'cooperative' approach. When the directors are considering appointing an administrator, they will consider, and discuss with an IP, whether the practitioner would consent to their preference in handling the insolvency of the company business. If the directors are conscious of such disinterest, they are likely to appoint another IP.[38]

Ideally, IPs would act ethically to protect their reputations as even-handed and effective negotiators of corporate solutions.[39] But in practice, the worry arises that appointors may tend to use IPs with low ethical sensitivity and 'more practical' approaches to the pursuit of bank-friendly turnaround proposals.[40] The concern is that insolvency practitioners, like other business individuals, are competing for business and are accountable for their contribution to the performance of the firms for which they work.[41] Due to market pressure, some may choose to act in a legally and technically correct way that could still be seen as unethical in order to get appointed. In addition, the low level of publicity and disclosure in private sales means that the reputation sanction may not be as critical as in the case of professional advisors involved in a public sale.

Another question arising here is whether banks, especially those holding a floating charge, have the right incentives to check possible undue influence by insiders. The answer to this question turns on to the strategic position of banks in insolvency and the impact of the pre-pack deals on their incentives. Having regard to their legal and financial capacity, the banks are the strongest players and in a key position to influence managerial behaviours, as well as the presiding administrators. With regard to their incentives in this situation it should be remembered that the principal priority of financial creditors is to recover their loans or

---

[38] See B Xie, 'Role of Insolvency Practitioners in the UK Pre-pack Administrations: Challenges and Control' (2012) 21 *INSOL International Insolvency Review* 85, 93.

[39] Finch, 'Doctoring in the Shadows of Insolvency', 707.

[40] Finch, 'Pre-packaged Administrations: Bargains in the Shadow of Insolvency or Shadowy Bargains', 584.

[41] J Cousins *et al.*, *Insolvent Abuse: Regulating the Insolvency Industry* (Association for Accountancy & Business Affairs, 2000) <http://visar.csustan.edu/aaba/INSOLVNTABUSE.pdf> accessed 30 July 2015, 19.

other claims.[42] Banks will probably be more inclined to a business sale if it constitutes the quickest route out of an unpredictable situation.[43] The pre-pack route often offers a concrete route to recovery for bank creditors and is one in which they are normally involved or consulted and therefore are likely to be the least affected party by the pre-arranged sale. Even in those cases where there is a low prospect of recovering money in full, the banks will be able to secure themselves a well-placed position in the pre-pack deals. It is therefore doubtful whether they will be monitoring the negotiation and the operation of the pre-pack sales rigorously.

In view of the above analysis, the practical implication of the pre-pack strategy brings new challenges that deserve some fresh thinking about the traditional profound reliance on the role of administrators. The concern, in short, is that when the insolvency practitioners exercise the delegated powers and extensive discretion granted under the administration regime, they are likely to encounter excessive influence and pressure from the management who likely has a vested interest in the insolvency process, especially in phoenix pre-packs. This is likely to impair their objectivity as disinterested office-holders.

TRANSPARENCY ISSUES IN PRE-PACK BUSINESS SALES

Given the aforementioned concerns in pre-pack business sales, it should be recognised that the whole panoply of statutory protections to excluded creditors mostly lies in the value of the information disclosed ex post facto, especially when there is no creditors' meeting to be called and general creditors are rarely consulted until being presented with a fait accompli to consider. A necessary level of information disclosure should be ensured in the documentation presented to outside creditors to enable them to assess and measure whether the practitioner has carried out his functions in a manner that has not improperly or unlawfully prejudiced their interests.[44] Furthermore, a meaningful exercise for creditors to hold the administrator accountable requires information about the administrator's actions and their reasons for taking those actions so as to assess

---

42 See Xie, 'Role of Insolvency Practitioners in the UK Pre-pack Administrations: Challenges and Control', 93.

43 G Cook and K Pond, 'Explaining the Choice between Alternative Insolvency Regimes for Troubled Companies in the UK and Sweden' (2006) 22 *European Journal of Law and Economics* 21, 34.

44 Frisby, *A Preliminary Analysis of Pre-Packaged Administrations*, 8.

whether their interests have been unfairly prejudiced and amount to a challenge if appropriate. This section will consider the statutory reporting requirements in administration and transparency issues in pre-packs – strictly speaking, the ex post information disclosure issue.

Ex Post Information Disclosure in Administration – Administrator's Statutory Duty to Explain

Administrators do not just have a duty to merely give reasons for their decisions but they also need to explain them. According to para.49(1) and (2) of Sch. B1, the administrator must make a statement setting out proposals for achieving the purpose of administration and it shall include his explanation as to why he is choosing a lower priority objective.[45] It is primarily through this explanation of his reasons that the administrator will show whether the legislative intention of prioritising corporate rescue was met and how he is complying with his duty to act in the interests of the creditors as a whole; and it is primarily this explanation which renders meaningful the statutory right (particularly) of junior creditors to determine whether they should call the administrator to account as to what, as noted, is the most fundamental and far-reaching of the decisions.[46]

Rule 2.33(2) of the IR 1986 further specifies the matters that the statement shall include, in summary:

(a) details relating to his appointment as administrator;[47]
(b) how it is envisaged that the purpose of the administration will be achieved and how it is proposed that the administration shall end;
(c) the manner in which the affairs and business of the company have, since the date of the administrator's appointment, been managed and financed and,

---

[45] Para.49 of Sch. B1 to the IA 1986 provides that the administrator's statement must, in particular –

(a) deal with such matters as may be prescribed, and
(b) where applicable, explain why the administrator thinks that the objective mentioned in paragraph 3(1)(a) or (b) cannot be achieved.

[46] Mokal, 'Administrative Receivership and Administration – an Analysis', 20.

[47] This includes the date of appointment and the person making the application of appointment, an account of the circumstances giving rise to the appointment of the administrator and the basis of the administrator's remuneration claim. Rule 2.33(2)(c)(e)(k) of IR 1986.

(d) where any assets have been disposed of, the reasons for such disposals and the terms upon which such disposals were made.

It should be noted that the statutory disclosure requirements in the administrator's proposals are mainly focused on the actions taken after the commencement of the procedure. The pre-determination nature of pre-packs suggests that actions taken prior to the administrator's official appointment and his rationale may indeed be a matter of concern. In this regard, the legislative amendments to the IR 1986 introduced in 2010[48] regarding expenses incurred prior to the appointment of the administrator imposes certain disclosure interests on general creditors.[49] According to the amendments, a statement in the administrator's proposals to creditors must be made to explain expenses and remuneration incurred, including details of the work done for which the fees were charged and an explanation of why the work was done before the company entered administration, and how it would further the achievement of the statutory objectives.[50] Nevertheless, it should be noted that in most pre-pack cases, the pre-appointment expenses and remuneration only need to be approved by secured creditors of the company when it is predicted that there is no distribution to be made to unsecured creditors.[51]

Another important associated document for creditors is the statement of affairs, which is often of fundamental importance to the formulation of the administrator's proposals to justify his choice and actions in discharging his duties properly. According to para.47 of Sch. B1, once appointed, the administrator shall by notice in the prescribed form require one or more relevant persons,[52] most usually the directors or manager of the

---

48 The Insolvency (Amendment) Rules 2010, SI2010/686.

49 A new rule 2.67A introduced addresses expenses uncovered prior to the appointment. Such sums are only payable in accordance with the provisions of expense of administration (r. 2.67) if (a) they have been identified as such in the administrator's proposals as provided for in r. 2.33(2)(ka), and (b) they have been approved by the creditors in accordance with r. 14.

50 R. 2.33(2)(2B).

51 R. 14.

52 'Relevant person' is defined in para.47(3) of Sch. B1 to the IA 1986. Those providing services to the company, most obviously its solicitor, accountants or auditors may also be called on to submit a statement of affairs or a statement of concurrence, as the employment defined includes a contract for service. L Doyle and A Keay, *Insolvency Legislation: Annotations and Commentary* (2009), 673. The Rule also allows for the non-disclosure in the statement of the administrator's proposals of information 'which could seriously prejudice the commercial interests of the company'.

company, to provide the administrator with a statement of the affairs of the company.[53] Where disclosure of the whole or part of the statement of affairs would prejudice the conduct of the administration, the administrator can apply for a court order sanctioning limited disclosure.[54] The most common example of such potential prejudice is where the statement of affairs or the proposal includes price-sensitive information from which competitors or any prospective purchaser might derive a commercial advantage and thus could prejudice the commercial interests of the company.[55] However, this may not be an entirely convincing ground for partial disclosure (or worse non-disclosure). Certainly commercial confidentiality might be a persuasive justification for non-disclosure while negotiations are still in progress, but this is not the case in a pre-packaged sale, as negotiations will have concluded and key arrangements will have been reached prior to disclosure of the administrator's reports.[56]

As suggested above, the laws do require comprehensive information disclosure to keep administrators accountable for their decisions. General creditors who are normally excluded from any participation in the process might be presented with a statement disclosing such information well in line with the requirements in the insolvency legislation. At the same time no significant assistance may be offered to them to fully understand whether the administrator has taken proper care of the best interests of the creditors as a whole and whether the business and its assets were properly marketed or whether the best possible price was obtained.

The duty to explain is mainly about spelling out the administrator's reasons for choosing a particular objective. As a result, the focus of the explanation of a pre-pack sale is often simply justified on the basis that selling a business as a going concern is likely to realise more value than on a break-up sale of assets and thus will achieve a better return for

---

[53] A further statement of concurrence may be considered appropriate where the administrator has doubts or concerns as to the information set out in the statement of affairs. R. 2.29(2) of IR 1986.

[54] Rule 2.30 of the IR 1986. It is suggested that mere administrative inconvenience which might arise from the disclosure of whole or part of the statement of affairs should not justify limited disclosure. The reference to 'prejudice[ing] the conduct of the administration' should, it is submitted, be interpreted as meaning 'would be likely to cause financial harm to those with an interest in the administration'. See Doyle and Keay, *Insolvency Legislation: Annotations and Commentary*, 673.

[55] Doyle and Keay, *Insolvency Legislation: Annotations and Commentary*, 673.

[56] Frisby, 'A Preliminary Analysis of Pre-packaged Administrations', 31.

creditors as a whole. But to offer a comprehensive explanation, the statement of administrator's proposals should not just demonstrate that the administrator had considered a number of issues, such as the soundness of the company, and the financing issue, but it should also present a full history of the company leading up to the arranged pre-packaged sale, an explanation of the decision on the price, and an analysis of the consideration and how it was apportioned between various asset groups.

Additional Disclosure Requirements for Pre-pack Sales – SIP 16

As far as information disclosure is concerned, the general situation in pre-packs was unsatisfactory, especially prior to the issue of the standard included in the Statement of Insolvency Practice 16 ('SIP 16').[57] Frisby suggested in her empirical study of pre-pack cases that the quality of the reports to creditors varied, but overall, 'the informative value of reports to creditors is somewhat haphazard'.[58] Some essential information, such as the identity of the purchaser of the business, the approach of administrator appointment and their pre-appointment involvement, was often missing.[59]

In January 2009, SIP 16[60] came into force as one of a series of guidance notes aiming at making the pre-pack administration process more transparent, stressing that unsecured creditors must be given a

57 The general picture could be seen from Frisby's empirical study of pre-pack cases in Frisby, *A Preliminary Analysis of Pre-packaged Administrations* published in August 2007. The sample used in this report comprised 639 cases, of which 412 are categorised as non-pre-packaged business sales, including 222 administration cases (52.9 per cent); 190 receivership cases (46.1 per cent); and 227 as pre-packs. The 227 pre-packs consist of 109 receivership cases (48 per cent) and 118 administration cases (52 per cent), which further contain 40 pre-Enterprise Act cases (33.9 per cent) and 78 post-Enterprise Act cases (66.1 per cent).

58 *Ibid*., 31–2. It is pointed out that the most common omission in relation to provision of information thought to be particularly useful to creditors was the identity of the purchaser, and that 'just over one third of the reports surveyed presented a reasonably full account of the practitioners' motives for preferring a pre-pack'.

59 *Ibid*., 13 and 30.

60 SIP 16 is issued under procedures agreed between the insolvency regulatory authorities acting through the Joint Insolvency Committee (JIC). It was commissioned by the JIC, produced by the Association of Business Recovery Professionals, and has been approved by the JIC and adopted by each of the regulatory bodies.

detailed explanation and justification as to why a pre-pack sale was undertaken.[61] Meanwhile, Dear IP 42 was issued by the Insolvency Service in October 2009 to provide guidance on information disclosure required under SIP 16. It provided additional guidance about the detailed requirements and required the notification to be sent out within 14 days of completion of the sale.

SIP 16 was essentially a salutary reminder to insolvency practitioners of their responsibilities, and it sought to influence the way in which they and company directors act in the context of pre-pack negotiations.[62] To promote a better understanding of the decision to use the pre-pack process, SIP 16 required administrators to explain to creditors the background to their appointment and the reasons why they considered that a pre-pack sale would be the best outcome for creditors. In particular, SIP 16 (2009) listed certain crucial information that should be provided to creditors when there is a pre-packaged sale.[63]

---

[61] Particularly, it addresses concerns that the process was 'shrouded in secrecy' from the creditors' point of view and that they were not always informed of the reasons for the pre-pack or shown that 'best value' had been achieved. See R3 News Room-Press briefing, *The Use of 'Pre-pack' Administration*, (22 January 2009), previously available at <https://www.r3.org.uk/newsandpress/default.asp?page=1&i=4&id=289#PressStory>, accessed 13 February 2009.

[62] Re *Kayley Vending* [2009] EWHC 904 (Ch), [12]. SIP 16 (2009) paras.5 and 6 of SIP 16(2009) specifically stated that practitioners are reminded of the potential liability of directors and others who caused the company to incur credit in the period prior to entry into administration (e.g. fraudulent or wrongful trading under ss 213 and 214 of the IA 1986) and of the duty of the administrator when realising assets to act in the interests of creditors as a whole. Further, it is emphasised that the directors of the company should be encouraged to seek independent advice, especially where there is a possibility of the directors acquiring an interest in the assets in the pre-packaged sale.

[63] In particular, the following information must be provided:

(a) The source of the administrator's initial introduction;
(b) The extent of the administrator's involvement prior to appointment;
(c) Any marketing activities conducted by the company and/or the administrator;
(d) Any valuations obtained of the business or underlying assets;
(e) The alternative courses of action that were considered by the administrator, with an explanation of possible financial outcomes;
(f) Why it was not appropriate to trade the business, and offer it for sale as a going concern, during the administration;
(g) Details of requests made to potential funders to fund working capital requirements;
(h) Whether efforts were made to consult with major creditors;

Given concerns about the disenfranchising of creditors' participation rights in the pre-packing process and limited marketing of the business sale that may be necessitated by commercial expediencies, any assessment of the appropriateness of the pre-pack process greatly depends on the quality and completeness of information disclosure after the event. These professional rules aim to promote best practice regarding information disclosure by making it mandatory for all pre-pack deals. The enhanced focus on information disclosure by SIP 16 is praiseworthy, but it should be noted that the enforcement of the new rules greatly depends on effective monitoring and control systems to detect any non-compliance with the requirements, and to ensure that any instances of abuse will be firmly dealt with.

The operation of SIP 16 at present is examined by the Insolvency Service with information received through three main channels, including: (a) SIP 16 reports from practitioners conducting pre-packaged sales, which is the same information they have provided to creditors; (b) their reports on the conduct of the directors and (c) complaints from members of the public, received through the Hotline telephone service and in writing. The overall compliance rate of IS reviewed sample cases in the first year since SIP was introduced in 2009 was 62 per cent; the figure increased to 75 per cent in 2010. For 2011, the figure was 68 per cent,[64] 65 per cent during the first six months of 2012 and 79 per cent in 2013.[65]

(i) The date of the transaction;
(j) Details of the assets involved and the nature of the transaction;
(k) The consideration for the transaction, terms of payment and any condition of the contract that could materially affect the consideration;
(l) If the sale is part of a wider transaction, a description of the other aspects of transaction;
(m) The identity of the purchaser;
(n) Any connection between the purchaser and the directors, shareholders or of any other entity into which any of the assets are transferred;
(o) Whether any directors had given guarantees for amounts due from the company to a prior financier, and whether that financier is financing the new business;
(p) Any options, buy-back arrangements or similar conditions attached to the contract of sale.

[64] The Insolvency Service, *Report on the Operation of Statement of Insolvency Practice 16: 1 January to 31 December 2011*, 3.

[65] It should be noted that a revised SIP 16 came into force on 1 November 2013. For the first two months of operation of the revised SIP 16, the overall compliance was 89 per cent. See the Insolvency Service, *2013 Annual Review of Insolvency Practitioner Regulation* (April 2014), 8.

In general, the impact of SIP 16 in providing greater information for creditors remains satisfactory in spite of the disappointment of no consistent improvement in compliance level. The latest industry report on its implementation indicates that there are still cases where insufficient information is provided concerning valuation, assets details and apportionment of sale consideration.[66] The nature of the assets and how values have been attributed to them, in particular the basis upon which substantial allocations are made to maintain goodwill, is crucial in forming a proper understanding of the pre-pack transaction. Inadequate provision of such information does not necessarily mean that the pre-pack itself was inappropriate or unjustified, but it often invites negative perceptions of the efficacy of the pre-pack actual process, as it is imperative for creditors to appreciate whether the best value has been obtained for the business and assets.

IS DISHONEST BEHAVIOUR CAPTURED BY THE CURRENT LEGAL FRAMEWORK?

The previous discussion examined concerns about pre-packs' vulnerability to abuse by insiders at the expense of general junior creditors, especially when the business is sold to connected parties. Limited marketing activities in pre-pack sales, and a lack of transparency in the pre-packing process and meaningful ex post facto information disclosure to the general creditors (and their exclusion from the pre-pack process) are the main factors that give rise to concerns that insiders might have manipulated the process in order to get an advantageous price to the detriment of general creditors during the accelerated sale process. Naturally, this begs the question whether there is adequate legal protection for unsecured creditors which they may be able to utilise if they have doubts about whether a pre-pack sale was not conducted in such a way as to obtain the highest possible price.

The legislative framework responds to the problems of abusive conduct in insolvency by seeking to impose duties on those who are supposed to be accountable. The following sections will examine the robustness of insolvency law in responding to those concerns in pre-packs, focusing on potential grounds for liability imposed on those who have been assisting in the implementation of pre-pack sales, namely company directors and

---

66 *Ibid.*, 7–8.

the administrator, if they do act in a dishonest manner, under the applicable statutory and common law framework.

Directors' Obligations at the Onset of Insolvency

A key concern in pre-pack arrangements relates to the active role directors play, and the enhanced influence they have in the pre-formal phase of negotiating a pre-pack sale and the possible conflict of interests arising when connected parties are the purchasers of the insolvent business. This section discusses the relevant directors' duties, questioning whether the design of these duties could offer worthwhile protection to unsecured creditors in the context of pre-pack sales. Generally, duties in the vicinity of insolvency could be covered by breach of general and common law duties and insolvency specific duties.

Directors' duty to creditors in common law

Traditionally in company law, fiduciary duties are imposed on corporate directors to deal with managerial opportunism.[67] A number of overlapping obligations are bundled together under the term 'fiduciary duty' to promote loyalty and protect the interests of intended beneficiaries.[68] It is well established in case law that a director owes a fiduciary duty to act bona fide in the best interests of the company.[69] From this stems the duty of directors, in times of financial distress, to take account of the interests of the company's creditors in their decision-making.[70] The reason is that

---

67 'A fiduciary is someone who undertakes to act for or on behalf of someone else in circumstances which give rise to a relationship of trust and confidence between the parties. The distinguishing obligation of a fiduciary is the obligation of loyalty.' See *Bristol and West Building Society v Mothow* [1998] Ch1 (CA) at 18.

68 Including the duty to act in good faith in the interests of the company; the duty to exercise directors' powers for the proper purposes; the directors' duty not to fetter their own discretion; and the duty not to place themselves in a position in which there is conflict between their duties to the company and their personal interests.

69 See *Re Smith and Fawcett Ltd* [1942] Ch 304; *Dorchester Finance Co. Ltd v Stebbing* [1989] BCLC 498. See also Finch, *Corporate Insolvency Law: Perspectives and Principles,* 499. Companies Act 2006 codifies directors' duties including the long-established fiduciary duties as well as the common law duty of care and skill into a statutory statement of seven general duties, which are set out in s 172 'Duty to promote the success of the company'.

70 A Keay, 'Directors' Duties to Creditors: Contractarian Concerns Relating to Efficiency and Over-protection of Creditors' (2003) 66 *Modern Law Review*

if the company is or seems to be, in financial distress, the shareholders are no longer the owners of the residual value of the company, having been, in effect, supplanted by the creditors.[71] One aspect of the directors' traditional fiduciary duties is to act bona fide in the interests of the company. As a result, the directors' duty to creditors is, arguably, of a fiduciary nature.[72] A number of English court decisions, which built on a series of Commonwealth cases,[73] found in favour of the idea that duties

665, 668–9. See also Finch, *Corporate Insolvency Law: Perspectives and Principles*, 501.

[71] See Armour, 'The Law and Economics of Corporate Insolvency: A Review'. A Keay, *Company Directors' Responsibilities to Creditors* (Cavendish, London 2006), 181–2. DG Baird, 'The Initiation Problem in Bankruptcy' (1991) 11 *International Review of Law and Economics* 223, 228–9. Amour and Mokal, 'Reforming the Governance of Corporate Rescue: The Enterprise Act 2002', 7. Where the company becomes factually insolvent, creditors displace shareholders as 'residual claimants'. It is well put by Goode stating that the true principle is not that the directors owe duties to creditors as well as to the company, but that when the company is insolvent or approaching insolvency the directors, in discharging their duty to act in the best interests of the company by maximising its value, must have regard predominantly for the interest of creditors, who now have the primary interest in the proper application of the company's assets. See Goode, *Principles of Corporate Insolvency Law*, para.12-15.

[72] Keay, *Company Directors' Responsibilities to Creditors*, 179. It was during the 1980s that directors' duties to creditors came to be seen. In the common law, notably, in the Australian case *Kinsela v Russell Kinsela Pty Ltd* [1986] 4 ACLC 215, Street CJ stated:

> 'In a solvent company the proprietary interests of the shareholders entitle them as a general body to be regarded as the company when questions of the duty of directors arise … But where a company is insolvent the interests of creditors intrude. They become prospectively entitled, through the mechanism of liquidation, to displace the power of the shareholders and directors to deal with the company's assets.' [1986] 4 ACLC 215 at 401. On directors' duties to creditors, see also, V Finch, *Directors' Duties: Insolvency and the Unsecured Creditor* in A Clarke (ed) *Current Issues in Insolvency Law* (Stevens & Sons Ltd., London 1991).

[73] Notable is *Walker v Wimborne* [1976] 50 ALJR 446 in which the Australian High Court spoke of 'directors of a company in discharging their duty to the company [having to] take account of the interest of its shareholders and its creditors'. Similarly, Cooke J in the New Zealand Court of Appeal in *Nicholson v Permakraft* [1985] 1 NZLR 242 concluded that directors' duties to the company 'may require them to consider inter alia the interests of creditors'.

to creditors flow from the traditional fiduciary duty to act in the best interests of the company.[74]

In *West Mercia Safetywear Ltd v Dodd*,[75] where the director effected a fraudulent preference and was found to be guilty of a breach of duty,[76] the decision of the Court of Appeal indicated that where a company is insolvent, a director's duty to act in the best interests of the company comprises a duty to protect the interests of the company's creditors. Also, in *Brady v Brady*,[77] where his Lordship considered the meaning of 'given in good faith in the interest of the company' in section 153(1)(b) of the Companies Act 1985, Nourse LJ stated that 'where the company is insolvent or even doubtfully solvent, the interests of the company are in reality the interests of the existing creditors alone'.[78]

On the other hand, it should be noted that some commentators hold the interesting view that directors' duties owed to creditors do not stem from the aforementioned traditional fiduciary duty to act in the best interests of the company, but rather from an independent, positive duty owed directly to creditors and founded on ordinary principles of directors' duty of care.[79] The importance underpinning the difference is whether the directors owe the duty to the creditors directly or if it has to be mediated

---

[74] For example, Lord Diplock in *Lonhro Ltd. v Shell Petroleum* spoke of 'the best interests of the company … [being] not exclusively those of its shareholders but may include those of its creditors'. [1980] 1 W.L.R. 627 at 634. In both the Court of Appeal and House of Lords decisions in *Brady v Brady*, Nourse LJ and by implication Lord Oliver indicated that directors needed to consider creditors' interests if they were to act in the interests of the company. [1988] BCLC 20 (C.A.). In the *Yukong* case, Toulson J considered that where a director acted in breach of his duty to the company by causing assets of the company to be transferred in disregard of the interests of its creditor or creditors, he was answerable through the scheme provided in the IA 1986 Section 212, but 'he does not owe a direct fiduciary duty towards an individual creditor nor is an individual creditor entitled to sue for breach of the fiduciary duty owed by the director to the company'. *Yukong Lines Ltd of Korea v Rendsburg Investments Corporation and Others* [1998] 2 BCLC 485 at 503.

[75] [1988] 4 BCC 30. The statement by Street CJ is also echoed in *Official Receiver v Stern* (No. 2) [2002] 1 BCLC 119 at 129–30.

[76] The director had, for his own purposes, made a transfer between accounts in disregard of the interests of the general creditors of the insolvent company.

[77] [1988] BCLC 20.

[78] *Ibid.*, at 40. Section 172(3) under the CA 2006 provides that this duty to act in good faith and to promote the success of the company has the effect of requiring directors, in certain circumstances, to consider or act in the interests of creditors of the company.

[79] Finch, *Corporate Insolvency Law: Perspectives and Principles*, 499–501.

through the company. Either way it is generally accepted that the duty is discharged indirectly, through the company and cannot be enforced by creditors.[80]

The time when the duty arises is equally important to identify the point at which directors are to be held accountable to the creditors' interests. Common law has yet to provide a clear statement on this issue. Judges may inevitably have to exercise discretion in assessing the point of doubtful solvency in particular contexts.[81] One way to identify an actual prospective insolvency might be derived from the statutory criteria, for example, the definition of inability to pay debts found in s. 123(2)[82] of the IA 1986, or by the cash flow test[83] provided by s. 123(1)(e).[84] Nevertheless, Cooke J, in the New Zealand Court of Appeal case *Nicholson*, went further suggesting that, although balance sheet solvency and the ability to pay capital dividends were important in assessing any actions taken, nevertheless:[85]

> As a matter of business ethics it is proper for directors to consider also whether what they will do will prejudice the company's practical ability to discharge promptly debts owed to current and likely continuing trade creditors ... because if the company's financial position is precarious the futures of such suppliers may be so linked with those of the company as to bring them within the reasonable scope of the directors' duty.

Andrew Keay pointed out that the duty to take into account the interests of creditors is triggered where 'the circumstances of a company are such that its directors know, or can reasonably expect, that the action upon

---

80 Keay, 'Directors' Duties to Creditors: Contractarian Concerns Relating to Efficiency and Over-protection of Creditors', 669.

81 *Ibid.*, 507.

82 This section adopts the liabilities test and the strict balance-sheet approach of total assets, exceeding total liabilities, that a company is deemed unable to pay its debts if it is proved to the satisfaction of the court that the value of the company's assets is less than the amount of its liabilities, taking into account contingent and prospective liabilities.

83 A company by such test is deemed unable to pay its debts 'if it is proved to the satisfaction of the court that the company is unable to pay its debts as they fall due'.

84 Finch, *Corporate Insolvency Law: Perspectives and Principles*, 506.

85 [1985] 1 NZLR 242, 249.

which they are going to embark could lead to the insolvency of the company, could be advantageous for the interests other than the creditors.'[86]

Directors' duties to creditors were also considered in the course of company law reform in the UK.[87] However, the government's White Paper 'Modernising Company Law'[88] in July 2002, considered that if there was a statement of duties to creditors in the statute then it would be incumbent on directors to make finely balanced judgments and they might err on the side of caution because of fear of personal liability, and this would be inconsistent with the rescue culture which the government was trying to foster. Nevertheless, the Companies Act 2006 through s. 172(3) of the CA 2006 stated that the duty imposed by the section under the title 'Duty to promote the success of the company' 'has effect subject to any enactment or rules of law requiring directors, in certain circumstances, to consider or act in the interests of creditors of the company'. This to some extent represents certain real development of principles dealing with the interests of creditors in legislation.

The current approach regulating the general duty to creditors is that the duty is a fiduciary one and is ex post in nature.[89] Since, as is commonly held, the duty to creditors derives from general duties owed to the company, breaches should properly be dealt with by the company. This means that before the company goes into administration, the duty is enforced by creditors mainly relying on the existing board to complain about the ill-treatment of creditors' interests.[90] Creditors *per se* are given a right of action only on winding up by virtue of a misfeasance action under s. 212 of the IA 1986, which allows proceedings where a director has been guilty of 'any misfeasance or breach of any fiduciary or other duty in relation to the company'.

---

[86] A Keay, 'The Director's Duty to Take into Account the Interests of Company Creditors: When Is It Triggered?' (2001) 25 *Melbourne University Law Review* 315, 334–8.

[87] In reviewing and proposing the reform of UK company law starting in 1998, the Company Law Review Steering Group (CLRSG) at one stage rejected the view that in legislation-regulating companies there should be a statement of principles concerning duties of directors. One of the primary reasons for the rejection was that a statement of principles placing a responsibility on directors to creditors might 'cut across section 214 of the Insolvency Act 1986'.

[88] DTI (Cm 5553-I, 2002). The White Paper is in two volumes, with the consultative document in Volume I and draft clauses of the proposed Companies Bill in Volume II.

[89] Keay, *Company Directors' Responsibilities to Creditors*, 197.

[90] Finch, *Corporate Insolvency Law: Perspectives and Principles*, 516.

Furthermore, the common law duty is owed to the general body of creditors, as a whole, rather than unsecured creditors individually or as a class. The interests of different groups of creditors in some insolvency circumstances may strongly conflict with each other. Unfortunately, there is no guidance to directors who have to balance between such competing interests. There has been concern that requiring this balancing of interests may result in directors using the requirement to maintain balance between conflicting interests as an opportunity to foster their own self-interests.[91] As Keay pointed out: 'on any balancing exercise the danger is that the director whose actions are likely to be reviewed will simply pay lip-service to the need to consider the interests of both shareholders and creditors, and then make the decision that he or she wants, possibly based on self-interest.'[92] Accordingly, investigating possible creditor remedies for abusive conduct in pre-pack sales at common law and in equity brings us to a blind alley, as the general creditors whose interests may be prejudiced will lack any control of the company to exercise the relevant remedy for breach of directors' duties. This finding means that we should now turn to examine grounds for liability under statutory law.

Potential statutory liabilities of directors at the onset of insolvency

Section 212 IA – summary remedy against delinquent directors, liquidators etc Section 212 provides much wider grounds for proceedings to be taken against any of the persons listed who have misapplied or retained or become accountable for any money or other property of the company, or been guilty of any misfeasance or breach of any fiduciary or other duty in relation to the company.[93] The right to make a petition

---

[91] Keay, *Company Directors' Responsibilities to Creditors*, 231.

[92] *Ibid.*, 232.

[93] Section 212 states that:

(1) This section applies if in the course of the winding up of a company it appears that a person who:

(a) is or has been an officer of the company,
(b) has acted as liquidator or administrative receiver of the company, or
(c) not being a person falling within paragraph (a) or (b), is or has been concerned, or has taken part, in the promotion, formation or management of the company,

has misapplied or retained, or become accountable for, any money or other property of the company, or been guilty of any misfeasance or breach of any fiduciary or other duty in relation to the company.

under s. 212 is conferred upon the official receiver or the liquidator, and upon any creditor[94] or contributory of the company. This provision refers not only to misfeasance, but also 'breach of any fiduciary or other duty'. For courts to order any contribution, the applicant must demonstrate that the company has suffered a loss.[95] It should also be noted that, for a creditor wishing to bring a claim under s. 212, any order can only be made to the benefit of the company, and not to the applicant.[96]

Could s. 212 provide junior creditors with certain protection to challenge suspicious behaviour by directors in the case of pre-pack sales to a connected party, by establishing a cause of action on the ground of directors' 'breach of any fiduciary or other duty', as directors have a duty to avoid conflicts of interests? Agency theory requires directors to act in the best interest of the company and not to place themselves in a position where their personal interests or duties to others are liable to conflict with their duties to the company. Section 175 of CA 2006 (duty to avoid conflicts of interest) establishes a statutory duty that replaces the no-conflict rule applying to directors. This duty covers all conflicts, actual and potential, between the interests of the director and the interests of the company.[97] In the case of pre-pack sales to a connected party, the conflicts between the interests of purchasing directors and the interests of the company are obvious, as in such a circumstance, relevant directors are liable to take advantage of their position and information to further their own ends when they have a strong self-interest to influence the outcome of the pre-pack negotiations.

Although this may be a strong case of a breach of the non-conflict duty, it could also be technically avoided. What happens frequently is that an interested director resigns before the commencement of the administration procedure and subsequently makes an offer to buy the

---

94 An instance of an application by a creditor is *Re Loquitur Ltd* [2003] EWHC 999 (CH), where the Revenue applied under s 212 IA 1986 for an order that R and J, former directors of a company, should pay a certain amount of money for misfeasance or breach of duty in declaring a dividend of that amount in favour of another company.

95 Doyle and Keay, *Insolvency Legislation Annotations and Commentary*, 263. See also *Re Derek Randall Enterprises Ltd* [1990] BCC 749, CA.

96 Doyle and Keay, *Insolvency Legislation Annotations and Commentary*, 264.

97 This includes conflicts relating to the exploitation of the company's property, information or opportunity for personal purposes. See para.339 of CA 2006: Explanatory Notes. The present law is that in all cases, conflicts of interest must be authorised by the members of the company, unless some alternative procedure is properly provided. See s 175(4)(b) of CA 2006.

business from the office-holders or other directors of the company.[98] So the actual sale will be effected by the administrator, rather than the directors themselves. As regards their previous involvement in the pre-pack negotiation, the suspicion of breach of the non-conflict rule (s. 239 of CA 2006) can be remedied by full disclosure on behalf of interested directors of the nature and extent of their interest to the board as soon as the transaction is proposed.[99]

Section 213 – fraudulent trading The provision of s 213[100] is an attempt to discourage directors from carrying on business at the expense of creditors. It provides that, if in the course of winding up a company, it appears that any business of the company has been carried on with intent to defraud creditors of the company or creditors of any other person or for any fraudulent purpose, any persons who were knowingly parties to the carrying on of the business in the manner mentioned above are to be liable to make such contributions (if any) to the company's assets as the court thinks proper. Nevertheless, this aim is severely restricted by the requirement of dishonest intent and the courts' insistence on strict standards of pleading and proof.[101]

The phrases 'with intent to defraud creditors' and 'for any fraudulent purpose' require a finding of actual dishonesty, which Maugham J characterised as 'involving, according to current notions of fair trading among commercial men, real moral blame'.[102] And also, the relevant defendant must have taken 'an active part in carrying on the relevant

---

[98] In this way, the sale will not need shareholder approval under s 190 of CA 2006 as a substantial property transaction. Walton, 'Pre-packaged Administrations – Trick or Treat', 114.

[99] See also the analysis in Armour, 'The Rise of the "Pre-pack": Corporate Restructuring in the UK and Proposals for Reform'.

[100] Section 213 of the IA 1986 provides:

(1) If in the course of the winding up of a company it appears that any business of the company has been carried on with intent to defraud creditors of the company or creditors of any other person or for any fraudulent purpose, the following has effect.

(2) The court, on the application of the liquidator may declare that any persons who were knowingly parties to the carrying on of the business in the manner above-mentioned are to be liable to make such contributions (if any) to the company's assets as the court thinks proper.

[101] Finch, *Corporate Insolvency Law: Perspectives and Principles*, 511.

[102] In *Re Patrick & Lyon Ltd* [1933] Ch 786, 790.

business of the company'.[103] In the first case on 'fraudulent trading', *Re William C Leitch Bros Ltd*, Maugham J directed that 'if a company continues to carry on business and to incur debts at a time when there is to the knowledge of the directors no reasonable prospect of the creditors ever receiving payment of those debts, it is, in general, a proper inference that the company is carrying on business with intent to defraud'.[104]

Section 214 – wrongful trading Section 214 imposes liability on directors on the basis that they failed to take the requisite action to protect creditors (i.e. take every step with a view to minimising the potential loss to the company's creditors they ought to have taken) when they knew or ought to have concluded that there was no reasonable prospect that the company would avoid going into insolvent liquidation.[105] The aim of regulating directors' conduct through the use of s. 214 is to stop directors from continuing to trade during troubled times and placing all of the unjustifiable risks at the creditors' expense.[106]

But what is meant by directors taking 'every step' to minimise potential loss to company creditors is not defined and it may be difficult for a director to know which actions they should take to diligently

---

[103] A Elleray QC in *Morphites v Bernasconi* stated that: 'In order to prove "intent to defraud creditors" or a "fraudulent purpose" for the purposes of s 213 of the 1986 Act the liquidator had to prove against a relevant defendant that he took an active part in carrying on the relevant business of the company, that in doing so he intended to defraud creditors or had some other fraudulent purpose and that he acted dishonestly.' [2001] 2 BCLC 1 at 2.

[104] [1932] 2 Ch 71, 77. Furthermore, in *R v Grantham* [1984] QB 675, the Court of Appeal held that a company also carried on business with intent to defraud creditors if it incurs credit when there is no good reason for thinking that funds will become available to pay the debts when they become due or shortly thereafter. [1984] QB 675, 681–4. See also S Mortimore QC, ed, *Company Directors: Duties, Liabilities, and Remedies* (OUP, Oxford 2009), para.29-155.

[105] Section 214(2)(b) and (3) of IA 1986. A director will not be liable to contribute under s 214 if the court is satisfied that the director took 'every step … with a view to minimising the potential loss to the company's creditors as he ought to have taken'. The onus is on the person concerned to show that he took the proper steps, not for the liquidators to prove that he did not.

[106] Finch, 'The Recasting of Insolvency Law', 92. See also A Keay, 'Wrongful Trading and the Liability of Company Directors: A Theoretical Perspective' (2005) 25 *Legal Studies* 431, 433. In *Re Purpoint Ltd* [1991] BCLC 491, Vinelott J suggested that this section was introduced to stop directors from continuing to trade while their companies are on a slide into insolvency and to allow a liquidator to recoup the loss to the company caused by the actions of the directors, so as to benefit the creditors as a whole. [1991] BCLC 491, 499.

discharge this duty. Generally, the test as to whether a director has taken every step depends on courts considering what has been done in light of the criteria contained in s. 214(4). It specifies that a director is judged not only by the knowledge, skill and experience that he actually has, but also by the 'general knowledge, skill and experience' that may reasonably be expected of a person carrying out the same functions.[107] This test of knowledge, skill and experience is a combination of the objective and the subjective.[108] It is suggested that the steps that directors might take are, among many: seeking the advice of insolvency practitioners; appointing an administrator; seeking up-to-date accounts and reports from executive directors; and ensuring that adequate inquiries are made of managers.[109]

The courts do not appear ready to impose liability on directors, particularly when the directors have sought and obtained advice from professionals. In most cases where directors have been found liable they have been found to have acted irresponsibly.[110] In *Re Welfab Engineers Ltd*,[111] which considered the position where a company was insolvent but had not been placed in the hands of a receiver, the court held that, if the directors have properly considered the possible courses of action open to them, and concluded reasonably that some form of insolvency proceedings are inevitable, and honestly and reasonably began the process of realising assets by sale, they are probably not to be judged by the higher standards applicable to insolvency practitioners. Moreover, to be held as having fully complied with the s 214(2) duty, directors must be able to show that they obtained a reasonable price. They are not, however, required to conduct a full-scale investigation of other offers, which might produce a better price.[112] Recent cases have shown that where a company

---

107 Section 214(4) provides that the directors are judged against the standard of a reasonably diligent person having both:

(a) the general knowledge, skill and experience that may reasonably be expected of a person carrying out the same functions as are carried out by that director in relation to the company, and
(b) the general knowledge, skill and experience that that director has.

108 Goode, *Principles of Corporate Insolvency Law*, para.12-37.

109 Doyle and Keay, *Insolvency Legislation: Annotations and Commentary*, 259.

110 *Ibid.*, 257.

111 *Re Welfab Engineers Ltd* [1990] BCLC 833.

112 J Birds *et al.*, *Boyle & Birds' Company Law* (8th edn, Jordans, 2011), 603. In the reasoning of his judgment, Hoffmann J argued that 'This seems to me in accordance with recent developments in insolvency law, such as the institution of administration, which are intended to encourage trying to save the business

is in financial distress and the directors are having to make a difficult decision as to whether they trade on or close down the company and go into liquidation, the courts will take note of the fact that the directors are facing an unenviable dilemma.[113]

It should be noted that only directors may be the subject to proceedings under s 214, although subsection (7) makes it plain that this includes shadow directors.[114] Goode has added that a director could be a controlling shareholder if interfering too regularly in the day-to-day management of the company, as he could be the controller of a company acting as de facto director. The same qualification can apply to a 'company doctor' who is brought in to extricate the company from its difficulties and now acts as a director or shadow director, and to a lending bank exercising control for the protection of its loans and security. They are all capable of being held to be a shadow director.[115]

Can creditors rely on ss. 213 or 214 to establish any potential liability of directors in relation to a pre-pack sale? The more realistic view is that they are probably unlikely to be of much assistance. Under the IA 1986, only liquidators are able to initiate action under s. 213 and s. 214 and one of the conditions that must be satisfied is that the company has gone into insolvent liquidation. Nevertheless, according to Walton and Umfreville's empirical research on pre-packs, nearly half of pre-packs (242 cases out of 497) moved from administration directly to dissolution pursuant to para. 84 of Schedule B1 IA 1986, which means there were no opportunities for the claims to be asserted by a liquidator.[116] Furthermore, even if a pre-pack ends in a liquidation, the directors would be able to rely on the statutory defence in subsection 214(3) to argue against being liable

---

rather than destroy it. Of course, directors are not entitled to sell the business to save their jobs and those of other employees on terms which would clearly leave the creditors in a worse position than on a liquidation. But I do not think that an honest attempt to save the business should be judged by a stricter standard.' [1990] BCLC 833 at 838.

[113] *Re Continental Assurance Co of London Plc* [2001] BPIR 733. See also Doyle and Keay, *Insolvency Legislation: Annotations and Commentary*, 259.

[114] It is said that the extension of liability to a 'shadow director' is of considerable importance as it entails that in many situations a parent company will be liable for the debts of its subsidiary, and so also may others who have been involved to a significant extent in the management of a company's affairs, for example, a company's bank. DD Prentice, 'Creditor's Interests and Director's Duties', (1999) 10 *Oxford Journal of Legal Studies* 265, 267–8.

[115] Goode, *Principles of Corporate Insolvency Law*, paras.12-27 to 12-33.

[116] Walton and Umfreville, *Pre-pack Empirical Research: Characteristic and Outcome Analysis of Pre-pack Administration*, 28.

insofar as they took every (reasonable) step with a view to minimising the potential losses to the company's creditors as, in negotiating a business sale as a going concern through a pre-pack, a higher overall return has been achieved for the creditors as a whole.[117]

Sections 216 and 217 – phoenix provisions These sections are designed to deal with the 'phoenix syndrome'[118] to cover those cases in which the privileges of limited liability are exploited. They impose personal liability where a director of a company that has gone into liquidation since he was appointed, or during the period of 12 months before the company went into liquidation, a director or shadow director is involved for the next five years in any way, either directly or indirectly, in the management of a company that has a name which the liquidating company was known by at any time in that 12-month period, or a name which is so similar as to suggest an association with that company.[119] Section 217 provides that the person who breaches s. 216 is jointly and severally liable for the debts of the successor company.[120]

Exceptions could be made if disclosure requirements are satisfied by giving notice to all creditors of the insolvent company that the successor company is aware of, and the relevant notice must be given and published no later than 28 days after completion of the sale.[121] What a petitioner

---

[117] Armour, 'The Rise of the "Pre-pack": Corporate Restructuring in the UK and Proposals for Reform'.

[118] Phoenix syndrome is defined as where a company 'trading under a particular name goes into liquidation or receivership, leaving its creditors behind, and then a new company, with much the same name and all the same assets run by the same people, takes over but shorn of its previous creditors'. See *Western Intelligence Ltd v KDO Label Printing Machines Ltd* [1998] BCC 472 at 473 per Jacob J.

[119] Section 216(1)(2)(3) of the IA 1986.In *Ricketts v Ad Valorem Factors Ltd* [2004] 1 BCLC 1, CA at [30], Simon Brown LJ said that the 'similarity between the two names must be such as to give rise to a probability that members of the public, comparing the two names in the relevant context, will associate the two companies with each other, whether as successor companies or as here, as part of the same group'.

[120] This includes the debts and other liabilities of the company incurred at a time when that person was involved in the management of the company, and such debts and other liabilities as incurred at a time when the person was acting or was willing to act on instructions. S 217(2) (3) of the IA 1986. It should be noted that there is no need for a director to be found guilty of a breach of s 216 before proceedings can be initiated under s 217.

[121] This requirement is set out in Rule 4.228(3)(a) of the IR 1986. Such notice must state the name of the person, his intention to be director of the

under s. 217 has to establish is that, where there are two companies trading under similar names and the respondent was a director of one of the companies that had gone into insolvent liquidation, the relevant director was either involved in the management of the other company, or acted on the instructions of someone whom he or she knew was liable under s. 216.[122]

Sections 238 and 239 – undervalued transactions or preference Liability of transactions at an undervalue under s. 238 may arise in connection with pre-liquidation transactions[123] the company entered into at the relevant time.[124] If the value of the amount paid in consideration, in monetary terms or money's worth, is significantly less than the consideration paid by the company, such a transaction is deemed to be at an undervalue, unless at the time of such liquidation transaction there were reasonable grounds for believing that the transaction would benefit the company.[125] Namely, s. 238 aims to prevent insolvent companies disposing of property at a lower than reasonable value just before winding up

---

successor company or be otherwise associated, his purchase of the business from the organising office-holder and the re-use of a prohibited name.

[122] Doyle and Keay, *Insolvency Legislation: Annotations and Commentary*, 266. *Inland Revenue Commissioners v Nash* [2003] EWHC 686 (Ch).

[123] 'Transaction' is defined by s 436 as including 'a gift, agreement or arrangement'.

[124] 'Relevant time' is defined in s 240 as the time at which a company enters into a transaction at an undervalue or gives a preference –

(a) in the case of a transaction at an undervalue or of a preference which is given to a person who is connected with the company (otherwise than by reason only of being its employee), at a time in the period of two years ending with the onset of insolvency,
(b) in the case of a preference which is not such a transaction and is not so given, at a time in the period of six months ending with the onset of insolvency,
(c) In either case, at a time between the making of an administration application in respect of the company and the making of an administration order on that application, and
(d) In either case, at a time between the filing with the court of a copy of notice of intention to appoint an administrator under paragraph 14 or 22 of Sch. B1 and the making of an appointment under that paragraph.

[125] Section 238(4) of the IA 1986 states: For the purposes of this Section and s 241, a company enters into a transaction with a person at an undervalue if –

(a) the company makes a gift to that person or otherwise enters into a transaction with that person on terms that provide for the company to receive no consideration, or (as a means of asset-stripping), thereby reducing the pool of assets which would be available to be distributed to creditors.[126] This is an important safeguard and is applied in connection to both administration and liquidation procedures.

The most critical element of an s. 238 remedy is to prove that the company entered into an 'undervalue' transaction. Office-holders must establish that the consideration the company received was 'significantly less' than what the company provided.[127] The term 'significantly less' has not been interpreted by the courts yet.[128] One attempt was made by Lord Scott in *Phillips v Brewin Dolphin Bell Lawrie Ltd*, suggesting that '[t]he value of an asset that is being offered for sale is, prima facie, not less than the amount which a reasonably well-informed purchaser is prepared, in arm's length negotiations, to pay for it'.[129] Accordingly, whether a transaction is a transaction at an undervalue pursuant to s. 238(4)(b) will depend on an estimation of what a well-informed and reasonable purchaser would be prepared to pay.

Section 239 can be used to seek the adjustment of a pre-liquidation transaction on the basis that it amounted to a 'preference'; namely, a situation where the company has given a preference to a creditor by the transfer of money or of some interest in property by a company to a creditor to settle an antecedent debt, and it benefits that creditor to the prejudice of other creditors by granting the preferred creditor a greater share of the diminished assets than that creditor would enjoy in liquidation.[130]

(b) the company enters into a transaction with that person for a consideration that the value of which, in money or money's worth, is significantly less than the value, in money or money's worth, of the consideration provided by the company.

Section 238(5) of the IA 1986: the court shall not make an order under this section in respect of transaction at an undervalue if it satisfied –

(a) that the company which entered into the transaction did so in good faith and for the purpose of carrying on its business, and
(b) that at the time it did so there were reasonable grounds for believing that the transaction would benefit the company.

126 Doyle and Keay, *Insolvency Legislation: Annotations and Commentary*, 293.

127 In *Re M C Bacon Ltd* [1990] BCLC 324, at 340–41.

128 Keay, *Company Directors' Responsibilities to Creditors*, 191.

129 *Phillips v Brewin Dolphin Bell Lawrie Ltd* [2001] 1 WLR 143 at [27].

130 Section 239(4) of the IA 1986. Keay, *Company Directors' Responsibilities to Creditors*, 187. A preference is where a transaction confers a priority of

Those two potential grounds for statutory liability provisions might offer some substantive assistance to address the price concern of business sales in pre-packs, especially when the sales are made to a connected party, on the basis of the transaction at an undervalue or preference. Nevertheless, there is a time restriction: the transactions eligible to establish liability must have been concluded at the time prior to the commencement of formal insolvency proceedings. This would rule out their relevance to pre-packs, as allegedly pre-packaged sales, although pre-arranged before the official appointment of the administrator, are conducted by the administrators post commencement of the statutory procedure.[131]

Summing up

To sum up, this section examined the potential grounds for directors' liability in pre-packaged sales under applicable statutory and common law duties, if they have acted in a dishonest manner. It suggests that most of the relevant provisions in the insolvency legislations apply only when the process enters into liquidation or administration or prior to the commencement of those proceedings, whereas, due to the pre-determined nature of pre-packs, there is a mismatch between those who arranged the pre-pack deals and those who executed them. As a result, the current

---

advantage on a creditor in relation to past indebtedness of the insolvent company and the advantage is given at the expense of other creditors who are owed debts at the time of transaction, thus preventing an equal distribution of the insolvent's property among the creditors. See Doyle and Keay, *Insolvency Legislation: Annotations and Commentary*, 297. In order for a liquidator to successfully attack a transaction as a preference, the liquidator has to prove a number of elements, including proof that:

(a) the transaction was entered into within the six months before the onset of insolvency or, if the respondent is a person connected with the company, within the two years prior to the onset of insolvency;
(b) the company has done anything which has the effect of putting the recipient of the preference into a position which, in the event of the company entering insolvent liquidation, will be better than the position he or she would have been in had the thing not been done;
(c) the company was influenced in deciding to enter into the impugned transaction by a desire to enable the recipient to have a preference; at the time, or as a result, of the giving of the preference the company was unable to pay its debts within the meaning of s 123, in other words insolvent.

[131] See also the analysis by Armour in 'The Rise of the "Pre-pack": Corporate Restructuring in the UK and Proposals for Reform'.

legal framework is inadequate when it comes to the protection of vulnerable junior creditors in pre-packs. This is an important loophole in the current regime in dealing with pre-packed business sales in administrations and it ought to be examined closely by policy-makers.

Challenging the Actions and Decisions of Administrators

Statutory claims against administrators

The right to challenge the decisions or actions of the administrator is granted to the company's creditors and others by paras.74 and 75 of Sch. B1 to the IA 1986. According to para.74(1), a creditor or member of a company in administration may apply to the court claiming that:

> (a) the administrator is acting or has acted so as unfairly to harm the interests of the applicant (whether alone or in common with some or all other members or creditors), or
> (b) the administrator proposes to act in a way which would unfairly harm the interests of the applicant (whether alone or in common with some or all other members or creditors).

Paragraph 74(2) affords any creditor or member the power to challenge the administrator for not performing his functions with reasonable speed or with efficiency. The basis for such a challenge corresponds to the administrator's duty to act as quickly and efficiently as is reasonably practicable.

For an application by a creditor or member of the company under para.74(1), the applicant should be able to establish that the conduct complained of has, or will, cause 'harm' to his interests and therefore an applicant must initially discharge the burden of establishing a tangible interest.[132] The applicant must also establish unfair harm in the sense that the conduct or proposed conduct of the administrator is not only harmful but unfairly harmful to the applicant, whether alone or in common with some or all other members or creditors.[133]

The criteria to determine unfairness may be found in common law. In *O'Neill v Phillips*[134] which concerns 'unfair prejudice' under the Companies Act, it was held by the House of Lords that 'the unfairness might

---

[132] Doyle and Keay, *Insolvency Legislation: Annotations and Commentary*, 698.

[133] *Ibid*. The term 'harm' must be understood as meaning 'prejudice', which is consistent with the meaning under para.3(4)(b) of the Sch. B1 of IA 1986.

[134] [1999] 2 All ER. This case is concerned about an action for unfair prejudice under s 459 of CA 1985 (now s 994 of CA 2006).

consist in a breach of the rules regulating the basis on which it had been agreed that the affairs of the company should be conducted or in using those rules in a manner which equity would regard as contrary to good faith'.[135] In *Four Private Investment Funds v Lomas and others*,[136] an application brought under para.74 of Sch. B1 by four (unnamed) hedge funds was to seek an order from the court requiring Lehman Brothers International (Europe)'s (LBIE) administrators to provide details of assets held as custodian by LBIE for the hedge funds and any sums owing by the hedge funds to LBIE. The court declined to make the order. It held that:

> the administrator must seek to balance the need to proceed with the administration in the interests of creditors as a whole against the desirability of responding to legitimate enquiries from individual creditors and others. But, in the absence of some plainly wrongful conduct on the administrator's part, it is for him to decide where the balance lies.[137]

In Lightman *et al* analysis of what constitutes unfair harm, it is demonstrated that the complaint may refer unfair harm to the interests of the applicant to be where the complaint arises because the administrator has taken a decision that serves the interests of a class of claimants X but harms those of another class Y.[138]

---

135 [1999] 2 All ER, at 976.

136 [2008] EWHC 2869 (Ch). The hedge funds argued that if they were not made aware of their financial position in relation to LBIE then they would be unable to fulfil their obligations in planning the fund's future management and it was likely that the funds would be wound down.

137 [2008] EWHC 2869 (Ch), para.48. It was recognised that harm would be caused to the hedge funds by the continued non-disclosure of their financial position. However, it was held that this harm was not unfair given that the administrators were focusing on carrying out their functions in the interests of LBIE's creditors as a whole. Devoting a disproportionate amount of time to a small group of creditors' issues at the expense of creditors as a whole would not fulfil that function. [2008] EWHC 2869 (Ch), para.39.

138 Lightman *et al., The Law of Administrators and Receivers of Companies*, 270. There are at least three possibilities:

(a) There is a statutory obligation in the particular circumstances that exist to prefer X over Y (for example, in the context of the statutory hierarchy of objectives provided in para.3 of Sch. B1): here, there is of course no unfairness. The administrator is merely complying with his statutory duty.
(b) The administrator is not under any duty to prefer X over Y, and further, at least one alternative way of making the decision was reasonably open to him which would not have required any trade-off between the respective

Paragraph 75 is dedicated specifically to any so-called misfeasance claim against an administrator. Under para.75, a creditor of the company can apply to the court to examine the conduct of a person who is, or purports or has been purported to be, the administrator of a company on the basis that the alleged administrator:

(a) has misapplied or retained money or other property of the company;
(b) has become accountable for money or other property of the company;
(c) has breached a fiduciary or other duty in relation to the company or
(d) has been guilty of misfeasance.[139]

Paragraph 75 provides a summary remedy against a person who has misapplied or retained or become accountable for any money or other property of the company, or been guilty of any misfeasance or breach of a fiduciary or other duty in relation to the company (rather than towards the individual who makes the application).[140]

A removal application can also be used as an indirect route to challenge the actions and decisions of insolvency practitioners in pre-packs. The power of the court to order the removal of an administrator is provided by para.88 of Sch. B1. In comparison to para.74 and para.75, the standard applied by the court to make an order of removal of the administrator under para.88 is lower. The court is ready to do this where the office-holder has lost the confidence of key creditors, though such order will not imply any misconduct by the administrator.[141] In the case of *Clydesdale v Smailes*,[142] David Richards J. ruled that it was appropriate to remove those administrators from office under para.88, because the

---

interests of X and Y: here, the administrator is open to the charge of unfairness.

The administrator is not under any duty to prefer X over Y, but the only choices open to him necessarily require trading off the interests of X against those of Y: here, the harm to Y's interests is unfair if it is disproportionate to the benefit to X's interests.

[139] Para.75(3) of Sch. B1 to the IA 1986. This provision applies not only to the administrator or former administrator but also to an individual whose appointment was actually invalid or void. See Doyle and Keay, *Insolvency Legislation: Annotations and Commentary*, 700.

[140] I Fletcher, *The Law of Insolvency* (4th edn, Sweet and Maxwell, London 2009), 596.

[141] D Milman, 'Judicial Reflections on the Administration Process: A 2010 Perspective' (2010) 283 *Company Law Newsletter* 1, 1–5.

[142] *Clydesdale v Smailes* (No. 1) [2009] EWHC 1745 (Ch), [2010] BPIR 62. In this case, the major creditor of the company alleged that the insolvency practitioner had been closely connected with the negotiations of the sale, that the

evidence demonstrated that the administrators had been intimately involved in the negotiations and it would have been difficult for them to conduct an independent review. Another important factor in the court's ruling is that the majority of creditors in value must support the removal. Nevertheless, it should be noted that the judge did not draw any conclusions on whether the sale was at an undervalue.[143]

One basis on which a challenge under para.75 might be mounted would be that the administrator did not expend sufficient effort to ensure that the price achieved for the sale was the best possible; this would imply a breach of his duty of care and possibly of his statutory duty to act in the interests of the creditors as a whole.[144] Yet, arguably, the removal application has little use in the context of pre-packs, as the pre-arranged business sale will be processed in advance of general creditors' knowledge of the deal. Naturally, introducing a new insolvency practitioner who will be highly paid at the expense of all creditors would be futile by that time. As a result, the provisions of paras 74 and 75 are unlikely to be used by creditors in challenging the administrators in the context of a pre-pack.

Common law duty – the duty to take reasonable steps to obtain a proper price

As mentioned earlier the insolvency officer has a duty to take reasonable steps to obtain a proper price in his business sale proposal. Millett J. (as he then was) held in *Re Charnley Davies Ltd*[145] that an administrator owed a duty to the company over which he was appointed to take reasonable care to obtain the best price that the circumstances, as he reasonably perceived them to be, permitted, including a duty to take reasonable care in choosing the time at which to sell the property.[146]

---

sale was at a gross undervalue and, in breach of SIP 16 and otherwise, the administrator had failed subsequently to conduct himself with independence.

143 The court rejected the allegations of impropriety made against the administrator, as 'it is impossible on this application to resolve the issue as to whether the sale was at a significant under value'. [2009] EWHC 1745 (Ch), [26].

144 Amour, 'The Rise of the "Pre-pack": Corporate Restructuring in the UK and Proposals for Reform'.

145 No. 2 [1990] BCLC 760.

146 In reaching this decision, Judge Millett J contrasted the position of the administrator with that of the mortgagee:

> 'It was common ground that an administrator owed a duty to a company over which he is appointed to take reasonable steps to obtain a proper price for its

Therefore, if nevertheless an administrator pursues a less advantageous sale, this could constitute a breach of the common law duty of care and possibly of his statutory duty to act in the interests of the creditors as a whole.

How could reasonable care be taken in order to get the best price reasonably obtainable in the condition they were in? In *Re British American Racing (Holdings) Ltd*,[147] the court stressed that the administrators would be bound to take steps to ensure that potential purchasers were aware that the assets were on the market and encourage them to make the highest bid possible.[148] The court also explained the need for the administrators to properly test the market. The administrator is under a duty to take reasonable care to obtain the best price that the circumstances permit, particularly taking reasonable care in choosing the time at which to sell the property. The conduct of an administrator is to be judged by the standards of a professional insolvency practitioner of ordinary skills.[149]

In ascertaining whether or not a proper price has been realised, the courts are unlikely to conceive the duty breached unless there is evidence of substantial undervalue. This again may also be largely a matter of opinion. Indeed, what is alleged to be an undervalue may merely be a difference in opinion of several valuers.[150] In *Cuckmere Brick Co Ltd v Mutual Finance Ltd*,[151] his Lordship remarked:

> I accordingly conclude, both on principle and authority, that a mortgagee in exercising his power of sale does owe a duty to take reasonable precautions to

---

assets. That is an obligation which the law imposes on anyone with a power whether contractual or statutory; to sell property which does not belong to him. A mortgagee is bound to have regard to the interests of the mortgagor, but he is entitled to give priority to his own interests, and may insist on an immediate sale whether or not that is calculated to realise the best price; he must "take reasonable care to obtain the true value of the property at the moment he chooses to sell it". See *Cuckmere Brick Co Ltd v Mutual Finance Ltd* [1971] 2 ALL ER 633. An administrator, by contrast, like a liquidator, has no interest of his own to which he may give priority, and must take reasonable care in choosing the time at which to sell the property. His duty is "to take reasonable care to obtain the best price that the circumstances permit".' [1990] BCLC 760, at 775.

147 [2005] 2 BCLC 234.

148 *Ibid.*, at 248.

149 See *Re Charnley Davies Ltd* [1990] BCLC 760.

150 *Ibid.*

151 *Cuckmere Brick Co Ltd v Mutual Finance Ltd* [1971] 2 ALL ER 633.

> obtain the true market value of the mortgaged property at the date on which he decides to sell it. No doubt in deciding whether he has fallen short of that duty the facts must be looked at broadly, and he will not be adjudged to be in default unless he is plainly on the wrong side of the line.[152]

The duty to take reasonable precautions to obtain a proper price is easily stated but less easily demarcated. Often, the idea is that the value of a business in administration is whatever is offered, amounting to an impenetrable defence to the charge that a proper price has not been obtained, because the standard is quite subjective and difficult to measure. It has been suggested that going-concern sales are unlikely to be open to attack on undervalue grounds unless this can be easily demonstrated, such as that the business had been sold to a person other than the highest offeror.[153]

Judging administrators' commercial decisions

It should be recognised that English courts are normally unwilling to interfere with or provide guidance on administrative matters or those involving the exercise of commercial judgment.[154] The courts will not seek to substitute their own judgment for the considered commercial judgment of the administrator if it seems that the administrator fulfilled his functions by giving thought to all relevant considerations and informing his decisions properly.[155] In the absence of manifest fraud or negligence the courts can rarely be expected to apply a high standard in reviewing insolvency practitioners' conduct.[156] The recent case *DKLL Solicitors v Her Majesty's Revenue and Customs*[157] illustrates that the

---

152 *Ibid.*, 646.

153 See S Frisby, 'The Law and Practice of Contractual Receivership' (PhD thesis, University of Nottingham 2000). This comment was made in the context of business sales in administrative receivership.

154 For instance, in *Re T & D Industries Plc*, Neuberger J stated: 'The importance of the decision and the time involved may well be such that the administrator should have what *[sic]* consultation he can with the creditors … Whether he should effect any consultation, with whom he should effect it, how he should effect it and what decision he should make following any consultation must be matters for him to decide by reference to the facts of the individual case.' [2000] 1 WLR 646, 658–9.

155 Goode, *Principles of Corporate Insolvency Law,* para.10-89.

156 A Walters and M Seneviratne, *Complaints Handling in the UK Insolvency Practitioner Profession* (Report for the UK Insolvency Practices Council, 2008) <http://papers.ssrn.com/sol3/papers.cfm?abstract_id=1094757> accessed 30 July 2015, 7.

157 [2007] EWHC 2067 (Ch).

courts tend to defer to the professional expertise of insolvency practitioners as regards formulation and execution of commercial strategy.[158]

With regard to the merits of a pre-pack sale, the general stance of the judiciary is that they are for the administrator to deal with and administrators' business judgements in commercial issues should not be interfered with lightly by the court and not without evidence of irrationality.[159] A number of cases have displayed a significant amount of faith in the professionalism of insolvency practitioners in conducting insolvency proceedings.[160] The court approach is designed to allow the administrator to act in a decisive way without fear of delays or second-guessing by the judge.[161] Nevertheless, in light of the rising controversy surrounding pre-packs, even in the absence of statutory amendments, the courts are likely to act more responsively to allegations of abuse of pre-pack processes and adopt a more sceptical approach. The question is, however, to what extent the courts can be expected to energetically oversee the business management approach followed by administrators and decisions in that context.

One of the difficulties facing the judiciary in undertaking such a task would be that the question of what amounts to the best price that is reasonably obtainable is largely a matter of opinion and business judgement. In assessing whether any allegation of an undervalue or abuse has any substance, the fact that some precautions should have been taken, or steps may have been taken,[162] may raise some interesting questions for further investigation. Yet they are unlikely to be deemed sufficient for the judiciary to hold administrators accountable for misconduct or abuse,

---

[158] Walters and Seneviratne, *Complaints Handling in the UK Insolvency Practitioner Profession*, 7.

[159] In cases such as *Re T & D Industries Plc*, the courts made it clear that administrators may have to make urgent commercial and administrative decisions and that it is not for the courts to make those decisions for them or to second-guess the judgments involved, provided that these are made in good faith. Further, in the DTI Explanatory Notes to the Enterprise Act 2002 (Chapter 40) para.648, it was suggested that the court will only interfere if bad faith can be established or the decision was one that no reasonable administrator would have taken.

[160] For instance, *Re T & D Industries Plc, Re Transbus International Ltd, Re Ballast Plc* [2004] EWHC 2356; [2005] 1 WLR 1928, *Clydesdale v Smailes*.

[161] See Finch, *Corporate Insolvency Law: Perspectives and Principles*, 399.

[162] For instance, the company was advertised for sale inappropriately, the specialist advice as to its value is not taken where such an independent valuation is needed.

unless there is evidence of manifest fraud or negligence in the insolvency practitioner's conduct.

To change the perceived 'judiciary leniency' to the administrators' judgements on commercial issues and promote public trust in pre-pack sales, the judiciary must be willing and capable to stimulate the production of clear arguments to challenge commercial decisions and be prepared to indicate the conditions under which the insolvency practitioners' business judgements and decisions should be deferred.[163] As suggested in the case *Re Hellas Telecommunications*,[164] where there is obvious evidence that a pre-pack sale would be an abuse of the administrator's power, the court could refuse to make an order, or make an order but give a direction to the administrator not to effect the proposed sale; while there is compelling evidence suggesting that the pre-pack sale is the best solution or the only real way forward, the court could grant the administrator a specific liberty to enter into the sale, leaving open the possibility that aggrieved creditors could challenge the administrator *ex post facto*.[165] In cases where there is no compelling evidence either way, it may be appropriate for the court, on a discretionary basis, to apply a less 'deferential' approach in judging the practitioners' actions. By doing so, it will send out a strong signal that administrators should make all reasonable efforts to attract potential purchasers and to ensure the best price that is reasonably obtainable, and any failure to do so may render their commercial decisions questionable or result in their removal from office.

Nevertheless, one cannot be too optimistic about the feasibility of addressing the prevailing concerns about pre-pack sales when aggrieved creditors resort to litigation. As far as unsecured creditors are concerned, it is hard to expect them to play an active role in initiating a lawsuit, rather than loudly complaining about perceived prejudice to their interests. To a small creditor, not only are the costs of legal action high, but successful recovery is uncertain, as he may not have sufficient information to effectively challenge the administrator's conduct, and in the event of successful recovery the proceeds will go to a general pool of assets from which, at best, he is only likely to receive an enhanced dividend.

---

163 Finch in her recent article suggested that the judiciary is expected to fulfil a facilitation/mediation role so that common understandings and expectations can be developed and different regimes of influence can be harmonised. See Finch, 'Pre-packaged Administrations and the Construction of Propriety'.

164 *Re Hellas Telecommunications* [2009] EWHC 3199 (Ch).

165 See judicial opinions expressed in [2009] EWHC 3199 (Ch) at [8].

CONCLUSION

This chapter focuses on pre-pack sales to connected parties, questioning its vulnerability to abuse by insiders at the expense of general junior creditors. The key concern is that, when the business is sold to a connected party, the pre-pack strategy creates the risk that, while the interests of the insiders are well aligned through the process, the interests of general unsecured creditors who are under-represented in the decision-making may be less well served. This may lead to a suboptimal business sale strategy through the pre-packing route where insiders may engage in morally or legally dubious activities during the accelerated sale process in order to get an advantageous price to the detriment of general creditors. This concern is fueled by the fact that often very limited marketing activity is carried out when businesses are sold to connected parties, and there is a more general transparency issue surrounding pre-packs, where the information disclosed ex post facto to creditors excluded from the negotiations may not have the necessary resources to properly assess whether the business sale has been carried out in a manner that has not improperly or unlawfully prejudiced their interests.

This chapter also examined the robustness of the UK's requisite legal framework in responding to those concerns. The analysis has focused on potential grounds to establish liability or provide a remedy under applicable statutory and common law duties to challenge those who have been assisting in the implementation of pre-pack sales, namely, company directors and the administrator, if they have acted in a dishonest manner. Arguably, protective provisions in insolvency legislations only apply where the complaint in question arises in the context of a case that has eventually reached liquidation or administration proceedings. Therefore, the current UK insolvency framework does not provide adequate monitoring mechanisms or remedial routes to respond to sensitive issues arising in the context of pre-packs due to a mismatch between those who arranged the pre-packaged deals and those who execute them.

The judiciary will continue to play a central role in ensuring that the legislative objectives of the procedure are met when judging how administrators have discharged their duties. Despite the perceived reluctance of UK courts to second-guess practitioners' business judgement on commercial issues, it is expected that the courts will take a more rigorous and sceptical approach to the question of whether reasonable precautions have been taken in decisions leading to pre-pack sales, given the current level of controversy the pre-pack practice has generated. Nevertheless, one cannot be too optimistic about the possibility of success when aggrieved creditors resort to litigation, due to litigation costs and the difficulty of a legal challenge.

As shown in this chapter, current arrangements may not be sufficient to provide a good balance between the need for an expeditious resolution of the company's financial distress and creditors' rights and expectations. It means UK policy-makers need to consider the feasibility of introducing a balancing act at some point in the process, either by enhancing the transparency of the process or by opening up legal routes to unsecured creditors to enable them to challenge prejudicial conduct more effectively. This is important not just on grounds of equity but also on grounds of efficiency. General creditors who might feel assured that misconduct within the pre-pack process and any resulting prejudice to their interests will give rise to liability will be less willing to find any obstacles to stop the pre-negotiated sale furthering the rescue objective.

4. Safeguards for creditors – an evaluation of UK reform initiatives

INTRODUCTION

The preceding chapter discussed a number of intrinsic risks surrounding the pre-pack practice. It highlighted the importance of ensuring that the commercial advantages of the pre-pack process, in the form of enhanced consideration for the sale of the business and a reduction in transaction costs, should be to the benefit of all creditors who have a tangible interest in the proceedings, particularly those who are excluded from the decision-making process. Nevertheless, the pre-determined nature of the pre-pack strategy makes the administration procedure less disruptive for management than the formal rules, and this raises questions about the danger of the alignment of interests between insiders at the negotiation stage and the impartiality of the administrator, particularly where the business is to be sold to a connected party.

A series of professional regulation amendments have been implemented to address strong criticism directed at the role of professionals in pre-packs. As mentioned earlier SIP 16 was issued in January 2009 and adopted by all the PRBs in response to creditors' concerns about pre-pack sales, and an updated version was implemented on 1 November 2013. This new standard seeks to impose new requirements on IPs. In conjunction with SIP 16, a revised Insolvency Code of Ethics[1] was introduced for all insolvency practitioners to adhere to. Nevertheless, critics have maintained that the professional guidance in the form of a SIP has failed to fully regulate the use of pre-pack sales. The Department for Business Innovation & Skills ('BIS') further released a Consultation paper in 2010 to invite views on whether more measures were needed to strengthen the transparency of, and confidence in, pre-packaged sales. Following that consultation, the IS published a draft of the Insolvency (Amendment) (No. 2) Rules 2011 ('the Draft Rules'), which was

[1] Insolvency Practitioners Association, *Ethics Code for Members* (London, November 2008).

intended to enhance the regulation of pre-pack insolvency sales to connected parties, but was effectively abandoned due to its poor reception from the profession. Meanwhile, attention was drawn to any required improvements in the effectiveness of the insolvency profession given the important role IPs played in the pre-pack process.

This chapter will look into the recent efforts to address concerns surrounding pre-packs in the UK and comment on the effectiveness of those initiatives in addressing those concerns, especially pre-pack sales to connected parties. The chapter is divided into four sections. Section 2 examines increased disclosure obligations that were recently incorporated into the revised SIP 16 and their effectiveness in limiting the room for abuse of the pre-pack process. Section 3 assesses the proposed measures in the Draft Rules 2011, and the more recent recommendations put forward by Teresa Graham CBE. Furthermore, section 4 looks into the recent initiatives in the insolvency profession to strengthen the regulatory regime for insolvency practitioners and enhance their accountability, and questions to what extent those efforts to build a more responsive and consistent regulatory and monitory system would entrench public confidence in pre-packs.

ENHANCING TRANSPARENCY THROUGH SIP 16

The Revised Version of SIP 16

An updated revision of SIP 16 came into effect from 1 November 2013 ('SIP 16 (2013)'),[2] introducing more timely and detailed disclosure requirements. The revised SIP 16 is not a major rewrite and does not seek to impose new requirements on insolvency practitioners. Many of the changes implemented have already been seen in the Insolvency Service's '*Dear IP*' guidance in 2009, but these points are now contained within the updated SIP itself, and the *Dear IP* guidance is consequently withdrawn.

The main changes include the requirement for a detailed narrative explanation and justification of the pre-pack sale that should be provided to creditors with the first notification to creditors and in any event within seven days of the date of completion of a pre-pack transaction.[3] The

[2] *Statement of Insolvency Practice 16: Pre-packaged Sales in Administrations* (2013) <http://www.insolvency-practitioners.org.uk/regulation-and-guidance/england-wales> accessed 30 July 2015.

[3] SIP 16 (2013), para.11.

earlier *Dear IP* guidance required the notification to be sent out within 14 days of completion of the sale. This should then be included in the administrator's Statement of Proposals filed at Companies House.

Furthermore, the information disclosure requirements under SIP 16 (2013) are more extensive and more structured, categorised into the different elements of the transaction, including: details of the alternative courses of action that were considered and any requests made to potential funders to satisfy working capital requirements; details of previous sales of the business or assets by office-holders in the previous (at least) 24 months and disclosure of any involvement by the administrator or the administrator's firm; more comprehensive information relating to the valuers, valuations obtained and the rationale behind the valuations; and details of sale consideration by asset categories. It is also required that the administrator should seek the requisite approval of the proposals by the affected creditors as soon as practicable after appointment.

It is worth noting that disclosure of valuations was improved in the updated guidance. The SIP 16 (2013) replaced a need to list 'any valuations obtained of the business or the underlying assets' to a more explicit requirement to give: the names, qualifications and confirmation of the independence of the valuers; the valuations themselves; a summary of the basis of the valuation adopted and a rationale for its use; and an explanation of any variance in the sale price from those valuations.

In general, the SIP 16 (2013) is not radically different from its predecessor and it mainly seeks to be more comprehensive about the information that should be disclosed to creditors and the time limits for such disclosures. Clearly, the more explicit and detailed statements required under SIP 16 (2013) will allow creditors to quickly identify a sale to connected parties and also to assess whether a proper market price was paid for the business and assets. Also the requirement to show that independent professional valuation advice has been obtained, and that any difference between the price obtained and the valuation advice is to be explained, addresses part of the real concern of a devalued sale. Therefore, both steps can improve the transparency of pre-pack business sales if the new standard is properly implemented.

Ensuring Compliance of SIP 16 Guidance

The effectiveness of the professional guidance to increase the transparency of pre-pack business sales greatly depends on effective monitoring and control systems to detect any non-compliance with those requirements, and to ensure that any instance of abuse will be firmly dealt with. With regard to compliance of SIP 16, the overall compliance rate was 69.8 per cent during the years since its introduction in 2009 till the revision in 2013.[4] The latest reports concerning the operation of SIP 16 (2013) implemented from November 2013 showed that for the first two months of operation of the revised SIP 16, 89 per cent of the cases reviewed were considered fully compliant with the updated requirements;[5] 78 per cent of pre-pack cases during 2014 were considered fully compliant.[6] The increased level of compliance rates suggests a very positive sign as regards the quality of the information disclosed to creditors.

It should be noted that the failure to comply with the SIP does not imply misconduct in the pre-pack sale itself. There are concerns raised by practitioners about the way the Insolvency Service judged reports that found them to be non-compliant, arguing that insolvency practitioners were 'not made aware of the criteria on which they are being judged by the IS, or indeed given any feedback on their reports'.[7] Furthermore, the quality of information flows is also important to enhance practitioners' accountability and procedural fairness.[8] There is certainly an argument that if the information is available, it should be provided. Nevertheless, there should be an awareness of the restraining factors that are likely to cause information flow disruptions in pre-packs. First, incumbent management constitutes the key reservoir of relevant information. But management may possess strong private incentives to preserve their control over the rescue process and therefore be disinclined to lay all their cards on the table.[9] Also, in some cases, there may be a hostile appointment where the administrator is appointed on short notice and may have little

---

[4] This figure was based on the reported overall compliance rates of SIP 16: 62 per cent full-compliance in IS reviewed sample cases during 2009; 75 per cent during 2010, 68 per cent during 2011, 65 per cent during the first six months of 2012, and 79 per cent during 2013.

[5] See the Insolvency Service, *2013 Annual Review of Insolvency Practitioner Regulation* (April 2014), 8.

[6] The Insolvency Service, *2014 Annual Review of Insolvency Practitioner Regulation* (March 2015), 14.

[7] The House of Commons Business, Innovation and Skills Committee, *The Insolvency Service: Sixth Report of Session 2012–2013* (HC 675, January 2013), para.79 at p 25. It is recommended that the IS amend its monitoring processes to include feedback to each IP and their regulatory body where SIP 16 reports have been judged to be non-compliant.

[8] Professor Finch pointed out that 'sound information flows are (also) essential if processes are to be open and accountable as well as procedurally fair'. Finch, 'Control and Co-ordination in Corporate Rescue', 379.

[9] *Ibid.*, 380.

time to investigate the full circumstances of the company.[10] In such cases the administrator will not have armed himself with all the requisite information at the time of drafting the statement. As a result, the information provided in the statement will be inadequate.

Nevertheless, in normal circumstances, the practitioners should be in a position to deliver a comprehensive justification of the use of the pre-pack strategy to all concerned. The bottom line behind the requirements of information disclosure is to inform creditors how decisions were made; it is not a check-list of disclosure requirements to be done in a perfunctory manner. There should be an awareness of the situation where formulaic explanations are devised in advance and routinely employed by practitioners in their statements to creditors, as the effectiveness of SIP 16 will otherwise suffer.[11]

Another issue that directly relates to the compliance concern is to ensure that any instances of abuse are firmly dealt with. Where the disclosures made by IPs are insufficient to give a full picture of the reasons for the pre-pack sale in line with the requirements of SIP 16, the Insolvency Service would write to the practitioner concerned for further information.[12] If the disclosure made gives rise to concerns about the conduct of the practitioner or if there appears to be a clear regulatory breach, they would be reported to their authorising bodies for consideration from a disciplinary perspective. Most instances of non-compliance are deemed to be minor. Examples of a minor breach would usually be a disclosure statement being sent a couple of days late or the sale consideration not being broken down across all asset categories; more serious cases would typically be several omissions from the disclosure or where no justification for the pre-pack sales is provided.[13]

Of the cases reviewed in 2013, 21 per cent were found to be not fully compliant with SIP 16. Of the total number of disclosures reviewed, involving 19 practitioners, 2.3 per cent were cases where more serious

---

[10] Frisby, 'A Preliminary Analysis of Pre-Packaged Administrations', 30.

[11] S Frisby, 'Balancing Interests in Administration: Contributions from the Courts and the Coalface – Creditors to Concede Individual Agendas' (2009) 24 *Butterworths Journal of International Banking and Financial Law* 198.

[12] In some instances this has been done without prior reference to the insolvency practitioners concerned where the breach is so unambiguous or serious that it warrants immediate consideration by the relevant authorising body. The Insolvency Service, *Report on the First Six Months' Operation of Statement of Insolvency Practice 16*, para.3.1.3.

[13] The Insolvency Service, *2013 Annual Review of Insolvency Practitioner Regulation*, 9.

breaches were identified and referred to relevant RPBs so that their SIP 16 disclosures could be considered from a regulatory and disciplinary perspective.[14] In 2014, 22 per cent were found to be non-compliance cases and 3 per cent of the total cases reviewed were referred to the relevant RPBs with a view to possible disciplinary proceedings.[15] In 2010, 2 per cent of cases were referred to the relevant RPBs, and 25 per cent of cases reviewed were found to be non-compliant.[16]

It should be noted that breach of SIP 16 is merely a professional disciplinary offence, as the SIP is embraced as professional guidance rather than a statutory requirement. It is up to the insolvency professional regulators to take any disciplinary action. Insolvency practitioners can be issued fines for non-compliance. From January 2010 to November 2012, it was recorded that there have been a total of six fines given to insolvency practitioners by their authorising bodies for breaches of SIP 16. The fines ranged from £250 to £2,500 with costs attached ranging from £250 to £2,167. In 26 other cases, the authorising bodies took regulatory action resulting in five consent orders without financial penalty and 21 formal warnings.[17] However, it has been recognised that the level of fines was an inadequate deterrent, which can be seen from the negligible impact on improving compliance levels and that non-compliance needs to be followed through with stronger penalties by way of larger fines and stronger measures of enforcement.[18]

LEGISLATIVE REFORM PROPOSALS TO REGULATE PRE-PACKS

The 2010 Consultation and Proposals

A Consultation paper was released on 31 March 2010 by the Department of Business, Innovation & Skills to invite views on whether new

---

[14] *Ibid.*, 8–9.

[15] The Insolvency Service, *2014 Annual Review of Insolvency Practitioner Regulation* (March 2015), 15.

[16] The Insolvency Service, *Report on the Operation of Statement of Insolvency Practice 16: 1 January to 31 December 2010*, 7.

[17] Written evidence submitted by the Insolvency Service to the BIS Committee, see House of Commons Business, Innovation and Skills Committee, *The Insolvency Service: Sixth Report of Session 2012–13*. Ev 67.

[18] House of Commons Business, Innovation and Skills Committee, *The Insolvency Service: Sixth Report of Session 2012–13*, para.77.

measures are needed to strengthen the transparency of, and confidence in, pre-packaged sales. Five options for regulating pre-packs were offered in the Consultation, ranging from radical to modest.[19]

One of the proposals under the 2010 Consultation paper suggested giving statutory force to the disclosure requirements currently required under SIP 16 by incorporating them into the Insolvency Rules by virtue of the powers in the IA 1986, thus providing greater penalties for non-compliance.[20] This would include a requirement to file the information at Companies House, which would place the details of pre-packs in the public domain. However, to achieve this, it would be necessary to define the precise circumstances or agreements that constitute a 'pre-pack', as the phrase is currently undefined under statute.[21]

Some of the proposals were more radical than ex post transparency of SIP 16, aiming to grant stronger powers to creditors or the court. To ensure that there would be an impartial office-holder to certify the appropriateness of the whole process and to identify and report any illegal conduct, one proposal in the 2010 Consultation paper was to restrict the exit of a pre-pack administration under compulsory liquidation, which would result in automatic scrutiny of directors' and administrators' actions by the Official Receiver ('OR'), who as an officer of the court and a public official would work independently to the insolvency practitioner. This would require the administrator to petition the court for compulsory liquidation. The OR has a statutory duty to investigate the causes of the company's failure and the business dealings and affairs of the company. As part of their investigation the OR would be able to scrutinise the pre-pack deal and properly review the previous insolvency practitioner's actions. They also have a statutory duty to report on the conduct of the directors.

---

[19] The five identified options are: 1. No change. 2. Giving statutory force to the disclosure requirements currently in SIP 16, and providing penalties for non-compliance. 3. Following a pre-pack administration, restrict exit to compulsory liquidation, so as to achieve automatic scrutiny of the directors' and administrators' actions by the Official Receiver. 4. Require different insolvency practitioners to undertake pre- and post-administration appointment work. 5. Require the approval of the court or creditors, or both, for the approval for all pre-pack business sales to connected parties.

[20] The Insolvency Service, *Consultation/Call for Evidence: Improving the Transparency of, and Confidence in, Pre-packaged Sales in Administration* (March 2010) <http://www.britishprint.com/downloads/managed/industry_info/Pre-pack_consultation_document_-_Final.pdf> accessed 30 July 2015.

[21] P Walton, 'Government Consultation: Is it Time to Re-pack the Pre-pack?' (2010) 273 *Company Law Newsletter* 3.

This proposal could bring independent scrutiny to pre-pack transactions and secure the independence of the IP from the pre-pack negotiations by being appointed directly by the court, but the downside is that this route would likely increase the cost of the procedure. It is cautioned that compulsory liquidation is a relatively expensive process and creditors would probably not welcome the idea of paying for two office-holders. In a scenario where there is no money left in the company after the pre-pack (which is likely), it appears that the cost of the winding up falls on the public purse.[22]

Another option in the 2010 Consultation paper was to require different insolvency practitioners to undertake pre- and post-administration appointment work. This proposal was designed to address the concern on the independence of administrators due to their pre-appointment involvement. Such previous engagement may influence the way the administrator manages the insolvent company when presiding over the consequent administration. The disadvantage of this proposal is the possible delay in executing the pre-pack, caused by the independent administrator needing to get up to speed with the proposed pre-pack sale and then spending time assessing its appropriateness. The follow-on appointment might be well justified on the basis of efficiency, as the IP has worked for a while and knows much more about the business than a newly introduced IP. This appears compliant with the provision that tightens the timescale to encourage a quick execution of administration procedure. Furthermore, a mandatory veto to an appointment would generally undermine the flexibility of the pre-pack strategy and this would be to the detriment of those cases where the pre-pack is done properly. The cost issue is another obvious concern with this proposal. Unsecured and secured creditors may not be convinced that paying two insolvency practitioners for doing what is essentially one job is necessary.[23]

The last option sought to address the concern surrounding pre-pack business sales to connected parties. It resolved to require the approval of the court or creditors, or both, for the approval for all such business sales to connected parties. Connected parties could be made personally liable for the debts of the purchaser in instances where sales were executed without the requisite approval. Under this suggestion, approval could be obtained by either requiring the administrator, on appointment, to obtain the consent of a proportion of unsecured creditors or of the court before executing the pre-pack sale to a connected party, or by requiring the

22 *Ibid.*
23 *Ibid.*

prospective administrator to seek the approval of unsecured creditors as part of the court application for approval to enter administration. Nevertheless, it was questioned that it would be considered to be inequitable for unsecured creditors to be able to influence the process where they have no direct financial interest in the outcome of the sale, as is the case in many insolvencies.[24]

The Draft of Insolvency (Amendment) (No. 2) Rules 2011

Following the 2010 Consultation on pre-packs, the Minister of BIS issued a statement in March 2011, suggesting new measures to control the pre-packing insolvency sales to connected parties. A key reform is that it requires administrators to give notice to creditors (a three-day notice period has been suggested) when they propose to sell a significant proportion of the assets of a company or its business to a connected party (whether or not in a pre-pack administration), in circumstances where there has been no open marketing of those assets. This requirement was intended to enable creditors to express concerns, which the administrator would need to consider, or to make a higher offer for the assets in question, and in cases where the circumstances justify it, apply to the court for injunctive relief.[25]

In June 2011 the Insolvency Service published a draft of the Insolvency (Amendment) (No. 2) Rules 2011 for consultation with interested stakeholders. Having discussed the merits and practical application of the proposed measures in the Draft Rules with interested parties, the Government through a written BIS Ministerial Statement announced that no new legislative controls on the pre-packs will be introduced at this time.[26] The Minister suggested in the Statement that, although it is 'apparent that concerns remain about the use of pre-pack sales', 'the Government is not convinced that the benefit of new legislative controls presently outweighs the overall benefit to business of adhering to the moratorium on regulations affecting micro-business which is an important plank of this Government's deregulatory agenda.'

---

[24] See the Insolvency Service, *Consultation/Call for Evidence: Improving the Transparency of, and Confidence in, Pre-packaged Sales in Administration.*

[25] The Written Ministerial Statement on Pre-packaged Sales in Administrations (House of Commons Hansard Ministerial Statements on 31 March 2011, cm 29WS).

[26] The Written Ministerial Statement on Pre-packaged Sales in Insolvency (House of Commons Hansard Ministerial Statements on 26 January 2012, cm 23WS).

The insolvency profession also expressed considerable concern about the potential practical effects of the application of the Draft Rules, considering it does not represent a proportionate way of achieving the transparency objective it was intended to achieve. In particular, practitioner commentators questioned the meaning and potential practical effects of the notice period:

> the new measures may be designed to protect vulnerable creditors, but it is far-fetched to believe that smaller creditors would be able to put together their own offer for a business within a few days, or be able to fund an urgent application to court.[27]
>
> Giving creditors, who may be crucial suppliers, three days' notice of a sale will give them ample opportunity not only to demand ransom conditions for further suppliers or to pursue retention of title claims aggressively to the detriment of ongoing trading. Both those situations can cripple a trading business and leave it incapable of rescue.[28]

The proposed new measures would not dramatically affect the power of administrators. They are, however, liable to reduce the extent to which his judgments can be put into effect. As mentioned earlier, a risk inherent in the three-day notice requirement is that it could create unintended incentives (for creditors who predict a low likelihood of recovery) to take hostile action and apply delaying tactics to the implementation of the deal. If processes are highly contested and slowed down, their effectiveness in rescue terms will be reduced. This would be at the cost of any creditors who have actual economic interests in the realisation of the business assets. If the only deal would be unworkable, it is doubtful whether there will be a better alternative option or a higher offer available for the company. The cost of the procedure and business

---

[27] See 'Industry Calls for Even Tougher Pre-pack Rules', *Estates Gazette News* on 2 April 2011, previously available at <http://business.highbeam.com/410547/article-1G1-253317771/03-news> accessed 3 December 2011. See also M Izza, 'What is the Future of Pre pack Administrations?' *ICAEW* Blog entry on 19 July 2011, previously available at <http://www.ion.icaew.com/insolvencyblog/22670> accessed 3 December 2011.

[28] See 'Pre-pack Changes will Create More Liquidations', *Insolvency News* on 1 April 2011, previously available at <http://www.insolvencynews.com/article/show/Pre-pack-changes-will-create-more-liquidations> accessed 3 September 2011.

operation, plus the destruction of value as a consequence of the failed deal will prove to be untenable.[29]

Furthermore, the notice mechanism is also criticised for resulting in the loss of relative privacy, which has been an attractive feature of the pre-pack practice. Indeed, the extensive disclosure of the details of pending business sales associated with the three-day notice period may be a concern for potential buyers. It would discourage their desire to buy the business or make them choose to reduce their offered price due to the substantial uncertainty involved. After all, information disclosure and transparency augment accountability, ensuring affected creditors that their interests are fairly taken into account – it is not about exposing the commercial negotiations for the entire business.

Nevertheless, in the highly controversial pre-pack sensoria, if ex post information disclosure proves inadequate to ensure fairness, there is a strong argument for legislative intervention by way of such a pre-view right to those affected, as the loss in value due to the prolonged process will be shared by the affected creditors who choose to vote down the pre-packed sale proposal. But the difficulty is that it is hard to define who those affected ones eligible to vote are, as the sale is not complete and the business is still in a negotiating process focusing on the ongoing commercial viability, and therefore accompanied by the uncertainty of its value. This would create another layer of controversy by giving certain creditors the power to influence the process where they have no direct financial interest in the outcome of the sale or any other possible options.

THE LATEST WAVE OF REFORM: GRAHAM'S RECOMMENDATIONS ON PRE-PACKS

In spite of the aforementioned fierce debate on pre-pack sales regulation, concerns about businesses sold back to the same management team continued to soar. Thus, the Secretary of State commissioned Teresa Graham CBE to undertake a review and her report, *Review into Pre-pack Administrations* ('the Graham Review'),[30] was published in June 2014. The conclusion of the review was that: 'there is a place for pre-packs in the UK's insolvency landscape … . There could – and should – be some

---

[29] B Xie, 'Role of Insolvency Practitioners in the UK Pre-pack Administrations: Challenges and Control' (2012) 21 *International Insolvency Review* 85, 98.

[30] T Graham CBE, *Graham Review into Pre-pack Administration: Report to the Rt Vince Cable MP* (June 2014) <https://www.gov.uk/government/publications/graham-review-into-pre-pack-administration> accessed 30 July 2015.

major improvements to how they are administered.'[31] But, as Graham argued, government legislation of pre-packs should be a last resort. She proceeded, however, to make six recommendations for improving the pre-pack framework, all of which require action on the part of insolvency regulators and the insolvency profession rather than government. One of the key recommendations is the establishment of a 'pre-pack pool' to provide a level of independent scrutiny of connected party pre-pack sales. Other recommendations concerned viability reviews of sales to connected purchasers, the strengthening of marketing and valuation rules, and the revision and monitoring of SIP 16.

Pre-pack Pool

One of the six recommendations of the Graham Review is the establishment of a pre-pack pool of experienced business people who could provide a level of independent scrutiny of connected party pre-pack sales. It is proposed that connected parties, on a voluntary basis, approach a pre-pack pool before the sale and disclose details of the deal, for a pool member to opine on. This would offer the connected party an opportunity to present the deal's outline and why it is necessary to proceed in this way to an independent person prior to administration, and therefore create independent scrutiny of the deal yet retain overall secrecy before the event.

Approaching the pool will be voluntary. When used, one member of the pool will be allocated to the case and review the supporting documentation provided by the applicant. The material to be presented to the pool member in order to comment on the deal will be decided on by the applicant. After scrutinising the documents, the pool member will issue a statement. If the statement is negative, the deal can still proceed, though the fact that a negative statement had been made would have to be referred to in the SIP 16 statement. A positive statement would also be referred to in SIP 16, bringing the fact that the deal had received some independent scrutiny to the attention of the creditors.[32]

It should be noted that this recommendation is aimed solely at connected pre-pack sales, and is available for all connected parties arranging a sale of all or part of the business in all circumstances before creditors are made aware of the sale.[33] With regards the cost, it is

---

[31] The Graham Review, Introduction.

[32] On the detail of the operation of the pre-pack pool, see the Graham Review, Recommendations.

[33] The Graham Review, Recommendations.

intended that the process be low cost and that the fee will be paid up front, by the connected party. The fee will also pay for the administrative costs associated with maintaining the pool.

This recommendation is being taken forward by an industry-led working group tasked with setting up the pool. The steering group is made up of a broad range of professional bodies, insolvency regulators and creditor representative groups.[34] In mid-December 2014, an advertisement for pool members was circulated and it is expected that pool will begin scrutinising sales to connected parties in the summer.[35]

Viability Review and the Revision of SIP 16

Authoritative empirical evidence suggested that a new company in a connected pre-pack sale is more likely to fail than a new company unconnected with those controlling the old company.[36] To curb fundamentally unviable businesses being allowed back into the marketplace via pre-pack sales, it is proposed that a 'viability review' of the new company is completed by the connected party on a voluntary basis prior to the commencement of the administration procedure. The viability review of the new company would state how the company will survive for at least 12 months from the date of the statement, and it will be accompanied with a short narrative, detailing what the new company will do differently from the old company to avoid failure again. In the event that the new

---

[34] The Pre-pack Pool Steering Group, Letter to the Secretary of State (6 March 2015) <https://www.google.co.uk/url?sa=t&rct=j&q=&esrc=s&source=web&cd=1&ved=0CCIQFjAAahUKEwiH5a7W_8bHAhVOLNsKHf4eAIk&url=http%3A%2F%2Fwww.insolvency-practitioners.org.uk%2Fdownload%2Fdocuments%2F1277&ei=V9LdVcfdDs7Y7Ab-vYDICA&usg=AFQjCNHUcQTeTEMwHIz4pSGTLFoCC9irRg> accessed 30 July 2015. Those include R3, ACCA, British Property Federation, Chartered Institute of Credit Management, Insolvency Practitioners Association, Institute of Chartered Accountants in England and Wales, Institute of Chartered Accountants of Scotland, and Institute of Directors.

[35] 'Cleaning up Pre-packs', Insolvency Service News on 12 March 2015 <https://www.gov.uk/government/news/cleaning-up-pre-packs> accessed 30 July 2015.

[36] The statistics found in the Walton and Umfreville's empirical study suggest, as summarised in the Graham Review, that, on average, the odds of failure were 2.4 times as high for trading administrations as they were for pre-packs; compared with sales not involving connected parties, the odds of failure, that is, the probability of failure divided by the probability of continued trading, were over three times as high for sales to a connected party, see the Graham Review, 51.

company should fail, the statement will be available to the new company's insolvency office-holder for reference when ascertaining if recovery action can be taken against the director.[37]

Furthermore, there are several supplementary recommendations in the Graham Review. First of all, SIP 16 is to be redrafted[38] to underpin and act as a vehicle for the delivery of Graham's package of recommendations, as the documents required by the preceding two recommendations are to be sent with the SIP 16 statement. Furthermore, two additional recommendations are made on marketing and valuation to provide additional guidelines to complement those already in SIP 16. On marketing, it is proposed that any deviation from the six principles of good marketing in pre-pack cases should be brought to creditors' attention. Regarding valuations, it is proposed that SIP 16 be amended to the effect that valuations must be carried out by a valuer who holds professional indemnity insurance and, where this is not the case, that they explain their reasons for choosing a valuer without such insurance.[39] It is also recommended that the Insolvency Service withdraws from monitoring SIP 16 statements and that monitoring be picked up by the RPBs, as it is believed that they are best placed to do so.

Enhancing the Accountability of Insolvency Professionals

In the current insolvency regulatory system, professional regulators have an important role to play in enforcing new professional standards and increasing public confidence in the economical and fair running of the pre-pack practice. This section first summarises the current regulatory model in the UK's insolvency profession, and then discusses relevant professional regulatory mechanisms, in responding to the call for an effective and consistent monitoring and complaint handling system. And lastly, it reviews the latest discussion on the reform of the insolvency profession.

---

[37] On the detail of the viability review, see the Graham Review, Recommendations.

[38] A redrafted SIP 16 is available in Annex A in the Graham Review.

[39] The reason for this recommendation, it is said, is that issuers of PII place their own stringent checks on those who apply cover. Creditors of an insolvent company can be better satisfied that a valuation executed by someone with such cover will represent a fair value for the business/its assets. See the Graham Review, 66.

The Current Regulatory Framework of Insolvency Profession

All IPs that could be appointed as office-holders have to belong to one of the RPBs. There are currently seven recognised bodies: the Institute of Chartered Accountants in England & Wales (ICAEW); the Insolvency Practitioners Association (IPA); the Law Society of England & Wales (LS); the Institute of Chartered Accountants of Scotland (ICAS); the Association of Chartered Certified Accountants (ACCA); the Institute of Chartered Accountants in Ireland (CAI); and the Law Society of Scotland (LSS). In addition, authorisation of IPs can also be made by the Secretary of State directly. The RPBs act as self-regulators in controlling their own qualified members. BIS acts as 'regulator of regulators' in relation to the RPBs with statutory power to grant and withdraw 'RPB' status[40] but exercises its monitoring functions through its executive agency, the Insolvency Service (IS).[41]

In particular, the IS advises on the form and effectiveness of insolvency legislation, ensuring that the RPBs regulate their members properly, with suitable rules that are effectively enforced, and supervise the regulatory process. It is responsible for the development of insolvency standards and professional and ethical guidance,[42] and conducts regular assessment visits to the RPBs to ensure that standards are maintained.[43] To support this, the IS has worked with the profession to establish the Insolvency Code of Ethics and Statements of Insolvency Practice (SIPs) with which IPs must comply. Furthermore, to address the problems of regulatory proliferation, complexity and the 'maze' of new standards, the Joint Insolvency Committee ('JIC') and the Insolvency Practices Council ('IPC') were put in place[44] to encourage consistency of approach across regulators and to promote common professional and ethical standards, and to make regulatory processes more efficient.[45]

---

[40] Walters and Seneviratne, *Complaints Handling in the UK Insolvency Practitioner Profession*, 3.

[41] V Finch, 'Insolvency Practitioners: Regulation and Reform' (1998) *Journal of Business Law* 334, 336.

[42] Insolvency Practitioners Association, 'Putting Better Regulation into Practice: Regulatory and Disciplinary Report 2005' (Report, 2005), para.3.4.

[43] Finch, 'Doctoring in the Shadows of Insolvency', 695–6.

[44] Their establishment was a result of the Insolvency Regulation Working Party's review *'Insolvency Practitioner Regulation – Ten Years On'* (1998 DTI).

[45] Finch, 'Regulating Insolvency Practitioners: Rationalisation on the Agenda' (2005) 18 *Insolvency Intelligence* 17, 18. The Joint Insolvency Committee contains representatives from all the RPBs. It works closely with the IPC,

The professional standards – code of ethics

IPs are given considerable authority and discretion to enable them to do their job. In turn, the exercise of such discretion carries a responsibility to act with the highest standards of integrity and impartiality.[46] The importance of maintaining independence and objectivity in the insolvency profession is promoted by the principles of the joint ethical code for IPs agreed and adopted by the RPBs, the Insolvency Ethical Guide adopted in January 2004. To achieve standardisation, and in conjunction with SIP 16, a revised Insolvency Code of Ethics[47] was introduced for all IPs to adhere to.

The new Insolvency Code of Ethics, as a standardised guide for all IPs, regardless of their authorising body, is intended to assist them in meeting their statutory obligations by providing professional and ethical guidance.[48] Failure to observe the Code may not, in itself, constitute professional misconduct, but will be taken into account when assessing the conduct of an IP.[49]

The Code sets down five fundamental principles: integrity; objectivity; professional competence and due care; confidentiality; and professional behaviour.[50] Practitioners are required to identify, evaluate and respond in

---

which is established to influence the professional and ethical standards of IPs and represents the public interest in the profession's standards.

46 M Chapman, 'The Insolvency Service's View of Regulation' (Winter 2005) *Recovery*, 24.

47 The Insolvency Service, *Insolvency Code of Ethics* (London, November 2008) <https://www.gov.uk/government/publications/insolvency-practitioner-code-of-ethics> accessed 30 July 2015. The new Code came into force on 1 January 2009.

48 *Insolvency Code of Ethics*, para.1.

49 *Insolvency Code of Ethics*, paras. 2 and 3.

50 *Insolvency Code of Ethics*, para.4. An insolvency practitioner is required to comply with the following fundamental principles:

(1) Integrity: an insolvency practitioner should be straightforward and honest in all professional and business relationships.

(2) Objectivity: an insolvency practitioner should not allow bias, conflict of interest or undue influence of others to override professional or business judgements.

(3) Professional Competence and Due Care: an insolvency practitioner has a continuing duty to maintain professional knowledge and skill at the level required to ensure that a client or employer receives competent professional service based on current developments in practice, legislation and techniques. An insolvency practitioner should act diligently and in accordance with applicable technical and professional standards when providing professional services.

an appropriate manner to any threats to compliance with the fundamental principles.[51] In all cases, an insolvency practitioner will need to exercise his judgement to determine how best to deal with an identified threat.[52]

The Code also describes some of the safeguards that IPs will need to consider implementing prior to accepting an appointment where there is a threat to the fundamental principles.[53] It is made clear that it will be

---

(4) Confidentiality: an insolvency practitioner should respect the confidentiality of information acquired as a result of professional and business relationships and should not disclose any such information to third parties without proper and specific authority unless there is a legal or professional right or duty to disclose. Confidential information acquired as a result of professional and business relationships should not be used for the personal advantage of the insolvency practitioner or third parties.

(5) Professional Behaviour: an insolvency practitioner should comply with relevant laws and regulations and should avoid any action that discredits the profession. Insolvency practitioners should conduct themselves with courtesy and consideration towards all with whom they come into contact when performing their work.

It is said that each of the fundamental principles set out in the Code is based upon and follows closely the fundamental principles contained in the *International Federation of Accounting Code*. The earlier Insolvency Ethical Guide also includes five fundamental principles: *Integrity, Objectivity Competence, Due Skill and Courtesy*. The JIC do not consider that the application of the revised fundamental principles will be materially different from the application of the fundamental principles contained in the Insolvency Ethical Guide.

[51] Paras. 31 and 32 of the Code require a practitioner to take reasonable steps to identify any circumstances that pose a conflict of interest, and the Code also requires to identify any threats to the principle of objectivity that may arise from a professional and personal relationship.

[52] *Insolvency Code of Ethics*, para.30. In exercising his judgment, a practitioner should consider what a reasonable and informed third party, having knowledge of all relevant information, including the significance of the threat and the safeguards applied, would conclude to be acceptable.

[53] The examples of safeguards listed in para.25 of *Insolvency Code of Ethics* are:

(a) involving and/or consulting another IP from within the practice to review the work done.

(b) consulting an independent third party, such as a committee of creditors, an authorising body or another IP.

(c) involving another IP to perform part of the work, which may include another IP taking a joint appointment where the conflict arises during the course of the insolvency appointment.

(d) obtaining legal advice from a solicitor or barrister with appropriate experience and expertise.

inappropriate for an IP to accept an insolvency appointment where there is a threat to the fundamental principles unless:

(a) disclosure is made, prior to the insolvency appointment, of the existence of such a threat to the Court or to the creditors on whose behalf the IP would be appointed to act and no objection is made to the IP being appointed; and
(b) safeguards are or will be available to eliminate or reduce that threat to an acceptable level. If the threat is other than trivial, safeguards should be considered and applied as necessary to reduce them to an acceptable level, where possible.[54]

It is always up to the IP to exercise his judgement to determine how best to deal with an identified threat.[55] The Code requires an IP to take reasonable step to identify any circumstances that pose a conflict of interests.[56]

(e) changing the members of the insolvency team.
(f) the use of separate IPs and/or staff.
(g) procedures to prevent access to information by the use of information barriers (e.g. strict physical separation of such teams, confidential and secure data filing).
(h) clear guidelines for individuals within the practice on issues of security and confidentiality.
(i) the use of confidentiality agreements signed by individuals within the practice.
(j) regular review of the application of safeguards by a senior individual within the practice not involved with the insolvency appointment.
(k) terminating the financial or business relationship that gives rise to the threat.
(l) seeking directions from the court.

It should be noted that the examples are not intended to be exhaustive. Neither will the examples given be applicable to all situations. It is also made clear that an insolvency practitioner may encounter situations where no safeguards can reduce a threat to an acceptable level. In such circumstances, an insolvency practitioner should conclude that it is not appropriate to accept an insolvency appointment.

54 *Insolvency Code of Ethics*, para.24.

55 *Insolvency Code of Ethics*, para.30.

56 Para.31 lists examples of where a conflict of interest may arise:

(a) an IP has to deal with claims between the separate and conflicting interests of entities over whom he is appointed.
(b) there are a succession of or sequential insolvency appointments.

In addressing the insolvency appointment following audit related work, the Code states that a significant professional relationship will arise where the IP has previously carried out audit-related work within the previous three years. The Code considers that it will not be appropriate for the IP who previously held such a relationship to take the appointment as an administrator. However, the Code clarifies that the acceptance of the appointment would normally not be inappropriate in the event of a pre-existing significant professional relationship where: (a) there has not been a direct involvement in the management of the company; (b) the practice had its principal client relationship with the creditor or other party, rather than with the company or proprietor of the business; and (c) the company was aware of this.[57]

The key concern in pre-packs is that interaction with insiders will significantly influence the independence of the IPs. Thus, para.51 of the Code is of further importance in relation to pre-packs. It is recognised that 'where the assets and business of an insolvent company are sold by an insolvency practitioner shortly after appointment on pre-arranged terms, this could lead to an actual or perceived threat to objectivity'. Such threats, the Code states, 'may be eliminated or reduced to an acceptable level by safeguards such as obtaining an independent valuation of the assets or business being sold, or the consideration of other potential purchasers'.

This ethical guidance for IPs is a standard not a rule and it is unclear if it can prove sufficient in the absence of strict monitoring. Therefore, key responsibility for preventing abuse rests with the complaint and monitoring system.

Monitoring, Complaining and Disciplinary Systems: The Merits and Demerits of Self-regulation

The regulation of insolvency practitioners in Britain is based on a dual regulatory approach combining both self-regulation by the profession, and independent oversight by the Government. Self-regulation is carried out by the RPBs, while oversight is carried out by the Secretary of State for BIS through its agency the Insolvency Service. The RPBs are empowered to establish a register of practitioners and to establish quality and ethical standards for practice and discipline, as well as disciplinary

---

(c) a significant relationship has existed with the entity or someone connected with the entity.

[57] *Insolvency Code of Ethics*, paras. 79-80.

and other sanctions to ensure that these standards are being met.[58] Monitoring is an important part of this regulatory structure. A Memorandum of Understanding has been agreed and signed by all the RPBs and the IS, requiring all professional bodies to subject authorised practitioners to monitoring in accordance with a Standard for Monitoring agreed between the Secretary of State and the RPBs.[59] The Memorandum of Understanding sets out the principles for monitoring IPs agreed between the Secretary of State and RPBs. The purpose of the monitoring is to facilitate the gathering of sufficient relevant information by a Body on the conduct and performance of the practitioners it authorises to enable an informed and unbiased decision to be made as to whether a practitioner is and continues to be, a fit and proper person to act as an IP.[60]

It is the responsibility of each of the self-regulatory bodies to ensure that their authorised IPs are monitored in accordance with the Principles for Monitoring.[61] In doing so, the RPBs have in place an ongoing process of desktop monitoring[62] and a scheme to undertake monitoring visits to their authorised practitioners.[63] Professional regulators are required to take reasonable steps to confirm satisfactory levels of compliance with all relevant aspects of insolvency law and practice and other legislation that may impact upon an individual while acting as an IP.[64]

---

58 M Seneviratne, *The Legal Profession: Regulation and the Consumer* (Sweet and Maxwell, London 1999), 26–30.

59 The Insolvency Service, *Principles for Monitoring of Insolvency Practitioners* <https://www.gov.uk/guidance/principles-for-monitoring-insolvency-practitioners> accessed 30 July 2015. The purpose of monitoring is to facilitate the gathering of sufficient relevant information by a regulator on the conduct and performance of the practitioners it authorises to enable an informed and unbiased decision to be made as to whether a practitioner is, and continues to be, a fit and proper person to act as an insolvency practitioner.

60 *Principles for Monitoring Insolvency Practitioners*.

61 *Ibid*., para.1.

62 Desktop monitoring means it will gather information relevant to the monitoring objective from both the practitioner and from sources independent of the practitioner.

63 The frequency of such visits will be determined using a risk-based approach. Normally each IP is subject to a monitoring visit once every three years.

64 Reference to insolvency law and practice includes but is not limited to Statements of Insolvency Practice; the Ethical Code; prevailing statutory and common law; the Body's bylaws, rules and regulations, and continuing professional education requirement. *Principles for Monitoring of Insolvency Practitioners*, para.5(A).

Complaint handling is principally concerned with maintaining and enhancing professional standards and ensuring that IPs licensed by a professional body remain fit and proper.[65] As a first step, there are in-house complaints procedures within large accountancy/law firms. They normally function as tools for the identification and centralised management of risk with the purpose of ensuring that any matter that could give rise to legal, regulatory or reputational risks is reported so that any potential legal claims[66] can be controlled centrally at firm level.[67] Therefore the in-house complaints handling procedures are not generally seen as redress mechanisms for complainants;[68] rather they are viewed as necessary and sensible mechanisms for protecting the firm.[69]

The principal channel is the RPBs' complaints and disciplinary process. Under the current regulatory model in the UK's insolvency profession,[70] complaints regarding unprofessional, improper or unethical behaviour by an insolvency practitioner shall be directed to his authorising RPB.[71] In general each RPB has a similar but slightly different structure for dealing with complaints and the appropriate RPB will decide if sanctions should be imposed.[72] The complaint letter should include full details of what has gone wrong or has not been handled properly. All RPBs have disciplinary committees, consisting of professional and lay membership, with powers to impose sanctions, and all have appeal committees/tribunals, with professional and lay membership, which hear appeals from members who do not accept the findings and/or

---

65 Walters and Seneviratne, 'Complaints Handling in the UK Insolvency Practitioner Profession', vi.

66 For example, negligence claims, that could result in the firm having to pay monetary compensation.

67 Walters and Seneviratne, 'Complaints Handling in the UK Insolvency Practitioner Profession', iv.

68 If the firm considers that a complaint is justified it may offer the complainant an apology and, in the case of advisory work, a complaint of inadequate professional service could conceivably lead to fee remission or discount. However, firms are not in the habit of making ex gratia consolatory payments for any distress or inconvenience that complainants may have suffered. *Ibid.*, 21.

69 *Ibid.*, iv.

70 See Insolvency Service, *Consultation on Reforms to the Regulation of Insolvency Practitioners* (February 2011), para.2.8.

71 *Ibid.*, para.3.4.

72 On the current complaints processes, see *Consultation on Reforms to the Regulation of Insolvency Practitioners*, Chapter 3. The complaint system is not an alternative to the legal remedies.

sanctions imposed by the Disciplinary Committee.[73] The appeal mechanisms of the RPBs may only be used by practitioners, who can appeal against determinations and penalties.[74] The complainant normally has no right of appeal against the determinations of the RPBs.

Taking the IPA as an example, all complaints investigated by the IPA will be considered by the Investigation Committee,[75] responsible for deciding whether a *prima facie* case is made out against the IP. A prima facie case is one where upon an examination of the complaint, the Committee is of the view that there is a sufficiently strong and evidenced case that the IP has breached statute, any issued Statements of Insolvency Practice or the IPA's Ethics Code for members.[76] If the Committee decides that there is no prima facie case made out against the IP, that brings the matter to an end and the complaint will be closed.[77] Where the Committee decides a prima facie case has been made out against an IP, the Committee may issue a warning to the IP or exercise its discretion to take no further action where it considers the errors or failings of the IP are minor or excusable.[78]

Where the Committee considers relevant errors or failings of the IP are serious enough to attract a disciplinary penalty, the Committee may issue an Order against him/her without the matter being determined by a

---

73 M Seneviratne and P Walters, *Complaints Handling by the Regulators of Insolvency Practitioners: A Comparative Study* (Report to the Insolvency Practices Council, 2009) <http://papers.ssrn.com/sol3/papers.cfm?abstract_id=1310791> accessed 30 July 2015, 58.

74 *Ibid.*, 60. It is noted that the process is different for lawyer IPs, where there is an appeal to the Legal Services Ombudsman for complainants dissatisfied with the way the Law Society handled the complaints.

75 The Committee is composed of insolvency practitioner members of the IPA and lay persons and no one from the IP's firm or anyone who is associated with him/her will take part when the complaint is considered.

76 Insolvency Practitioner Association, *Complaints Procedure* <http://www.insolvency-practitioners.org.uk/complaints-procedure/complaint-procedure> accessed 30 July 2015.

77 The complainant may ask for the complaint to be referred to an independent Reviewer of Complaints, who acts independently of the IPA. If the Reviewer agrees that there has been a failure by the Committee to follow correct procedure and/or its decision was not one the Committee could reasonably have arrived at on consideration of the facts before it, the Reviewer may ask the Committee to reconsider the complaint.

78 There will not be any publicity of the warning but any warning issued will remain on an IP's record for three years and may be taken into consideration should further failings be identified. *Ibid.*

Disciplinary Committee Tribunal,[79] if the IP accepts the Committee's findings. The terms of any Consent Order are at the discretion of the Committee and may include an Order that the IP be reprimanded and may also include a financial penalty by way of a fine and a contribution to the costs of the IPA in dealing with the complaint. For the most serious cases of professional misconduct and for cases where an IP has declined to accept a Consent Order, the Committee will usually refer the complaint for a hearing before a Disciplinary Committee Tribunal. If the Tribunal dismisses a complaint then that decision is final and brings an end to the proceedings. If the Disciplinary Committee finds that a complaint is proved, whether in whole or in part, it may impose an Order on the IP, which may include exclusion from membership and the withdrawal of his/her insolvency licence. The IP can appeal against the decision to the Appeal Committee.[80]

Seneviratne and Walters compared complaints handling and disciplinary systems of insolvency regulators with those of the regulators of other professions,[81] and suggested that complaints procedures in the RPBs are regulatory mechanisms rather than redress mechanisms for individual complainants[82] and the accountant RPBs do not systematically provide redress for service complaints.[83] Where complaints seem to be justified and do not present issues of serious misconduct warranting disciplinary action, the insolvency regulators seek to resolve them, either through their established conciliation mechanisms, or informally and on an *ad*

---

[79] The Disciplinary Committee Tribunal consists of at least two ordinary members and one lay member.

[80] Appeal Committee Tribunals are conducted on a similar basis to Disciplinary Committee Tribunals but are usually chaired by a judge, barrister or solicitor, accompanied by two ordinary members and two lay members.

[81] Seneviratne and Walters, *Complaints Handling by the Regulators of Insolvency Practitioners: A Comparative Study*. Five comparative systems are: the Bar Standards Board; the Royal Institution of Chartered Surveyors; the General Medical Council; the Primary Care Trusts of the National Health Service; and the Financial Ombudsman Service.

[82] *Ibid.*, 60.

[83] It said that the ACCA is an exception as it can require its members to pay compensation up to a maximum of £5,000 if a complaint against them is found proved. However, it will only be awarded if the matter is referred to the Disciplinary Committee, and that committee makes an award. The award is for any inconvenience suffered as a result of the member's failure to observe proper standards, rather than to compensate for any financial loss suffered. *Ibid.*, 61.

hoc basis.[84] As Walters and Seneviratne pointed out, while withdrawal of an IP's licence or restrictions imposed on it may benefit the public at large, they do not provide any tangible redress to the individual who has complained.[85]

The complaints and disciplinary procedures of the regulators are focused on conduct issues about alleged infringement of the legislation, SIPs, and professional ethics and standards.[86] Generally, the RPBs will not consider complaints about the amount of an IP's remuneration or other commercial disputes (providing the actions complained of have been properly approved in accordance with the law and relevant SIPs) as this is seen as a court function.[87] Also, making complaints against their members is not a substitute for seeking damages or other redress through the courts.[88] It is suggested that isolated incidents of non-compliance with an SIP would be seen as fairly minor, and there would not be disciplinary action in order to withdraw authorisation although the IP would be given guidance in relation to this. If, however, complainants revealed non-compliance on a systemic basis, the RPB would take action, because this would be evidence of incompetence or misconduct.[89]

Failures of self-regulation and the need for an independent body

Effective and efficient monitoring and complaints handling procedures are encouraged to ensure that professional requirements and standards are met. Yet, professional bodies' dual role of promoting and, at the same time, regulating the profession has shown little effectiveness in pushing the profession to the highest standard and protecting affected stakeholders.[90] First, there is the traditional criticism against self-regulation which also holds true in this context. In principle, the capacity of a self-regulation agency to make rules governing the activities of an

---

[84] Walters and Seneviratne, *Complaints Handling in the UK Insolvency Practitioner Profession*, 73.

[85] *Ibid.*, 74.

[86] *Ibid.*, 56–9. Generally, the RPBs will not investigate allegations in relation to remuneration, the reason given for rejecting these types of complaint is that the legislation provides a mechanism for challenging remuneration; the remedy is a court challenge.

[87] The Office for Fair Trading, *The Market for Corporate Insolvency Practitioners: a Market Study* (June 2010), para.5.25.

[88] Walters and Seneviratne, *Complaints Handling in the UK Insolvency Practitioner Profession*, 59.

[89] *Ibid.*, 55.

[90] PJ Arnold *et al.*, *Insolvency, Market Professionalism and the Commodification of Professional Expertise* (Colchester 2003).

association or profession may itself constitute an abuse if it lacks democratic legitimacy in relation to members of the association or profession. The potential for abuse becomes intolerable if, and to the extent that, the rules affect third parties. It is accurately argued that if the self-regulation agency's functions cover policy formulation, interpretation of the rules, adjudication and enforcement (including the imposition of sanctions) as well as rule-making, there is a fundamental breach of the separation of powers doctrine.[91]

Secondly, there is the issue of conflicts of interest. The UK's insolvency industry is dominated by self-regulated organisations, which have received strong criticism over the duality of their role.[92] In the case of the regulation of IPs, the RPBs have been accused that they have little interest in eliminating the 'conflicts of interest' and abuses. The claim is that the RPBs as regulators are the promoters, protectors and defenders of their members and are therefore strongly influenced by those to be regulated, therefore the entire regulatory system is under the control of the IPs.[93] It is argued that the insolvency practices are shaped by the internal culture of the accountancy and law firms, but the firms are highly secretive in terms of their charge-out rates, conflicts of interests and internal organisational structure.[94]

Furthermore, given that there is no single, uniform procedure for handling complaints against IPs, nor is there an insolvency ombudsman, concerns have been expressed in particular about the potential for wasteful duplication of effort across the RPBs in relation to ongoing

---

[91] A Ogus, *Regulation: Legal Form and Economic Theory* (Oxford University Press, Oxford 1994), 108. See further AC Page, 'Self-Regulation: The Constitutional Dimension' (1986) 49 *Modern Law Review* 141, 163. I Harden and N Lewis, *The Noble Lie: The British Constitution and the Rule of Law* (Taylor & Francis Ltd, London 1988), Chapter 6.

[92] Such criticism centres around allegations that: 'they favour the regulated group and ignore the broader public interest; they are designed with large, well-organised, well-resourced enterprises in mind and fail to deal with those who really need to be regulated; their procedures tend to exclude third parties; they are low on accountability; they have anti-competitive effects; they tend not to enjoy public confidence; and their investigative, enforcement and sanctioning processes tend to be weak.' See V Finch, 'Corporate Governance and Cadbury: Self-Regulation and Alternatives' (1994) *Journal of Business Law* 51, 57.

[93] J Cousins *et al.*, *Insolvent Abuse: Regulating the Insolvency Industry* (Association for Accountancy and Business Affairs, Essex 2000), 14. It is held that the RPBs are trade associations and their main mission is to secure economic advantages for their members.

[94] *Ibid.*, 11.

monitoring and complaints handling and for inconsistencies of regulatory response to professional misconduct.[95] These concerns, coupled with wider fears that professional self-regulation of IPs may lack sufficient independence and objectivity to safeguard the public interest and foster public confidence, have led to occasional calls for the establishment of a single regulator or of an independent oversight and complaints handling mechanism.[96]

In 2010, the Office of Fair Trading ('OFT') investigated the corporate insolvency profession and made several suggestions including the introduction of a single complaints body,[97] followed by the IS's consultation on reforms to the regulation of insolvency practitioners.[98] It suggested that the current system lacks a fully independent framework for handling complaints and the present regulatory mechanisms fail to provide a consistent complaint and review process which can work as an accessible and cost-effective alternative to court.[99] In addition, the OFT found that there was a lack of trust in the current complaint and review mechanisms.[100] To increase the efficacy and consistency of after-the-event review, the OFT proposed the establishment of an independent complaints handling body with the ability to review fees.[101] Furthermore,

---

[95] Finch, *Corporate Insolvency Law: Perspectives and Principles*, 168.

[96] Walters and Seneviratne, 'Complaints Handling in the UK Insolvency Practitioner Profession', 4.

[97] The Office for Fair Trading, *The Market for Corporate Insolvency Practitioners: a Market Study* (June 2010).

[98] The Insolvency Service, *Consultation on Reforms to the Regulation of Insolvency Practitioners* (February 2011).

[99] *The Market for Corporate Insolvency Practitioners: a Market Study*, paras. 2.32, and 7.8. This, the OFT argues, discourages complaints by unsecured creditors.

[100] Over half of unsecured creditors did not know how to complain about the insolvency process. In a survey of insolvency practitioners by the OFT, 41 per cent of the respondents did not believe that the current regulatory system dealt effectively with rogue IPs; and 45 per cent believed that it dealt with poor behaviour inconsistently. See *The Market for Corporate Insolvency Practitioners: a Market Study*, para.5.36.

[101] Insolvency Service, *Consultation on Reforms to the Regulation of Insolvency Practitioners,* para.3.14. Apart from the need for establishing an independent complaints body, the OFT also identifies a range of issues to be addressed to improve the effectiveness and efficiency of the regulatory regime and enhance the power of unsecured creditors in insolvency proceedings with proposals of improvements to the regulatory structure and amending some of the detailed insolvency provisions. On the detailed recommendations, see *The Market for Corporate Insolvency Practitioners: a Market Study*, Chapter 7.

concern was expressed in the OFT report that the IS's dual role as oversight regulator of RPBs and a direct regulator hinders its ability to carry out its oversight role and buttress the regulatory framework.

Following the OFT's report, a consultation was launched seeking views on further reforms to the regulation of IPs.[102] The consultation proposed four specific models for an independent complaints body.[103] Responses to the consultation have indicated that a single first tier independent complaints body model was favoured, and respondents generally favoured the introduction of a 'single portal' to receive all complaints to improve accessibility and consistency.[104] In December 2011, the Minister of BIS placed a statement in Parliament setting out the broad direction of reforms concerning the insolvency profession. The statement sends out a key message of support for a single regulator and conveys the intention of the Secretary of State to withdraw direct authorisation of IPs and strengthen its competence as oversight regulator so as to have more wide ranging powers of monitoring and sanctions over the RPBs.[105] The same statement expressed the intention to strengthen and simplify processes for handling complaints. Clearly, the statement opened new avenues for complaint and redress while closing an important loophole in the self-regulation framework.

The new Complaints Gateway launched in June 2013

Following the Minister's Statement on reforms to the insolvency profession, the Insolvency Service set up a new single gateway through which complaints about IPs are directed in the first instance. The single Complaints Gateway covers five of the seven regulatory professional

[102] The Insolvency Service, *Consultation on Reforms to the Regulation of Insolvency Practitioners* (February 2011).

[103] Model 1: a single first tier body; model 2: an independent appeals body; model 3: an independent decision-making body; and model 4: an independent decision-making body overlaid with an investigative appeal function. The consultation also sought views on a number of issues associated with the structure of the present regime, including: the introduction of regulatory objectives; the role of the Insolvency Service as a direct regulator; the powers of the oversight regulator; standard setting and the role of the Insolvency Practices Council.

[104] Insolvency Service, *Consultation on Reforms to the Regulation of Insolvency Practitioners: Summary of Consultation Responses* (December 2011), paras. 3.6-4.3.

[105] See Insolvency Service News, *Minister Sets Out Future Direction for Reforms of Insolvency Practitioner Regulation* (Insolvency Service News on 20 December 2011).

bodies, including ICAEW, IPA, ACCA, ICAS and CAI, as well as IPs regulated by the Secretary of State. This covers approximately 92 per cent of all UK IPs. The Complaints Gateway does not cover complaints made against IPs in relation to insolvency procedures governed by Northern Ireland legislation. These complaints need to be made directly to the relevant authorising body of the IP concerned.

It should be noted that the Insolvency Complaint Gateway is a central hub for complaints about IPs in order to provide an independent and standardised method for complainants to access the complaints system. Complaints can be made by completing an online complaints form or through the IS Enquiry Line. Complaints coming in to this Gateway will be considered if there is an indication of a breach of the insolvency legislation, Statements of Insolvency Practice, RPB regulations and guidance or code of ethics. The allegations should be capable of being supported with evidence. If it is established that the complaint relates to an activity or behaviour which may result in the IP being liable to disciplinary action, it will then be passed on to the body that authorises and regulates the relevant IP for further consideration.

Furthermore, the IS published the 'Common Sanctions' guidance[106] to provide transparency and consistency to the sanctions system. When complaints are referred to relevant authorising bodies, each RPB will follow its own disciplinary processes. The 'Common Sanctions' guidance sets out the possible sanctions for various infringements/misconduct by the insolvency practitioner to make sure that outcomes are as consistent as possible across RPBs. It gives an indication of the level of sanction[107] for various breaches of the IA 1986, other relevant legislation, the SIPs and the Insolvency Code of Ethics to be imposed. Each disciplinary committee or tribunal will refer to these and use its own judgement to set a sanction appropriate to the circumstances of the individual case.

For each type of complaint there is a suggested starting point for the sanction and a range of financial sanctions. The starting point is not a tariff for the complaint but it simply indicates where the committee or tribunal might start when it looks at all the aggravating and mitigating factors[108] relevant to deciding the penalty. Similarly, the committee or

---

[106] For general information, see the Insolvency Service, *Common Sanctions Guidance* <https://www.gov.uk/government/publications/disciplinary-sanctions-against-insolvency-practitioners/common-sanctions-guidance> accessed 30 July 2015.

[107] *Ibid.*

[108] The Guidance also provided a non-exhaustive list of aggravating factors and mitigating factors, see *ibid.*

tribunal will be guided by the range of sanctions but will not be bound by the range. For instance, if the committee or tribunal has identified the relevant category of complaint as a material failure to comply with the previsions of a SIP, for which the starting point for financial sanction according to the indication of sanction is a fine of £5,000, the committee or tribunal might start with the indicative sanction and then takes into account any aggravating and mitigating factors before deciding whether it is appropriate to reduce or increase the penalty. The committee or tribunal may decide on a more or less severe penalty than the starting point depending on all the circumstances of the case. The indicative range of financial sanction for this category of complaint is £500–£7,500, which will guide the committee or tribunal when deciding the actual penalty but should not be regarded as setting either a maximum or minimum sanction. The final penalty decided might fall below or above the range depending on all the circumstances of the case.

According to the first year report,[109] the Gateway received around 950 complaints in its first year operation, 75 per cent of which were referred to the relevant authorising body for consideration. Between June and December 2014, 547 complaints were received and 72 per cent were referred to the authorising bodies.[110] According to the statistics in the first year report, 25 per cent of those referred cases were administration and 13 per cent (96 complains) were breaches of ethical guidance, 40 per cent of which involved conflict of interests.[111]

The 2014 Consultation on Strengthening the Regulatory Regime and Fee Structure for Insolvency Practitioners

Building on earlier consultations, the 2014 consultation paper[112] sets out proposals to: strengthen the regulatory framework through the introduction of clear regulatory objectives; enhance the IS's powers as the oversight regulator to deal with misconduct and abuse; take a backstop power to introduce a single regulator for the insolvency profession; and

---

109 Insolvency Service, *Report on the First Year of the Complaints Gateway* (Report, August 2014).

110 Insolvency Service, *2014 Annual Review of Insolvency Practitioner Regulation* (March 2015), 10.

111 *Report on the First Year of the Complaints Gateway*, 10–11.

112 Insolvency Service, *Consultation on Strengthening the Regulatory Regime and Fee Structure for Insolvency Practitioners* (February 2014).

change the way that IP fees are set to ensure better returns for unsecured creditors.[113]

To address concerns about the number of regulatory bodies dealing with a relatively small insolvency profession and the resulting potential for inconsistency, a single independent regulator for IPs has been proposed to replace the current system of RPBs. Nevertheless, is also recognised that moving to such a single regulator structure would involve significant time and cost and may not be done without further detailed analysis and consultation as well as secondary legislation.

The strong argument in favour of widening the power of the Secretary of State as the oversight regulator

The previous analysis has revealed several loopholes in the way IPs are supervised. I argue here that as a first step, the dual role of the IS (which both authorises IPs directly and acts as oversight regulator) ought to be reformed. The Secretary of State should stop authorising IPs directly. This would also go a long way to create consistency in the regulation of IPs. Secondly, it has been recognised that the lack of appropriate and proportionate powers of sanction leaves the oversight regulator in a weak position and undermines the credibility of the regulatory regime.[114] Although the seven PRBs are recognised as such and regulated by the Secretary of State, the Secretary of State can currently employ only one sanction against an RPB: withdrawal of its recognition of that RPB. But the application of such a radical sanction could be disproportionate in all but the most serious circumstances and has never been used.[115] It is therefore proposed that the Secretary of State should have a range of sanctions available so that proportionate action can be taken when the Secretary of State is satisfied that an RPB has not acted in a way which is compatible with the regulatory objectives. The proposed powers include: directing an RPB to take certain steps to counter the adverse impact of any failure to act compatibly with its objectives; imposing a

---

[113] *Consultation on Strengthening the Regulatory Regime and Fee Structure for Insolvency Practitioners*, 3.

[114] The Secretary of State currently has only one sanction against an RPB which is not regulating effectively and that is to withdraw its recognition as an RPB.

[115] *Consultation on Strengthening the Regulatory Regime and Fee Structure for Insolvency Practitioners*, para.42.

financial penalty of an appropriate amount;[116] and publishing a statement reprimanding the RPB for its failure to act in a way that is compatible with its regulatory objectives.[117]

In addition to new powers to sanction an RPB, to address the perception that the current disciplinary procedures for IPs are not always effective in delivering fair and prompt outcomes for those affected, it was also proposed to grant the IS, acting on behalf of the Secretary of State, the power to directly sanction an IP on public interest grounds. This would include the power to apply to the court directly to sanction an IP who is authorised by an RPB.[118] Sanction on public interest grounds may, for instance, be justified where an IP has failed to comply with the body of legislation and rules to such an extent that this has particularly serious consequences for the reputation of the profession and the insolvency regime. The principal responsibility for dealing with poor behaviour by IPs would remain with the RPBs.

Currently, the key changes that are expected to be introduced between October 2015 and April 2016 by the Small Business Enterprise and Employment Bill are the introduction of regulatory objectives, as well as enhanced powers for the IS as oversight regulator to the existing RPBs.[119] It was said that the idea of introducing a single regulator to replace the existing RPBs has not been ruled out and there will be a reserve power to allow the Secretary of State to designate a single body as the regulator for IPs at the appropriate time.[120]

---

[116] This would apply where it is satisfied that the RPB has failed to comply with a requirement imposed by a direction given by the Secretary of State or by a provision of the IA 1986 or its subordinate legislation.

[117] *Consultation on Strengthening the Regulatory Regime and Fee Structure for Insolvency Practitioners*, para.62.

[118] *Ibid.*, para.80. In terms of procedure vis-à-vis the application of sanction powers, it is proposed that, where the Secretary of State is satisfied that it is in the public interest to take direct action, it will give notice to the IP and the authorising RPB of its intention to apply to the court for a sanction against the IP. The sanction may be a financial penalty in the form of an order or/and a non-financial penalty, for example a warning, a severe reprimand, suspension or revocation of authorisation as an IP. If the proposed sanction is not agreed by the IP, the Secretary of State will apply to the court for an order to impose the sanction.

[119] Those powers include: to direct a RPB to take action; to impose a financial penalty on a RPB; reprimand a RPB; and where it is in the public interest, apply to the court to directly sanction an IP. See Insolvency Service, *Annual Review of Insolvency Practitioner Regulation 2014*, 21.

[120] *Ibid.*

Fee and remuneration of IPs

The issue of IP fees is important in relation to pre-packs, as if it is left unchecked, there is a risk that IPs are themselves sharing in the pre-pack surplus unfairly by charging higher fees at the expense of creditors. It is therefore important to ensure there are adequate constraints and control on IP fees. An IP's remuneration can be set on a time-cost basis, as a percentage of realisations or as a fixed fee. It is the IP who proposes which basis they wish to take their remuneration under and the creditors vote on the proposal. In the majority of cases, IPs take their remuneration on a time-cost basis, which requires creditors to have considerable knowledge and understanding of the insolvency process in order to question the amount of time spent, as well as the grade of staff used to carry out a particular piece of work.[121] Under the current system, IP fees are usually charged on an hourly rate without an indication of the work that will be done or the length of time it is expected to take.[122]

The Insolvency (Amendment) Rules 2010 requires IPs to engage with creditors to reach a collective agreement on remuneration. In administration, if no distribution to unsecured creditors is expected, fees are to be approved by all secured creditors and 50 per cent of preferential creditors (where there is a distribution to them); if secured creditors are over-secured, fees must be approved by unsecured creditors. With pre-packs, it is often the case that secured creditors are to be repaid in full, and the negotiation over fees will be with unsecured creditors.

Although no empirical study has yet examined whether pre-packs are associated with higher fees on a like-for-like basis, the general picture is that in a typical insolvency case, an amount paid to the IP is nine per cent higher when secured creditors are unaffected by the fees charged than when they are affected, according to the findings in the OFT's report on IP fees.[123] This finding was supported by another independent review led by Professor Elaine Kempson into IP fees, published in July 2013. It

---

[121] *Consultation on Strengthening the Regulatory Regime and Fee Structure for Insolvency Practitioners*, para.91. Professor Kempson highlights four main areas of concern among stakeholders, those being the actual hourly charge out rates and what they include, inefficient working and staff management, time recording and cost-ineffective working. See E Kempson, *Review of Insolvency Practitioner Fees* (Report to the Insolvency Service, July 2013), para.5.2.

[122] Insolvency Service Press Release, *More Transparency for Fees Charged in Insolvency* (3 March 2015) <https://www.gov.uk/government/news/more-transperancy-for-fees-charged-in-insolvency> accessed 30 July 2015.

[123] *The Market for Corporate Insolvency Practitioners: a Market Study*, 57 and footnote 88.

suggested that the current system of controls on IP remuneration work as intended where a secured creditor, often a bank, plays an active part in an insolvency but it does not work as competitively where control lies in the hands of unsecured creditors collectively as there is no 'identifiable' client.[124] Where the IP is working for a number of unsecured creditors, most of which have no involvement with the process, there is little effective oversight of the work undertaken by IPs, and costs are higher as a result.[125]

It has been highlighted in Kempson's review that the existing codes of practice and associated regime for compliance monitoring is inadequate when it comes to remuneration and independent oversight to ensure that time changed is for work that is necessary and properly performed.[126] The RPBs do not currently play a role in or monitor the level of IP fees. The only recourse open to creditors is the court, which is costly and time-consuming.[127] To enhance monitoring by the regulators, it is proposed in the 2014 Consultation to give the RPBs a regulatory role in monitoring fees to require the RPBs to provide a check and balance against the level of fees charged and take a full role in assessing the fairness of an IP's fees.[128]

Also, to simplify the fee structure and align IP fees and unsecured creditors' interests more closely, it is proposed in the Consultation that

---

[124] Kempson, *Review of Insolvency Practitioner Fees*. Kempson in her review offers a wide range of options for reform, including transparency measures and increasing creditor engagement which concern the availability of sufficient and clear information for creditors and the timing of this information to encourage greater engagement by unsecured creditors; simplifying the fee structure by changing the basis of time and rate basis for remuneration to either having a percentage of realisations as the presumed basis for charging fees in all cases or using different bases for different aspects of a case; and enhanced monitoring and oversight of fees by ensuring the regulators exercise a greater degree of compliance monitoring of fees. The full recommendations can be found in Chapter 6 of *Review of Insolvency Practitioner Fees*.

[125] Similarly, Armour argued that, in contrast to secured lenders, unsecured creditors are typically dispersed, ill-informed and one-off participants in insolvencies. As a consequence, they are poorly positioned to control administrators' fees. See Armour, 'The Rise of the "Pre-pack": Corporate Restructuring in the UK and Proposals for Reform'.

[126] *Review of Insolvency Practitioner Fees*, Chapter 6.

[127] *Ibid.*

[128] *Consultation on Strengthening the Regulatory Regime and Fee Structure for Insolvency Practitioners*, paras 97 to 101 on proposed measure on enhanced monitoring by the regulators. This would be done via the usual monitoring visits and complaint handling processes.

the Insolvency Rules on requirement to set the basis of remuneration should be amended to require office-holders to take their remuneration either as a percentage of realisations or as a fixed fee in all insolvency cases except those where a creditors' committee is established or secured creditors will not be paid in full.[129]

In March 2015, the Government announced that measures will be introduced to provide more transparency for fees charged in insolvency cases, which will come into effect from October 2015.[130] It is said that, where IPs' fees are based upon time costs, they will be required to provide an upfront estimate of their fees for creditor approval, before they can take their fees. IPs will not be permitted to draw fees in excess of the approved estimate unless creditors give further approval. This will therefore act as a cap on fees.[131]

To sum up, the controversy of pre-pack sales has tested the public confidence in the insolvency profession, and inspired a set of restrengthening measures to improve transparency of the process by imposing even more comprehensive ex post information disclosure requirements, and to strengthen the role of professional regulation in playing a particular effective part in their respective capacities. While the effect of these changes on providing a solid safeguard for the general unsecured creditors in pre-packs can only be properly evaluated in the fullness of time, as a first and firm step in the right direction, they should greatly improve public confidence in sanctioning insolvency practitioners' questionable conduct and behaviour in pre-pack practice in the instances of abuse.

CONCLUSION

The participation of the debtor's management in negotiating asset sales with prospective purchasers, often a connected party, along with the

---

[129] This proposal should not apply in the case of IVAs, CVAs and MVLs. Where the office-holder seeks to take their remuneration as a percentage of realisations, approval of a simple majority in value of creditors voting will be required. Similarly where the IP seeks to take remuneration as a fixed amount, they will be required to seek approval.

[130] Insolvency Service, *Annual Review of IP Regulation 2014*, 7. These changes affect administration, CVL, compulsory liquidation and bankruptcy. Those changes apply to England and Wales only.

[131] House of Commons Written Statement, *Measures to Improve Transparency in Insolvency Practitioner Fees and Handling of Cases in the Courts* ((HCWS325 on 3 March 2015).

speed and lack of transparency in this process, leaves room for potential self-dealing that may go undetected without cautious judicial consideration of which groups are benefiting from these sales.

The Draft Rules 2011 intended to include extra regulation on pre-pack sales to connected parties, with the proposed measure of a three-day notice requirement to offer creditors a pre-view right where the pre-pack sale to a connected party is highly suspicious of undervalue. Nevertheless, it was abandoned for being seen by the professionals as too restrictive and would create a legal setting that impedes administrators from pursuing their statutory objectives expeditiously. Although there is a strong argument that in the highly controversial pre-pack sensoria, there probably will be a need for legislative intervention by way of such a pre-view right to those affected, especially where ex post information disclosure proves inadequate to ensure fairness, the difficulty is that it is hard to define who those affected ones eligible to vote are, due to the uncertainty of the value of the ailing business. This would create another layer of controversy by giving certain creditors the power to influence the process where they have no direct financial interest in the outcome of the sale or any other possible options.

Apart from possible legislative intervention, more efforts have been made to focus on enhancing the transparency of the accelerated sale process through comprehensive ex post information disclosure requirements and accountability through reform of the regulatory regime of the insolvency profession.

SIP 16 is a comprehensive guide for the provision of relevant information to creditors, especially the updated 2013 version with its more extensive and more structured information disclosure requirements. In spite of the effort to make it more comprehensive to ensure the quality of information, the effectiveness of SIP 16 guidance significantly depends on its compliance and enforcement, especially an effective monitoring system to detect any non-compliance and to ensure that any instance of abuse will be dealt with firmly. Due to its professional guidance nature, a breach of SIP 16 at present is merely a professional disciplinary offence, and it is the discretion of the PRBs to take any disciplinary action. It is therefore important to construct a more responsive and consistent regulatory and sanction system that will apply a rigorous approach in the evaluation of IPs' actions and behaviour, with additional costs made available for the instances of abuse that are detected.

One issue to the very problem in connected pre-pack sales is to safeguard the impartiality of the office-holders to ensure the IPs involved in the negotiations are impartial and accountable, as they are in the front line of setting up and processing the pre-pack sales. Strengthened measures are being introduced through an increasing amount of professional regulation aimed at improving visibility and accountability. A complaints gateway is now in operation to make procedures for handling complaints more straightforward and more efficient. 'Common Sanctions' guidance has been published to provide transparency and consistency to the sanctions system.

Furthermore, following the 2014 Consultation, foreseeable legislative reforms will introduce more strengthened measures, such as conferring the Secretary of State, as oversight regulator, increased powers to sanction RPBs so that they will adequately fulfil their regulatory functions. This is supplemented with a reserve power for the Secretary of State to designate a single insolvency regulator to authorise and regulate all IPs when necessary. Furthermore, reforms will also be made to control insolvency practitioners' fees by requiring them to provide an upfront estimate of the fees for creditor approval. While the effect of these changes can only be properly evaluated in the fullness of time, they should greatly improve public confidence in the role of professional regulation playing a particular effective part in their respective capacities.

PART III

Pre-packs in the USA

5. Pre-packaged reorganisaton under Chapter 11

INTRODUCTION

This part extends the present analysis to the US bankruptcy[1] law notwithstanding that the institutional arrangements governing insolvency in the USA and the UK are significantly different. More importantly, in tandem with a similar trend in the UK, use of pre-packaged bankruptcy filings or of the 'pre-packing route' to bankruptcy proceedings has seen a considerable rise in the number of cases in the USA.[2] The term pre-packaged bankruptcy filings generally refers to restructurings of financially distressed companies through Chapter 11 proceedings commenced after the negotiation of a plan of reorganisation and the solicitation of the necessary affirmative votes on the plan. For the purposes of this book it will be referred to as the 'pre-packaged Chapter 11 proceedings'. The 'pre-packing route' to bankruptcy proceedings refers to a sale of all or substantially all of the debtor's assets pre-confirmation of a Chapter 11 plan through section 363(b) of the US Bankruptcy Code. For the purpose of this book it is referred to as 's 363(b) pre-plan sales'.

Accordingly, Part 3 is composed of two chapters. This chapter deals with pre-packaged Chapter 11 proceedings as a fast track alternative to the traditional Chapter 11 reorganisation. Chapter 6 deals with s 363(b) pre-plan sales through a Chapter 11 procedure. For completeness of analysis, the conventional Chapter 11 procedure will be discussed first to provide some background to the ensuing discussion of the pre-pack route

[1] In the US, insolvency of a company is described as bankruptcy whereas in the UK such a description is only applied to individuals.

[2] It is said that between 1990 and 2009 pre-packaged and pre-arranged bankruptcy constituted between 26 per cent and 34 per cent of all cases filed. Since 2010, 44 per cent were pre-packaged or pre-arranged. See DG Baird, 'Chapter 11's Expanding Universe' (2015) 87 *Temple Law Review* 975, 978. According to BankruptcyData.com in 2009, public companies filed 30 pre-arranged bankruptcies, in which many creditors approved a reorganisation plan prior to a filing. This represented a 300 per cent increase on 2008 figures.

and comparisons with the UK procedure. Furthermore, the chapter examines the circumstances normally surrounding a pre-packaged Chapter 11 reorganisation and, in particular, the factors that have contributed to its popularity. Then it considers the implications of pre-petition solicitation for the protection of the interests of claimholders that are constituted under a conventional Chapter 11 framework. Finally, the chapter explores the differences between the US pre-packaged Chapter 11 proceedings and the UK pre-packaged administration.

CHAPTER 11 OF THE US BANKRUPTCY CODE

Brief History of the Chapter 11 Regime

The first comprehensive federal bankruptcy statute in the United States was the Bankruptcy Act of 1898, which was directed towards liquidation rather than reorganisation.[3] Bankruptcy reorganisation in the USA originated from the equity receivership of railroads that began during the late nineteenth century.[4] The railroad reorganisation procedure was codified in 1933 and in 1934 as a general corporate reorganisation that was added to the Bankruptcy Act of 1898. The main benefit of this reform was that the main features of the practice in equity receivership were preserved.[5] Then, corporate reorganisation law changed dramatically following the New Deal Reform policies aimed at reviving the US economy in the aftermath of the Great Depression.[6] Most notably a new Chapter X was

---

[3] The Bankruptcy Act, Ch 541, 30 Stat. 544 (1898). It was amended several times on a piecemeal basis and revised substantially by the Chandler Act in 1938, Ch 575, 52 Stat. 840. The Chandler Act remained in effect until it was superseded by the Bankruptcy Reform Act of 1978, Pub. L. No. 95-598, 92 Stat. 2549.

[4] When the railroads were trapped in financial distress there were no bankruptcy reorganisation provisions in state bankruptcy law that could be used directly to reorganise the railroad enterprise. To maximise the value of investment, the parties creatively used the equity receivership as the legal mechanism. See BA Markell, 'Owners, Auctions, and Absolute Priority in Bankruptcy Reorganization' (1991) 44 *Stanford Law Review* 69, 74–5.

[5] *Ibid.*, 83.

[6] The Great Depression stirred populist mistrust and hostility toward Wall Street and led to enormous pressure for reform and government intervention that ultimately resulted in the New Deal. Consistent with the trends in the development of US bankruptcy legislation, the economic collapse spurred a push for reform. See HR Miller and SY Waisman, 'Does Chapter 11 Reorganization

added to the 1898 Bankruptcy Act by the Chandler Act of 1938, which was to regulate the reorganisation of large public corporations. In addition, the Chandler Act introduced a new reorganisation chapter: Chapter XI, which was designed to be used for smaller companies. A remarkable difference between the two proceedings is that Chapter X required the mandatory appointment of a trustee to replace the existing management while Chapter XI was designed to leave incumbent management in control.[7]

The current Bankruptcy Code, Title 11 of the United States Code, was enacted in 1978 by section 101 of the Bankruptcy Reform Act of 1978 and completely replaced the Bankruptcy Act of 1898.[8] It fundamentally reformed the corporate reorganisation law and unified the two corporate reorganisation chapters into one, Chapter 11 of the 1978 Code. It has been amended several times since 1978 with the most significant recent changes enacted in 2005 through the Bankruptcy Abuse Prevention and Consumer Protection Act of 2005.[9] The current Bankruptcy Code comprises nine chapters, including the initial eight chapters (1, 3, 5, 7, 9, 11 and 13) of the Bankruptcy Reform Act of 1978 and Chapter 12 added by the Bankruptcy Reform Act 1986. Chapter 7 provides liquidation proceedings available for businesses and consumer bankrupts; Chapter 11 of the Bankruptcy Code 1978 is the most widely-known company reorganisation regime.

Key Stages of the Chapter 11 Reorganisation Procedure

A Chapter 11 reorganisation procedure can be initiated by a voluntary petition for relief under Chapter 11 filed by the debtor company.[10] Alternatively, it can be triggered by an involuntary petition filed by at least three unsecured creditors in a standard case, or by a single unsecured

---

Remain a Viable Option for Distressed Businesses for the Twenty-First Century?' (2004) 78 *American Bankruptcy Law Journal* 153, 167.

7 DA Skeel, Jr., 'An Evolutionary Theory of Corporate Law and Corporate Bankruptcy' (1998) 51 *Vanderbilt Law Review* 1325, 1374.

8 Title 11 of the United States Code ss 101-1330 (1982 & Supp. IV 1986) (hereafter the 'US Bankruptcy Code'). It became effective, for the most part, on 1 October 1979.

9 The amendments include: Bankruptcy Tax Act 1980, Bankruptcy Amendment Act of 1984, Bankruptcy Judges, United States Trustees and Family Farmer Bankruptcy Act of 1986, Bankruptcy Reform Act of 1994, and a lot of specific bankruptcy legislations were presented between 1986 and 1994. Chapter 12 was specifically intended to aid farmers.

10 S 301 US Bankruptcy Code.

creditor in lower value cases.[11] Upon the filing of a bankruptcy petition, the debtor will obtain immediate protection from creditors' individual debt-collection actions.[12] The automatic stay preserves the debtor's assets for the operation of the collective bankruptcy procedure to force claimholders to bargain collectively for a reorganisation plan to turnaround the business or otherwise to maximise the value of debtor's overall recovery through the implementation of the reorganisation plan.

Debtor in Possession and its exclusive power in proposing a plan

As already explained the key property of the US Chapter 11 procedure is to allow the management of the ailing company to retain control of the company during the reorganisation process.[13] The debtor becomes a Debtor in Possession (DIP) by default upon a Chapter 11 Reorganisation filing; only in exceptional situations will an outside trustee be appointed.[14] The debtor, by virtue of s 1107(a) of the US Bankruptcy Code, is given all the rights, duties and powers of a Chapter 11 trustee except the investigative duties. The DIP is also subject to the limitations placed on a Chapter 11 trustee.

In simple terms the DIP is the fiduciary of the estate and is accountable for all property received.[15] For its power of administering the estate, the DIP is obliged to supply information about the estate and the estate's administration if requested by a party in interest and should file with the court a final account of its administration of the estate.[16] The DIP's powers with respect to the use, sale or lease of property of the estate are governed by s 363. The DIP can run the business in the ordinary way, such as engaging in selling, leasing property or obtaining unsecured credit, and is not required to send notice or obtain court approval except for 'cash collateral', for which the DIP must obtain the lienholder's

---

[11] S 303 US Bankruptcy Code. The order for relief in such cases can only be granted by the court upon proof of statutory grounds.

[12] S 362 US Bankruptcy Code.

[13] Although the existing management can run the business in the ordinary way, court approval will be required for substantial asset sales. See s 361 US Bankruptcy Code. For the relative merits of the US DIP model and the British PIP model, see D Hahn, 'Concentrated Ownership and Control of Corporate Reorganisations' (2004) 4 *Journal of Corporate Law Studies* 117; V Finch, 'Control and Co-ordination in Corporate Rescue' (2005) 25 *Legal Studies* 374.

[14] The DIP may be replaced by a trustee only for cause such as fraud, gross mismanagement and incompetence. S 1104(a)(1) US Bankruptcy Code.

[15] S 323 US Bankruptcy Code.

[16] See s 1107(a) and s 704(2), (7), (9) US Bankruptcy Code.

consent or court approval in any case.[17] Furthermore, the DIP's power as regards transactions within the ordinary course of business can be limited by an interested party, usually the debtor's creditors, seeking a court order restraining the managers' ability to make decisions or conduct company affairs.[18] Where transactions out of the ordinary course of business are involved, such as substantial assets sales, the DIP must obtain court approval and notify the creditors.[19]

The interests of secured creditors are safeguarded by constraining via s 363(e)) the debtor's authority to use, sell or lease estate property as is necessary to provide adequate protection of the secured creditor's interests in the property.[20] Section 361 provides some examples of 'adequate protection' safeguards which include periodic cash payments and the replacement of security interests on other property, although, *stricto sensu*, the concept itself is not defined. It should however be stressed that it is only the value of the collateral that enjoys 'adequate protection'. The interests of unsecured creditors in the proceeds of unencumbered assets are protected by s 1112(b), which only allows the court to convert the case into a Chapter 7 case if there are substantial and continuing losses that cannot be resolved.

With an automatic stay to prevent creditors from collecting their claim or enforcing their liens, the DIP enjoys an exclusivity period of 120 days following the filing of the petition, during which the debtor ought to propose a reorganisation plan.[21] When exclusivity expires, or the debtor's

---

[17] S 363 (c)(2)-(4) US Bankruptcy Code. The DIP must segregate and account for any cash collateral in its possession, custody or control pursuant to s 363(c)(4) and provide adequate protection for the secured creditor's interest in the cash collateral properly. A specialised hearing procedure is also available under s 363(c)(3) for the debtor to obtain emergency relief in compelling cases while protecting the interests of the secured creditor.

[18] Ss. 336(c) and 1108 US Bankruptcy Code.

[19] S 363 US Bankruptcy Code.

[20] If the party that is affected by the proposed action objects, the court will determine whether the protection provided is adequate.

[21] S 1121 US Bankruptcy Code. The court may extend this period for up to 18 months. The period is terminated if the court appoints a trustee. Plan negotiations typically are conducted primarily between the debtor and one or more official committees appointed shortly after the filing of the debtor's bankruptcy petition, although any party in interest may seek to participate in negotiations. Once the debtor reaches agreement with its major constituencies on a plan that appears to have the necessary support to be confirmed, the plan will be filed with the bankruptcy court. See MD Plevin *et al.*, 'Pre-Packaged Asbestos Bankruptcies: A Flawed Solution' (2003) 44 *South Texas Law Review* 886.

plan fails to get acceptance, any party in interest can file a plan.[22] Within 180 days after the date of the order for relief, the debtor has the exclusive right to solicit acceptances for its plan. On the request of an interested party, after notice has been given and a hearing has taken place, the court may reduce or extend the 120-day or the 180-day period for cause.

By excluding competing reorganisation plans proposed by other parties during the exclusivity period, the DIP is given a special advantage in obtaining acceptance of their plan. This advantage is premised on dual grounds. First, it removes creditors' power to compare the debtor's proposals against other possibilities or plans,[23] since a non-debtor party who may wish to submit a competing plan must wait until the exclusivity period ends. Secondly, bankruptcy bargaining among interested parties can be more structured within the exclusivity period in the absence of competing plans. For the company's creditors, choosing to reject the plan proposed by the debtor means further delays. First, the exclusivity period provides the debtor with the power of strategic delay, as the debtor has primary control of the length of time of the initial exclusivity period used for proposing a plan and soliciting acceptance of the plan. Any failure of the proposed plan would lead to an extra delay for the formulation of the competing plans since the exclusivity period prohibits the competing plans from being proposed simultaneously with the debtor's plan. Delays are expensive for the bargaining parties. Secondly, by rejecting the plan and forcing the debtor to revise the draft plan and solicit acceptance of the revised plan, the uncertainty surrounding the plans of the non-debtor parties remain the same. It is unlikely that these will bear the cost of delay without knowing the result of it, since during the whole period it will be unknown whether there is room for acceptance by creditors of their alternative plans. Thus, in the circumstances, creditors 'are more likely to vote for the debtor's proposal rather than risk unknown delay'.[24]

Plan acceptance and voting by classified claimholders

After filing the plan, the debtor must try to get the plan accepted. Before soliciting acceptance of the plan, the debtor must prepare a written

---

[22] S 1109(c) US Bankruptcy Code provides that if more than one plan meets all the rules of Chapter 11, the bankruptcy judge shall consider the 'preferences of creditors and equity security holders in determining which plan to confirm'.

[23] See *In Re Century Glove, Inc.*, 860 F.2d 94 (3rd Cir. 1988). The court commented that the exclusivity period limited this ability and thus provides special favour to the debtor's plan.

[24] 860 F.2d 94, 102, footnote 9.

disclosure statement and persuade the court to approve it.[25] The disclosure statement should meet the 'adequate information' standard set forth in s 1125(a)(1)[26] to allow the claimholders to make an informed judgement about the plan and whether to vote in favour or against it. A hearing will be scheduled to consider the sufficiency of the disclosure statement.[27] Once the statement is approved, the debtor will distribute it to eligible holders of claims and interests and may begin seeking acceptance of the plan from various classes of claimholders.

In the plan, claimholders are grouped into classes based on the nature of their claims or interests.[28] The claims or interests may be placed in a particular class only if the claim or interest being included is substantially similar to the other claims or interests of the class. Generally, a plan will classify claim holders as: secured creditors, unsecured creditors entitled to priority, general unsecured creditors and equity security holders. Equity is always a separate class. All claims or interests in a specific class should receive the same treatment unless the holder of a particular claim or interest agrees to less favourable treatment.[29]

The reorganisation plan must also specify any class of claims or interests that is or is not impaired.[30] Under Chapter 11, all classes have the right to vote on the reorganisation plan, except the classes that are impaired or the classes that will receive nothing under the reorganisation

---

[25] S 1125(b) US Bankruptcy Code.

[26] 'Adequate information' is defined in s 1125(a)(1) as: 'information of a kind, and in sufficient detail, as far as is reasonably practical in light of the nature and history of the debtor and the condition of the debtor's books and records, that would enable a hypothetical reasonable investor typical of holders of claims or interests of the relevant class to make an informed judgment about the plan'.

[27] The draft plan and the disclosure statement shall be mailed only to the debtor, any trustee or committee appointed, the Securities and Exchange Commission and any party in interest who requests in writing a copy of the statement or plan. Any objections to the disclosure statement must be filed and served on the debtor, any trustee or committee, the Securities and Exchange Commission, the United States Trustee and any other entity designated by the court at any time before the disclosure statement is approved. See r. 3017 of Federal Rules of Bankruptcy Procedure.

[28] S 1122(a) US Bankruptcy Code.

[29] S 1123(a)(4) US Bankruptcy Code.

[30] The concept of 'impairment' of claims or interests is defined in the s 1124 US Bankruptcy Code. Generally speaking, a class is unimpaired if it consists only of claims that the plan does not restructure.

plan.[31] A class of claims is unimpaired where the plan leaves a claimholder's legal, equitable and contractual rights unaltered.[32] By making a class unimpaired, the plan proponent actually avoids negotiation with the claimholders in that class.

Acceptance of a plan generally requires approval from all impaired creditor classes and shareholders. For each impaired class, acceptance of the plan requires approval from two-thirds in amount of claims and more than half in the number of each class of claimholders. This is a rather strict requirement but it does safeguard the representativeness of the decision. In the case of equity interests, two-thirds of shares voting must favour the plan. Under Chapter 11 shareholders are considered interested parties with a claim, but subordinate to that of creditors. In contrast, English administration proceedings do not consider the claim of shareholders at all. Finally, each claimholder of the unimpaired classes is conclusively presumed to have accepted the plan, therefore solicitation of acceptances with respect to an unimpaired class from the claimholders of such a class is not required.[33]

The role of creditor committees

The appointment of a committee of unsecured creditors is mandatory in a Chapter 11 case. Creditor committees are designed to represent the interests of certain claimholder classes during the negotiation. US law treats the creditor committee as an important creditor empowerment mechanism enabling creditors to protect their own interests, since in the usual case no trustee or examiner is ever appointed and the creditors' committee is the only participant in the case that can carry out an investigation of the debtor's financial condition and of the debtor's chances for a successful reorganisation.[34] Therefore, the creditors are required to take a proactive role in the bankruptcy process and monitor the treatment of their claims.

Chapter 11 specifically requires the United States Trustee to appoint a committee of creditors holding unsecured claims as soon as practicable in every case[35] and US law grants bankruptcy courts the authority to order the appointment of additional creditors' committees and an equity

[31] Classes that will receive nothing under the plan are deemed to reject the plan. S 1126(g) US Bankruptcy Code.

[32] S 1124(1) US Bankruptcy Code.

[33] S 1126(f) US Bankruptcy Code.

[34] R Jordan and W Warren, *Bankruptcy* (2th edn, The Foundation Press 1989), 730.

[35] S 1102(a) US Bankruptcy Code.

security holders' committee, if such committees are necessary to 'assure adequate representation of creditors or equity security holders'.[36] Moreover, creditor committees are given broad powers by s 1103(c) of the US Bankruptcy Code, including investigating the acts, conduct, assets and financial condition of the debtor, the operation of the debtor's business and the desirability of the continuation of such business, and participating in the formulation of a plan and so forth. The most important right of creditors' committees is to negotiate with the debtor in possession or the trustee about the terms of the reorganisation plan. If no agreement can be reached, the creditors' committee may submit a rival plan and solicit acceptances for that plan.[37] The committee will perform an advisory role in that it will make recommendations to those it represents with regard to how major issues are to be decided, and collect and file acceptances of the reorganisation plan.[38]

Court confirmation of a reorganisation plan and the 'cram-down' exemption

Once the votes have been received, the bankruptcy court will hold a hearing to confirm the plan.[39] The court hearing is compulsory and it is the final opportunity for any party in interest to object to the proposed plan.[40] For dissenting creditors, if they believe that the vote of the impaired class was improperly obtained, they can seek to disallow it on good faith grounds explicitly provided for in s 1126(e). This provision allows the court to disqualify an entity whose acceptance or rejection of a plan was not given in good faith, or was not solicited or procured from voting in good faith or from voting in accordance with what is provided in the Bankruptcy Code.

Furthermore, to confirm the plan, the court will scrutinise the plan to determine whether the plan complies with the list of requirements specified under s 1129. The court will confirm the plan if the plan has

---

[36] S 1102(a)(2) US Bankruptcy Code. ES Adams, 'Governance in Chapter 11 Reorganisations: Reducing Costs, Improving Results' (1993) 73 *Boston University Law Review* 581, 614.

[37] Jordan and Warren, *Bankruptcy*, 731.

[38] S 1103(c)(3) US Bankruptcy Code.

[39] Confirmation of a reorganisation plan generally follows the approval of disclosure statement and the solicitation of votes. In cases where the debtor is a small business and elects to be treated as a small business under s 1121(e), after soliciting acceptance, a debtor can combine the hearing on the disclosure statement with the confirmation hearing. See s 1125(f) US Bankruptcy Code.

[40] S 1128 US Bankruptcy Code.

gained a unanimous vote of all impaired classes of claims or interests and if it also meets all the applicable requirements under s 1129(a). To protect dissenting creditors, s 1129(a) requires that the plan may only be confirmed by the court if it satisfies the feasibility test which is based on two tests: (1) the possibility that the plan is to be followed by liquidation must be ruled out, and (2) the need for further financial reorganisation must similarly be ruled out.[41] Attached to the confirmation process is also a best interest test (so-called 'no-creditor worse off' test), which requires that each dissenting member of the impaired class receives a distribution that has a present value no less than what he would receive under a hypothetical liquidation on the effective date of the plan.[42] It should be noted that the best interest test is applied to each dissenting member of an impaired class rather than to the class as a whole.

Furthermore, to be confirmed, the plan should disclose any payment for the services or for costs and expenses in connection with the plan and the case.[43] Also, s 1129(a)(5) provides that the plan must disclose: the identity and affiliations of the top managers of the reorganised debtor; any of the debtor's affiliations that participate in a joint plan or the successor of the debtor participating in the plan; the identity of the insiders that will be employed in the reorganised debtor; and the compensation to be paid to such insiders.

Under certain circumstances where the plan satisfies all requirements of s 1129(a) but fails to secure a unanimous vote from all impaired classes, the court may use the 'cram down' provision of s 1129(b) to prevent a particular class holding out by forcing the dissenting class to accept the plan. Confirmation of a plan over a class dissent is known as a cram-down of the plan. This power can only be used where at least one impaired and non-insider[44] class has accepted the plan and more than one claim is impaired. An important statutory requirement for a court cram-down is that the plan does not 'discriminate unfairly, and is fair and equitable with respect to each class of claims or interests that is impaired under, and has not accepted, the plan'.[45] The condition that the plan is 'fair and equitable' is further defined by s 1129(b)(2). In determining whether a plan discriminates unfairly, the focus will be on whether the

---

41 S 1129(a)(11) US Bankruptcy Code.

42 S 1129(a)(7)(ii) US Bankruptcy Code.

43 S 1129(a)(4) US Bankruptcy Code.

44 The term 'insider' is defined in s 101(31) US Bankruptcy Code in a broad sense and include officers, directors and any other person in control of the debtor company.

45 S 1129(b)(1) US Bankruptcy Code.

legal rights of a dissenting class are protected in a manner consistent with the treatment of other classes whose legal rights are intertwined with those of the dissenting class.[46] The separately classified but substantially similar claims should be treated in the same way under the 'no unfair discrimination' requirement.

Naturally, the fair and equitable requirement is designed to protect the basic interests of the non-consenting classes of claims or interests in a court 'cram-down. It should be noted that s 1129(b)(2) provides separate 'fair and equitable' 'cram-down' standards for non-consenting classes of holders of secured, unsecured claims and equity holders. For dissenting secured classes, 'fair and equitable' means the secured property must be kept intact and the collateral value preserved so that the class can receive the full value of their collateral under the plan.[47] For dissenting unsecured and equity classes, unless they are paid in full, the standard is that no class junior to them is entitled to receive or retain anything under the plan.[48]

Confirmation of a plan has the effect of ceasing the automatic stay[49] and all prior claims and interests against the debtor are replaced by the new terms under the plan. The legal effects of the confirmation of a plan are specified in s 1141 including: the terms of the plan that bind all affected parties, whether or not their claims and interest are impaired, and whether or not they voted in favour of or against the plan;[50] that the confirmation vests all the property of the estate to the debtor, except as otherwise provided; and that the confirmation discharges the debtor from any pre-confirmation debt and terminates all rights and interests of shareholders subject to certain exceptions.[51]

Use of a trustee in Chapter 11 reorganisations

An outside trustee is appointed in Chapter 11 proceedings only in exceptional cases. Section 1104 US Bankruptcy Code specifies that a trustee can be appointed on grounds of suspected fraud, dishonesty or

---

46 KN Klee, 'All You Ever Wanted to Know about Cram Down Under the New Bankruptcy Code' (1979) 53 *American Bankruptcy Law Journal* 133, 142–3.

47 S 1129(b)(2)(A) (2005) US Bankruptcy Code.

48 S 1129(b)(2)(B)(C) US Bankruptcy Code.

49 S 362(c) US Bankruptcy Code.

50 S 1141(a) US Bankruptcy Code.

51 In particular for a limited company, the existence of a written waiver of discharge executed by the debtor after the order for relief under Chapter 11 under s 1141(d)(4).

gross mismanagement provided that a large number of bondholders or shareholders have not objected to an appointment of a trustee by the court.[52] In practice, the courts are generally extremely reluctant to appoint a trustee, especially in bigger cases. Upon the court's determination that the appointment of a Chapter 11 trustee is appropriate, it is the duty of the United States Trustee,[53] after consultation with the parties, to appoint one disinterested person,[54] other than the United States Trustee, to serve as the Chapter 11 trustee, and the appointment must be approved by the court.[55] Since Chapter 11 trustees are also responsible for managing a distressed operating business, the United States Trustee usually prefers turnaround managers to lawyers or accountants as the appointee.[56] Unsecured creditors may seek the election of a trustee if they are dissatisfied with the United States Trustee's selection.[57]

---

[52] S 1104(a)(1) US Bankruptcy Code.

[53] The United States Trustee is charged with the responsibility of supervising the administration of cases and trustees in cases under chapters 7, 11, 12 and 13 of title 11 of the US Bankruptcy Code. It acts in the public interest to promote the efficiency, and to protect and preserve the integrity, of the bankruptcy system. See US Department of Justice, Chapter 11 Trustee Handbook, May 2004.

[54] The term 'disinterested person' is defined in s 101(14): The trustee or examiner must not be one of the following: a creditor, equity security holder or insider; an investment banker for any outstanding security of the debtor; an investment banker for a security of the debtor within three years prior to the filing of the petition, or an attorney for such an investment banker in connection with the offer, sale or issuance of a security of the debtor; a present or former (with the two years prior to the filing of the petition) director, officer or employee of the debtor or of the debtor's investment banker; or a person holding an interest materially adverse to the interest of the estate or of any class of creditors or equity security holders, by reason of any direct or indirect relationship to, connection with, or interest in the debtor or the debtor's investment banker or attorney for the debtor's investment banker.

[55] The court shall order the appointment of a Chapter 11 trustee at any time after a case is filed, but before a plan is confirmed, upon a motion of any party in interest or the United States Trustee, if after notice and a hearing the court finds: (1) that cause exists, or (2) that such appointment would be in the best interest of creditors, equity security holders, and other interests of the estate. See s 1104(a) US Bankruptcy Code. S 1104(d) requires the United States trustee to consult with the parties in interest prior to the appointment. Although the United States Trustee is not required to select one of the candidates nominated by the parties, the qualifications of the persons recommended and the views of parties in interest will be given due consideration.

[56] WD Warren and DJ Bussel, *Bankruptcy* (6th ed., New York 2002), 596.

[57] Pursuant to s 1104(b) and 702(b), creditors may elect one person to serve as trustee in the case if election of a trustee is requested by creditors with voting

Upon the appointment, the DIP's exclusive right to file a reorganisation plan is terminated, even if it is still within the statutory exclusivity period.[58] As an independent third party, the Chapter 11 trustee assumes management and control of the bankruptcy estate from the debtor, and serves as a fiduciary charged with protecting the interests in the bankruptcy estate of all parties, including all classes of creditors and the debtor.[59] The responsibilities a Chapter 11 trustee must take on include: operating the debtor's business; investigating the debtor's business and financial affairs; and filing a report of his findings, as well as performing administrative tasks relevant to the proceedings.[60] If the Chapter trustee is operating the debtor's business, then the trustee may generally use, sell or lease property of the estate to the extent that such transactions are in the ordinary course of the debtor's business.[61]

PRE-PACKAGED CHAPTER 11 PROCESS

A 'pre-packaged' Chapter 11 describes the procedure of devising a plan of reorganisation and soliciting acceptances to such a plan prior to the

---

power on the election of a trustee holding 20 per cent of the claims eligible to vote at an election. Pursuant to s 702(a), creditors are eligible to request and vote in an election only if they hold general unsecured claims that are allowable, undisputed, fixed, liquidated and entitled to distribution under specified Code sections. Further, as specified in s 702(a)(2)(3) a creditor will not be permitted to vote if the creditor is an insider or holds an interest materially adverse to the estate and its other creditors.

58 Ss 343 and 521 US Bankruptcy Code.

59 US Department of Justice, Chapter 11 Trustee Handbook, May 2004, p 19.

60 Ss. 1108 and 1106(a) US Bankruptcy Code. The statutory duties of a Chapter 11 trustee set forth in s 1106 incorporates by reference certain Chapter 7 trustee duties as specified in s 704. The applicable duties prescribed by s 704 include the obligations to: (2) be accountable for all property received; (7) unless the court orders otherwise, furnish such information concerning the estate and the estate's administration as is requested by a party in interest; (8) if the business of the debtor is authorised to be operated, file … periodic reports and summaries of the operation of such business; and (9) make a final report and file a final account of the administration of the estate with the court and the United States Trustee. In addition to the duties described in s 704, s 1106(a)(2) also requires a trustee to investigate the acts, conduct, assets, liabilities and financial condition of the debtor, the operation of the debtor's business and the desirability of the continuance of such business, and any other matter relevant to the case or to the formulation of a plan.

61 S 363(c)(1) US Bankruptcy Code.

formal filing for Chapter 11 protection.[62] It is permitted by s 1126(b) of the Bankruptcy Code that a debtor company can formulate a plan of reorganisation and solicit acceptance of the plan prior to its filing for Chapter 11 protection.[63] In practice, the debtor following the pre-packaged route usually files for bankruptcy after the main impaired classes of creditors have approved a draft plan of reorganisation recorded in a comprehensive written agreement comprising a plan of reorganisation and a disclosure statement.[64]

The idea of taking the pre-pack route to a Chapter 11 reorganisation is to allow the contentious and time-consuming work of negotiating a reorganisation plan to be carried out prior to filing under Chapter 11 so that the company can spend as little time in bankruptcy as possible. Ideally, all issues concerning the reorganisation are resolved prior to commencement of the bankruptcy case, leaving only the procedural steps required to confirm the plan of reorganisation that have already been negotiated and agreed upon. In reality, the degree of pre-filing plan negotiation and solicitation of votes varies depending on the size, complexity and preferred confidentiality of the case. There are two typical situations in respect of vote solicitation in a pre-packaged Chapter 11. One is often referred to as 'pre-negotiated' or 'pre-arranged' Chapter 11 where a plan of reorganisation is negotiated among the parties prior to

---

62 MS Kirschner *et al.*, 'Pre-packaged Bankruptcy Plans: The Deleveraging Tool of the '90s in the Wake of Old and Tax Concerns' (1991) 21 *Seton Hall Law Review* 643, 644, footnote 8. In contrast to pre-packaged cases, there are also pre-negotiated cases, where some debtors negotiated the terms of their representatives prior to bankruptcy, but did not solicit usable votes prior to filing or did not solicit them from all impaired creditor classes. See T Eisenberg and LM LoPucki, 'Shopping for Judges: An Empirical Analysis of Venue Choice in Large Chapter 11 Reorganizations' (1999) 84 *Cornell Law Review* 967, 976.

63 11 U.S.C. 1126(b) US Bankruptcy Code:

(b) For the purposes of subsections (c) and (d) of this section, a holder of a claim or interest that has accepted or rejected the plan before the commencement of the case under this title is deemed to have accepted or rejected such plan, as the case may be, if –
   (1) the solicitation of such acceptance or rejection was in compliance with any applicable non-bankruptcy law, rule or regulation governing the adequacy of disclosure in connection with such solicitation; or
   (2) if there is not any such law, rule or regulation, such acceptance or rejection was solicited after disclosure to such holder of adequate information, as defined in section 1125 (a) of this title.

64 See TJ Salerno and CD Hansen, 'A Prepackaged Bankruptcy Strategy' (1991) 12 *Journal of Business Strategy* 36, 38.

the filing, but no formal solicitation of votes occurs until after the filing of the Chapter 11 petition.[65] The other is 'pre-voted' Chapter 11 where the debtor company files the plan of reorganisation and the outcome of the vote at the same time as their Chapter 11 bankruptcy petition after receipt of all requisite acceptances.

Varying Degrees of Pre-packing: Pre-negotiated v Pre-voted

In a 'pre-negotiated' Chapter 11, the votes will be solicited after the Chapter 11 petition has been filed. The disclosure statement and plan can be filed with the bankruptcy court immediately upon commencement of the Chapter 11 case. The company will then seek the approval of the bankruptcy court for a disclosure statement, solicit votes on the plan and seek an order from the court confirming the plan. As the plan has been negotiated, the vote solicitation process can occur promptly after the bankruptcy court has approved the disclosure statement for distribution to creditors and shareholders.

In some circumstance, initial solicitation of plan acceptance may have been conducted with key or major creditors before the bankruptcy filing. Upon obtaining their consents, the debtor and creditors often enter into 'lock-up' or 'cooperation' agreements in which creditors agree to vote for the plan at a time when a court approves disclosure statements. After the court approves the disclosure statement, the debtor can continue to solicit all requisite votes for the plan, and creditors may also solicit rejections of the plan. Then a confirmation hearing is scheduled quickly. In such circumstances, vote solicitation is actually completed after the debtor files for Chapter 11 relief.

In a 'pre-voted' Chapter 11, solicitation of all requisite acceptances is actually completed before the filing. The debtor company files the plan of reorganisation and the outcome of the vote at the same time as their Chapter 11 bankruptcy petition after receipt of all requisite acceptances. Chapter 11 is entered to complete necessary procedural steps, including approval of the disclosure statement used in the pre-petition solicitation of votes, official tabulation of votes received and determination of the feasibility of the plan in order for it to be effective and binding on all parties. In such a situation, the first thing for the court to do is to hold a combined hearing upon approval of the disclosure statement, acceptance of the reorganisation plan and confirmation of the plan. At the hearing,

65 AN Resnick and HJ Sommer (ed), *Collier Guide to Chapter 11: Topics and Selected Industries* (LexisNexis, 2015), para.5.02.

the court is required to find that the solicitation of acceptances and rejections was in compliance with the relevant rules.[66]

Requirements on Pre-petition Solicitation of Votes

Pre-petition solicitations can only be recognised by the court if they comply with the relevant laws and rules and the requirements for disclosure of sufficient information. The bankruptcy court must ensure that all impaired creditors and equity security holders were in fact solicited,[67] and that the solicitation period was reasonable and the disclosure was adequate under s 1126(b).[68]

Procedural requirements

Federal Rule of Bankruptcy Procedure 3018(b) sets forth the minimum procedural requirements for pre-petition solicitation. For the pre-petition vote of a claimholder to be valid, the bankruptcy court must be satisfied that the pre-packaged plan and disclosure statement were transmitted to substantially all creditors or stakeholders in the same class, and that the solicitation period in which time was allowed for the vote to be made was not 'unreasonably short'.

If the debtor did not solicit claimants who have the right to vote on the pre-packaged plan, the debtor must give them an opportunity to vote; otherwise the claimants may be able to successfully challenge the plan on appeal.[69] As to those interested parties who were not included in the pre-petition plan negotiations, and whose interests are therefore not

---

66 Particularly s 1126(b) of the US Bankruptcy Code and r. 3018 of Federal Rules of Bankruptcy Procedure.

67 R. 3018(b) of Federal Rules of Bankruptcy Procedure sets up the requirement that the bankruptcy court will not approve the acceptance or rejection of the plan by a holder of a claim or interest if, after notice and hearing, the court finds that the proposed plan had not been transmitted to substantially all impaired creditors and impaired equity security holders.

68 Kirschner *et al.*, 'Pre-packaged Bankruptcy Plans: The Deleveraging Tool of the '90s in the Wake of Old and Tax Concerns', 668. R. 3018(b) of Federal Rules of Bankruptcy Procedure requires that creditors and equity security holders must be given a reasonable time to accept or reject the plan of reorganisation. While r. 3018 does not set forth a time period for the pre-petition solicitation, it was held that compliance with the 25-day notice period (set in r. 2002(b)(2) of Federal Rules of Bankruptcy Procedure) required for confirmation of a plan in a normal Chapter 11 case should be sufficient.

69 This is corresponding to the requirement in r. 3018(b) of Federal Rules of Bankruptcy Procedure that pre-petition votes accepting or rejecting a plan 'shall

reflected in the proposed plan, they may delay or derail confirmation by objecting to the plan, thereby depriving the debtor of some or all of the anticipated benefits of the pre-pack.[70] The effects of the voting will legally bind all claimholders unless the court determines that inadequate disclosure was made or the voting was improperly conducted. Such a court decision can result in the invalidation of votes and the need to re-disclose and re-solicit if the restraints on pre-petition solicitation are not satisfied.

Adequacy of disclosure

For acceptances solicited and received prior to the commencement of the case to be recognised for the purpose of plan confirmation, the vote must have been solicited with adequate disclosure. According to s 1126(b), adequacy of disclosure is determined under applicable non-bankruptcy law or if there is no such applicable law, in accordance with the concept of 'adequate information' defined in s 1125(a) of the Bankruptcy Code. In practice, the debtor will often draft a disclosure statement that meets the standards of s 1125 although the debtor is not technically obligated to do so.

'Adequate information' is defined in s 1125(a)(1) as:

> information of a kind, and in sufficient detail, as far as is reasonably practical in light of the nature and history of the debtor and the condition of the debtor's books and records, that would enable a hypothetical reasonable investor typical of holders of claims or interests of the relevant class to make an informed judgment about the plan.

The statement typically contains a valuation of the debtor or an appraisal of the debtor's assets, which is subject to the scrutiny of the bankruptcy court.[71] There is no prescribed format for disclosure statements, although in considering the meaning of 'adequate information', courts have developed lists of topics that should be discussed in the disclosure statement, including: a description of debtor's business; reasons for the company entering into financial difficulty and possible measures that could be taken to remedy this situation; historical and current financial information; material post-petition events; outline of the plan; means of

---

not be deemed to have accepted or rejected the plan if the court finds after notice and hearing that the plan was not transmitted to substantially all creditors'.

[70] Plevin *et al.*, 'Pre-Packaged Asbestos Bankruptcies: A Flawed Solution', 889.

[71] S 1125(b) US Bankruptcy Code. The court may approve a disclosure statement without a valuation of the debtor or an appraisal of the debtor's assets.

effectuating the plan; securities to be issued, if any; projections, if any; post-confirmation management and control; insider and affiliate claims, and transactions with insiders/affiliates; disputed claims; ongoing legal proceedings involving the debtor; tax consequences for the debtor; the existence and future of any committees; and a liquidation analysis.[72]

What constitutes 'adequate information' must be considered in conjunction with the concept of a hypothetical investor typical of holders of claims or interests of a relevant class.[73] Thus, what constitutes adequate disclosure for a particular class of claimants will vary depending on the availability of information to and the level of sophistication of the claimants in the class.[74] The courts will take a practical approach as to what is necessary under the circumstances for each case, such as the cost of preparation of the statements, the need for relative speed in solicitation and confirmation, and of course, the need for investor protection.[75]

Where the court finds that the disclosure statement is inadequate in some respects, the debtor will have to amend and redistribute it, and re-solicit plan acceptances, resulting in potentially lengthy delays in confirmation.[76] Furthermore, an objection to confirmation or approval of the disclosure statement and solicitation process can raise complex litigation issues under the Bankruptcy Code that may delay the confirmation process and result in extensive hearings or a trial. To avoid the additional restraints on pre-petition solicitation and associated risks, the debtor has a strong incentive to make every effort to comply with the applicable disclosure standards.

Promoting the Use of Pre-packs – The Bankruptcy Abuse Prevention and Consumer Protection Act 2005

The conventional Chapter 11 procedure as designed in the Bankruptcy Code 1978 was often criticised for being time consuming, expensive and inefficient.[77] It was broadly accepted that the 'one-size-fits-all' approach to business reorganisation adopted in the 1978 Code has proven not so

---

[72] US Department of Justice, *Chapter 11 Trustee Handbook* (May 2004) <https://www.justice.gov/sites/default/files/ust/legacy/2011/07/13/Ch11Handbook-200405.pdf> accessed 30 January 2016, 55.

[73] S 1125(a)(2) US Bankruptcy Code.

[74] *Chapter 11 Trustee Handbook*, 56.

[75] *Ibid.*, 55.

[76] S 1125(b) US Bankruptcy Code.

[77] See Baird, 'The Uneasy Case for Corporate Reorganisations'. M Bradley and M Rosenzweig, 'The Untenable Case for Chapter 11' (1992) 101 *Yale Law*

successful and the design of Chapter 11 for big cases has caused unreasonable delay and burdensome costs in most cases.[78] To encourage more use of pre-packaged re-organisations under Chapter 11, the Bankruptcy Abuse Prevention and Consumer Protection Act 2005 (the BAPCPA 2005)[79] revised some of the key provisions of the Bankruptcy Code 1978.

Section 1125 of the Bankruptcy Code was revised by the BAPCPA 2005 to streamline the disclosure statement process and grant it more flexibility, dispensing with a disclosure statement if the plan itself contained adequate information. Section 408 of the Act 2005 also added a new subsection (g) to s 1125 which gave a party explicit statutory authority to solicit acceptances or rejections prior to a bankruptcy case being filed.[80] Furthermore, s 341 was revised by the BAPCPA 2005 to provide that, upon request of a party in interest and after notice and a hearing, the court may order a meeting of creditors or equity security holders not to be convened if the debtor has filed a plan for which acceptances have been solicited prior to commencement of the case. This is designed to prevent needless delays in the Chapter 11 pre-pack process, to minimise costs and to increase efficiency. In theory, the meeting is to provide creditors with an opportunity to examine the debtor's position and obtain important information. However, in the context of a pre-pack, the comprehensive requirement on information disclosure and pre-petition solicitations renders the s 341 meeting less meaningful. Moreover, there is more flexibility in the disclosure statement process brought by the amendment to s 1125 for small business cases. Section 431 of the BAPCPA 2005 expressly permits the court to conditionally approve a disclosure statement, and allows the debtor to solicit acceptances of the plan based upon such conditioned approval.

Although the pre-packed way of reorganisation under Chapter 11 appears to be more desirable, especially with the increased flexibility and

---

Journal 1043. MJ White, 'Does Chapter 11 Save Economically Inefficient Firms?' (1994) 72 *Washington University Law Quarterly* 1319.

[78] E Warren and JL Westbrook, 'Financial Characteristics of Businesses in Bankruptcy' (1999) 73 *American Bankruptcy Law Review* 499.

[79] Legislation passed on 20 April 2005.

[80] The provision permits that votes to accept or reject a plan of reorganisation may be solicited from a holder of a claim or interest before commencement of the cases if the votes are solicited in a manner complying with applicable non-bankruptcy law, for example the applicable registration and disclosure requirements under the relevant securities laws. 11 U.S.C. 1126(b) US Bankruptcy Code.

legislative endorsement lent to it, the reputation of a pre-packaged Chapter 11 reorganisation as a speedy and efficient process may be theoretical as it has not been frequently used in practice.[81] Its limited use may be attributed to the contingent nature of pre-petition solicitations. The essential condition for pre-petition solicitation to be recognised is compliance with applicable securities laws, including the nature of the disclosure made in connection with the solicitation and the procedures followed in making such solicitation. Invalidation of pre-petition solicitation will result in a re-solicitation conducted post-petition, which would be subject to s 1125(b) of the Bankruptcy Code, requiring the prior approval by the bankruptcy court of the disclosure statement used in such solicitation. This process can substantially lengthen the Chapter 11 case. In addition, the company is subject to further uncertainty as to the outcome of the re-solicitation.

CORPORATE RESCUE THROUGH PRE-PACKS – COMPARING US PRE-PACKAGED CHAPTER 11 REORGANISATION WITH UK PRE-PACKAGED ADMINISTRATION

As already mentioned, companies with limited financing options seeking to minimise the administrative costs associated with full-fledged statutory procedures are increasingly opting for pre-packaged bankruptcies in an effort to fast-track the process. There is a similar trend in the UK insolvency landscape, although the respective circumstances of fostering the new pre-packing practice are different. Nevertheless, due to the differences in the institutional arrangements governing their main rescue-oriented procedures in these two jurisdictions, the respective abilities of their existing legal insolvency regulation framework to adopt the changes and absorb the challenges brought by the pre-packing strategy differ substantially.

Primarily, although both countries believe that reorganisation law can be justified by the fact that assets used in a going concern are more valuable than those same assets sold for scrap, the procedural objectives

[81] See S Takagi, *Recent Developments of Restructuring Schemes and Practices in the US, the UK, Germany and France, Comparative Study* (International Insolvency Institute publication) <https://www.iiiglobal.org/sites/default/files/recentdevelopmentsfrestructuringschemesand_practiceskadomaecheck.pdf> 30 January 2016.

of their main rescue-oriented procedures do not see eye-to-eye as there are important discrepancies.

Chapter 11 of the US Bankruptcy Code aims at reorganisation and rehabilitation of the debtors, concerned mainly with promoting the survival of the corporation as a going concern, at least the maintenance of its core business.[82] This traditional use of Chapter 11 reorganisation is different conceptually from the UK Administration procedure which is a multi-faceted procedure.[83] Although rescuing the company as a going concern is set as the top priority, saving businesses rather than corporate shells as going-concerns through a sale of all or substantially all assets of the debtor to a new owner, or just liquidating their assets piecemeal when that operation can make creditors better off, are all encouraged in the UK Administration procedure.

US Chapter 11 as a Negotiation Forum

The US Chapter 11 is essentially designed as a bargaining-oriented procedure, providing a forum for the incumbent management to negotiate the terms and conditions of reorganisation with its creditors and other interested parties.[84] Therefore, the overriding procedural objective of a Chapter 11 case is to formulate and obtain confirmation on a reorganisation plan agreed between relevant parties. To achieve the goal, substantial rights are given to the company's incumbent management to continue running the business while a reorganisation plan is being constructed. Furthermore, the central goal of Chapter 11 rescues – to promote economically viable companies to recovery and maintain their business as a going concern – can be achieved through negotiations between relevant parties, even if the resulting arrangement reduces the proceeds available to creditors. Chapter 11 imposes no duty on

---

[82] It is said that the motive for introducing the Chapter 11 procedure was to increase the possibility that the company would emerge as a going concern from the reorganisation process. See J Franks and W Torous, 'Lessons from a Comparison of US and UK Insolvency Codes' (1992) 8 *Oxford Review of Economic Policy* 70, 75.

[83] N Martin, 'Common-Law Bankruptcy Systems: Similarities and Differences' (2003) 11 *American Bankruptcy Institute Law Review* 367, 396.

[84] McCormack, *Corporate Rescue Law – An Anglo-American Perspective*, 88.

management (or the court) to liquidate the company, even if the value obtained in liquidation is greater than the going-concern value.[85]

Of course, reorganisation negotiations are often steeped in uncertainty and success often hinges upon evaluation of risk and a willingness to accept that risk. The bargain-oriented nature of Chapter 11 reorganisation is necessarily designed with certain mechanisms to facilitate the debtor's negotiations for a successful outcome. A few carefully selected features of the Chapter 11 procedure that promote successful outcomes are examined below.

Unique mechanisms to facilitate company rescue efforts

(a) DIP by default to encourage early filing The DIP mechanism, together with granting management the exclusive privilege of proposing a reorganisation plan, was designed to 'incentivise' the debtor to file for Chapter 11 reorganisation at an early stage,[86] so they fear no loss of control.[87] Any possible delay in filing for reorganisation could prejudice the interests of the company and its investors and the right timing for achieving a successful reorganisation could be missed.[88]

Yet it is worth noting that empirical evidence challenges the assumption that it helps the debtor's managers to keep their position of control and their job during the reorganisation procedure and in the future, once the reorganisation is completed. According to Betker's study of 75 bankruptcy reorganisation cases which had their reorganisation plans confirmed during 1982 and 1990, only 25 per cent of the original CEOs who held office two years before default survived on emergence from bankruptcy.[89] Gilson, who studied 69 publicly held companies that filed for bankruptcy under Chapter 11, found that only 29 per cent of the original top managers of those companies survived over the four-year

[85] See Franks and Torous, 'Lessons from a Comparison of US and UK Insolvency Codes', 78.

[86] N Petrovski, 'The Bankruptcy Code, Section 1121: Exclusivity Reloaded' (2003) 11 *American Bankruptcy Institute Law Review* 451, 485. RL Weston, 'The Exclusivity Period in Section 1121: How Exclusive Is It?' (1990) 11 *Cardozo Law Review* 639, 650.

[87] KN Klee, 'A Brief Rejoinder to Professor LoPucki' (1995) 69 *American Bankruptcy Law Journal* 583, 586.

[88] Weston, 'The Exclusivity Period in Section 1121: How Exclusive Is It?', 651.

[89] BL Betker, 'Management's Incentives, Equity's Bargaining Power, and Deviations from Absolute Priority in Chapter 11' (1995) 68 *Journal of Business* 161, 174.

period starting two years before the date of bankruptcy filing.[90] If one assumes retaining their jobs is a high priority for managers, this empirical evidence may suggest that managers have relatively little power to keep their jobs during and especially after bankruptcy reorganisations. It is suggested that the reason for changing management is premised not only on business considerations but also on ethical norms dictating that someone must take the blame for the massive loss that leads to bankruptcy reorganisation.[91]

(b) The court's power to order a creditor 'cram-down' One of the challenges of the corporate rescue process is how to accommodate divergent classes of claims or interests and deal with their different incentives in risk taking. The negotiation-oriented process would be unlikely to go very far when dealing with a traditional, highly contentious Chapter 11 reorganisation, where complex, litigious disputes among hundreds of creditor groups with sharply divergent interests exist. To deal with the problem of holdout creditors, the court may grant, upon the proponent's requests, a 'cram-down' power over dissenting votes of impaired classes, in addition to a separation of the unimpaired classes that are conclusively presumed to accept the plan. This way the dissenting class is prevented from holding out, instead being forced to accept the plan. But it won't be easy. As said earlier, there are several statutory requirements in s 1129 of the Bankruptcy Code that must be satisfied before an opponent class can be crammed down.

(c) Priority of DIP financing One significant innovation of the US way of corporate rescue is the opportunity for a company that has filed for Chapter 11 protection to obtain DIP financing under s 364 of the Bankruptcy Reform Act of 1978. The ability to obtain financing is a critical element in the attempt to successfully reorganise a company as it may guarantee keeping its supply channels open and allowing the business to continue with less disruption, which will in turn provide confidence about the viability of the financial conditions of the company.

---

90 SC Gilson, 'Management Turnover and Financial Distress' (1989) 25 *Journal of Financial Economics* 241, 247.

91 LM LoPucki and WC Whitford, 'Corporate Governance in the Bankruptcy Reorganization of Large, Publicly Held Companies' (1993) 141 *University of Pennsylvania Law Review* 669, 694.

DIP loan proceeds may only be used as working capital and obtaining such financing is subject to formal court approval.[92]

Obtaining new funds is usually difficult for a financially troubled company, since the risk of increased indebtedness is high. The advantage to the lender of this post-petition financing mechanism under the US law is that this lending generally has 'superpriority' status in comparison to existing debts, which gives a compelling reason for potential lenders to engage in DIP loans.

Section 364 of the US Bankruptcy Code provides a set of complicated continuing financing provisions granting a progressive hierarchy of priorities to post-petition lenders. The security and seniority of the DIP financing is structured in 4 subsections. The subsections 364 (a) and 364(b) provide the DIP lender with the administrative expense priority status, which implies that the DIP lending is unsecured but enjoys the first priority along with other administrative claims such as professional fees and costs of administering the estate of the company with the class of unsecured loans. Section 364(a) provides the prospective lender an automatic administrative priority under s 503(b)(1) where the DIP has incurred unsecured debt in the ordinary course of business. If the credit extension is not in the ordinary course of business, the court, after notice and a hearing, may approve the new loan transaction under s 364(b). Although administrative priority is convenient, its status alone will not assure repayment where the total amount of administrative expenses exceeds the value of the estate's unencumbered assets; normal priority expense treatment for a Chapter 11 loan will entitle the lender only to a *pro rata* share of those assets.[93]

Subsection 364(c) provides: a super-administrative priority over all other administrative claims under s 503(b) and s 507(b); a lien on unencumbered property of the estate;[94] and a junior lien on property of the assets that is subject to a pre-petition lien.[95] If all estate property is encumbered, the repayment to super-priority debt will become hopeless in fact. The liens in this category do not interfere with the existing

---

[92] To obtain DIP financing the debtor needs to make a motion for authorisation to obtain the loan pursuant to the Federal Rule of Bankruptcy Procedure 4001(c)(1). The motion is usually filed upon or shortly after the commencement of Chapter 11 and is required to be served upon any official committee and upon the United States trustee.

[93] JU Schorer and DS Curry, 'Chapter 11 Lending: An Overview of the Process' (1991) 47 *Secured Lender* 10, 15–16.

[94] S 364(c)(2) US Bankruptcy Code.

[95] S 364(c)(3) US Bankruptcy Code.

priority ordering of the debtor's assets and the new lenders' secured property will survive dismissal or conversion of the case into Chapter 7, if the Chapter 11 case fails. The court must be convinced of: (1) the impossibility of obtaining prospective loans from merely granting administrative priority or superpriority; (2) the compelling necessity for the funds; (3) the desirable purpose the funds will pursue; and (4) the conclusion that the proposed financing is in the best interests of creditors; and then approve the liens.[96]

Subsection 364(d) provides the highest level of security, allowing a senior or equal lien on the property of the estate that is already subject to a prior lien. Such a lien is referred to as a 'priming lien' and can only be approved after stringent conditions are met. In order to grant this sort of first lien that will subordinate prior lienholders, the court must be convinced that the DIP is unable to obtain credit under s 364(c) and that the subordinated lienholder's interests are adequately protected in accordance to s 361.[97] Despite the stringent conditions, the majority of DIP financing is made under subs. 364 (c) or (d) in practice.[98]

UK Administration: A Conservative Approach to Corporate Rescue

The US bankruptcy law has based its governance structure on a regulatory system with much intervention from the bankruptcy courts; in contrast, the English procedure is built on a foundation of a long tradition of the use of independent, expert professionals. Unlike the US system

---

[96] L Qi, 'Availability of Continuing Financing in Corporate Reorganisations: the UK and US perspective' (2008) 29 *Company Lawyer* 162, 163.

[97] It is difficult to achieve this 'adequate protection' as establishing an equal security or a superior security on the same collateral reduces the security level of the pre-petition lienholders. In practice, courts rely on the value of the collateral to see if there is adequate protection for the pre-petition lienholders. For instance, *In Re Snowshoe*, 789 F.2d 1085, 1090 (4th Cir. 1986) the appellate court approved the district court's permission to allow a trustee to obtain additional credit of $2 million by granting senior lien on property of the estate pursuant to 364(d) over an objection of the existing lienholder based on the findings that the objecting creditor was owed a loan between $13 and $14 million dollars and the estate was worth over $19 million dollars. Also, in *Anchor Sav. Bank FSB v Sky Valley, Inc.*, 99 B.R. 117, 119 (N.D. Ga. 1989), the court authorised a superpriority financing of approximately $425,000 over a property worth $8 million which was on collateral to secure a loan of $3 million. See more on JJ White, 'Death and Resurrection of Secured Credit' (2004) 12 *American Bankruptcy Institute Law Review* 139.

[98] S Dahiya, *et al.*, 'Debtor-in-Possession Financing and Bankruptcy Resolution: Empirical Evidence' (2003) 69 *Journal of Financial Economics* 259, 266.

where the incumbent management is allowed to remain in office as a debtor-in-possession, the UK legislation involves the employment of a trustee as an independent officer of the court who replaces management in office to take control of the business, affairs and assets of the debtor, and to propose and effectuate a reorganisation plan. Not only does the law give extensive discretion to administrators and envisages that the administrator is suitably qualified and once appointed, free to act without court involvement except where directions are sought, but the English judiciary is generally unwilling to be put into a position where it would have to make commercial decisions on the administrator's proposals. This is quite different to the US law where the bankruptcy courts play a central role in bankruptcy proceedings, closely supervising all aspects of corporate bankruptcy.

The UK administration procedure is multi-faceted. This is manifested by its provision for a hierarchical list of possible objectives for the procedure. The UK administration procedure is, in general, about saving the business, rather than the company shell. The overriding objective of the UK insolvency law, that is, the maximisation of the value of the company and its assets and the repayment of creditor's claims, prevails. Furthermore, notwithstanding the UK government's goal to enhance the prospects of a successful company rescue, administrators have not been provided with any effective apparatus to achieve it. It is fair to say that in comparison to the US reorganisation law, the UK administration proceedings have ambiguous effects in promoting risk taking in corporate rescues, and therefore the operation is still a very conservative one.

The Pre-packed Approach: Opportunity or Challenge?

Pre-packs in corporate rescue are used as an innovative approach to overcome the holdout problem in informal workouts by entering a formal procedure to solidify the outcome of private negotiations. It allows the company to steer the process with a clearly prearranged exit strategy that will minimise the time it will need to be in the formal proceedings. Although both are tagged as pre-packs, the underlying issues with the UK pre-packs and the US pre-packs are significantly different. Compared with the UK pre-pack administration, the US pre-packed Chapter 11 reorganisation is more regulated and it retains most of the safeguard mechanisms built to protect the procedural fairness of a standard Chapter 11 reorganisation, e.g. impaired creditors' voting rights, and court sanctions on significant decision-making in the process.

Compared with the 'light touch' approach of the UK courts in the administration procedure, the US's heavy reliance on judiciary supervision appears to be an advantage in regulating the pre-formal stage of pre-packs. Because of the existence of the judicial approval mechanism under Chapter 11, the US pre-packaged Chapter 11 regulates the pre-formal stage by imposing additional restraints on pre-petition solicitation, voting with information disclosure requirements and giving interested parties the chance to be heard prior to its implementation. This warrants creditors having a place in the negotiation table and therefore performing a certain supervisory role. Furthermore, a pre-packaged plan of reorganisation follows the same basic voting procedures of a conventional Chapter 11 case. If the disclosure was adequate, to be binding on all creditors, the court must be satisfied that the plan has been accepted by the required majority of creditors, or that it is fair and equitable and does not unfairly discriminate.[99]

In contrast, in the context of UK pre-packaged administration, the pre-formal stage that is the most worrisome is left unregulated. The pre-pack strategy, perhaps unintentionally, places the whole matter exclusively in the hands of inside players and precludes the junior creditors from any substantial input into the rescue plan. This, coupled with the fears of the occasional phenomena of administrators' self-serving alliance with well-placed creditors or managers, raises concerns that, in the absence of a judicial approval mechanism, due to the pre-determination nature of pre-packs, creditors are rendered unable to challenge the sale before it is too late.

CONCLUSION

Companies with limited financing options seeking to minimise the administrative costs associated with the full-fledged Chapter 11 procedure are increasingly opting for pre-packaged bankruptcies in order to fast-track the process. A pre-packaged Chapter 11 reorganisation speeds up the process by allowing pre-petition solicitation to be recognised if it has been conducted in accordance with the principles of the law and has fulfilled the legal requirements of information disclosure. The most essential work left then, upon filing of the petition, is for the court to

---

99 S Phillips and A Kaczor, 'The Benefits of UK-style Pre-packs and Comparisons with Other Jurisdictions' (2010) 7 *International Corporate Rescue* 328.

examine the adequacy of the disclosure that is designed to allow parties voting on the plan to make an informed judgment.

Although both are tagged as pre-packs, the underlying issues with the UK pre-packs and the US pre-packs are significantly different. The US pre-packed Chapter 11 reorganisation is more regulated, retaining most of the safeguard mechanisms built to protect the procedural fairness under a standard Chapter 11 reorganisation. In contrast, in the UK pre-pack context, the original device for procedural inclusiveness and decision-making democracy in a standard administration procedure, notably creditors' voting on the pre-pack arrangements, is often readily circumvented. Also, as mentioned earlier, compared to the 'light touch' approach of the UK courts in the administration procedure, the US's heavy reliance on judiciary supervision appears to be an advantage in regulating the pre-formal stage of pre-packs. Because of the existence of the judicial approval mechanism under Chapter 11, the pre-packaged arrangements can remain subject to the same set of requirements with those non-pre-packed ones, whereas the pre-packaged arrangements in the UK context are more capable of establishing a single way forward and building a strong but self-serving case for whatever has been decided with a reduced level of inclusiveness, raising controversy on its procedural fairness, if not on the fairness of the outcomes.

6. Pre-plan sales under s 363(b) in Chapter 11

INTRODUCTION

Reorganisation through either the traditional Chapter 11 or its pre-packed path is not the best way to deal with distressed companies in practice. Value realisation through business sales is a fast, cheaper solution to deal with a company in financial difficulties, and, unsurprisingly, it is often the preferred route to realise value. This is especially true in times of crisis. The credit crunch did not only mean more bankruptcies in the USA, but it also pushed a larger number of financially troubled companies into asset sales and liquidations, because they were unable to raise the debtor in possession (DIP) financing that troubled companies need to try to re-emerge from bankruptcy. So a large number of undertakings had to sell assets on a more expedited basis. In this context, section 363(b) pre-plan sales, where all or a substantial part of the debtor company's assets are sold prior to the confirmation of the reorganisation plan, have become even more useful and customary in recent years and they may well replace the main route for Chapter 11 reorganisation plans. The recent use of s 363 pre-plan sales as a substitute for the traditional Chapter 11 reorganisation of large global companies like *General Motors*, *Chrysler* and *Lehman Brothers*[1] reflects such a dramatic trend in the bankruptcy arena.

This chapter looks into s 363(b) pre-plan sales in a Chapter 11 reorganisation procedure, the other 'pre-packing route' in bankruptcy proceedings in the US. It is divided into five parts, including the present introduction. Part 2 looks at the workings of s 363 pre-plan sales under Chapter 11, and explains its advantages for business sales in comparison with business sales under a reorganisation plan. It also discusses the

[1] See *In Re Lehman Bros. Holdings Inc.* 415 B.R. 77 (S.D.N.Y. 2009) affirming the sale made under s 363. Following the 2008 collapse of *Lehman Brothers*, and almost immediately after Lehman filed for bankruptcy, its European investment banking and capital markets operations were sold to *Barclays Capital, Inc.*

scepticism and caution that accompanies this accelerated sale process, which mostly relates to concerns about the debtor taking advantage of the very different and arguably lower standard of creditor protection of s 363 than that applied to in-plan sales. Section 363 pre-plan sales can deprive creditors of any say in the allocation of the debtor's assets. Part 3 examines the standards the US courts apply when determining whether a particular s 363 pre-plan sale is permissible, and inquires whether the judicial scrutiny is adequate and effective in striking a balance between authorising s 363 sales where appropriate and addressing the scepticism of potential abuse when parties evade Chapter 11's safeguards embedded in the plan confirmation process. Part 4 refers to the recent proposals of addressing the issues highlighted by the ABI Commission to Study the Reform of Chapter 11. Part 5 compares the practical and recurring issues surrounding s 363(b) pre-plan sales in the US with those in the UK pre-pack context. It specifically examines, critically evaluates and contrasts the different approaches within their respective legislative frameworks in ameliorating the concerns of abuse raised in the accelerated sale process in insolvency.

ASSET SALES UNDER CHAPTER 11 AND S 363(B) PRE-PLAN SALES

In reorganisations, asset sales can take place either prior to any bankruptcy petition or during the bankruptcy procedure. In the case of a Chapter 11 reorganisation, the US Bankruptcy Code provides two separate and distinct sets of provisions under which a Chapter 11 DIP or trustee may sell property free and clear of claims or interests.[2] Section 363 of the Bankruptcy Code governs sales within or outside the ordinary course of business of the debtor company; in particular, subsection 363(b) governs sales outside and prior to a reorganisation plan. Section 1123(a)(5)(D) governs sales made as part of a plan of reorganisation (hereafter referred as in-plan sales).[3] As sales pursuant to s 1123(a)(5)(D)

---

[2] Nevertheless, sales outside bankruptcy can be challenged under state law as fraudulent conveyances when creditors think the sale price is inadequate. The risks of fraudulent conveyance are eliminated when the asset sale is conducted under bankruptcy court supervision, since s 548 of the US Bankruptcy Code, which grants the trustee the power to avoid fraudulent transfers, applies only to pre-petition transfers.

[3] Pursuant to s 11232(a)(5)(D) US Bankruptcy Code, a company may implement a reorganisation plan through the 'sale of all or any part of the

are accomplished in the context of a plan, they require a debtor to satisfy plan confirmation requirements, including approval of a disclosure statement and creditor acceptance by the voting of applicable classes of creditors and a good faith requirement.

Section 363 grants the trustee or DIP the right to use, sell or lease property of the estate under certain conditions. Property of the estate may be sold free and clear of existing claims.[4] Sales are allowed in two situations under this section: one is for sales within the ordinary course of business of the debtor governed by s 363(a), without prior notice to creditors or an opportunity for a hearing;[5] and the other is for sales outside the ordinary course of business governed by s 363(b), subject to a certain level of scrutiny from creditors and the bankruptcy court.[6] It should be noted that although courts frequently use the auction process as a means to ensure the best and highest price in asset sales, the language of s 363 and of the bankruptcy rules do not expressly require an auction and public sale process. Therefore, a s 363 sale can be undertaken by means of a public auction or through a private sale, depending on whichever vehicle is most likely to result in the highest and best offer for the assets in question.

Procedural Requirements for s 363(b) Pre-plan Sales

Section 363(b) does not automatically authorise the sale of all or substantially all assets of the debtor's estate in a Chapter 11 reorganisation. However, the courts have acknowledged that this constraint is subject to exceptions, especially where the particularity of the case concerned demonstrates the necessity of the sale to serve the best

---

property of the estate'. Further, s 1123(b)(4) provides that 'a plan may ... provide for the sale of all or substantially all of the property of the estate, and the distribution of the proceeds of such sale among holders of claims or interests'.

4 S 363(f) US Bankruptcy Code.

5 S 363(c)(1) US Bankruptcy Code.

6 There is no clear test for determining when a sale is in the 'ordinary course of business'. However, two tests have been developed under the case law: the 'vertical dimension' test under which the court focuses on the specific transaction and determines whether it is of a type that the parties in interest reasonably expect the debtor to conduct in the ordinary course of its business and the 'horizontal dimension' test, where the court focuses on a comparison between the debtor's business and businesses in the same industry to determine whether the proposed transaction is in the ordinary course of such business. See SD Consins, 'Chapter 11 Asset Sales' (2002) 27 *Delaware Journal of Corporate Law* 835, 841–2.

interests of the estate. It is further acknowledged that imposing strict rules upon authorisation of asset sales may prohibit parties from acting quickly, resulting in an adverse impact on the value of the assets concerned.[7]

Where a s 363(b) sale encompasses the sale of all or substantially all of a debtor's assets, it must comply with the notice and hearing requirements of s 363(b) of the Bankruptcy Code and of relevant rules under the Federal Rule of Bankruptcy Procedure (hereafter 'the Bankruptcy Rules'). Those requirements are intended to provide creditors with an opportunity to examine the price and other terms of the proposed sale and afford parties sufficient time to object, and where necessary, prepare for a hearing on the propriety of the sale.

The Bankruptcy Rule 2002(a)(2) requires that notice is given to all interested parties before the proposed sale of assets outside the ordinary course of business. Such notice has to be served, at a minimum, 21 days before the sale in question, unless the court reduces the notice period.[8] Courts generally permit debtors to shorten the notice time based on the exigencies of a particular case provided that the reduced notice period is sufficient to ensure that all interested buyers have an opportunity to bid for the assets.[9] Individual creditors, creditor committees, United States Trustees, as well as potential buyers, can object to proposed sales and bidding procedures under the Bankruptcy Rule 6004(b). Once before the court, the creditor, or other eligible objectors, may present their arguments, and the court has the opportunity to decide whether the transaction is permissible.

---

[7] The Second Circuit in *In re Lionel Corp.* 722 F.2d 1063 (2d Cir. 1983) noted that 'the bankruptcy machinery should not straightjacket the bankruptcy judge so as to prevent him from doing what is best for the estate'. It was acknowledged that the likelihood of maximising value for one debtor may necessitate a different method for another. Therefore, the court affirmed that 'to further the purposes of Chapter 11 reorganisation, a bankruptcy judge must have substantial freedom to tailor his order to meet differing circumstances'. See 772 F.2d at 1069.

[8] The Bankruptcy Rule 2002 also provides that notice must include 'the time and place of any public sale, the terms and conditions of any private sale and the time fixed for filing objections'.

[9] RM Fishman and GE Gouveia, 'What's Driving Section 363 Sales after Chrysler and General Motors?' (2010) 19 *Norton Journal of Bankruptcy Law and Practice* 351, 355.

Beyond the Federal Rules, there are local bankruptcy rules made by district courts providing court-specific procedural rules governing proposed s 363 sales to help streamline procedures.[10] These local rules often provide greater details about such issues as to: who must receive notice; how long before a hearing notice must be given; how objections can be made; how public versus private sales will be conducted; and which connections, relationships and compensation must be disclosed, etc.[11] Nevertheless, those court-specific procedural rules are not uniform across jurisdictions.

Advantages of s 363(b) Pre-plan Sales and a Few Concerns

Not surprisingly, in practice, s 363 sales are the preferred method of selling assets in the context of Chapter 11 bankruptcy cases.[12] Compared to asset sales as part of a confirmed Chapter 11 reorganisation plan, s 363(b) pre-plan sales are much more straightforward, and are therefore quicker and cheaper, and less risky and uncertain, as these sales bypass the potentially cumbersome process of classification of creditors into appropriate classes and obtaining the consent of creditors.

Like in-plan sales under s 1123 via s 1141(c), s 363(b) transactions are 'free and clear of all claims and interests of creditors' via s 363(f). But where transactions under s 1123 are subject to a constellation of requirements prior to their approval, a s 363(b) transaction only requires 'notice and a hearing' before the bankruptcy judge, allowing it to circumvent the disclosure and equity requirements that are, otherwise, necessary for the approval of a reorganisation plan. After the requisite notice is served and the hearing has been granted, the purchase agreements of pre-plan sales face only court approval, rather than the more time-consuming confirmation by several classes of creditors. This offers the critical benefit of speed for the s 363(b) pre-plan sale process. In this case, sales are

---

[10] Each district court acting by a simple majority of its district judges may make and amend rules governing practice and procedure in all cases and proceedings within the district courts' bankruptcy jurisdiction subject to relevant Acts of Congress.

[11] JA Wilkerson, 'Defending the Current State of Section 363 Sales' (2012) 86 *American Bankruptcy Law Journal* 591, 597. For a dated but informative survey of the court rules that go beyond the Federal rules of Bankruptcy Procedure, see GW Kuney, 'Let's Make It Official: Adding an Explicit Pre-plan Sale Process as an Alternative Exit from Bankruptcy' (2004) 40 *Houston Law Review* 1265.

[12] Fishman and Gouveia, 'What's Driving Section 363 Sales after Chrysler and General Motors?', 352.

typically completed within two to three months,[13] whereas creditor confirmation of a reorganisation plan may span several years. For example, the sales of GM and Chrysler businesses under s 363 took forty and forty-two days respectively, which proves this point.[14]

Nevertheless, conducting a s 363 sale prior to the Chapter 11 plan confirmation often gives rise to concerns that the accelerated route to asset sales grants the debtor disproportionate control over the sale and therefore ample opportunity to engage in questionable transactions and unfair dealings due to the absence of creditor confirmation. Confirmation of the plan is a relatively democratic process, requiring a debtor to propose a reorganisation plan and work with creditors to obtain their approval, hence providing a much greater level of participation and protection to creditors than a s 363(b) sale does.

First of all, in-plan sales are subject to the s 1125 requirement of disclosure statements describing the terms and conditions of the plan to enable claimholders to make a meaningful evaluation on the proposed sales. In a s 363(b) sale, there is a lack of an equivalent adequate disclosure requirement and it is substituted with an obligatory notice and hearing. However, it should be noted that a s 363(b) pre-plan sale may be approved by a bankruptcy court without an actual hearing if the notice is given properly and if such a hearing is not requested in a timely manner by a party in interest or if there is insufficient time to hold a hearing before the sale is effected.[15] Moreover, though proper notice should be given to creditors, it is doubtful that the claimholders would be supplied with sufficient knowledge about how the s 363(b) transaction in question would impact on their claims given that all essential preparations for the sale of business are conducted within a rather limited timeframe.

Furthermore, in an in-plan business sale, the plan, even if approved by claimholders' votes, still needs to be confirmed by a bankruptcy court and the court can only do so if the plan meets the comprehensive requirements of subsection s 1129(a) of the Code. This requires, among other things, that the sale is in the best interests of creditors and is accepted by all impaired classes of creditors, or that it has the support of at least one class of impaired creditors and is fair and equitable. On the other hand, while s 363(b) sales also require court approval, the statute itself provides no guidance as to the standards that courts are to apply for

---

[13] RE Steinberg, 'Seven Deadly Sins in S 363 Sales' (2005) 24 *American Bankruptcy Institute Journal* 22, 22.

[14] *General Motors* filed its Chapter 11 petition on 1 June 2009 and the sale of its assets under s 363(b) was approved on 5 July 2009.

[15] S 102(1)(b) US Bankruptcy Code.

approving or disapproving the sale, notwithstanding the rigorous requirements during Chapter 11 plan confirmation. The courts, in exercising discretionary power, have to form their own views while trying to balance the authority to sell all or substantially all of a debtor's assets against the potential for abuse when parties evade Chapter 11 safeguards.

To illuminate this contrast further, the next section looks into those guidelines established under case law on how to approach s 363(b) transactions. It then considers whether those guidelines are adequate and effective in helping the courts to strike a balance between sanctioning s 363 sales and preserving the fundamental Chapter 11 protections embedded in the reorganisation plan confirmation process to address the scepticism that often surrounds s 363(b) sales.

JUDICIAL SCRUTINY OF S 363(B) PRE-PLAN SALES

Despite the aforementioned silence in the statute on the standards that courts should apply for approving or disapproving a 363 sale, the provision itself contains nothing that could limit a judge's broad authority under s 105(a), which allows the court to:

> issue any order, process or judgment that is necessary or appropriate to carry out the provisions of this title. No provision of this title ... shall be construed to preclude the court from, *sua sponte*, taking any action or making any determination necessary or appropriate to enforce or implement court orders or rules, or to prevent an abuse of process.

Certain guidelines have been established in case law on how to approach s 363(b) transactions, although no court offers fixed or more concrete standards with which they can analyse these transactions, and neither has the Supreme Court shown an intention to provide lower courts with a concrete set of standards. Said guidelines informing judicial scrutiny mainly focus on two key issues: (1) on the sound business justification analysis and, (2) on the sub rosa prohibition analysis.

The *Lionel* Sound Business Justification Standard

The prevalent standard for court approval of s 363(b) sales is the sound business justification standard (also known as 'sound business purpose' or 'business judgment'), articulated by the Second Circuit in *In re Lionel*

Corp.[16] In its seminal decision, the court recognised the danger of 'swallowing up Chapter 11's safeguards' through the disposition of an important asset under s 363(b) without a sound business justification. Thus, the court held that there must be 'a good business reason' for approval of the sale of a substantial asset by the debtor outside a reorganisation plan.[17] The Second Circuit in this case instructed bankruptcy judges to consider the following factors for determining the propriety of a proposed sale of a debtor's assets under s 363(b):

- the proportionate value of the asset to the estate as a whole;
- the amount of time that has elapsed since the filing of the petition;
- the likelihood that a plan of reorganisation will be proposed and confirmed in the near future;
- the effect of the proposed sale on a future plan of reorganisation;
- the proceeds to be obtained from the dispositions vis-à-vis any appraisals of the property;
- which of the s 363 alternatives, use, sale, or lease, the proposal envisions; and
- most importantly, perhaps, whether the asset is increasing or decreasing in value.[18]

---

[16] *Committee of Equity Security Holders v Lionel Corp.* (*In re Lionel Corp.*) 772 F.2d 1063 (2d Cir. 1983). In this case, the debtor proposed to sell its most significant asset – 82 per cent of the common stock of its solvent, profitable, publicly traded subsidiary corporation. Four days after proposing the sale, the debtor filed a plan of reorganisation that was conditioned on the pre-confirmation sale and the distribution of the sale proceeds to creditors. The bankruptcy court approved the sale prior to plan confirmation based primarily on the insistence of the creditors' committee and the court's perception that failure to approve the sale would delay reorganisation for at least one year.

[17] The Second Circuit in determining whether to affirm the sale's authorisation reasoned that 'there must be some articulated business justification, other than appeasement of major creditors, for using, selling or leasing property out of the ordinary course of business before the bankruptcy judge may order such disposition under section 363(b)'. The court held that The *Lionel* creditors' committee on the sale in this case did not constitute a sufficient business justification because (1) as a matter of fact, there was no evidence that the sale could not be completed pursuant to a plan at the same price and (2) as a matter of law, approval of the sale at the behest of the creditors' committee ignored the equity interests required to be weighted and considered under Chapter 11. See 722 F.2d 1063, at 1070–71.

[18] 772 F.2d 1063 at 1071.

As suggested by the Second Circuit, the last factor, namely the fluctuation of the value of the asset, was the determining criterion in establishing that there was no good business justification for the sale in this case because it was considered that the common stock that was the subject of the sale was not falling in value.[19] Under this 'change of value' test, judges can form their decisions according to the unique circumstances surrounding each debtor's case, in order to determine how to satisfy the objectives of bankruptcy law. Where there is not sufficient evidence to suggest an urgent need to sell assets that are quickly decreasing in value, courts may conclude that it is in the best interests of the estate to delay the sale until confirmation of the reorganisation plan.[20]

It is clear in the original guidelines that there was an emphasis on the standard of strict emergency and perishable goods to justify the necessity of a sale. An example of such an urgent need to sell can be found in the case *In re Baldwin United Corp*,[21] where the court considered that the sale of partnership interest constituting 40 per cent of debtor's assets articulated a sound business justification. It acknowledged that the nature of such interest would, if not sold promptly, only impede reorganisation and would lose value as an asset in the long term.[22]

The Sub Rosa Doctrine

The sale cannot be a sub rosa[23] plan of reorganisation, whereby a transaction or agreement commits such a substantial part of the debtor's assets that it would de facto predetermine the terms of a reorganisation plan sale, dictate the terms of a plan or otherwise restructure creditors' rights.[24] In other words, it would be a sub rosa plan in the way that the size of a pie to be shared by stakeholders may be fixed in

---

19 772 F.2d at 1071–2.

20 J Uziel, 'Section 363(b) Restructuring Meets the Sound Business Purpose Test with Bite: An Opportunity to Rebalance the Competing Interests of Bankruptcy Law' (2011) 159 *University of Pennsylvania Law Review* 1189, 1202.

21 *In re Baldwin United Corp.*, 43 B.R. 888 (Bankr. S.D. Ohio 1984).

22 43 B.R. 888 at 905–6.

23 The Latin phrase *sub rosa* here means 'confidential, secret, not for publication'.

24 'The debtor and the bankruptcy court should not be able to short-circuit the recruitments of Chapter 11 for confirmation of a reorganisation plan by establishing the terms of the plan sub rosa in connection with a sale of assets.' See *Pension Benefit Guar. Corp. v Braniff Airways, Inc.* (*In re Braniff Airways, Inc.*), 700 F.2d 935 at 940 (5th Cir. 1983).

advance, without the drafting and voting procedures of the plan in place. The rationale is that the fast-paced route side-steps creditor protections in Chapter 11.[25] If the sale agreement does determine core s 1129 features, it can do so only if the court fashions a makeshift safeguard – a substitute that is overall consistent with what is mandated by s 1129.[26]

The reach of this restriction was exemplified by the case *In re Braniff Airways, Inc.*[27] In this influential case on s 363 sub rosa plans, the Fifth Circuit of the US Court of Appeal found that a proposed sale was impermissible because it dictated the terms of any future reorganisation plan.[28] In this case, the debtor, a well-known commercial airline, sought to sell nearly all of its assets, including airplanes, terminal leases and landing slots, to another airline in exchange for travel scrip, unsecured notes and profit-sharing in the new airline. The terms of the sale set restrictions of the use of the travel scrip,[29] and also dictated that secured creditors must vote their deficiency claim in favour of any proposed plan that the unsecured creditors' committee supported. Further, it was required that the debtor and its officers, directors and secured creditors were to receive a release of all claims by all parties.[30]

The Fifth Circuit Court of Appeals, in reviewing the approval of the sale by the district court and the bankruptcy court, held that the transaction could not be authorise under s 363(b). The court identified three specific factors on which it premised its decision: (1) the proposed transaction and restrictions it attached 'had the practical effect of

---

[25] S Takagi, 'Recent Developments of Restructuring Schemes and Practices in the US, the UK, Germany and France' (2011) Eleventh Annual International Insolvency Conference <http://www.iiiglobal.org/sites/default/files/media/36 Recent_Developments_of_Restructuring_Schemes_Shinjiro_Takagi.PDF> accessed 30 July 2015.

[26] MJ Roe and DA Skeel, 'Assessing the Chrysler Bankruptcy' (2010) 108 *Michigan Law Review* 727, 736.

[27] *Pension Benefit Guar. Corp. v Braniff Airways, Inc.* (*In re Braniff Airways, Inc.*), 700 F.2d 935 (5th Cir. 1983).

[28] The proposed sale provided for the release of claims by all parties against the debtor, its secured creditor and its officers and directors and would have required the secured creditors to vote a portion of their deficiency claim in favour of any future reorganisation plan approved by the unsecured creditors' committee. See 700 F.2d at 940.

[29] It was required that the travel scrip be used in the debtor's reorganisation, and the scrip could only be issued to former employees, shareholders or, to a much lesser extent, unsecured creditors. 700 F.2d 935 at 939.

[30] 700 F.2d 935 at 939–40.

dictating some of the terms of any future reorganisation plan';[31] (2) it prevented creditors from exercising their right to vote on the plan as contemplated by Chapter 11; and (3) it released all claims against the debtor, therefore altering creditor rights.[32]

The *Branniff* case involved a rather disruptive transaction with some distinct factors. Although the terms or effect of a pre-confirmation transaction may threaten to subvert the protections of Chapter 11, it should be noted that the sale of all or substantially all of a debtor's assets via s 363(b) does not in itself dictate the terms of a subsequent plan. As the Second Circuit in the *Lionel* case pointed out:

> Every sale under s 363(b) does not automatically short-circuit or side-step Chapter 11, nor are these two statutory provisions to be read as mutually exclusive.[33] The bottom line here is whether the terms of the sale constitute an attempt by the debtor to circumvent the distribution scheme of the Bankruptcy Code. In other words, whether the terms allocate and/or distribute the sale proceeds among creditors and equity holders contrary to the Code's priority scheme.[34]

Three years after the *Branniff* case, the Fifth Circuit revisited the sub rosa question in *In re Continental Air Lines, Inc.*[35] and refined the criteria employed by the courts when judging whether a s 363(b) sale is a sub rosa plan of reorganisation. On appeal, the Fifth Circuit affirmed the decision of the bankruptcy court and of the district court, and found that the debtor had adequate business justification for entering into the lease agreement. The Fifth Circuit reasoned:

> When an objector to a proposed transaction under s 363(b) claims that it is being denied certain protection because approval is sought pursuant to s 363(b) instead of as part of a recrganisation plan, the objector must specify

[31] 700 F.2d 935 at 940.

[32] *Ibid.*

[33] 722 F.2d at 1071.

[34] See *In re Trans World Airlines, Inc.*, 2001 WL 1820326 at 11 (Bankr. D Del 2 April 2001). An example can be the case *In re Iridium Operating LLC*, 478 F.3d 452 (2d Cir. 2007), where the Second Circuit held that a settlement in the course of bankruptcy proceedings was inappropriate because it distributed assets to prepetition creditors as part of the agreement, and the settlement allowed the negotiating parties to sidestep the fair and equitable standard as well as the absolute priority rule of the bankruptcy plan confirmations. See 478 F.3d 453 at 462–5.

[35] *Institutional Creditors of Continental Air Lines, Inc. v Continental Air Lines, Inc.* (*In re Continental Air Lines, Inc.*) 780 F.2d 1223 (5th Cir. 1986).

> exactly what protection is being denied. If the court concludes that there has in actuality been such a denial, it may then consider fashioning appropriate protective measures modeled on those which would attend a reorganisation plan.[36]

Clearly, the Fifth Circuit in its holding in *Continental* provided a refined method for approaching a sub rosa objection: (1) it placed the burden on the objecting party to identify the actual protection that would be lost if the court approved the transaction; (2) where there is some actual concern that creditors may not be treated fairly, the court is permitted to construct a remedy that provides protection to parties in interest without wholly denying the proposed transaction.[37] Therefore, unless the transaction is, in effect, a de facto plan, the judge is allowed to give a sub rosa objection ample consideration by creating a remedy that maintains creditors' rights. Additionally, the Fifth Circuit also made it clear that a transaction that cannot be approved as part of a plan should not be approved outside a plan.[38]

RECENT REFINEMENT OF JUDICIAL STANDARDS IN APPROVING S 363 PRE-PLAN SALES

Financially distressed companies have been increasingly looking to s 363(b) for a faster, less burdensome and cheaper resolution to their financial ailments since the Second Circuit set forth its seminal decision in *Lionel* in 1983. The increasing popularity of sales under s 363(b) in the bankruptcy landscape in recent years was noted by Judge Steen in *In re Gulf Coast Oil Corp.*:[39]

> Unprecedented liquidity in the capital markets, investment strategies that include significant claims trading in large case, alleged 'loan to own' strategies, active participation in bankruptcy cases by hedge funds and other non-bank lending entities, and venue selection based on a court's perceived propensity to approve §363(b) sales without requiring satisfaction of Chapter

---

[36] 780 F.2d at 1228.

[37] CA Sloane, 'The Sub Rosa Plan of Reorganisation: Side-stepping Creditor Protections in Chapter 11' (1999) 16 *Bankruptcy Development Journal* 37, 49–50.

[38] *Ibid.*, 49. 'The bankruptcy court may have lacked statutory authority to authorise the leases if the [objectors] could have defeated a plan of reorganisation containing the leases or may have had to condition certain terms of any lease.' See 780 F.2d at 1228.

[39] *In re Gulf Coast Oil Corp.*, 404 B.R. 407 (Bankr. S.D. Tex. 2009).

> 11 confirmation requirements have altered the landscape of Chapter 11 in large cases. While these factors have initially appeared in the very large cases, the practice in smaller cases has followed the lead of the larger cases … the result has been a huge increase in motions to sell substantial parts (or all) of the estate under s 363(b) prior to plan confirmation.[40]

Nevertheless, given the fact that no court has offered any fixed standards on ascertaining a proper s 363(b) transaction, there has been increasing concern as regards the broad and variable applications of the business justification standard behind the increased number of sale approvals.

Arguably, these cases have stretched the limits of the original *Lionel* sound business justification standard. Under the original standard, there was a clear emphasis on strict emergency and perishable goods to restrict debtor's wider use of s 363 assets sales. However, recently there has been a movement away from the emergency and cause restriction toward adopting more liberal standards for approving s 363 sales, as evidenced in the Second Circuit's recent revisit of the s 363 pre-plan sale issue in *In re Chrysler LLC*.[41]

The Problematic Approach of *In re Chrysler* and *General Motors*

The Second Circuit in *In re Chrysler LLC* applied the *Lionel* business justification standard in approving the sale of substantially all of the assets of *Chrysler LLC* and its subsidiaries, and upheld the bankruptcy court's approval of the sale of the company to *Fiat* over the objections of certain creditors. Unlike the facts in *Lionel*, the *Chrysler* bankruptcy involved all of *Chrysler*'s assets. The Second Circuit held that the proposed sale of *Chrysler* assets under s 363(b) met the *Lionel* business justification standard threshold for four reasons. (1) unlike the sale in *Lionel*, which had multiple bidders involved, *Fiat* was the sole bidder for *Chrysler*'s stock. (2) the potential commercial benefits existing between Chrysler and Fiat integration must be taken into account. (3) the transaction was time-sensitive and it demanded a quick sale. (4) failure of the sale would have undermined *Chrysler*'s reorganisation, which would have led to the Chapter 11 plan being converted to a Chapter 7

---

[40] 404 B.R. 407 at 415–19.

[41] *Ind. State Police Pension Trust v Chrysler LLC* (*In re Chrysler LLC*), 405 B.R. 84 (Bankr. S.D.N.Y. 2009) affirmed, 576 F.3d 108 (2d Cir. 2009). In this case secured creditors advanced one of the major objections to the proposed pre-plan sale: that the sale benefited certain unsecured creditors more than those with collateral.

liquidation plan, resulting in a near systemic halting of *Chrysler*'s operations.[42]

In its reasoning, the Second Circuit took into consideration: that the proposed sale was the only viable going-concern option and the only alternative to a liquidation that would net substantially less for creditors than the proposed sale; that any material delay in effectuating a sale would result in substantial additional losses; and that the debtor's extensive repetition of marketing efforts, in addition to the opportunity for competing bids, ensured that reasonable value was given for the assets.[43] It emphasised the clear presence of the deterioration of the going-concern value of *Chrysler* and the consequent need for a prompt sale of the business.[44]

Furthermore, there was a sub rosa issue. In this case, the s 363(b) sale was contested by the Pension Trust on grounds that it constituted a sub rosa, and thus it amounted to a 'secret plan' to reorganise *Chrysler*'s assets that should have been conducted within *Chrysler*'s reorganisation plan under Chapter 11 of the Code. But the court asserted the proposed s 363(b) transaction was not a sub rosa plan because the debtor would receive more than fair value in return for the sale of assets to *Fiat,* based on the valuation and the fact that *Fiat* was the only entity willing to help *Chrysler*, which otherwise might have been forced into a total liquidation, and all the sales proceeds would be distributed according to the Chapter 11 priority scheme.[45] The court also stated that the executory contracts New *Chrysler* would take over through the sale did not violate the priority rules of a Chapter 11 plan, even though they received more favourable treatment than other creditors in the same class or in a higher class.[46]

The same bankruptcy court which heard *Chrysler* allowed a s 363(b) transaction in the General Motors ('GM') case under which GM would sell most of its assets to a government-sponsored buyer to whom it would also assign the health and welfare benefits of GM employees.[47] GM

---

[42] See 405 B.R. at 95–7. See also MA Karam, 'The Chrysler Bankruptcy and Future of 363(b) Transactions' (2011) XI *Houston Business and Tax Law Journal* 395, 420.

[43] 405 B.R. at 96–8.

[44] 405 B.R. at 119.

[45] 405 B.R. at 97–8. A valuation determination of Chrysler's assets if liquidated was 800 million dollars, while Fiat purchased the assets for two billion dollars.

[46] 405 B.R. at 98–9.

[47] *In re General Motors Corp*., 407 B.R. 463 (Bankr. S.D.N.Y. 2009).

struck the agreement for the sale following government-sponsored attempts to restructure out of court. The US and Canadian governments were the only entities willing to extend financing for the transaction, on the condition that such financing would be used within a six-week time period after which they would rescind the offer. The court asserted that its decision to disallow the transaction in question would result in liquidation, which would produce considerably less value for GM's assets.[48] The court enumerated a number of reasons that justified the transaction as a sound business decision in order to satisfy the *Lionel* standard: (a) avoidance of the costs of a lengthy Chapter 11 process, (b) stemming the losses of GM's plummeting stock value, (c) the governments' short time frame for offering to sponsor the sale, and (d) the looming effects of bankruptcy and ensuing liquidation.[49] As to the bondholders' sub rosa accusation, the court noted that since the proceeds of the sale would be allotted to creditors according to the Chapter 11 priority scheme,[50] their claim was unsubstantiated.

It has been argued, following both decisions, that the US courts applied the business justification analysis established in *In re Lionel* inconsistently, relying on this principle only for factual comparisons.[51] Both *Chrysler* and GM arguably stretched the limit of what is permissible in traditional s 363 sales.[52] The strict emergency and perishable goods rationales used to justify an urgent need to sell were replaced by justifications on the basis of the costs of a lengthy formal procedure, fear of limited offers and the looming effects of a total liquidation. Also, in applying the sub rosa doctrine, a loose *Braniff* standard was adopted to

---

[48] A liquidation sale would produce between six and ten billion dollars of value for GM's assets, whereas the 363(b) transaction would provide GM with 45 billion dollars.

[49] 407 B.R. 463, at 491–3.

[50] 407 B.R. 463, at 481–2.

[51] K Korres, 'Bankrupting Bankruptcy: Circumventing Chapter 11 Protections Through Manipulation of the Business Justification Standard in s 363 Asset Sales, and a Refined Standard to Safeguard Against Abuse' (2013) 63 *Florida Law Review* 959, 971.

[52] Commentators criticize the courts in *Chrysler* for allowing s 363 sales as substitutes for reorganisation and for denying creditors the right to actively negotiate to enhance their own interests. See DA Skeel Jr., 'Why the Chrysler Deal Would Horrify a New Dealer' (2009) American Enterprise Institute Scholar Posts <http://www.aei.org/publication/why-the-chrysler-deal-would-horrify-a-new-dealer/> accessed 30 July 2015.

allow s 363(b) transactions to proceed unless they undoubtedly restructured priority schemes within Chapter 11.[53]

The current application of judicial scrutiny in permitting s 363(b) sales is held to be open to manipulation and thus insufficient when it comes to providing adequate protection against the vulnerabilities of s 363 abuse. This happens because the business justifications presented by the bankruptcy courts generally centre on saving time or money. Consequently parties can manipulate the courts' application of the principle of business justification by creating an immediate necessity, which often serves as an overriding factor when weighing the potential misuses of s 363 sales.[54] As businesses struggle or approach failure, they have the ability to manufacture an emergency by delaying bankruptcy filings until the last possible moment.[55] Furthermore, as the hurdle to achieving a 363(b) sale is no more than a mere notice and a hearing, because the transaction occurs outside the sphere of a Chapter 11 plan, it is doubtful whether the requirements of notice and hearing serve as a sufficient substitute for the Chapter 11 plan safeguards of disclosure, voting, acceptance and confirmation.

The Refined Standard of *Gulf Coast Oil*

In *In re Gulf Coast Oil Corp.*, the Bankruptcy Court for the Southern District of Texas was confronted with the issue of whether to authorise the proposed sale of all of the debtor's assets to its sole secured creditor.[56] The court shed light on recent developments in bankruptcy and expressed concern that 'the concept of debtor reorganisation and rehabilitation is in peril'.[57] It recognised that the evolving nature of s 363 sales necessitated legal guidelines that would address these concerns. In light of current trends, the court included in its inquiry a determination of

---

[53] Karam, 'The Chrysler Bankruptcy and Future of 363(b) Transactions', 425.

[54] Korres, 'Bankrupting Bankruptcy', 973.

[55] *Ibid.*, 974.

[56] The debtor here, *Gulf Coast Oil*, encompassed several affiliated companies. It denied the debtor's motion to sell on the grounds that the debtors had failed to demonstrate a good business reason for the need to sell the company prior to a plan confirmation. It considered that the debtor's proposal lacked evidence of deterioration of the assets or justification for using s 363 to pursue the sale of the debtor's business to its single secured lender.

[57] *In re Gulf Cost Oil Corp.*, 404 B.R. at 419.

'whether safeguards are necessary to protect rights that could be exercised in the context of plan confirmation'.[58]

To guide this analysis, Judge Steen in *In re Gulf Coast Oil Corp.*[59] provided a nonexclusive list of factors that could be considered when determining whether to approve a s 363(b) sale prior to confirmation of a Chapter 11 plan, including:

1. evidence regarding the need for an immediate sale;
2. the business justification for the sale and sale process occurring separate from the plan confirmation process;
3. the satisfaction of due process through the participation of official committees of creditors and equity interest holders;
4. an asset purchase agreement that is designed to facilitate competitive bidding;
5. the existence of an active market and aggressive marketing efforts;
6. the disinterestedness of a debtor's fiduciaries;
7. whether the sale includes the debtor's 'crown jewel';
8. whether the purchaser is seeking extraordinary protections, such as successor liability protections, that a Chapter 11 plan might provide;
9. the burden of proposing a sale as part of confirmation of a Chapter 11 plan;
10. whether the sale generally benefits the estate or just select creditors;
11. whether Chapter 11 protections can be fashioned as part of the sale; and
12. whether adverse interests are represented and the information is adequate for a judge to authorise the sale.[60]

Without altering the essence of the sound business justification test established in *Lionel*, the bankruptcy court of the Southern District of Texas presented a more comprehensive set of guidelines that confer on judges a broad authorisation of judicial discretion to balance the competing interest of efficiency and creditor protection in a variety of circumstances.[61]

---

[58] 404 B.R. at 423.

[59] *In re Gulf Coast Oil Corp.*, 404 B.R. 407 (Bankr. S.D.Tex. 2009).

[60] 404 B.R. at 422–7.

[61] The court in *Gulf Coast Oil* acknowledged the requirement that bankruptcy judges 'weigh all of the facts and circumstances of the case'. 404 B.R. at 423.

The framework the bankruptcy court adopted in *Gulf Coast Oil* integrated several new factors into the analysis, which heightens scrutiny in order to ensure a fair and reasonable price for pre-plan s 363(b) sales.[62] In approving asset sales in bankruptcy proceedings, courts generally require that the purchase price be fair and reasonable.[63] Reasonableness of the purchase price in a proposed s 363 sale is not easy to judge. Traditionally, courts have held that fair and valuable consideration is given in a bankruptcy sale when the purchaser pays 75 per cent of the appraised value of the assets.[64] In the updated framework provided in *Gulf Coast Oil*, considerations of whether the proposed purchase agreement facilitates competing bids or whether the assets in question have been aggressively marketed in an active market are highlighted as indicators of whether these sales will receive maximum value for the estate.[65]

Nevertheless, although a market test may to some extent dictate the fair price for the asset and prevent abuses that stem from undervaluation,[66] the speed of the s 363(b) sale process purportedly discourages the submission of competing bids, even if there are any other willing buyers. Due to the fast pace of s 363(b) sales, it is often required that any competing bids be submitted within a matter of days. This impedes a true market valuation of the assets.[67] As a quick sale will likely preclude an effective market test and the safeguards that the test ensures, apart from considering a debtor's efforts in marketing its assets when judging the reasonableness of the purchase price, the updated guidelines also require judges to consider the disinterestedness of the debtor's fiduciaries which

---

[62] For example, in *Gulf Coast Oil*, one reason the court denied a motion by related debtors to approve an auction procedure and a proposal to sell substantially all of their assets under s 363 was that the court was concerned that the marketing process demonstrated that there was not an active market to ensure that the debtors' assets were being sold for a fair price. See 404 B.R. at 428.

[63] Fishman and Gouveia, 'What's Driving Section 363 Sales after Chrysler and General Motors?', 354.

[64] *In Re Abbotts Dairies of Pennsylvania, Inc.*, 788 F.2d 143 at 149 (3d Cir. 1986).

[65] 404 B.R. at 424. The fourth, fifth and sixth factors in the thirteen factors list.

[66] Professor Barry E Adler advocated putting all large s 363(b) sales through a stringent market test to ensure fair price and prevent abuse, see Oversight of TARP Assistance to the Automobile Industry: Field Hearing Before the Congressional Oversight Panel, 111th Cong. 97-108 (2009).

[67] AJ Warburton, 'Understanding the Bankruptcies of Chrysler and General Motors: a Primer' (2010) 60 *Syracuse Law Review* 531, 567.

necessarily involves an investigation into the underlying relationship between the debtor and the purchaser.

Concerns Remain

There is a growing concern that the use of s 363(b) sales increases the ability of insiders to engage in self-dealing or selling to outsiders at below market value in return for side benefits, because of the quick timeline, claimholders' limited access to information and lack of involvement in the preparation of the sale.[68] A study has shown that in eleven out of thirty reorganisations under examination, the CEO of the selling company was able to secure a side benefit, such as severance payments, continued employment or a paid consulting position.[69]

The court in *Gulf Coast Oil* noted that 'if entities that control the debtor will benefit, or will potentially benefit, from the sale the court must carefully consider whether it is also appropriate to defer to their business judgment'.[70] To ameliorate these concerns and safeguard against self-dealing and abuse, the sixth factor in the *Gulf Coast Oil* guidelines requires the court to examine the interest of these parties when assessing a debtor's business judgment and any connection between the debtor and the purchaser. The consideration of the disinterest of fiduciaries controlling the debtor serves to discern whether a transaction is tainted by insider dealing and collusion or not. This also marks the difference between the sound business justification standard and the emergent *Gulf Coast Oil* standard, with the former built on the assumption that DIPs fulfil their fiduciary duties to creditors and the latter based on the notion that DIPs are unwilling or incapable of seeking high value in bankruptcy.[71]

In summary, in spite of the aforementioned attempts to refine the original sound business justification standard, it essentially remains the same discretionary and broad method for reviewing s 363(b) sales. No

---

68 It has been argued that the debtor in possession may have conflicts of interest that encourage selling to insiders or affiliated companies and may yield deals that provide a windfall for third parties at the expense of creditors. See HR Miller and SY Waisman, 'Does Chapter 11 Reorganisation Remain a Viable Option for Distressed Businesses for the Twenty-First Century?' (2004) 78 *American Bankruptcy Law Journal* 153.

69 LM LoPucki and JW Doherty, 'Bankruptcy Fire Sales' (2007) 106 *Michigan Law Review* 1, 13.

70 404 B.R. at 424.

71 Wilkerson, 'Defending the Current State of section 363 Sales', 594.

court has offered fixed guidelines on how to approach s 363(b) transitions, and the Supreme Court has not shown an intention to provide lower courts with a more concrete set of guidelines. As a result, courts approach cases using a variety of factors, which produces a large degree of variance in the weight given to each of these considerations.[72]

Inconsistency concerns acutely emerged in the recent aggressive use of s 363 pre-confirmation sales and were noted by the Commission established in 2012 by the American Bankruptcy Institute (ABI) to study the reform of Chapter 11. It suggested that most courts employ some form of heightened scrutiny in approving sales of substantially all of a debtor's assets under s 363 of the Bankruptcy Code, but that review may 'simply turn on whether the debtor in possession has a 'good reason' for the proposed sale under the circumstances of the particular case'.[73] It considered that such a standard is a much different and arguably lower standard than that applied to confirmation of a Chapter 11 plan in the cram-down context, where the debtor must establish that the plan satisfies all of the relevant requirements under s 1129(a), including good faith, the best interests of creditors test, and also does not discriminate unfairly and is fair and equitable with respect to each dissenting impaired class under s 1129(b).[74] Reflecting on the differences between a section 363 sale process and the Chapter 11 plan process, the Commission recommended some fundamental changes in order to afford creditors the same level of protection in the s 363 sale process and in the Chapter 11 plan process.

THE S 363 SALE PROPOSALS OF THE ABI COMMISSION

In 2012 the American Bankruptcy Institute (ABI) established a Commission to Study the Reform of Chapter 11 ('the Commission') to comprehensively evaluate US business reorganisation laws. The Commission was formed to respond to shifts in the financial market trends, corporate structures and credit and derivatives products since the Bankruptcy Code's adoption in 1978, and comprised leading bankruptcy

[72] Uziel, 'Section 363(b) Restructuring Meets the Sound Business Purpose Test with Bite', 1195.

[73] American Bankruptcy Institute, *Final Report of the ABI Commission to Study the Reform of Chapter 11* (2014) ('the ABI Commission Report') <https://abiworld.app.box.com/s/vvircv5xv83aavl4dp4h> accessed 30 July 2015, 205.

[74] *Ibid.*, 205–6.

practitioners, professors and judges.[75] Its Final Report and Recommendation ('the ABI Commission Report') was released on 8 December 2014 and was the result of an in-depth, two-year review of Chapter 11 by the Commission and 13 topical advisory committees. The chief objective of the report was: to identify ways to reduce barriers to entry for debtors; facilitate more efficient resolution of disputed matters; enhance debtors' restructuring options; incorporate checks and balances on the rights and remedies of debtors and creditors; and create an alternative restructuring scheme for smaller businesses.[76]

The ABI Commission Report referred to a sale of all or substantially all of a debtor's assets as a '363x sale'. It recognised the perceived increase in the number and speed of asset sales under s 363 and a corresponding decrease in stand-alone reorganisations.[77] The ABI Commission Report contended that s 363 sales were occurring too quickly, often only for the benefit of secured creditors, and denied debtors and junior creditors sufficient time to examine other restructuring alternatives.[78] To address the purported potential negative consequences of such quick sales, including the potential adverse impact on the possibility of holding a robust auction, and the limited time window for offering

---

75 It was established in recognition of the 'general consensus among restructuring professionals' that the time has come to evaluate US business reorganisation laws to correspond to numerous changes that have occurred since the Bankruptcy Code was enacted in 1978, including companies having more complex corporate structures with more leverage, companies' asset values being driven less by hard assets and more by services, contracts, intellectual property and other intangible assets, the greater prevalence of multinational operations, and perceived increase in the costs associated with Chapter 11. See the Need for Reform at page 12 of the ABI Commission Report.

76 *Ibid.*, 6.

77 It noted that high professionals' fees, among other factors, have encouraged debtors to pursue alternatives to traditional Chapter 11 reorganisation, such as s 363 asset sales on an expedited basis. See the ABI Commission Report, 58.

78 It states that: 'Such a sale may (i) not facilitate a robust auction, (ii) not allow the debtor sufficient time to explore a stand-alone reorganisation or other restructuring alternatives, and (iii) take advantage of a decline in the applicable markets without giving parties in interest a reasonable time to assess the likelihood that such markets will rebound during the pendency of the debtor's Chapter 11 case. The Commissioners also acknowledged the problems with insufficient notice and opportunity for parties in interest to assert meaningful objections or perform reliable asset valuations within the abbreviated time frames of a quick sale.' The ABI Commission Report, 87.

sufficient notice limiting the opportunity to perform reliable asset valuations or raise meaningful objections, it proposed a greater degree of scrutiny, longer timetables and certain other requirements that are more commonly found in connection with confirmation of a Chapter 11 reorganisation plan.

60-day Moratorium on Sales of Substantially All Assets

To address the concern that rapid sale processes provided insufficient time to market the assets thoroughly so that interested bidders could participate and maximise value, the Commission sought to reintroduce the 'breathing spell'. This would afford parties in interest (and competing bidders) a reasonable period of time to assess the proposed sale. It was recommended that the trustee or DIP should not be permitted to conduct an auction of, or receive final approval of such a sale transaction within 60 days after the petition date or date of the order for relief, whichever was the longer. It further specified that the court should not shorten the 60-day moratorium unless the trustee or a party in interest 'demonstrate[d] by clear and convincing evidence that there [was] a high likelihood that the value of the debtors assets [would] decrease significantly' within those 60 days, and the court found that the proposed sale satisfied the standards set forth in the principles for 363x sales.[79]

The principles recommended by the Commission were consistent with standards imposed on reorganisation plans under s 1129 including a requirement that: the sale complies with the applicable provisions of the Bankruptcy Code; the sale has been proposed in good faith; and the debtor must retain proceeds sufficient to fund administrative expenses incurred through the closing of the sale.[80]

It is clear that the proposed changes to lengthen the s 363 sale process by implementing a 60-day moratorium were designed to allow debtors and junior creditors sufficient time to examine other restructuring alternatives. But by doing so, it inevitably would rebalance power and control among secured creditors, debtors and unsecured creditors in favour of the debtor and unsecured creditors. This, however, has been criticised that it would likely only serve to harm secured creditors while providing little to no benefit to junior creditors.[81] This is because mandating additional time

---

79 *Ibid.*, 83.

80 *Ibid.*, section VI.B.

81 Chapman and Cutler LLP, 'Twin Daggers: Proposed 363(x) Amendments and Revisions to Adequate Protection Provisions Would Significantly Erode Secured Creditors' Recoveries' (Client Alert, January 2015).

for s 363 sales would necessitate additional financing in order to allow the debtor to operate during the moratorium period. While such changes may increase a debtor's ability to obtain post-bankruptcy financing over the objection of the secured creditor, they could, at the same time, also significantly erode secured creditors' collateral value.[82]

Modifications to the Absolute Priority Rule

The Commission brought up a novel concept of Redemption Option Value based on its view that, except in small and medium-sized company cases, the absolute priority rule should be altered by providing a mechanism for an immediately junior, otherwise 'out of the money' class of creditors to receive distributions under a plan and from 363x sales based on the possibility that the value of the reorganised entity may appreciate after the plan's effective date or entry of the 363x sale order.[83]

The Commission expressed the view that the absolute priority rule can result in an allocation of value among creditors 'in an arguably random manner depending on the timing of the value realisation event' i.e., plan confirmation.[84] According to the Commission, if the assets are valued 'during a trough in the debtor's business cycle or the economy as a whole', the valuations used to support the plan distributions will value the reorganised entity at a low point in the valuation cycle. Accordingly, under the absolute priority rule, junior creditors and interest-holders could lose their rights against the estate and receive no value on account of their claims simply because of the time of the valuation. Arguably, this could prove unfair to junior stakeholders who would then be foreclosed from participating in any future appreciation of the value of the assets sold or in the going-concern value of the reorganised entity when the business cycle and general economic conditions improved.[85]

Similarly in the context of a 363x sale, the debtor's estate may be monetised at value far below what the estate could be worth at a later date to the prejudice of stakeholders standing lower in the pecking order of priorities.[86] The Commission therefore concluded that 'relying on a valuation [during such a trough] may result in a reallocation of the

---

82 *Ibid.*
83 See the ABI Commission Report, section VI.C.1.
84 *Ibid.*, 213.
85 *Ibid.*, 213–14.
86 *Ibid.*, 214.

reorganised firm's future value in favour of senior stakeholders and away from junior stakeholders' under current law is 'subjectively unfair'.[87]

To remedy this perceived unfairness and allow junior creditors to benefit from an increase in the debtor's value that takes place after plan confirmation or a s 363 sale, the Commission proposed that senior creditors should set aside a form of compensation for the immediately junior class in the event the debtor's enterprise value surpasses the amount of senior claims during a three-year period, a so-called 'redemption option'. The redemption option starts on the petition date and refers to a notional 'purchase' of the debtor's enterprise, with a strike price equal to the full amount of the senior creditor's claim.[88] Namely, in the context of s 363 sales, senior creditors would be required to share, as compensation to junior creditors, an amount calculated on the value of the company if acquired within a reasonable period of time after the effective date of a Chapter 11 plan or a 363x sale order minus the value of senior debt claims; it is not a percentage or fixed payment to junior creditors. The court would determine the value of the redemption option based on the evidence presented by the parties at a hearing under s 1129(b) or s 363x.[89] It should be noted that if the immediately junior class objects to the sale, they would not be entitled to the redemption option value.

The principle behind this recommendation is that an immediately junior class that might otherwise be permanently cut off from receiving value should be entitled to an allocation of value attributable to such class that reflects the possibility that the value of the company might have been sufficient to pay the senior class in full with interest and provide incremental value to such immediately junior class within a reasonable period of time after the effective date of a Chapter 11 plan or a 363x sale order.[90] The ABI Commission Report stressed that the recommended principles are not intended to alter the order of creditor priorities. Nevertheless, it is intended to provide a new conceptual framework for an adjustment to the current absolute priority rule, denying the effect of the current determination of reorganisation value

---

[87] *Ibid.*, 207.

[88] *Ibid.*, 208. The Report notes that possible methods of paying the redemption option value include 'pursuant to the plan or section 363 sale order in the form of cash, debt, stock warrants or other consideration'. See the ABI Commission Report, 210.

[89] *Ibid.*, 210.

[90] *Ibid.*, 208.

based on the fortuity of timing of the reorganisation or sale on cutting off alternative distributional possibilities.

As Professor Michelle Harner commented, this new concept is intended to mitigate valuation fluctuations caused by the timing of a valuation-realisation event in Chapter 11, and its simple objectives are to provide a full return to classes 'in the money' on the value-realisation date, and also to 'double-check' whether any value might remain for the first class that appears to be 'out of the money' on that date.[91] As the ABI Commission Report admitted, the conceptual principle of allocating a redemption option value to the immediately junior class requires further development to determine whether and how it should be applied in more complex contexts, for example where a senior class is entitled to less than all of the firm's enterprise value.

COMPARISON BETWEEN THE US 363(B) PRE-PLAN SALES AND THE UK PRE-PACK SALES AND THEIR APPROACHES IN ADDRESSING POTENTIAL ABUSE

Both the UK pre-pack sales and the US pre-plan sales aim at value realisation through going-concern disposals on an expedited basis. There are, however, clear differences between pre-plan sales and pre-pack sales. First of all, a s 363(b) pre-plan sale is not really a pre-pack by definition, at least in the form that these take place in the UK. As explained in Chapter 2, the UK 'pre-pack' process has the effect of moving the playing field of insolvency negotiations and decision-making to the shadow of law, resulting in a certain level of pre-determination. The private feature in the US pre-plan sales is not so obvious, as the negotiations may take place post-petition.

Also, there are substantial differences in the formal procedures under which respective sales are carried out. As discussed in the previous chapter, the formal rescue-oriented procedures in the two jurisdictions exhibit significant differences in terms of institutional arrangements. One of the fundamental differences is that Chapter 11 is based on debtor-in-possession whereas in UK administration the board of directors loses their managerial powers and functions to the administrator. Yet the

---

[91] MM Harner, 'Chapter 11 Reform: Refining the Tools Available to Rehabilitate Distressed Business' (29 January 2015) Columbia Law School's Blog on Corporations and the Capital Markets <http://clsbluesky.law.columbia.edu/2015/01/29/chapter-11-reform-refining-the-tools-available-to-rehabilitate-distressed-businesses/> accessed 30 July 2015.

differences are not as important when Chapter 11 and UK reorganisation proceedings are used for fast-track business sales. The UK pre-packaged administration goes halfway towards a debtor-in-possession governance model, as it allows a transfer of functions from the administrator to the existing management. Not only the board or its officials continue to direct the affairs of the company during the negotiation of the sale in the context of a pre-pack administration, but also the deal for the sale of company assets is often put in place by existing management in advance of the official appointment of an administrator. Therefore, the role of administrator as representative of interests of the creditors as a whole is accordingly significantly weakened. At the same time, the substitution of the functions of the administrator in the UK pre-packs is not as extensive under US law, where DIP powers are also not restricted to the pre-formal negotiation stage as is the case in the UK.

In spite of the discussed differences in the timing of taking pre-arranging measures and the governance models of requisite formal procedures, the issues underlying the two expedited sale processes are remarkably similar. By pre-arranging a deal at the pre-formal stage, UK pre-pack sales circumvent time-consuming and expensive administration proceedings to offer an attractive streamlined process for value realisation. Similarly, the US pre-plan sales offer the opportunity to sidestep creditor approval requirements by disguising the reorganisation as an s 363(b) asset sale, in which significant transactions greatly limit possible options for plan formulation. Therefore, both processes involve a certain disenfranchisement of creditors as the latter do not vote on substantive asset sales. At the same time, both processes have raised the spectre of a debtor company taking advantage of a loophole or ambiguity within the respective legislative framework to keep its creditors from having any say on how the debtor allocates its assets, since a fundamental guarantee of the formal process is fairness in allocations achieved through negotiations between and voting by all interest holders.

The principal risk involved in both sale processes is leaving ample room to powerful creditors and the debtor to exercise excessive influence and control over relevant transactions by dictating favourable terms or prices for a pre-arranged asset sale at the expense of junior or unsecured creditors who lack the ability to protect their own interests. The fact that this risk remains appreciable is a continuous matter of concern both vis-à-vis protection of junior or non-dominant creditors and in terms of denying or bypassing due process, a fundamental principle underlying statutory bankruptcy procedures.

While there are undeniable justifications relating to speed and secrecy in the sale process, it is both critical and desirable to include additional safeguards vis-à-vis creditor protection and to ensure that the sale will not be negotiated in a manner which is likely or calculated to prejudice the interests of the company or of its creditors as a whole. There are two mechanisms to provide necessary checks and controls to rebalance the increased control of the debtor and the weakened position of creditors in the pre-pack process. The obvious one is to offer affected parties pre-view rights and an opportunity to file objections to the proposed sale as a direct means of safeguarding their own interests. Another means to safeguard creditors' interests is ex ante judiciary or other independent scrutiny and supervision.

Claimholders' Pre-view Right

In the US pre-plan sales, although the need for a speedy bypassing of the standard protections provided under the traditional Chapter 11 reorganisation is recognised, claimholders' pre-view rights are not completely eroded. Sales of assets outside the ordinary course of business requires judicial authorisation under s 363(b) of the Bankruptcy Code, as well as giving notice to the creditors' committee. Then, the requirement for a hearing provides an avenue for creditor complaints, since it grants all substantially affected stakeholders, who were not part of the negotiations, certain pre-view rights and the opportunity to file objections to the proposed sale. Nevertheless, the proposed transaction may be approved by bankruptcy courts without an actual hearing, if the notice is given properly and such a hearing is not requested by a party in interest in a timely manner or if there is insufficient time for a hearing to be commenced before the sale is concluded.

As already mentioned, the recent Report of the ABI Commission recommended a 60-day moratorium on sales of substantially all assets so as to create a 'breathing spell' to afford parties in interest (and competing bidders) a reasonable period of time to assess the proposed sale. Such a proposal is designed to allow the debtor sufficient time to explore a stand-alone reorganisation or other restructuring alternatives, although it has been criticised that such a proposal would seriously increase the cost of the proceedings.

In comparison with the US pre-confirmation sales, the entirely disenfranchised position of junior creditors in a UK pre-pack sale deserves some sympathy. The pre-determination feature of pre-packs means that the creditors' meeting would be left meaningless in giving creditors the opportunity to consider the administrator's proposals when they are presented with a fait accompli when they receive the statement of proposals, although in the event of disgruntled creditors, there are avenues for creditors to file their complaints or objections with the relevant regulatory bodies and/or the court by way of complaints or litigations against the conduct of the administrator.

Judicial or Independent Sanction and Scrutiny

Another feature of US pre-plan sales is the role of the bankruptcy courts. In a context that time is of the essence and a market test is either impossible or impractical, heightened judicial reviews should be in place to substitute for such a test. Due to the significant role the bankruptcy courts play in determining and scrutinising whether a particular s 363 sale is appropriate, judicial discretion serves as a powerful mechanism to counteract recent concerns. In the context of pre-plan sales, the case law has also been evolving in providing effective guidelines in distinguishing permissible s 363 sales from those that open the bankruptcy process to potential abuse. It has been questioned whether it would be effective for the UK to adopt an enhanced judicial role in approving pre-plan asset sales that is similar to the US regime as a model so that key weaknesses can be ameliorated by closer judicial scrutiny.

In the UK by contrast, insolvency professionals are put in charge of an administration procedure. The administrator, as the court officer, may apply to the court for directions in connection with his functions, but mainly for serious legal or procedural problems.[92] In general, the administrators enjoy a considerable breadth of discretion in relation to business decision-making and the courts have been placing a significant amount of faith on the professionalism of insolvency practitioners in their governing of insolvency proceedings. In ameliorating the concerns of abuse raised in the context of pre-pack sales to connected parties, we have seen an enormous amount of effort being made to strengthen the accountability of the insolvency practitioners involved in the process as a means to safeguard creditors' interests.

CONCLUSION

The lack of liquidity in the credit markets that followed the 2008–2009 global financial crisis, which also triggered a wave of corporate failures, made it very hard for debtors to find DIP financing for a period. That meant that debtors had to sell assets on a more expedited basis. Value realisation by way of substantial asset sales prior to a Chapter 11 plan

---

92 Para. 63 of Sch. B1 to the IA 1986.

confirmation under s 363 can be implemented and completed more quickly and at a far lower cost than a sale done as part of a plan of reorganisation, because the latter requires compliance with all of the detailed confirmation requirements under s 1129 of the Code, including approval of a disclosure statement and successful solicitation and voting on the plan.

Pre-plan confirmation sales provide undeniable benefits to struggling businesses, especially in emergency situations. Nevertheless, the increasing popularity of s 363 pre-plan sales as a substitute for true reorganisations has inspired growing debate that has weighted efficiency against protection of parties' interests and intensified concerns about potential abuses by parties attempting to game the system to benefit themselves. The US debate is similar to that surrounding the UK pre-pack practice, as both processes aim at value realisation through going-concern sales on an expedited basis, with denial of creditor participation in the process.

In certain urgent circumstances, the procedural rights of certain creditors may have to be compromised in order to retain procedural efficiency and expertise, especially where exclusivity in commercial decision-making can contribute to the substantive aim of a rescue offering maximised realisations for creditors. So to a certain degree limitations on creditors' participation rights can be justified. However, the need for expedition is not a justification for abandoning proper standards of due process, which should be enshrined in any formal legal procedure including pre-packaged sales.

Also, there is an integrity and fairness issue to consider. Creditors' loss of control over the process may have a negative impact, on lenders generally and even healthy businesses, when the bankruptcy process deprives creditors of their promised return, the prospect of a debtor's failure looms larger in the eyes of future lenders to future businesses. The standards applied when approving or denying a pre-arranged transaction must afford creditors and other parties safeguards that will maintain the underlying principles of corporate rescue and ensure accountability and fairness to the disenfranchised parties. This is also essential to instill credibility in the system to deter abuse and managements' greed.

There are two mechanisms to provide necessary checks and controls to rebalance the increased control of the debtor and the weakened position of creditors in the pre-pack process. One is to offer affected parties pre-view rights and an opportunity to file objections to the proposed sale as an important means of safeguarding their own interests. Nevertheless, the provision of pre-view right could generate high costs in the form of unnecessary delays and seriously undermine the flexibility of the process.

Another means to safeguard creditors' interests is ex ante judiciary (or insolvency professionals acting as court-officers) scrutiny.

US law has premised its governance structure on a regulatory system that attracts much intervention from the bankruptcy courts, evidenced by court-oriented information disclosure and plan confirmation standards. In the context of pre-plan sales, US case law has also been evolving in an attempt to offer effective guidelines in distinguishing permissible s 363 sales from those that involve potential abuses. In contrast, the English procedure is built on a long tradition that involves the use of independent, expert professionals. In the absence of any pre-view right in the pre-pack sale context, primary emphasis has been placed on the accountability of the insolvency practitioners involved in the process as a means to safeguard creditors' interests.

Although the process adopted by each jurisdiction is different, it is clear that both the USA and the UK are taking a more stringent approach to pre-plan and pre-pack sales to ameliorate the concerns of abuse. This is, undoubtedly, a positive step in accepting and ensuring that the accelerated sale path through a formal procedure can serve as a vehicle to preserve the going-concern value of a failing business, as an economically efficient alternative to the traditional idea of corporate rescue.

PART IV

Pre-packs in Europe

7. The use of the pre-pack approach in key European jurisdictions

INTRODUCTION

Important reforms have been implemented recently in some of the biggest European jurisdictions, including Germany, France, the Netherlands, Spain, Italy, Austria, etc.[1] The wave of reforms is systematic, not incidental. On the one hand, these reforms were made against the backdrop of the financial crisis during which the current insolvency law regimes proved to be inadequate to meet the challenges of the changed economic environment. In particular, the rapid growth of insolvencies as a result of the economic recession has revealed the absence of an

[1] The Spanish insolvency system was reformed through Law 22/2003 of 9 July, on Insolvency (the Spanish Insolvency Act), which has been effective since 1 January 2004. There have been several amendments to the Spanish Insolvency Act, the most important ones being: the amendment introduced by Royal Decree: Law 3/2009 of 27 March; Law 38/2011 of 10 October; and Law 14/2013 of 27 September. One important amendment introduced by Law 38/2011 was to provide debtors who are in a negotiation process with their main creditors with an additional period for continuing these out-of-court negotiations. During this time, distressed debtors can negotiate a proposal for an agreement (*propuesta anticipada de convenio*) or an out-of-court formal refinancing agreement (*acuerdo de refinanciación formal*) ('Formal Refinancing Agreement') with their creditors. Furthermore, it introduced the DIP financing concept incorporated by the new section 84.2.11 of the Spanish Insolvency Act, giving priority to any new funds made available to the debtor under a Formal Refinancing Agreement. The Italian Bankruptcy Act (Royal Decree No. 267 of 16 March 1942) had also gone through material changes in recent years, with the introduction of the out-of-court debt restructuring plan (*piano attestato di risanamento*) in Article 67, para.3(d) of the Act; the debt restructuring agreement (*accordo di ristrutturazione dei debiti*) in Article 182-bis of the Act; and a more efficient pre-bankruptcy agreement procedure (*concordato preventivo*) in Article 160 of the Italian Bankruptcy Act. Austria's Insolvency Law Reform Act came into force on 1 July 2010 with the main objective to prevent companies from delaying filing insolvency proceedings and to improve the chances of successfully restructuring a company.

effective corporate rescue framework. On the other hand, the promotion of the corporate rescue approach also appears to be at the top of the insolvency law reform agenda of the EU legislators. In their capacity of providing common rules dealing with important conflict-of-law issues such as international jurisdiction, recognition and applicable law, EU policy-makers also serve at the European level as a driver behind domestic legislative changes and harmonisation. Increased insolvency forum shopping activity across Europe, where debtor companies have moved to another jurisdiction in order to benefit from fast-track restructuring options and/or director-friendly procedures, has posed a significant challenge for national legislators in Europe. Continental European authorities have essentially embarked on a major initiative to revise national substantive laws in order to enhance the availability of corporate rescue tools as alternatives to liquidation.

The general theme of those recent reforms is to improve the requisite legal framework with a view of enabling further development of coherent and functional rules for corporate rescue. The new frameworks normally include the introduction of relevant statutory procedures that help the parties to negotiate more effective solutions when a business becomes financially distressed. In this way they promote cooperation of formal and informal rescue measures and ease restrictions about the choice of procedures for liquidation and restructuring. Requisite reforms enhance the efficiency and effectiveness of the overall process since pre-insolvency restructuring options and flexible procedure conversion became available in a timely manner. In particular, the availability of systematic support for the identification of refinancing priorities, for the facilitation of complementation of the reorganisation plan and for cram-down mechanisms, strongly augment the effectiveness of the corporate rescue process in the European jurisdictions that have recently implemented the reforms discussed below.

This chapter focuses on pre-pack or equivalent mechanisms that have been implemented or under consideration in selected European jurisdictions, namely, France, Germany and the Netherlands, aiming at providing fast-tracked rescue-oriented proceedings in order to minimise the administrative costs associated with full-fledged statutory procedures. France, Germany and the Netherlands were chosen because they have developed relatively mature corporate insolvency legal systems and represent a broad spectrum of debtor- and creditor-oriented insolvency traditions. It should be borne in mind that there are significant differences between insolvency laws across these countries, especially as regards creditors' priorities and set-off rights. As an area of law dealing with matters of high economic, political and sometimes social relevance, insolvency law rules reflect the hierarchies of values and interests in each jurisdiction and the balance policy-makers strike between different policy goals and interests according to their own policy options and economic needs.[2] The policy dimension of the domestic insolvency law is out of the scope of the discussion here, as are the detailed substantive insolvency rules.

This chapter aims to provide an analysis of the use of pre-pack or equivalent mechanisms to facilitate the success of corporate rescue in the legal frameworks of the aforementioned jurisdictions. The central objective of this analysis is to identify the strengths and weaknesses of each system in utilising the pre-pack and alike approaches in corporate rescue while providing adequate safeguards to creditors. In particular, the analysis will focus on such legal issues as: the nature of the pre-insolvency negotiation platform; the objective and the effects of outcomes of the pre-insolvency negotiations; accountability of the process; and the level of creditor participation.

PRE-PACK LAW AND PRACTICE IN FRANCE

French law is heavily geared towards the preservation of ailing businesses, encouraging companies to adopt measures that enable them to detect and deal with any difficulties at an early stage, so that a turnaround could be possible.[3] The French insolvency legislations contained in Book VI of the Commercial Code in its current form was originally enacted in

---

2 On the relation of national social security policies and the distributive insolvency rules, see FM Mucciarelli, 'Not Just Efficiency: Insolvency Law in the EU and Its Political Dimension' (2013) 14 *European Business Organization Law Review* 175. See also J Garrido, 'The Distributional Question in Insolvency: Comparative Aspects' (1995) 4 *International Insolvency Review* 25.

3 A pre-insolvency intervention system, formerly called 'Amicable Settlement' (*reglement amiable*), later renamed Conciliation, which dealt with diagnosis and prevention of insolvency was introduced by the Prevention of Business Difficulties Law in 1984. Furthermore, the Insolvency Law of 1985, inspired by the United States Bankruptcy Reform Act of 1978, introduced the twin-track approach of having judicial rescue (*redressement judiciaire*) and judicial liquidation (*liquidation judiciaire*) proceedings as the primary procedures applicable to insolvent debtors. On French insolvency law history, see P Omar, 'The Progress of Reforms to Insolvency Law and Practice in France' and M Campana, 'A Critical Evaluation of the Development and Reform of the Corporate Rescue Procedures in France' in KG Broc and R Parry (eds) *Corporate Rescue in Europe: An Overview of Recent Developments from Selected Countries in Europe* (Kluwer Law International, 2004).

1985 and amended in 1994.[4] Substantial changes were brought by Law No. 2005-845 of 26 July 2005 (the Law of 2005), which drew further attention to the idea of corporate rescue. Most noticeably, it introduced an entirely new procedure called '*Sauvegarde*', which came into effect in January 2006. Furthermore, Ordinance 2008-1345 of 18 December 2008 (the Ordinance of 2008) made the *Sauvegarde* proceedings more accessible to companies in difficulty and, more generally, it enhanced the flexibility of its different corporate restructuring procedures. It also clarified the rules governing the composition and operation of creditors' committees and bondholders.

In October 2010, the French insolvency law underwent further reform, with the introduction of an 'accelerated financial safeguard procedure' (*Procédure de Sauvegarde Financière Accélérée*), which essentially amounted to a form of pre-pack restructuring.[5] This procedure is available to debtors who started *Conciliation* proceedings after 1 March 2011. Most recently, Ordinance 2014-326 of 12 March 2014 (the Ordinance of 2014) further created a new 'accelerated safeguard procedure' (*Procédure de Sauvegarde Accélérée*),[6] which is designed to encompass all creditors and not only financial creditors. This section will start with an overview of the relevant pre-insolvency rescue procedures available under French law, and then introduce the new fast-track options, followed by a critical discussion of the features of the French version of pre-pack restructuring.

The Relevant Pre-insolvency Rescue Procedures

Having undergone serious transformation in the restructuring and business rescue arena, the French corporate rescue framework has gradually become both quite sophisticated and complicated. The principal restructuring and corporate rescue regimes can be divided into the pre-insolvency procedures and the judicial or in-court procedures. The

---

[4] The 1994 amendments (Law 94-475 of 10 June 1994) had two main aims; the first was to improve corporate rescue procedures, especially to reinforce those measures at the pre-insolvency stage dealing with informal arrangements. The second aim was to redress some of the rights of creditors during insolvency proceedings. See Omar, 'The Progress of Reforms to Insolvency Law and Practice in France', 52. See also A Sorensen and P Omar, *Corporate Rescue Procedures in France* (Kluwer Law International, 1996), 28.

[5] The 'accelerated financial safeguard procedure' was created by Law No. 2010-1249 of 22 October 2010 on banking and financial regulation (*Loi de Régulation Bancaire et Financière*) (Articles 57 and 58) and was codified in Article L628-1 and L628-7 of the French Commercial Code.

[6] It entered into force on 1 July 2014.

pre-insolvency procedures include *mandat ad hoc* and *conciliation*, which are intended to facilitate negotiations between the debtor and its main creditors on a confidential and contractual basis, with a view to reaching an agreement and avoiding liquidation at an early stage, prior to facing a real threat of insolvency. The judicial or in-court procedures, which, in particular, offer an automatic moratorium, include the *Sauvegarde* procedure and the judicial rescue (*redressement judiciaire*) procedure. Different from the judicial rescue procedure, the *Sauvegarde* procedure is available to companies that are not technically insolvent by the test of cessation of payments (*cessation des paiements*).[7]

Mandat ad hoc

The *mandat ad hoc* procedure was formally introduced by the Law of 2005[8] but in practice it had existed for many years.[9] The procedure is usually initiated by a request from the ailing company to the presiding judge of the Commercial Court (*Tribunal de Commerce*) to determine the appropriate steps necessary to remedy the situation, provided that the company is not in a state of insolvency by the test of cessation of payments even though it may have acute or foreseeable difficulties.[10] The presiding judge of the court may, at the debtor's request, appoint a special commissioner (*mandataire ad hoc*) and define his duties.[11] The

---

[7] The insolvency test in French law is essentially a cash-flow test, i.e. whether a company is able to meet its payment obligations as they fall due for payment with its available assets. The judicial rescue proceedings can be opened at the request of the debtor, at the latest within 45 days following the cessation of payments. In addition, where conciliation proceedings have failed, the court will seek to intervene and may open the judicial rescue proceedings. Arts L621-12 and L631-1 of the Commercial Code.

[8] By art. 4 of the Law of 2005, introducing new paragraph II in art. L611-2 of the Commercial Code.

[9] It was a practice developed by courts in Paris in the early 1950s using their inherent jurisdictions. See P Omar, 'Reforms to the Framework of Insolvency Law and Practice in France: 1996–2006' in KG Broc and R Parry (eds) *Corporate Rescue: An overview of Recent Developments* (Kluwer Law International, 2nd edn, 2006), 140.

[10] Art. L611-2 of the Commercial Code. Accompanying the request, the company must supply the court with a plan stating the measures the company is going to take in order to repay its debts and also its plans for restructuring its business.

[11] Art. L611-3 of the Commercial Code. The main duties of the special commissioner typically involve reporting to the presiding judge of the court on the economic and financial situation of the debtor company and assisting the company in reaching an agreement of repayment and restructuring with its

debtor may propose the name of a special commissioner it wishes to appoint when applying to the court.[12] Management of the company during the process remains in the hands of the existing board.

This pre-insolvency procedure is contractual in nature; the initiation of the procedure has no moratorium effect and therefore does not give rise to any suspension of creditors' rights or remedies. Nevertheless, it offers significant flexibility for informal and private negotiations between the debtor company and its creditors, as this procedure is confidential and non-public, thus, it allows negotiations between the debtor company and its creditors to be carried out without attracting undue public attention which may have a catastrophic effect on the company's financial position.[13] Arguably, it is a useful procedure that may be used to reach a pre-packed restructuring agreement prior to the commencement of a formal procedure with a cram-down mechanism to bind the dissenting minority, such as *Sauvegarde*, in order to solidify the outcome of private negotiations.

Conciliation

The *Conciliation* proceedings were introduced by the Law of 2005,[14] available to businesses experiencing legal, financial or economic difficulties, actual or forecast, or businesses that have not been insolvent for more than 45 days.[15] The procedure is opened by the presiding judge of the Commercial Court, who, upon the request of the troubled company, shall appoint a conciliator (*conciliateur*), usually following a suggestion

---

creditors. In order to retain the impartiality of the special commissioner, the Law of 2005 limits the scope of appointments by preventing those remunerated by the business as well as judges of the Commercial Court from being appointed within a prescribed period: two years for individuals and five years for judges. Art. 10 of the Law of 2005, introduced the new art. L611-13 of the Commercial Code.

[12] Art. L611-3 of the Commercial Code.

[13] There is no specific time frame within which the process must be completed. This is subject to the discretion of the President of the Court and allows the debtor company to negotiate with its creditors without time pressure to devise a viable reorganisation plan. If an agreement has been reached between the debtor and the creditors, the proceedings may be transferred to the Conciliation proceedings to validate the agreement by the court.

[14] Its predecessor, the amicable settlement (*règlement amiable*) has been significantly changed in order to improve the procedure and make it more attractive to debtors.

[15] Art. L611-4 of the Commercial Code (inserted by art. 5 of the Law of 2005).

from the debtor company.[16] The main mission of the conciliator is to assist the debtor in its negotiations with relevant stakeholders (e.g. creditors, employees) in order to reach an agreement, which would ensure the continuation of the company's business.[17] During the process, the debtor remains in charge of running its business, since the *conciliator* has no power to interfere in the management of the business. Unlike the special commissioner whose length of office is at the discretion of the presiding judge of the court, the conciliator can only be appointed for a maximum of four months and this period may only be extended, by one month, in exceptional circumstances.[18]

Similar to *Mandat ad hoc*, the *Conciliation* procedure is confidential and will be disclosed only to those parties involved in the negotiation. There is no automatic stay of payments, therefore other creditors are not barred from taking legal action against the debtor to recover their claims.[19] If the parties reach an agreement (the *Conciliation Agreement*), they will be able to seek the endorsement of the *Conciliation* Agreement by a formal judgment of the court, upon the joint petition of the parties. There are certain conditions that the *Conciliation* Agreement has to meet for it to be endorsed by the court, including that: the debtor is not insolvent or the agreement terminates such situation; the terms and conditions of the agreement are such as to ensure the continuation of the debtor's business; and the agreement does not prejudice the interests of creditors that are not parties to it.[20]

---

[16] Art. L611-6 of the Commercial Code. Usually, the special commissioner in *Mandat ad hoc* and a conciliator in *Conciliation* are judicial administrators registered on a national list (the Union for the Kidicial Administorrs or the National Council of Receivers (ASPAJ) and Judicial Administrators (CNAJMJ)) apart from several exceptions.

[17] Art. L611-7 provides that 'the conciliator may suggest any proposal, which is relevant to the preservation of the business, the pursuit of economic activity and the maintenance of employment'.

[18] Art. L611-6 of the Commercial Code.

[19] But the Ordinance provides that where a creditor makes a formal demand for its debt during the conciliation proceedings, the debtor may make application to the court under art. 1244 of the French Civil Code with a view to obtaining payment grace periods if it wishes.

[20] Art. L611-8 of the Commercial Code. Before ruling upon the approval of the agreement, the court shall hear or duly summon to the judge's chambers: the debtor, the creditors who are party to the agreement, the representatives of the works council, the conciliator and the Public Prosecutor's Office. Art. L611-9 of the Commercial Code.

Where a court endorsement of the *Conciliation* Agreement is sought, the decision recording the agreement shall not be subject to publication formalities and shall not be appealed against.[21] What is more significant is that, in cases where the debtor subsequently goes into other insolvency proceedings, i.e. the *Sauvegarde* proceedings, the judicial rescue proceedings or judicial liquidation, lenders making new money and/or suppliers making trade credit available to the debtor under the court-endorsed *Conciliation* Agreement for the purposes of ensuring the continuation and long-term future of the business will benefit from a priority ranking before all other claims prior to the commencement of the *Conciliation* proceedings in those insolvency proceedings (the 'privilege de conciliation').[22] Nevertheless, this provision shall not apply to contributions made by shareholders or partners in the form of a capital increase.[23]

Sauvegarde

Sauvegarde is an entirely new procedure which was introduced by the Law of 2005[24] aiming at improving the chances of survival of companies facing financial distress. Similarly with the *Mandat ad hoc*, it may only be initiated by a court order at the request of the debtor company and only if the company is solvent.[25] To open the proceedings, the company is required to show that it is faced with difficulties that it is not able to overcome.[26] Although used for solvent companies, unlike the *Mandat ad hoc* or *Conciliation*, the initiation of *Sauvegarde* proceedings will trigger an automatic moratorium during an observation period for a maximum

---

[21] Art. L611-8 of the Commercial Code.

[22] Art. L611-11 of the Commercial Code.

[23] Art. L611-11 of the Commercial Code. The priority before all debts arising prior to the opening of conciliation is decided according to the ranking provided in II of art. L622-17 and II of art. L641-13.

[24] Arts L620-1 to L625-9 of the Commercial Code.

[25] If it appears, after the commencement of the proceedings, that the debtor was already in a state of cessation of payments at the time the commencement order was issued, the court shall covert the *Sauvegarde* proceedings to the *redressement judiciaire* proceedings. Art. L621-12 of the Commercial Code.

[26] It was originally required that the debtor company must show it is faced with difficulties that it is not able to overcome and the nature of which are capable of leading to cessation of payments. Article 12 of Ordinance of 2008 has relaxed the latter condition, only requiring proof of difficulties that it cannot overcome.

duration of six months,[27] under the protection of which the debtor is permitted to propose a recovery plan.

Following the commencement of the *Sauvegarde* procedure, the court shall appoint: (1) an supervisory judge *(juge-commissaire)*, mainly responsible for supervising the speedy progress of the proceedings and the protection of the parties' interests,[28] (2) a court-appointed receiver (*mandataire judiciaire*) who will act on behalf and in the general interest of the creditors,[29] and (3) an administrator ('*administrateur judiciaire*') to supervise or assist the incumbent management who will continue being in charge of the ailing business to help it overcome its financial difficulties.[30] The supervisory judge may appoint up to five controllers from among the creditors requesting to be appointed.[31] The controllers' role is to assist the supervisory judge in his duty of supervising the management of the business and the court-appointed receiver in his functions.[32] The controllers will not be paid for their duties.[33]

To make the *Sauvegarde* procedure more attractive and more accessible to companies in difficulty, the aforementioned 2008 Ordinance introduced a number of measures that aimed to enhance the powers of the debtor's existing management, including their ability to propose a specific administrator[34] and to make an application to the court to dispose of assets outside the ordinary course of business, or to seek to substitute security or sell part of the business during the moratorium period. In the *Sauvegarde* proceedings, it is the debtor, assisted by the administrator, who presents proposals to creditor committees. The Ordinance of 2008 further provides that any creditor that is a committee member may also submit proposals to the debtor and the administrator.

---

[27] It may be renewed once by a reasoned decision at the request of the debtor, the administrator or the Public Prosecutor. Art. L621-3 of the Commercial Code.

[28] The duties of the supervisory judge are specified in art. L622-20 of the Commercial Code.

[29] Art. L621-9 of the Commercial Code.

[30] Art. 23 of the Law of 2005, amending art. L622-1 of the Commercial Code. The court shall not be bound to appoint an administrator where the proceedings relate to a debtor whose number of employees and turnover net of tax are below the thresholds provided for by a *Conseil d'Etat decree*.

[31] Where he appoints several controllers, he must ensure that at least one of them is chosen from among the secured creditors and one from among the unsecured creditors. Article L621-10 of the Commercial Code.

[32] Art. L621-11 of the Commercial Code.

[33] *Ibid.*

[34] Art. 14 of the Ordinance of 2008.

Subject to certain thresholds referring to the size of a company's turnover and number of employees,[35] two creditor committees are required to be established: (1) the committee of credit institutions and (2) the committee of main suppliers of goods or services. These should be appointed within 30 days from the commencement order.[36] The debtor must, within a period of two months (renewable once) from the date of the committees' creation, present its proposals for drawing up the draft plan. Creditors' committees must generally vote on a plan at the latest within 30 days from its receipt, and the decision of each committee to approve the draft plan is taken by a two-thirds majority of overall debt claims of members of that committee who have voted on the debtor's plan.[37] Bondholders vote in a general meeting on the plan that has been adopted by both creditor committees.[38]

The role of the court during the *Sauvegarde* proceedings is rather limited, mainly consisting of its power to validate the plan adopted by the committees, and it must do so in conformity with the suggestions of the two creditor committees. In approving the plan as adopted by the committees the court must check that the interests of all creditors are sufficiently protected, and to this effect it can veto the plan if necessary.[39] Once the court has finally endorsed the plan, this becomes binding upon all members of the committees.[40] However, non-participating creditors are not bound by the decisions of the committees. Creditors who are not members of the committees must be consulted in parallel as to the

---

[35] That is, if the debtor (a) has more than 150 employees or (b) has a turnover of more than 20,000,000 and (c) its accounts are certified by a statutory auditor or carried out by a certified public accountant. Nevertheless, the insolvency judge can decide to create committees even though the thresholds are not met.

[36] Art. L626-30 of the Commercial Code. The committees are established by the administrator. Each supplier of goods or services shall be a member *ipso jure* of the committee of the main suppliers where its claims account for more than 3 per cent of the total claims of suppliers.

[37] Art. L626-30 of the Commercial Code. The Ordinance removed the former requirement of 51 per cent in number of creditors.

[38] Bondholders' decision is taken by a two-thirds majority of the aggregate amount of bond claims held by bondholders that voted at the bondholders' general meeting on the proposal.

[39] Art. L626-31 of the Commercial Code.

[40] Art. L626-29 to 35 of the Commercial Code.

strategy of settling the debts owed to them, for instance reduction of the debt with shorter deferral or full repayment over a longer period.[41]

It is worth noting that, similarly to *Conciliation*, in the *Sauvegarde* proceedings, creditors who have made a contribution of fresh funds to the debtor or performed essential executory contracts in order to support the continued operation of a distressed company after the issue of the commencement order are conferred a super-priority by the Law of 2005.[42] Nevertheless, the supervisor judge shall allow the provision of such funds only to the extent necessary for the continuation of business operations during the moratorium period, and the requisite decision is subject to publicity requirements.[43]

New Fast-track Options: the *Sauvegarde Financiére Accélérée* Procedure and the *Sauvegarde Accélérée* Procedure

To increase insolvency law flexibility, the French legislator implemented an evolutionary reform of the *Sauvegarde* procedure, providing a fast-track option, the *Sauvegarde Financiére Accélérée* ('SFA') in the beginning of 2011.[44] This fast-track procedure draws from practical experience and essentially offers an option that allows a restructuring with financial creditors, mainly banking establishments and bondholders, leaving the trade creditors unaffected,[45] and allowing the debtor to operate the day-to-day business of the company under circumstances that are as normal as possible.

There are certain pre-conditions that a company has to meet in order to take advantage of this procedure: (1) the company's accounts must be certified by a statutory auditor or prepared by an accountant; and (2) the company's turnover must equal or exceed €20 million per year, or the

---

[41] Art. L626-33 of the Commercial Code. The court cannot impose a reduction of the debt on creditors refusing the debtor's proposals, but only a rescheduling (not exceed ten years) or deferral of payment.

[42] Art. L611-12 of the Commercial Code. These claims will be paid in priority in the following order: claims of wages and salaries; loans and claims arising from the performance of continued contracts and where the other party accepts deferred payments; and all other claims, according to their priority.

[43] Art. L622-17 of the Commercial Code.

[44] It is contained in Art. L628-1 and L628-7 of the Commercial Code.

[45] B Laufer, *An Economic Analysis of the German Bankruptcy Code in the Context of the European Reform Movement*, Masters Thesis MSc International Finance at HEC Paris 2012 <http://www.professionsfinancieres.com/sites/default/files/docsupload/u213/M%20Benjamin%20LAUFER.pdf> accessed 30 January 2016, 44.

company must have 150 or more employees on the date of filing for the SFA.[46] Apart from those pre-conditions, a company that wishes to invoke this procedure must convince the court that the restructuring plan will not only address the financial difficulties it faces, but will also gain a qualified majority vote[47] from both the committee of creditors and the general meeting of bondholders.

Unlike the standard stand-alone *Sauvegarde* procedure, this fast-track procedure, initiated on the request of the debtor, directly follows on from the *Conciliation* proceedings during which a restructuring is negotiated.[48] The debtor should show that a draft plan aimed at ensuring the sustainability of the company has been prepared and that it is likely to receive sufficiently broad support from the creditors concerned.[49]

As mentioned earlier, the *Conciliation* procedure is a contract-based confidential procedure which requires the unanimous consent of creditors involved in the negotiations. Due to its contractual nature, a holdout problem may arise when recalcitrant creditors are unsatisfied with the negotiations and exercise their power to prevent the adoption of a plan where unanimity is required.

The fast-track procedure is introduced to act as a counterweight against such holdout powers of the dissenting minority creditors, by converting a *Conciliation* Agreement that does not have unanimous creditor approval into a mandatory restructuring plan that will be conferred with binding effect to all creditors involved if it can secure a qualified majority vote. As trade creditors are excluded from the discussions, they are not summoned to vote on the plan, and only financial creditors and potentially the bondholders vote on the plan.[50] As a result, the plan, if adopted, does not bind trade creditors. Also, the payment of the trade claims will not be frozen or rescheduled. The time limit of establishing the relevant committees is reduced from fifteen days in the standard *Sauvegarde* procedure to eight days.[51]

To obtain the court's approval on the restructuring plan, the same voting procedures as with the standard *Sauvegarde* procedure should be

---

[46] Arts. L628-1 and L626-29 of the Commercial Code.

[47] This is based on the total value of the claims of all the eligible creditors who actually take part in the voting.

[48] Art. L628-1 of the Commercial Code.

[49] *Ibid.*

[50] Art. L628-4 of the Commercial Code. The 15-day period for setting out the committee of credit institutions in the standard *Sauvegarde* proceedings shall be reduced to 8 days in the fast-track route.

[51] Art. L628-4 of the Commercial Code.

followed. After the court's approval to proceed under an SFA, the financial creditors have one month (with a possible extension of another month)[52] to vote on and adopt the restructuring plan in the banking establishments' committee and among the bondholders, respectively, instead of six months under the standard procedure (with the possibility to extend this period by a further six months).[53]

Most recently, the Ordinance of 2014 created a new *Sauvegarde Accélérée* procedure *('AS')*,[54] which is designed to encompass all creditors, not only financial. As in the case of the AFS, the AS procedure is available to a debtor company which is in *Conciliation* and has succeeded in presenting a plan approved by a sufficient (two-thirds) majority of creditors to form the basis for the initiation of *Sauvegarde* – this opens the possibility for the plan to be approved by creditor committees once the AS proceedings have opened.[55] The plan must be approved by the committees within a maximum period of three months of the opening of proceedings, in contrast to one month in the case of an AFS.

The French Pre-packs in the Form of *AFS* and *AS*

The two fast-track options are introduced to further enhance the dynamics of the French restructuring practice to facilitate the anticipation and treatment of corporate distress. The accelerated procedures have created pre-pack routes via a combination of two pre-insolvency rescue procedures to enable troubled companies to restructure their debts in a speedy manner. Initiation of *Conciliation* proceedings is a mandatory prerequisite for the fast-track procedures. This would provide incentives for company directors to take early steps in order to avert a crisis, as there is a clear requirement for the company to be solvent and the managerial power of the existing board will not be affected in *Conciliation*. Moreover, the proceedings are confidential and allow a restructuring plan to be negotiated and prepared without being made public. Further, to overcome the holdout problem, given the contractual nature of the

---

[52] Art. L628-6 of the Commercial Code.

[53] Instead of requiring the 20 and 15 days' notice of the meetings of the committee of banking establishments and assembly of bondholders, respectively, under the standard safeguard procedure, only 8 and 10 days' notice, respectively, need be given under the accelerated procedure.

[54] It entered into force on 1 July 2014.

[55] Norton Rose Publications, *Upcoming Changes To French Insolvency Law* <http://www.nortonrosefulbright.com/knowledge/publications/116292/upcoming-changes-to-french-insolvency-law> accessed 30 January 2016.

Conciliation proceedings, the outcome of the negotiations in *Conciliation* will be solidified by the *Sauvegarde* proceedings, which require a two-thirds majority vote from affected creditors to approve pre-negotiated plans. A positive vote for the plan at this stage will also bind the dissenting creditors.

Put simply, the French pre-pack is a combination of a pre-insolvency contractual settlement proceeding aimed at providing the debtor and its creditors with a confidential negotiation platform and a formal plan confirmation procedure. In comparison with UK pre-pack administration, although the negotiation platform in the French pre-pack is also contractual and confidential in nature, it is more court-supervised. The negotiation is conducted under the supervision of the presiding judge of the court. Furthermore, the company's directors negotiate its debts with the affected claimholders under the aegis of a conciliator who is appointed by the presiding judge of the court to provide assistance to the debtor with a view of achieving a successful negotiation of the company's debts. Court supervision at the negotiation stage introduces essential accountability safeguards to the restructuring process.

Moreover, at the plan confirmation stage, creditors' committees are required to be established to vote on the pre-negotiated plan. The plan has to obtain qualified majority approval from affected claimholders and also has to be validated by the court to ensure that the interests of all creditors are sufficiently protected and appropriate notice has been given to all parties.[56] In comparison with the UK pre-pack method, the level of 'pre-packing' in the French pre-pack approach is relatively lower than its UK counterpart. Essentially, the French approach merely aims to speed up the process by shortening the timeline of setting up creditor committees and taking the required vote. In contrast, there is a real element of pre-determination in a UK pre-pack, since the pre-arranged plan could often bypass creditors' voting rights and be executed immediately once the administration procedure commences, with no need for court sanction.

It should be noted that the French pre-packs offering fast-track options are preventive tools under the supervision of the court to allow troubled companies to deal with their difficulties in a preventive way. It is therefore geared towards securing the rescue of the company instead of rescuing the business through a going-concern sale, as is the case with the UK pre-pack process. In this respect, the French pre-pack is similar to the US pre-packaged Chapter 11 reorganisation. Also, to ensure the

---

[56] Art. L626-31 of the Commercial Code.

continuation of the business while attempting to obtain an approval of the pre-negotiated restructuring plan, the French pre-pack also offers certain privileges to new money made available during the *Conciliation* proceedings prior to formal court approval of the plan. One of the key differences between a French pre-pack and a US Chapter 11 pre-pack is that the operative voting in France takes place after commencement of the *Sauvegarde* proceedings for plan confirmation, not before. Therefore, a pre-pack arrangement in France is more similar to a US-style of pre-negotiated plan.[57]

THE USE OF THE PRE-PACK METHOD IN THE NETHERLANDS

The Statutory Rescue Procedure and the Use of the Pre-pack Approach in Dutch Restructuring and Insolvency Practice

The current Dutch Bankruptcy Act (*Faillissementswet*) came into force in 1896 and it has not been thoroughly revised since then, although recently the government announced that it is necessary to draft a new bankruptcy law given developments in insolvency practice.[58] The Act provides for two types of insolvency proceedings vis-à-vis companies that face financial difficulties: (1) bankruptcy proceedings (*faillissement*) that are aimed at liquidating the debtor's assets for the recovery of its creditors; and (2) the suspension of payments proceedings (*surseance van betaling*) aiming at rescheduling the debts of a financially distressed company whose business is still economically viable by offering a plan of composition to the creditors.[59]

---

[57] A Sorensen and A Tetley, 'French Pre-packs: Key Stages and Their Related Issues' (2010) 7 *International Corporate Rescue* 7.

[58] It was announced that three new Acts would be implemented: the Act on the Continuity of Companies I: Pre-pack proceedings; the Act on the Continuity of Companies II: Composition outside bankruptcy proceedings; and the Act on the Continuity of Companies III: Duty for suppliers to continue to supply in bankruptcy. The draft bill on the Continuity of Enterprises II was published in 2014, proposing a restructuring procedure to restructure the company through a compulsory composition, similar to the English Scheme of Arrangement and the US Chapter 11 proceedings.

[59] To make an application for suspension of payments status in the Dutch courts, the debtor must foresee that it will not be able to continue paying its debts when they fall due in the near future. Art. 214 of the Dutch Bankruptcy Act.

To make an application for suspension of payments in the Dutch courts, the debtor must foresee that the company will not be able to continue paying its debts when they fall due in the near future.[60] Upon a request from the debtor company, the court may grant a preliminary suspension of payments and set a date for a court hearing to determine whether the suspension should be granted on a more permanent basis.[61] At the same time, it will appoint an administrator (*bewindvoerder*) who, together with the debtor, will administer the debtor's affairs,[62] and at the request of the administrator, will appoint a supervisory judge (*Rechter-commissaris*) to advise the administrator upon his request.[63] This will trigger a suspension of payments against ordinary creditors, but leave preferential and secured creditors unaffected unless the court has granted a cooling-off period.[64] The suspension of payments proceedings are not confidential. Upon the granting of a provisional moratorium, information will be published immediately in the Government Gazette.[65] Any proposed settlement or arrangement with the affected creditors must be approved by a normal majority of all recognised and admitted creditors whose claims represent at least 50 per cent of the total amount of the admitted claims.[66] It is suggested that this statuary rescue procedure rarely ever fulfilled its goal and companies that do ask for suspension of payment are generally declared bankrupt within a few weeks after the initial decision on the suspension of payments request.[67]

---

[60] Art. 214 of the Dutch Bankruptcy Act.

[61] Art. 215 of the Dutch Bankruptcy Act. The length of time that a company remains under suspension of payment protection varies significantly depending on the objective being pursued and the size and complexity of the procedure, but in most cases, the provisional phase may last for a few days or a week, and if a suspension on payment is granted indefinitely, the district court shall set its duration at one and a half year at most. Art. 223 of the Dutch Bankruptcy Act. See also BG Arends and JA van der Meer, *Restructuring and Insolvency 2006/07: The Netherlands*, available at <https://www.holla.nl/mediamanagement/user/publicaties/422.pdf> accessed 30 January 2016, 121.

[62] Directors' powers are not suspended during this period, but they must govern the company and manage the estate in cooperation with and with authorisation from the administrator. Arts 215(1) and 228 of the Dutch Bankruptcy Act.

[63] Art. 223a of the Dutch Bankruptcy Act.

[64] Art. 232 of the Dutch Bankruptcy Act.

[65] Art. 216 of the Dutch Bankruptcy Act.

[66] Art. 268 of the Dutch Bankruptcy Act.

[67] It has been said that in 95 per cent of cases where a suspension of payments had been granted in 2004 ended without a settlement and with

Although there are only a few legal instruments available under the Dutch statutes, the practitioners and the judiciaries have adopted a rather flexible approach in dealing with insolvencies.[68] Dutch courts have taken the lead and are becoming increasingly inventive in assisting companies in financial distress to restructure and make a new start.[69] Thus, court-coordinated pre-packaged restructurings are not uncommon in the Netherlands. Although the pre-pack process has not gained any footage in Dutch insolvency legislation, in practice, most Dutch district courts are willing to cooperate with the appointment of a silent trustee ('*Stille Bewindvoerder*') upon request of a company in distress to facilitate the striking of a possible restructuring agreement in order to preserve the value of the business and minimise the negative consequences of corporate failure.

The silent trustee is appointed by the district courts in a confidential manner. The silent trustee will be informed of the ongoing negotiations with the relevant stakeholders (usually secured creditors and potential buyers), and will be given access to all necessary information and offered all cooperation that he requires to assess the possibilities of a restructuring.[70] Once the stakeholders have reached an agreement, often a sale arrangement, the company enters into bankruptcy proceedings, and the silent trustee will then be officially appointed as the bankruptcy trustee by the district court following the commencement of formal bankruptcy

---

insolvency declared. See Arends and Meer, *Restructuring and Insolvency 2006/07: The Netherlands*, 121.

[68] European Commission, *Evaluation of Member State Procedures for Financial Reconstruction of Enterprises in Financial Distress* (Report 2010), v.

[69] Judgment on *Schoeller Arca Systems* group ('SAS') restructuring in 2009 set the first Dutch-law precedent of a pre-pack whereby the sale of a Dutch holding company pre-agreed between the buyer, the company and its senior lenders is enforced, even though its subordinated bridge lenders opposed the proposed sale. The court approved the private sale process of SAS to a newly created entity owned by the existing PE sponsor, disregarding junior lenders' concerns over the valuation. For a summary of this restructuring case, see Clifford Chance Client Brief, 'The Way Forward where Value Breaks in the Junior Debt – a Ruling from the Dutch Courts' (Client briefing, September 2009) <http://www.cliffordchance.com/content/dam/cliffordchance/PDF/value_breaking_in_the_junior_debt.pdf> accessed 30 January 2016.

[70] B Rumora-Scheltema *et al.*, 'Dutch Pre-pack Alternatives on the Rise' <http://www.lexology.com/library/detail.aspx?g=a04ba290-dbf2-428a-bb2a-32ce2b0716aa> accessed 30 January 2016.

proceedings. It follows that any pre-arranged transaction will be effectuated by the trustee. Typically, the time between the opening of bankruptcy proceedings and the signing and closing of the transaction is very short – often on the same day.[71]

Introducing an Explicit Legal Framework for Dutch Style Pre-packs – the Appointment of a 'Prospective Trustee' in the (Draft) Act on Continuity of Companies I

The increasing popularity of the pre-pack practice has prompted Dutch legislators to look into the possibility of codifying the appointment of a silent trustee within an explicit legal framework to ensure that viable enterprises in financial difficulties have access to restructuring proceedings in order to prevent insolvency. Within the broad legislative programme of promoting the 'continuity of companies', to further facilitate pre-packs and create a statutory basis for this practice, in October 2013, the Dutch Minister of Security and Justice presented a draft bill for an Act on the Continuity of Companies I (*Wet Continuïteit Ondernemingen I*),[72] which aims to provide a statutory basis for the appointment of a silent trustee.

In the bill, a silent trustee is addressed as a 'prospective trustee' (*Beoogd Curator*). The bill provides guidance as to the conditions under which a prospective trustee can be appointed, and also addresses such issues as the duration of the silent insolvency, transparency, reporting and accountability duties of the prospective trustee, and the applicability of claw-back provisions in the period between the appointment of the silent trustee and the actual insolvency proceedings.

According to the bill, the appointment of a prospective trustee should be at the request of the debtor company. It is required that the request has to clarify why the appointment of a prospective trustee is preferable to immediate bankruptcy. The request also needs to describe the intentions of the pre-pack proceedings through a milestone-plan, which will be subject to a prima facie examination. It is specified in the draft Act that a request will be granted if it is likely that such an appointment will be in

---

71 *Ibid.*

72 A copy of *Memorie van Toelichting Wet Continuïteit Ondernemingen I* is available at <http://www.rijksoverheid.nl/documenten-en-publicaties/kamerstukken/2013/10/22/memorie-van-toelichting.html> accessed 30 January 2016.

the interests of the creditors as a whole[73] or in the public interest, or if the continuity of the business and the preservation of jobs will be served by such an appointment.[74] If satisfied, the court will appoint a prospective trustee and a prospective supervisory judge for a specific term. The appointment will not be made public and the decision cannot be appealed.[75] It should be noted that the 'prospective trusteeship' does not constitute a new insolvency regime. Simply put, the court appoints the person (the prospective trustee) who, if the company were to be declared bankrupt, would be appointed as the trustee, or as the administrator if the company were to apply for a suspension of payments.

Similarly with the existing silent trusteeship practice, the prospective trustee has no authority over the company, nor is he an agent of the company; the debtor (through its directors) retains the exclusive possession of its assets.[76] The prospective trustee represents and acts in the interests of all of the company's creditors, aiming at either working out a restructuring plan if it is realistic and in the best interest of creditors, or ensuring that the best value for the company's assets will be realised if bankruptcy is unavoidable.[77] He is not obliged to follow instructions from the debtor or from one or more of its creditors.[78]

Although not an adviser of the debtor company, the main purpose of the appointment, prior to the formal opening of the bankruptcy or suspension of payments proceedings, is to provide certainty to the parties' negotiation for an agreement and allow the business to continue without unnecessary interruption.[79] The debtor can consult with the prospective trustees on questions such as: whether or not certain business

---

[73] This could be established by showing that the expected outcome of a pre-arranged sale would exceed the liquidation proceeds of the assets.

[74] *Memorie van Toelichting Wet continuïteit ondernemingen I, F* Article 363(1).

[75] *Ibid.*, Article 363(5).

[76] Government of the Netherlands, 'Opstelten Facilitates Restart of Companies' (website News on 22 October 2013) <http://www.government.nl/news/2013/10/22/opstelten-facilitates-restart-of-companies.html> accessed 30 January 2016.

[77] H Buruma, 'Draft Legislation on Pre-pack Sales by a "Proposed Trustee" in the Netherlands' (News Update on 25 October 2013) <http://www.houthoff.com/uploads/tx_hhnewsletters/Insolvency_News_Update_Oct_2013.PDF> accessed 30 January 2016.

[78] *Memorie van Toelichting Wet continuïteit ondernemingen I, F* Article 365(1).

[79] Government of the Netherlands, 'Opstelten Facilitates Restart of Companies'.

performances or repayments of debts will be challenged by the trustee once the company enters into the formal proceedings; and whether certain preparations are necessary in order to speed up the restructuring and reduce the disadvantageous consequences of potential bankruptcy proceedings.[80] The debtor company should provide the prospective trustee with all relevant information for him to formulate their responses to these questions.[81] The prospective trustee, at the end of his appointment term, shall report its findings to the Office of the Court, and his report will be made available to the public when the formal insolvency proceedings commence.[82]

The Features of Dutch Pre-pack in the Form of the Prospective Trusteeship

The Dutch prospective trusteeship provides the relevant parties with certainty as regards the validity of their private negotiations prior to the opening of a formal insolvency procedure. In doing so, it prevents the company business from unnecessary interruption while a restructuring plan is put together. First, the company may ask the prospective trustee to give his view on certain matters, such as the effect of transactions carried out by the company at the pre-formal stage on creditor interests and the risk that such transactions may be annulled on the basis of fraudulent preference in consequent insolvency proceedings. Such declarations provide more certainty when parties negotiate the sale of a certain part of the business at the pre-insolvency stage. Secondly, the company may also ask the prospective trustee to give his view on the proposed transaction and his willingness to close the pre-arranged deal of business sales, once the company is declared bankrupt and he is appointed by the district court as a trustee or, if the company were to apply for a suspension of payments, as administrator.

This makes it possible for the assets and the business of a company to be sold immediately after the bankruptcy is announced. This also gives certainty to the stakeholders prior to the bankruptcy and leads to a faster conclusion of the asset transaction without the business having to cease

---

80 *Memorie van Toelichting Wet continuïteit ondernemingen I, F* Article 365(2).

81 *Ibid.*, Article 365(3)

82 *Ibid.*, Article 364(3).

its activities or the uncertainty that the trustee will annul certain transactions.[83]

The Dutch prospective trusteeship in many ways resembles UK pre-packs. Both allow a continuation of business while a restructuring plan is been putting together by keeping the on-going negotiation confidential. Furthermore, both allow essential preparation work to be done prior to the opening of a formal insolvency procedure with the assistance of a prospective trustee, so that the whole process can be sped up to minimise costs. The company will file a petition for bankruptcy when the arrangements are completed and the prospective trustee will be appointed as a trustee who can then effectuate the arrangements.

In spite of the resemblance, in contrast to a UK pre-pack, the Dutch prospective trusteeship under the draft Act involves more judicial intervention from the outset. First, there is certain judicial scrutiny about the purpose of the petition for the appointment of a perspective trustee. This would provide a certain degree of assurance for the pre-pack route to be used for appropriate purposes justified by particular circumstances. Secondly, the prospective trustee can only be appointed by the court.

In contrast, in the UK pre-pack process, the debtor company and/or its directors have more power in the appointment of an administrator. Furthermore, the legal status and duties of the prospective trustee are clearer than those of the insolvency practitioner involved in the pre-formal stage of a UK pre-pack. The prospective trustee is not an agent of the company, having no authority over the company. He is a court-appointed expert who enters into an agreement with the debtor company during the pre-formal stage to investigate the feasibility of the restructuring options and to help the debtor to identify the most effective way of restructuring. The salary of the prospective trustee will be paid by the debtor company and his salary will be paid with the same priority as administrative expenses in the event of bankruptcy.[84] The prospective trustee serves as an independent supervisor to ensure maximum preservation of value for the benefit of the creditors of the company. The prospective trustee's court appointment brings essential accountability to the secretive pre-formal stage and makes the whole process less controversial.

---

[83] De Brauw Blackstone Westbroek, Options for a Speedy Restructuring through Bankruptcy (website publication on 11 November 2013) <http://www.debrauw.com/newsletter/pre-pack-prospective-bankruptcy-trustee-in-the-netherlands-options-for-a-speedy-restructuring-through-bankruptcy/#> accessed 30 January 2016.

[84] *Memorie van Toelichting Wet continuïteit ondernemingen I, F* Article 366.

PRE-PACKS UNDER THE GERMAN INSOLVENCY CODE

Historically, German insolvency law has not been rescue-friendly. The protection of creditors was an important aspect of its court-driven insolvency procedures; in particular, the position of secured creditors has traditionally been very strong.[85] The law gave secured creditors strong incentives to trigger formal bankruptcy proceedings to liquidate the debtor company rather than maintaining it as a going concern. This resulted in an obvious lack of a rescue culture in Germany. In recent years, however, corporate insolvency law in Germany has undergone considerable changes.

The current German Insolvency Code was introduced in 1994 and came into effect in January 1999.[86] The 1994 reform aimed to limit the powers of secured creditors.[87] The core of the 1994 reform is the implementation of the insolvency plan proceedings ('*Insolvenzplanverfahren*'), which is devised to encourage parties to reach an arrangement with the aim of maintaining the company, although the fundamental objective of the satisfaction of the creditors remains paramount.[88] A general flaw pervading the 1994 insolvency law was that the court and the court-appointed trustee held significant control over the insolvency process, resulting in perceived impracticability and uncertainty for both

---

85 Secured creditors generally could enforce claims against immovable and movable assets in their possession unless the court imposed a stay upon request of the administrator, and this gave them strong incentives to trigger formal bankruptcy.

86 For an English translation of the German Insolvency Code (InsO), see <http://www.gesetze-im-internet.de/englisch_inso/englisch_inso.html#InsOengl_000P270> Accessed 30 January 2016.

87 The new Code repairs several inefficiencies inherent in the old procedure that often caused liquidations of economically viable debtors. For example, the Code introduces an automatic stay of three months on secured claims and considers a bankruptcy plan reorganisation an equitable alternative to formal liquidation. See more on P Jostarndt, *Financial Distress, Corporate Restructuring, and Firm Survival: an Empirical Analysis of German Panel Data* (Deutscher Universitats-Verlag 2007), 2–3.

88 As s.1 InsO makes clear, the insolvency plan proceedings is another tool provided for parties dealing with financial distress equivalent to other forms of insolvency procedures.

incumbent management and creditors at a sensitive point in the debtor company's history.[89]

More recently, to make German insolvency law more competitive, the 'Act for the Further Facilitation of the Reorganization of Companies' (*Gesetz zur weiteren Erleichterung der Sanierung von Unternehmen, ESUG*) was enacted (in December 2011) with a view to facilitating the reorganisation of companies in financial distress.[90] In order to facilitate the realisation of a pre-packaged insolvency plan, the ESUG introduced the new 'protective shield proceedings' *(Schutzschirmverfahren),* the German version of a pre-pack.

The Uniform Insolvency Proceedings and the Rescue-oriented Insolvency Plan Proceedings

German insolvencies follow uniform insolvency proceedings, within which there are several courses that can be followed in the search for the best opportunity to satisfy the creditors' claims.[91] In general, insolvency proceedings can be divided into two distinct stages: (1) the preliminary insolvency proceedings and, subsequently, (2) the final insolvency proceedings. The preliminary insolvency proceedings begin with the filing of the petition and usually last up to three months, during which the court has to gather all the information necessary to determine if the prerequisites for commencing insolvency proceedings are met.[92] In most cases in which insolvency proceedings are initiated, the courts appoint a preliminary insolvency administrator *(vorläufiger Insolvenzverwalter).*

The preliminary proceedings end when a court order initiating the commencement of the actual insolvency proceedings is made. An administrator *(Insolvenzverwalter)* will generally be appointed to replace the debtor's management and take control of all company affairs.[93] There is an express requirement that the insolvency administrator must be an independent natural person who is particularly experienced in business

---

[89] See B Laufer, *An Economic Analysis of the German Bankruptcy Code in the Context of the European Reform Movement*, 30.

[90] The material provisions of the Act came into force on 1 March 2012.

[91] Insolvency proceedings can be initiated against any natural or legal person.

[92] The debtor files an insolvency petition on the grounds of impending illiquidity ('drohende Zahlungsunfähigkeit') or over-indebtedness ('Überschuldung').

[93] S Sax and C Weidner, *Reform Act on Restructuring Insolvent Companies: Upcoming Changes* (Clifford Chance Newsletter, December 2011).

affairs and independent of the creditors and the debtor.[94] As an alternative to the administration of the debtor's business by an insolvency administrator, the insolvency court may grant the use of self-administration (*Anordnung der Eigenverwaltung*) on the request of the debtor, which allows management to remain in charge of the debtor's business under the supervision of a court-appointed trustee (*Sachwalter*). Nevertheless, these proceedings have rarely been used in Germany. The insolvency courts have shown considerable reluctance to order self-administration in insolvency proceedings.[95] It should be noted that following the uniform insolvency proceedings, the rules for certain procedural requirements are in general the same regardless of whether there was debtor self-management or insolvency administrator-led restructuring or liquidation. For example, the requirements for the approval of an insolvency plan after the opening of insolvency proceedings and the classifications of voting creditors are in any scenario the same.

The insolvency plan proceedings are part of the uniform insolvency proceedings which allow for different ways of disposing of the insolvent estate and distributing to the parties concerned the settlement of the creditors' insolvency claims other than those contained in the regular insolvency proceedings. It can be seen as an extension of the 'old' executive law with a focus on liquidation to accommodate the new approach focusing on reorganisation.[96] In the insolvency plan proceedings, both the debtor and the insolvency administrator (*Insolvenzverwalter*) are entitled to submit an insolvency plan to court.[97] An insolvency plan shall consist of a declaratory part that describes the measures taken after the opening of the insolvency proceedings and a constructive part that determines how the legal positions of the parties involved would be

---

[94] S 56(1) InsO. It also states that the requisite independence shall not already be ruled out on account of the fact that:

1. the person's name was put forward by the debtor or by a creditor,
2. the person in question had given the debtor advice of a general nature on the course and consequences of the insolvency proceedings prior to the request for the opening of insolvency proceedings being filed.

[95] Sax and Weidner, 'Reform Act on Restructuring Insolvent Companies: Upcoming Changes'.

[96] J Klein, 'Pre-pack Administration: a Comparison between Germany and the United Kingdom: Part 2' (2012) 33 *Company Lawyers* 303, 304.

[97] Submission by the debtor may be connected with a request to open insolvency proceedings; the administrator shall submit such plan if the creditors' assembly has charged him to do so. Ss 217 and 218 InsO.

changed.[98] The court will then arrange a hearing for the voting on the plan and the voting rights of the creditors.[99] Similar to the US Chapter 11 reorganisation, to ensure that creditors with different claims and interests are considered, eligible claims are divided into different voting groups. For an insolvency plan to be accepted, in each group the majority of creditors with voting rights have to agree to the plan and the sum of claims held by these creditors must be at least half of the value of claims held by all creditors with voting rights.[100]

In standard insolvency plan proceedings, the plan is submitted after the opening of the insolvency proceedings. Nevertheless, s 218 of the German Insolvency Code permits an insolvency plan to be prepared in advance of the opening of the formal insolvency procedure, allowing it to be submitted in conjunction with the request to open insolvency proceedings. In this way, the statutory process is sped up and the duration of the actual insolvency plan proceedings is reduced as the work for the preparation of the insolvency plan and discussion of its content with the most important creditors is done prior to the opening of the formal proceedings. Furthermore, it allows negotiations to take place away from the public eye and therefore avoid the risk of a prejudicial impact on the value of the company due to the usual negative reception of news of financial distress.

Considering their expected loss of control, debtors have limited incentives to file a pre-packaged bankruptcy petition.[101] The extremely poor survival chances for a bankrupt debtor in Germany are consistent with my finding that distressed firms only rarely make use of their option to file a pre-packaged bankruptcy petition.[102]

The 2011 Reform and the New 'Protective Shield Proceedings'

On 27 October 2011, the German Parliament passed the 'Act for the Further Facilitation of the Reorganization of Companies' (*Gesetz zur weiteren Erleichterung der Sanierung von Unternehmen, ESUG*), which was further enacted on 7 December 2011.[103] It is marked as a substantial reform to make German insolvency law more competitive with a view to

---

98 Ss 220–21 InsO.

99 S 235 InsO.

100 S 244 InsO.

101 Jostarndt, *Financial Distress, Corporate Restructuring, and Firm Survival: an Empirical Analysis of German Panel Data*, 77.

102 *Ibid.*, 111.

103 The material provisions of the Act came into force on 1 March 2012.

facilitating the reorganisation of insolvent companies. To do so, it tackles the obstacles that exist in the Insolvency Code for the reorganisation of a company by: encouraging early filing for insolvency; strengthening the influence of creditors on the proceedings, including the selection of an insolvency administrator; providing easier access to self-administration; introducing new 'Protective Shield' proceedings *(Schutzschirmverfahren)*; and extending and streamlining the insolvency plan proceedings.

Key measures to facilitate the reorganisation of financially distressed companies

In order to allow creditors to have more influence in the early stages of insolvency, a new form of statutory creditor participation via a provisional creditors' committee (*vorläufiger Gläubigerausschuss*) has been introduced via section 22a InsO.[104] Appointment of a provisional creditors' committee by the insolvency court is only required if the debtor company meets certain criteria regarding the size of its business and if the debtor's business has not been discontinued.[105]

Furthermore, prior to the ESUG reform, the insolvency court was entitled to choose the insolvency administrator in its sole discretion.[106] This to some extent produced uncertainty as regards the success of early negotiation efforts and of whether the administrator supports the agreed plan. However, now under the ESUG, prior to the appointment of the insolvency administrator and of the preliminary insolvency administrator,

---

[104] The court shall establish a preliminary creditors' committee at the debtor's or creditors' request for ordinary companies. It will be obligatory for companies of a specific size: a preliminary Creditors' Committee shall be set up during preliminary insolvency proceedings where the debtor company satisfies two of the following three requirements: a balance sheet total in excess of EUR 4,840,000, revenues of at least EUR 9,680,000 in the twelve months prior to the last balance sheet date and/or fifty or more employees.

[105] S 22a InsO. It is required that the debtor must satisfy at least two out of the three following criteria in the previous business year:

1. A minimum balance sheet total of 4,840,000 euros after deduction of an amount entered erroneously on the asset side within the meaning of section 268 subsection (3) of the Commercial Code (*Handelsgesetzbuch*);
2. A minimum of 9,680,000 euros sales revenues in the twelve months prior to the balance sheet date;
3. At least fifty employees on an annual average.

[106] Ss 56 and 57 InsO. Creditors only have the right to request the replacement of the administrator. But in practice, the courts often involved the creditors in the decision about the administrator.

the insolvency court may request comments from the provisional creditors' committee.[107] The provisional creditors' committee is entitled to provide the criteria for the appointment of the potential administrator and the court has to take such criteria into account.[108] Where the provisional creditors' committee unanimously agrees on a person to act as the insolvency administrator, the court can only refuse the proposal if the proposed person is unfit to be an administrator.[109]

In fact, it was very common for the German insolvency courts to reject insolvency practitioners who had advised the debtor at a pre-insolvency stage because, according to their view, an insolvency practitioner who was involved in the preparation of an insolvency plan prior to the filing for insolvency lacks the independence required by s 56 InsO. After the 2011 reform, s 56(1) InsO expressly provides that it is no longer considered as a conflict of interest or lack of independence of the insolvency administrator if the person suggested by the debtor or any of the creditors had previously advised the debtor about the insolvency procedure and its consequences.

This amendment can be crucial for the rescue of a company as it is usually important that debtors are advised and supported by an administrator with whom they have built a relationship of trust during previous transactions. In addition, it adds to the efficiency of the procedure because a person who knows the circumstances of the company and was already involved in the preparation of the plan and discussed the details with the major creditors will be able to reorganise the company in a shorter time and more cost-efficiently, and needs no further time to gain an insight into the situation. Another important objective of the insolvency reform was to promote the use of self-administration by limiting the insolvency court's ability to refuse to order self-administration.[110] The ESUG makes it clear that the court may refuse to grant a self-administration order only where there are known concrete grounds to hold that self-administration would negatively affect the creditors' position.[111] The provisional creditors' committee will have decisive influence on the court's decision to grant an order of self-administration with the

---

[107] S 56a (1) InsO.

[108] S 56a (1) InsO.

[109] S 56a(2) InsO.

[110] Prior to the reform, a court would permit self-administration only if it is convinced that the procedure will not be deferred or will not otherwise adversely affect creditors. S 270(2)3 InsO.

[111] S 270(2)2 InsO.

right to be heard by the insolvency court before the court decides on the self-administration petition filed by the debtor.[112]

The ESUG reform has also extended the array of restructuring options in an insolvency plan, for example, by facilitating conversion of debt into equity with relaxed requirements on the protection of shareholders' rights.[113] Furthermore, to reduce individual creditors' holdout powers, protection of minorities has been revised in the form of section 251 to make rejection of an insolvency plan more difficult if funds have been set aside to compensate disadvantaged claimants.[114]

The new 'Protective Shield Proceedings'

To encourage earlier filings for the opening of insolvency proceedings and therefore increase the chances for a successful restructuring, the ESUG introduced a new concept, the so called 'Protective Shield Proceedings' ('*Schutzschirmverfahren*'), in Section 270b InsO to enable potentially illiquid (as opposed to being actually illiquid) and/or over-indebted debtors to put together an insolvency plan in self-administration under the supervision of a provisional insolvency monitor (*vorläufiger Sachwalter*) prior to the opening of insolvency proceedings. The debtor must have requested self-management, and the intended restructuring should not manifestly lack the prospect of success.[115]

---

[112] If the committee supports the petition, the court generally cannot refuse to order self-administration on the grounds that it would adversely affect the creditors. In addition, the committee will be entitled to demand the revocation of self-administration (S 270(3) InsO).

[113] S 225a InsO. In such a case, the shareholders will have a voting right to support or reject the proposed insolvency plan. However, should they not approve the plan, they can nevertheless be crammed down, if the dissenting shareholders are not put in a worse position than without the plan following its implementation. Whether the shareholder receives compensation out of the 'cash reserves' shall be decided in regular court proceedings outside the insolvency proceedings. See B Bähr *et al.*, *The New German Laws Governing the Restructuring of Companies* (White&Case NewsAlert June 2011) <http://www.whitecase.com/sites/whitecase/files/files/download/publications/alert_the_new_german_laws_governing_the_restructuring_of_companies_-_it-s_time_for_change.pdf> accessed 30 January 2016.

[114] Funds can now be set aside in case an affected creditor is able to demonstrate that he has been placed in a worse position as a result of the insolvency plan. The creditor should receive compensation out of these funds, which will be settled outside insolvency proceedings in future, thus no longer preventing the plan procedure being concluded.

[115] S 270b(1) InsO. The debtor is required to provide certification, provided by a professional who is experienced in insolvency matters or with comparable

Provided that the aforementioned pre-conditions are met, upon the request of the debtor, the court may order to grant a deadline (no more than three months) for submission of the insolvency plan. At the same time, the court shall appoint a provisional insolvency monitor to supervise the debtor during the Protective Shield proceedings. The debtor is entitled to propose a specific individual as provisional insolvency monitor and the insolvency court may only reject this proposal if the person is clearly unsuitable for the position.[116]

In order to facilitate the restructuring, under the Protective Shield proceedings, the debtor will be granted a maximum period of three months to prepare a restructuring plan while enjoying the protection of a quasi-moratorium. On application of the debtor the insolvency court may order that compulsory enforcement measures taken by the creditors be temporarily suspended during the Protective Shield proceedings.[117] During the debtor-in-possession management, the debtor is subject to the supervision of the provisional insolvency monitor who must give his consent to any business transactions that exceed the course of the debtor's ordinary business operations. Furthermore, the law does not require the order granting the Protective Shield proceedings to be published. However, the decision of the insolvency court ordering debtor-in-possession management after the opening of insolvency proceedings shall always be published.[118]

The order shall be revoked before the deadline expires if the envisaged restructuring no longer has prospects of success, or if the provisional creditors' committee requests that the order be revoked.[119] If no provisional creditors' committee has been appointed, any creditor can make such a request on the basis of prima facie evidence that the proceedings will have a detrimental effect on the creditors.[120] The debtor or the provisional insolvency monitor has a legal obligation to notify the court immediately when the debtor becomes insolvent.[121]

---

qualifications, which provides evidence that the debtor is not already insolvent and that the intended restructuring does not manifestly lack the prospect of success.

[116] S 270b(2) InsO.

[117] S 270b(2) InsO. This does not, however, extend to compulsory enforcement measures in respect of immovables.

[118] S 273 InsO.

[119] S 270b(4) InsO.

[120] *Ibid.*

[121] *Ibid.*

After expiry of the deadline or revoking the order, the court shall take a decision regarding the opening of insolvency proceedings. The debtor shall submit the insolvency plan to the court in the former situation. Insolvency proceedings are then opened whereupon the company's creditors will take a vote on the insolvency plan. The requirements for the approval of the insolvency plan after opening insolvency proceedings are the same regardless of whether it was drawn in the course of Protective Shield proceedings or not.

If an order of self-management is granted, an insolvency monitor shall be appointed instead of an insolvency administrator.[122] The insolvency monitor will mainly verify the company's financial position and monitor the management team and its spending.[123] The insolvency monitor may object to transactions that are concluded in the course of the debtor's ordinary business.[124] Furthermore, the debtor shall obtain the consent of the creditors' committee for transactions of particular importance to the insolvency proceedings.[125]

The Features of the German Pre-pack in the Form of Protective Shield Proceedings

In general, the reforms introduced by the ESUG will significantly improve the chances of successful restructuring for German companies. The broader accessibility of self-administration and new protective shield proceeding will provide companies in financial difficulties with an incentive to take restructuring action at an earlier point in time without being concerning about loss of control. Furthermore, by creating a pre-insolvency preparation space, a pre-packed insolvency plan will be in place in good time for creditors to vote on at the opening of insolvency proceedings. This allows consultation and negotiation with creditors to take place in a relatively private but more flexible environment than in the insolvency proceedings.

In comparison to a UK pre-pack, the plan formulation stage of the German pre-pack is not completely private, but rather court-supervised. First, the initiation of the Protective Shield proceedings is subject to prior court checks to confirm that all necessary criteria have been met and that the prospect of restructuring would not be futile. The court may revoke its order before the deadline of the Protective Shield proceedings expires

---

122 S 270c InsO.
123 S 274(2) InsO.
124 S 275 InsO.
125 S 276 InsO.

if the envisaged restructuring no longer has prospects of success. Secondly, there is a court-appointed provisional insolvency monitor, an independent person who supervises the debtor during the Protective Shield proceedings and who is accountable to the court. The introduction of the provisional insolvency monitor encourages active monitoring of management behaviour, which may foster a proper level of director and management loyalty. Furthermore, attendant scrutiny provides a certain level of assurance for the creditors' interests during the process of plan formulation.

Judicial supervision is essential in terms of accountability. The plan formulation stage in a pre-pack is hardly a collective forum as a formal inclusive insolvency procedure, but it may have the same function in deciding the fate of the company, as any agreements on the company's way forward at that stage often foreclose alternative courses of action that may be otherwise available. Leaving the plan preparation space completely private entails a risk that certain key parties may push for solutions that may prejudice less powerful creditors. The scrutiny of DIP decisions under the Protective Shield proceedings also creates the necessary checks and motivation for the DIP to avoid practices that may stain the process.

Generally speaking, the German pre-pack in the form of Protective Shield proceedings is relatively preliminary in terms of levels of 'pre-packing' as compared with its counterparts in the UK or the USA. The law only allows for submission of the plan, it does not offer the possibility of recognised voting on the plan prior to the opening of the insolvency procedure. Unlike the US pre-packaged Chapter 11 where 'pre-voting' on the plan is accepted with binding effect, provided that relevant requirements are satisfied, a prepared plan under the German law has to go through a hearing and discussion and a vote on the plan in the court before it can be effectuated. Therefore, it is arguable that the German pre-pack is less pre-determined than its UK or US counterparts. This, nevertheless, does not mean that the whole process provides parties with less certainty. Although everything very much depends on verification and voting on the plan in the consequent proceedings, the supervision exercised by the provisional insolvency monitor over the process and the court primary verification of the pre-conditions for initiating the pre-packing proceedings are, to some extent, reassuring to parties involved in the negotiation of the predictability of the outcome.

CONCLUSION

This chapter has critically examined reforms of the insolvency framework in three key continental jurisdictions (France, the Netherlands, and Germany), which have introduced new and improved procedures that may promote corporate rescue and increase the chances of a successful rescue. Requisite reforms especially focus on new approaches for the integration of the pre-packing strategy to formal insolvency procedures to facilitate the formulation of the restructuring plan.

Recent reforms in French law have introduced two fast-track procedural options: (1) the *Sauvegarde Financiére Accélérée* proceedings and (2) the *Sauvegarde Accélérée* proceedings. The two fast-track procedures promote pre-packed restructurings via a combination of, on the one hand, contractual yet court-supervised *Conciliation* proceedings in which a restructuring plan can be negotiated and prepared confidentially, and on the other, the court-driven confirmation *Sauvegarde* proceedings, where the pre-established plan can be speedily approved. In the Netherlands, the pre-packing practice takes the form of the appointment of a silent trustee, who is meant to provide companies with certainty via-à-vis their confidential negotiation with relevant parties prior to the opening of formal insolvency proceedings and prevent the company business from unnecessary interruption while a restructuring plan is being put together. The German form of 'pre-pack' was introduced by the ESUG 2011 in the form of the 'Protective Shield Proceedings', under which the debtor will be granted a maximum period of three months to prepare a restructuring plan in self-administration under the supervision of a provisional insolvency monitor while enjoying the protection of a quasi-moratorium prior to the opening of insolvency proceedings.

It is clear from the reforms in the three jurisdictions that the use of pre-packing strategy has become the core of legislative efforts to make national insolvency laws more rescue-friendly and flexible. By providing debtors with a pre-insolvency preparation space prior to the commencement of formal insolvency proceedings, the law can enhance the possibility of a successful rescue in two ways: (1) it encourages early treatment of financial difficulties at the earliest stage; (2) it facilitates the efficient setting up of a restructuring plan. This can be done in two ways: (1) by bringing certainty to the parties' pre-insolvency preparation efforts by arranging for a court-appointed expert to investigate the feasibility of restructuring options and help the debtor company identify the most effective way to restructure itself during the pre-formal stage; or (2) by facilitating the negotiation process by putting in place a quasi-moratorium. The latter results in the temporary suspension of compulsory enforcement measures taken by creditors during the pre-insolvency preparation stage while keeping deliberations confidential at this sensitive stage.

There are distinct differences between the new pre-pack approaches implemented in the surveyed continental jurisdictions and the UK's pre-pack administration. First of all, the objects of the examined fast-track procedures are mainly to save the company through restructuring, and facilitation of complete disposal of a company's assets tends to be the exception to the rule, whereas the UK pre-pack is marked with the object of complete disposal of a company's assets. Secondly, the surveyed European pre-pack measures are largely incorporated within (rather than attached to) the insolvency framework and therefore they are better regulated than the pre-pack practice in the UK. Not only is there a certain amount of court scrutiny from the outset, but also there is some court-coordinated control keeping the balance of competing interests throughout the process. On the one hand, this allows the trade-off between the requirement for speedy action and creditor participation to be satisfied in a measured and supervised way. On the other hand, immediate effectuation of the pre-packed arrangements is unlikely, as the restructuring plan has to go through a court hearing and obtain approval from relevant claimholders before it becomes binding.

Due to these substantial differences, the fundamental problems facing the UK form of pre-packs and its continental counterparts are different. The use of the pre-packing strategy to accomplish substantial asset sales raises a host of complaints ranging from arguments that it represents an abuse of the reorganisation process by certain insiders, to the systematic undervaluation of assets, to concerns regarding the institutional competency of insolvency professionals to impartially administer the process for the best interests of creditors as a whole. In contrast the concerns surrounding the continental European pre-packs refer to concerns to make insolvency legislation more rescue-friendly and procedurally efficient, in particular, as a way of mitigating creditor power in order to better advance the restructuring outcome. Put in a different way, the existential question concerning UK pre-packs, as examined in Chapter 3, is whether the new mechanism encourages premature business sales and therefore does not produce as much value as traditional reorganisations; the tension lies in the room the procedure allows for increased managerial power and inadequately checked conflicts of interest. The existential question concerning the surveyed European jurisdictions is rather how to harness this new mechanism to ensure a delicate balance between creditor control and the need to afford debtors more power and allow them more room to manouevre in the process of restructuring negotiations.

In spite of those general differences, the one thing in common between the UK and continental pre-pack approaches is that none of them has an ex ante judicial approval mechanism implemented for substantively evaluating the economics of relevant rescue arrangements. This is indicative of a judicial trend away from the substantive review of the fairness of business arrangements and the recognition of the courts' institutional limitations in determining the attractiveness of a particular transaction in business terms. A common procedural safeguard in the continental pre-pack approaches is to place a neutral and well-informed party to serve as a proxy for creditors in the course of the pre-pack negotiations. This ensures that rigorous monitoring of requisite decision-making and existing safeguards in the legal constraints will not be summarily discarded.

There is such a lack of impartial monitoring in the UK law regarding pre-packs as to create a risk that pre-formal negotiations are carried out in a self-serving manner by insiders. UK law places its full faith in a neutral decision-making body, namely, the administrator. But this proves ill-suited to addressing conflicts of interest issues in connected sales as the assumption that the administrator will fulfil the neutral decision-making function becomes questionable when it comes to the delicate matter of business sales to connected parties. Lessening the controversy necessitates establishing a level playing field at the pre-packing stage with appropriate sanitising measures to cleanse the taint of connected pre-pack sales and adequately check and frustrate questionable business sale arrangements. Therefore, UK insolvency law and practice that has taught its European counterparts the value of corporate rescue and business restructurings in lieu of debilitating liquidations may now have something to learn from the continental approaches to pre-packs. This is especially the case with the credible and impartial monitoring of pre-pack administrations that augments its credibility and thus its attractiveness.

8. Pre-packs and insolvency forum shopping

INTRODUCTION

Companies are increasingly becoming more globalised, hence the increasing incidence of cross-border insolvency. In any cross-border case involving a formal insolvency procedure, stakeholders will assess which jurisdictions are available for the proceedings, considering the advantages of forum shopping for an optimal jurisdiction. Cross-border forum shopping, in simple terms, involves identifying an optimal jurisdiction for a restructuring or insolvency so as to take advantage of the availability of a more favourable legal position in the desired jurisdiction. To do so, companies may move their centre of main interests ('COMI') to the jurisdiction with the more favourable restructuring or insolvency regime.

The attractiveness of the insolvency regime of a particular jurisdiction is often assessed by reference to the speed of the restructuring process; the degree of control; the scope of directors' duties; the flexibility of the proceedings; and the possibility to cram down dissenting creditors, bearing in mind the markedly different restructuring and insolvency processes in different jurisdictions. The pre-pack administration in the UK has proved a popular target of insolvency forum shopping for companies who are mindful to effectuate a quick pre-packed business sale through the UK administration procedure.

This chapter first explains the mechanics of COMI shifting for the purpose of insolvency forum shopping in the EU context under the relevant laws, and then considers why the UK insolvency regime, especially the pre-pack administration, is appealing to foreign companies. In doing so, it uses a concrete case as an example to examine which steps, in preparing for a COMI shifting, have effectively convinced English courts to grant administration orders allowing companies to proceed with a pre-pack sale. The chapter will also evaluate the implications of such decisions and draw lessons for the legislators. Furthermore, this chapter looks at the recent changes to the EC Regulation (1346/2000) on Insolvency Proceedings. This section is followed by a critical evaluation of the interplay between the pre-pack regimes and competition to introduce more flexible and rescue-friendly insolvency proceedings at the national law level.

INSOLVENCY FORUM SHOPPING BY MEANS OF REBUTTING THE COMI PRESUMPTION UNDER THE EU LAW

Two key instruments, the UNCITRAL Model Law on Cross-Border Insolvency (the 'Model Law') and EC Regulation (1346/2000) on Insolvency Proceedings ('the EIR'),[1] are of particular importance to cross-border insolvency proceedings. The Model Law, adopted by the United Nations Commission on International Trade Law in 1997, is designed to assist countries in equipping their insolvency laws with a modern framework for handling cross-border insolvency proceedings and encourage cooperation and coordination between jurisdictions. The EIR came into effect in May 2002 as a European law measure fully binding EU Member States (apart from Denmark, which has opted out) with direct effect.[2]

The EIR confers jurisdiction to open main insolvency proceedings[3] on the courts of the EU Member State where a debtor's COMI is situated.[4] The Preamble to the EIR states that COMI should correspond to 'the

---

[1] It should be noted that the EIR is to be replaced by *Regulation (EU) 2015/848 of the European Parliament and of the Council of 20 May 2015 on Insolvency Proceedings (recast).*

[2] References to 'EU member state' in the remainder of this chapter should be taken to mean an EU Member State other than Denmark. EIR applies where the debtor (including a corporation or individual) in the insolvency proceedings is not a credit institution, an investment company or an insurance company and the COMI of the debtor is within the territory of a Member State of the EU.

[3] Main proceedings for the purposes of the EIR are defined as 'collective insolvency proceedings' and are listed in Annex A to the EIR. Those relevant to corporate insolvencies in the UK are: winding up by or subject to the supervision of the court; CVL (with confirmation by the court); administration (including out-of-court appointments) and CVA.

[4] The Preamble at sub-paragraph 12 and art. 3(1) of EIR. Similarly, under the UNCITRAL Model Law on Cross-Border Insolvency, a 'foreign main proceeding' means a foreign proceeding taking place in the state where the debtor has the centre of its main interests. See art. 2 and art. 20 of the Module law. Therefore, the two instruments use the same concept of COMI as the basis for recognising main insolvency proceedings.

place where the debtor conducts the administration of his interests on a regular basis and is therefore ascertainable by third parties'.[5] Article 3(1) of the EIR states that in the case of a company, 'the place of its registered office shall be presumed to be its COMI in the absence of proof to the contrary'.

This presumption as to COMI may be rebutted in appropriate circumstances. The then European Court of Justice ('the ECJ') (now the Court of Justice of the European Union)'s decision in *Re Eurofood*[6] confirmed that only factors which are both objective and ascertainable by third parties could rebut the presumption that a company's COMI was in the same country as its registered office.

As to which factors that are ascertainable by third parties, Lewison J. in the *Stanford International Bank Ltd* case[7] states that: '... what was ascertainable by a third party was what was in the public domain, and what a typical third party would learn as a result of dealing with the company.'[8] It is worth noting that 'third parties' usually meant the potential creditors, such as financial lenders and trade suppliers for a trading company, and does not include investors. According to Proudman J. in the English High Court case *Kaupthing Capital Partners II Master LP Inc.*:[9] '[t]he investors are not the type of third parties that the ECJ in

---

5 The Preamble at sub-paragraph 13 of EIR.

6 *Re Eurofood IFSC Ltd* [2006] ECR 1-03813. *Eurofood* had its registered office in the International Financial Services Centre, Dublin, and the company was a wholly owned subsidiary of *Parmalat SpA*, which was the Italian incorporated parent of the *Parmalat Group*. The sole function of *Eurofood* was to raise finance for the Group. As the Irish High Court granted a winding-up order on the petition of its creditor, the Bank of America, the Italian court declared *Eurofood* insolvent and asserted jurisdiction to open main proceedings on the basis that *Eurofood*'s COMI was located in Italy. One of the questions the Irish Supreme Court had, referring to the ECJ with regard to the interpretation of the EIR, was what are the governing factors for determining the COMI when the registered office of a parent company and its subsidiary are located in different Member States.

7 *Re Stanford International Bank* [2009] EWHC 14, [2010] EWCA Civ 137. The Company, Stanford International Bank Limited, was incorporated in Antigua and Barbuda. Office-holders were appointed by both the US and Antiguan courts (a receiver in the case of the US, liquidators in the case of Antigua) in respect of the Company. Both sets of office-holders applied to the High Court in England for recognition of their respective proceedings, each of them alleging that the proceedings in which they had been appointed were the 'foreign main proceedings'.

8 [2009] EWHC 14, at [70].

9 *Kaupthing Capital Partners II Master LP Inc, Re* [2010] EWHC 836 (Ch).

Eurofood or the Court of Appeal in *Stanford* had in mind. The investors are insiders within the partnership, equivalent to the shareholder or contributories of the company, rather than persons doing business with the partnership.'[10]

More recently, the ECJ's decision in *Interedil*[11] applied the principles of the *Eurofood* decision in the event of a registered office's relocation before the filing for insolvency, attributing greater significance to the place of the company's central administration.[12] In considering generally how the presumption could be rebutted, it suggested that if the bodies responsible for the management and supervision of a company are in the same place as its registered office, and the management decisions of the company are made in the same place as its registered office, and the management decisions of the company are taken in a manner that is ascertainable by the third parties, the presumption cannot be rebutted. However, if it can be demonstrated that the 'place in which an entity's central administration' is located somewhere other than the registered office, then the presumption can be rebutted.[13] Nevertheless, the ECJ in this case neither definitively defined COMI nor set out a full list of relevant objective factors and considerations to rebut the registered office presumption. In light of specific circumstances of individual cases, this is open for an interpretation of the facts by national courts.

The relevant time for determining the location of the debtor's COMI, according to the ECJ decision in *Re Staubitz-Schreiber*,[14] is the time of filing the petition requesting the court to open insolvency proceedings. This means, although the Recital 4 of the EIR states its intention to avoid incentives for the parties to transfer assets or judicial proceedings from

---

10 [2010] EWHC 836 (Ch) at [22].

11 *Interedil Srl (in liquidation) v Fallimento Interedil Srl, Intesa Gestione Crediti SpA* [2011] EUECJ C-396/09; [2011] BPIR 1639. In that case, an Italian company (*Interedil*) decided to transfer its registered office to London and cancelled the Italian registry. It was registered in the English Companies House as an 'overseas company', having only a 'place of business' in England. At the moment of the filing, *Interedil* still had assets and liabilities in the state of origin, Italy.

12 The ECJ held that the fact that a company has assets in the Member State of origin may only rebut the presumption if 'a comprehensive assessment of all the relevant factors makes it possible to establish, in a manner that is ascertainable by third parties, that the company's actual centre of management and supervision and of the management of its interests is located in that other Member State'. [2011] EUECJ C-396/09 at [53].

13 [2011] EUECJ C-396/09 at [51].

14 *Re Staubitz-Schreiber* [2006] EUECJ C-1/04, [2006] ECR I-701.

one Member State to another, seeking to obtain a more favourable legal position, there is nothing to stop a debtor from making an eve of bankruptcy move of COMI to another jurisdiction so as to take advantage of a more favourable legal regime and to open main insolvency proceedings there.[15]

RELOCATING COMI TO ACHIEVE A PRE-PACK SALE UNDER THE UK LAW

A popular target of insolvency forum shopping is the corporate insolvency procedures available in the UK, in particular, administration, as well as CVA.[16] Those procedures are available to a company: (1) registered in England and Wales or Scotland under the CA 2006; (2) incorporated in another EEA state or (3) not incorporated in an EEA state but having its COMI in a Member State (excluding Denmark).[17]

The popularity of those procedures in the UK insolvency law regime is not surprising, as Lord Drayson said in a House of Lords debate:

---

[15] Recital 4 of EIR states: 'It is necessary for the proper functioning of the internal market to avoid incentives for the parties to transfer assets or judicial proceedings from one Member State to another, seeking to obtain a more favourable legal position (forum shopping).'

[16] For example, *Schefenacker*, the ultimate holding company of a global automotive products manufacturer, was a German registered company. It completed its financial restructuring, taking the form of a debt-for-equity swap through a UK CVA by mid-2007. A CVA was chosen not only because it is one of the insolvency procedures recognised under the EIR, but also because it was the fastest way to achieve the desired outcome. As commented by the advisor of the bondholders in this case: '[t]he insolvency process in Germany is not organised for doing the kind of compromise deal that we wanted to achieve … It is normally set up to realise the assets and distribute the proceeds.' Furthermore, the company's acting chief executive during the restructuring process also commented: 'a potential obstacle in the German system is that the insolvency court can appoint a judge with no prior knowledge of the case to oversee the process. This can delay the restructuring and potentially damage the operating performance of the business. In the UK creditors and company have a say in the appointment of restructuring professionals.' See I Simensen, '*Schefenacker* Restructuring Holds up a Mirror to Cross-border Differences', *Financial Times* on 11 October 2007 <http://www.ft.com/cms/s/0/a6487d54-7794-11dc-9de8-0000779fd2ac.html#axzz3kZkUmIyK> accessed on 30 January 2016.

[17] Para.111(1A) of Schedule B1 and s 1(4) of the Insolvency Act 1986, following the Insolvency Act 1986 (Amendment) Regulations 2005 SI No. 2005/879.

> Our policy as a Government is to be as open as possible, to encourage businesses to relocate to the United Kingdom and not to put up any unnecessary barriers to that investment (…) Independent studies by the World Bank have shown that the United Kingdom's insolvency framework is highly regarded above that of the United States, Germany and France particularly on the basis of its protection to creditors, the costs of proceedings and the speed with which the process is able to be carried out.[18]

The Attractiveness of Pre-packs in Insolvency Forum Shopping

A significant portion of cross-border insolvency migration towards English jurisdictions is done to benefit from the pre-pack administration, with the purpose of effectuating a quick sale.[19] Despite the criticism voiced in previous chapters regarding the transparency of the process and the balance of interests protected by it, pre-pack administrations present a unique attractiveness to interested parties. Most importantly, they offer more control and a better certainty of the process from the perspectives of both the debtor and certain creditors. For the debtor, it allows the management board to engage in strategic planning with regard to the restructuring of the debt and initiate negotiations as early as possible without losing its control over the company. Furthermore, the debtor company and/or its directors have been conferred by the EA 2002 with enhanced powers to appoint an administrator out-of-court simply by filing documents at court and without any judicial scrutiny, whereas in many other jurisdictions, the office-holder of insolvency proceedings must be selected and appointed by the court. In this respect, the UK administration procedure is more management-friendly.

Certainty also comes from the fact that pre-packs allow quick completion of the prearranged deal with limited court intervention. Where a sale of the ailing business and/or assets is negotiated and agreed prior to the commencement of the administration procedure, the sale may take place immediately following the appointment of the administrator. Interested parties can not only avoid a lengthy formal procedure but also any recourse to the court's decision-making to approve the pre-arranged deal

---

[18] House of Lords debate on 11 March 2010, columns 342 and 343 Lords Hansard.

[19] Examples of such cases include the restructuring of the IT company *Damovo*, which involved a COMI relocation from Luxembourg to England in order to carry out an administration pre-pack sale, and most recently, the restructuring of *Hellas Telecommunications (Luxembourg) II SCA*, similarly involving a COMI migration from Luxembourg to England in order to effect a pre-pack administration.

before its execution, especially where the administrator is appointed out-of-court. Also, the UK law is relatively straightforward. Although rescuing the company is also promoted, the overreaching priority of maximisation of creditor return prevails when considering the merits of the pre-arranged sale arrangement by either the administrator or the court. While pre-packs can be open to abuse, it has been recognised as a valid process by the UK judiciaries, provided that the transaction is structured so as to reflect the value of the business.

Moreover, the hybrid route offers a unique flexibility which makes the procedure comparatively efficient and cost-effective. It allows negotiations to be carried out in secret, which would minimise disruption of the company's business and therefore preserve the value of the business. Furthermore, it is seen as more flexible than its continental counterparts in overcoming the holdouts by minority creditors.[20] Unsecured creditors in the UK have very few control rights and have no say in the appointment of the administration. They will only be involved if there are some funds available for distribution to them, and there is no expressed legal obligation for the administrator to consult with them prior to the formal commencement of the procedure.

The *Hellas II* Case and its Implication

Under EIR English courts only have jurisdiction to open administration proceedings in respect of a foreign company if its COMI is in the UK, which is presumed to be determined on the basis of where its registered office is situated. It is therefore necessary, in order for the pre-pack administration sale to be carried out, for the foreign company's COMI to be shifted from where it was registered to the UK. Although the direct way to move a company's COMI to another EU Member State is to move the company's registered office, which is governed by national law rather than EU law,[21] a more convenient way to enable a pre-pack restructuring

---

20 G McCormack, 'Jurisdictional Competition and Forum Shopping in Insolvency Proceedings' (2009) 68 *Cambridge Law Journal* 169, 185.

21 A series of ECJ cases (such as Case C 212/97, *Centros Ltd v Erhvervs-og Selskabsstyrelsen* ECR [1999] I-1459; Case C 208/00 *Überseering* [2002] ECR I-9919; Case C 167/01 *Inspire Art* [2003] ECR I-10155; Case 81/87 *Daily Mail* [1988] ECR 5483, Case C 411/03 *SEVIC* [2005] ECR I-10805, *Case C 210/06 Cartesio Oktato es Szolgaltato bt* [2008] ECR I-9641) attempted to curb national legislation which may restrict the ability of a company to move its COMI from the perspective of companies' mobility within the European Union.

under English Law is often done by rebutting the presumption of coincidence between COMI and the registered office.

This section attempts to ascertain the main considerations involved in determining whether a company's COMI has been effectively transferred to the UK in order to allow a pre-pack arrangement to proceed with reference to recent case law. In the most prominent relevant case of *Hellas Telecommunications (Luxembourg) II SCA* ('*Hellas II*'),[22] English courts decided that the COMI of *Hellas II* had been effectively transferred from Luxemburg to England and made an administration order to allow a pre-pack sale to be effected despite the fact that the company's registered office remained in Luxembourg.

The *Hellas* group was one of the largest integrated telecom operators in Greece.[23] The principal trading company within the Hellas group was *WIND Hellas Telecommunications SCA* ('*WIND Hellas*'). *Hellas II* was the parent company of *WIND Hellas*, and it had no operational role. The *Hellas* group's financial performance deteriorated during the course of 2009 as a result of competitive pressures in the marketplace and it subsequently entered into restructuring negotiations.[24] Meanwhile, the group and key stakeholders[25] took certain steps to address the mounting financial pressures, including entering into a standstill agreement with some creditors.[26]

Due to the ongoing crisis in the microeconomic environment in Greece, a series of initiatives was undertaken by the group to assess its restructuring alternatives beginning in May 2009, and this culminated in a restructuring proposal involving a sale of the shares in *WIND Hellas* owned by *Hellas II*.[27] To facilitate the implementation of a successful

---

22 In *Re Hellas Telecommunications (Luxembourg) II SCA* [2009] EWHC 3199.

23 The group was founded in 1992 in Greece and was established as the technology leader of the Greek mobile telephony market. It is part of Weather Investments, a global telecommunication group.

24 C Pilkington *et al.*, 'WIND Hellas: A Complex Restructuring in a Global Recession' (March 2011) *White & Case PLC Magazine* <http://www.whitecase.com/sites/whitecase/files/files/download/publications/article_wind_hellas_complex_restructuring.pdf> accessed 30 January 2016.

25 Including a steering committee of the group's revolving credit facility lenders and an *ad hoc* committee of the senior secured noteholders.

26 C Pilkington, *et al.*, 'WIND Hellas: A Complex Restructuring in a Global Recession'.

27 See K Buckley, 'WIND Hellas: Pre-packs and COMI Shift; Abuse or Innovation?' (2010) 25 *Butterworths Journal of International Banking and Financial Law* 342, 342.

sale, it was proposed that the proposed sale of the shares in *WIND Hellas* should be conducted by means of a pre-pack administration of *Hellas II*, the main shareholder and holding company of *WIND Hellas*.[28]

In order to achieve this, the group would need to move the COMI of *Hellas II* from Luxembourg, where the company's registered office was located, to the UK to avail itself to English judicial insolvency procedures. From early August 2009, the group took steps to ensure that the COMI shift was supported by a sufficient number of 'objective and ascertainable' factors to third parties as suggested in the ECJ's decision in *Re Eurofood* for the purpose of rebutting the COMI presumption.

Relevant measures included: relocating its head office and principal operating address to London; opening its main operating bank account in England; appointing new directors who were British nationals and UK residents and holding all board meetings in London; notifying all creditors, relevant parties and bodies of its move to London and issuing certain press releases about the relocation to that effect; holding all negotiations with creditors in London; ensuring that all correspondence was sent and administrative functions were conducted from London; and registering with Companies House as a foreign company with a UK establishment and ensuring that it became a resident in the UK for tax purposes, etc.[29]

Hellas II submitted its application on 17 November to the High Court for an administration order. On 26 November, the High Court issued its decision that the company had successfully shifted its COMI from Luxembourg to England, granted the administration order and went on to give the administrators liberty to enter into the proposed pre-pack sale. As contemplated, the administrator completed the sale shortly on 27 November.

The court noted that the COMI of *Hellas II* had been moved deliberately and expressly from Luxembourg to England in August and, following such move, Lewison J. treated the presumption that *Hellas II*'s COMI was in Luxembourg as having been rebutted. He was satisfied that the COMI was in England at the time of the hearing and was ascertainable by third parties. In considering whether there was a real prospect of

---

[28] See Slaughter and May, *Financial Restructuring of Wind Hellas* (December 2009) Financing Briefing <https://www.slaughterandmay.com/media/893777/financing_briefing_financial_restructuring_of_wind_hellas_dec_09.pdf> accessed 30 January 2016.

[29] See [2009] EWHC 3199, [4]. See also A Cohen, '*Eurofood* for Thought: Additional Guidance on COMI in Practice' (2012) 1 *Journal of International Banking and Financial Law* 52.

achieving one of the statuary purposes of the administration procedure, the court highlighted that by putting *Hellas II* into administration and effecting a pre-pack sale of its assets, it would be likely to attain the secondary purpose, namely achieving a better result for *Hellas II*'s creditors as a whole than if *Hellas II* were to be wound up immediately. The conclusion was particularly based on the court's acknowledgement of the factors that the proposed pre-pack sale was realistically the only way forward and that it was the only bid that had commanded the support of the necessary groups of creditors.[30]

Implication of the *Hellas II* Case

In this particular case, the English High Court, in applying the ECJ's propositions in *Eurofood* and *Interedil* that factors considered to rebut the COMI assumption must be identified by reference to criteria that are both objective and ascertainable by third parties, noted that the most important factor on which its decision was premised, among all the factors, was that all the negotiations took place in England. As Lewison J. explained:

> The purpose of the COMI is to enable creditors in particular to know where the company is and where it may deal with the company. Therefore, it seems to me that one of the most important features of the evidence, which is the feature I mention next, is that all negotiations between the company and its creditors have taken place in London.[31]

It must be pointed out that this does not necessarily mean that the place where the negotiations of restructuring take place is the most important factor in COMI shifting. The analysis should be based on the specific circumstances of each individual case, e.g. the nature of the debtor company, against the said established criteria. It should also be noted that *Hellas II* was a holding company with very limited functions, therefore factors that are objective and ascertainable by third parties are relatively easier to establish than those for an operating company. It would have been much more difficult to make a COMI transfer for an operating company with its physical location of employees and assets than a financial holding company.[32]

---

30 [2009] EWHC 3199, [7].

31 [2009] EWHC 3199, [5].

32 RJ de Weijs and MS Breeman, 'Comi-migration: Use or Abuse of European Insolvency Law?' (2014) 11 *European Company and Financial Law Review* 495, 503.

ENABLING PRE-PACK SALES THROUGH COMI-SHIFTING – ABUSE OR INNOVATION?

Companies may want to take advantage of this and move their COMI to the UK in order to benefit from the availability of a pre-pack or other favourable restructuring and insolvency regimes. But is insolvency forum shopping to ensure a more favourable outcome in terms of company restructuring/insolvency beneficial to creditors? Do they obtain a better deal? In other words, should there be certain mechanisms in place to distinguish abusive COMI-shifting, that should be prohibited or discouraged, from those permissible ones, and if yes, what are the parameters against which such distinction should be made so as to curb abusive COMI-shifting? This is an interesting question on which opinion is divided.

Possible Test for Abusive COMI-migration and Problematic Application

It has been proposed to address *abusive* COMI-migration by invoking the general principle of abuse of EU law, which has emerged from CJEU case-law.[33] The requisite test involves both an objective and a subjective element. The objective test, as first formulated by the CJEU in *Emsland-Stärke*,[34] refers to whether the purpose of the relevant European Community law has been achieved. The subjective test refers to evidence of intention to obtain an advantage from those rules by artificially creating the conditions laid down for legal forum shopping.[35]

The EIR contains two main goals which may conflict with each other: (1) the efficient and effective administration of cross-border insolvencies aims at maximising the value of the company's net assets to satisfy creditors' claims, and (2) preventing forum shopping in order to ensure predictability fosters the efficiency of credit contracts.[36] On this basis

---

33 H Eidenmüller, 'Abuse of Law in the Context of European Insolvency Law' (2009) 6 *European Company and Financial Law Review* 1, 9. See also Weijs and Breeman, 'Comi-migration: Use or Abuse of European Insolvency Law?', 508.

34 Case C 110/99, *Emsland-Stärke GmbH v Hauptzollamt Hamburg-Jonas* ECR 2000 I-11569.

35 Weijs and Breeman, 'Comi-migration: Use or Abuse of European Insolvency Law?' 506.

36 Eidenmüller, 'Abuse of Law in the Context of European Insolvency Law', 14.

Eidenmüller submits that whether COMI-migration qualifies as abusive or not depends:

> … on whether the COMI shift contributes to maximising the net assets available to satisfy creditors' claims. If it does, it surely cannot be considered abusive. … COMI shifts that evidently benefit either the debtor at the expense of its creditors or some creditors at the expense of others are suspicious. Such COMI shifts are driven by *distributive considerations* and not by the goal of maximising the net assets available to satisfy creditors' claims. If a COMI shift is evidently effected in order to enrich the person(s) initiating it at the expense of other stakeholders, the shift is abusive. Speaking very crudely, it all comes down to the question of whether a COMI shift is driven by considerations of efficiency (no abuse of law) or considerations of claiming value, i.e. distributive concerns (abuse of law).[37]

Nevertheless, Weijs and Breeman pointed out that Eidenmüller failed to discuss the problem case where a shift might aim at not only increasing the value of net assets but also advancing the ranking of certain interests in the distribution scheme.[38] This is a realistic scenario where shareholder loans would be treated as subordinated in some European jurisdictions such as Germany or Italy but would be upgraded to normal insolvency claims if the insolvency proceedings opened in a jurisdiction, such as the UK, which has no rules treating shareholder loans as subordinated claims.[39]

The argument put forward by Eidenmüller was refined by Weijs and Breeman who argued that COMI-migration should be allowed if its aim was to benefit from different rules on overcoming holdout behavior, most notably rules on reorganisation plans; that COMI-migration should also be allowed if it is aimed at benefiting from rules on preventing a strategy of the commons, most notably rules on liquidating assets and preferences. On the other hand, they accurately hold that COMI-migration would contravene basic insolvency law principles if it aimed to change the order of distribution by altering the ranking of certain claims such as the aforementioned shareholder loans.[40]

There are some differences between Eidenmüller's criteria and the refined ones. First the consideration of efficiency by Eidenmüller was

---

[37] *Ibid.*, 16.

[38] See Weijs and Breeman, 'Comi-migration: Use or Abuse of European Insolvency Law?' 495–530.

[39] *Ibid.*, 524 and footnote 116.

[40] *Ibid.*, 495–530. Their conclusions are based on an analysis of the common pool problems and protection of pre-insolvency entitlements for the creditors bargain theory perspective.

defined as overcoming holdout behaviour and preventing a strategy of the commons in the refined criteria. Another even bigger difference is that the refined criteria make it clear that COMI-shifting with the intention of bringing about a different distribution scheme should be deemed as abusive forum shopping even when it leads to an increase in net asset value.

These efforts to establish a clearer test to identify abusive insolvency forum shopping by way of COMI-migration are welcome, but there is concern that prohibition on 'abusive' COMI-shifting might generate significant costs, as the application of any such test would be surrounded by considerable uncertainty. Armour has argued that, given the inherent elasticity of the concept of COMI, national courts of the inbound jurisdiction, when considering whether they have jurisdiction for the opening of insolvency proceedings, might be tempted to elude and confuse the question of whether COMI has shifted at all with that of whether a *prima facie* shift should be struck down as being abusive.[41]

But even so the application of the refined criteria is not unproblematic in practice. The determination of whether the criteria for abuse of COMI-shifting are satisfied will be left to the national courts of the inbound jurisdiction, in the context of considering whether they have jurisdiction for the opening of insolvency proceedings. This may create a very problematic situation. There is no current CJEU case-law applying the abuse of law as a principle of Union law in the field of insolvency law. Also national insolvency laws present remarkable divergences.[42] When considering whether a particular COMI-shifting is abusive or not based on distributive concerns, the judge of the inbound jurisdiction ought to consider whether there is an intention to advance certain creditor interests at the expense of others, i.e. whether forum shopping aims at being deliberately detrimental to the interests of certain groups of stakeholders. Detriment ought to be determined by reference to the rules of distribution schemes under national insolvency law in the outbound jurisdiction, instead of one's own law.

---

[41] It is argued that: '… Given the inherent elasticity of the concept of COMI, it seems likely that courts might be tempted to elide – and confuse – the question of whether COMI has shifted at all with that of whether a prima facie shift should be struck down as being abusive.' See J Armour, 'Abuse of European Insolvency Law? A Discussion' in R de la Feria and S Vogenauer (eds) *Prohibition of Abuse of Law* (Hart Publishing, Oxford 2011), 165.

[42] Weijs and Breeman, 'COMI-migration: Use or Abuse of European Insolvency Law?' 507.

This is not always an easy task given the substantial distinction between the national insolvency laws and policy, be it the primacy of creditor wealth maximisation or the promotion of interests of all stakeholders.[43] It further raises the risk that national courts may implement the EIR while promoting the overriding objectives of their national insolvency law. In doing so national courts would run the risk of simplifying national insolvency law objectives to a single standard that may not be shared among Member States. For instance, pre-packs are used to capture the going-concern surplus thereby maximising the net asset value. This may be seen as consistent with the overriding objective of the UK law to provide an efficient and workable 'rescue' mechanism. Schedule B1 of the Insolvency Act 1986 has specifically created a very practical and flexible process whereby rescuing the business serves as an overriding objective of the law in order to secure a better result for the company's creditors as a whole than would be likely if the company was wound up. This is different with jurisdictions that have greater regard for the insolvency impact on labour and other social and economic issues. For instance, one of the primary objectives of French insolvency law is the preservation of employees' jobs.[44]

Furthermore, the standard in court sanctions may differ due to differences in national insolvency laws. In a UK pre-pack administration context, as noted by the court in *WIND Hellas*, the merits of a pre-pack administration are for the administrator to deal with, although such a court order would not provide complete immunity to the administrators from any subsequent challenge launched by creditors.[45] Furthermore, in

---

[43] An example is the consideration and treatment of company employees' interests in insolvency proceedings. There is an emphasis on employment protection, but trying to save jobs in the French approaches to corporate rescue and insolvency, while achieving the best return for creditors, which favours creditors as a whole, is arguably an uncompromisable goal under the UK insolvency law. On how national social policies affect the aims of corporate rescue with regard to the relative favouritism of the safeguarding of employment, see JL Gant, 'Social Policy and Insolvency: Struggles towards Convergence' (2014) 2 *Nottingham Insolvency and Business Law e-Journal* 49.

[44] KVW Stone, 'Labor and the Global Economy: Four Approaches to Transnational Labor Regulation' (1995) 16 *Michigan Journal of International Law* 988, 1005.

[45] In his reasoning, Lewison J in the *Hellas II* case stated: 'It seems to me that in general the merits of a pre-pack sale are for the administrator to deal with; and the creditors, if sufficiently aggrieved, have a remedy in the course of the administration to challenge an administrator's decision. It may on the evidence be obvious that a pre-pack sale is an abuse of the administrator's powers, in

cases where proceedings are opened without a court decision, e.g. an out-of-court appointment of an administrator, the obligation of judging the criteria for abuse would be judged by the administrator as the insolvency office-holder, namely the very officer whose impartiality may be in question.

Recent Reform of EIR to Curb Abusive Insolvency Forum Shopping

EIR's jurisdiction rules have been criticised for allowing forum shopping by companies through abusive COMI-relocation. It was noted in the Commission's Impact Assessment of the EIR:

> In the absence of harmonisation at EU or international level, Member States' insolvency laws and procedures vary considerably and offer a range of advantages and disadvantages to companies and individuals. For example, the flexible regime for restructuring companies offered by English law, and, in particular, the pre-packaged administration sales which enables a company to restructure by wiping out some of its creditors and converting into a new company shorn of its liabilities, attracts companies from other European jurisdictions.[46]

At a more macro-level, to judge the current trend of COMI-shifting to enable a pre-pack restructuring under the UK law, one may have to admit that the UK pre-pack restructuring may have worked, albeit imperfectly. It possesses unique advantages in addressing the challenges currently faced in the markets, in particular, value deterioration and uncertainty in prolonging court-driven proceedings. Its popularity in the cross-border insolvency domain reveals a sharp demand for quasi-formal restructuring which can offer a flexible pre-insolvency negotiation platform and efficient and effective recognition and execution of the pre-agreed arrangements. The tendency of other European countries, as seen in the previous chapter, to provide their insolvency law with a friendly pre-arranged procedure, either by introducing a similar pre-pack process in

---

which event the court could refuse to make the administration order or could direct the administrator not to complete a pre-pack sale. At the other end of the spectrum it may be that it is obvious that a particular pre-pack is on the evidence the only real way forward, in which case the court could give the administrator liberty to enter into the pre-pack, leaving open the possibility that a sufficiently aggrieved creditor could nevertheless challenge the administrator's decision ex post facto.' [2009] EWHC 3199 at [8].

[46] European Commission, *Impact Assessment: Accompanying the Document-Revision of Regulation (EC) No. 1346/2000 on Insolvency Proceedings* (Report, COM 2012 744 final), 21–2.

their legislation or by simply recognising the practice in the same context as the UK, suggests, at least, the acknowledgement of such demand.

On 12 December 2012, ten years after its introduction, the European Commission presented a Report to the European Parliament, the Council and the European Economic and Social Committee on the application of the EIR.[47] Against the background of a changing political and economic environment, and in recognition of the increased use and development of pre-insolvency techniques which focus on protecting the debtor and promoting a rescue culture, the European Commission proposed to amend the EIR with a number of reforms to improve the efficiency of the European framework for resolving cross-border insolvency cases.[48] The final text of the reform, known as Regulation (EU) 2015/848 of the European Parliament and of the Council of 20 May 2015 on insolvency proceedings (recast) ('the recast Regulation'), was published in the Official Journal on 5 June 2015 (OJ L 141/19). The recast Regulation entered into force on 26 June 2015 but only applies to relevant insolvency proceedings from 26 June 2017.

One of the essential elements of the recast Regulation is clarifying the jurisdiction rules in determining COMI to reduce the cases of forum shopping through abusive and non-genuine COMI-shifting. It is not clear what constitutes an abusive COMI-shifting, but it is said that: 'it is necessary for the proper functioning of the internal market to avoid incentives for the parties to transfer assets or judicial proceedings from one Member State to another seeking to obtain a more favourable legal position to the detriment of the general body of creditors.'[49] It seems to

---

[47] European Commission, *Report from the Commission to the European Parliament, the Council and the European Economic and Social Committee on the Application of Council Regulation (EC) No. 1346/2000 of 29 May 2000 on Insolvency Proceedings* (Report, COM 2012 743 final) <http://ec.europa.eu/justice/civil/files/insolvency-report_en.pdf> accessed 30 January 2016.

[48] European Commission, *Proposal for a Regulation of the European Parliament and of the Council amending Council Regulations (EC) No. 1346/2000 on Insolvency Proceedings* (COM 2012 744 final). The main elements of the Commission's proposal included: extending the Regulation to cover hybrid and pre-insolvency proceedings; clarifying the jurisdiction rules in determining COMI; providing for a more efficient administration of insolvency proceedings by improving cooperation between main and secondary proceedings; improving publicity of proceedings and standardising the lodging of claims in cross-border insolvency cases; and providing a coordination of insolvency proceedings concerning insolvency of groups of companies.

[49] The recast Regulation, Preamble sub-paragraph 5.

suggest that COMI relocations for the benefit of the general body of creditors are not abusive and non-genuine and therefore will be permitted.

The recast Regulation complements the definition of COMI as: 'the place where the debtor conducts the administration of his interests on a regular basis and which is ascertainable by third parties. In the case of a company or legal person, the place of the registered office shall be presumed to be the centre of its main interests in the absence of proof to the contrary.'[50]

The recast Regulation clarifies the circumstances in which the presumption that the COMI is located at the place of its registered office can be rebutted, which is based on the '*Interedil*' decision:

> In the case of a company, it should be possible to rebut this presumption where the company's central administration is located in a Member State other than that of its registered office, and where a comprehensive assessment of all the relevant factors establishes, in a manner that is ascertainable by third parties, that the company's actual centre of management and supervision and of the management of its interests is located in that other Member State.[51]

Furthermore, it sets a time limit on when the presumption about COMI can be rebutted as a safeguard to prevent abusive forum shopping. 'This presumption shall only apply if the registered office has not been moved to another Member State within a period of three months prior to the request for the opening of insolvency proceedings.'[52] So, if the registered office is moved within a period of three months prior to the request, the presumption cannot be rebutted. In addition, the proposal requires the court to examine its jurisdiction *ex officio* prior to opening insolvency proceedings and specify the grounds on which the jurisdiction of the court is based.[53]

Another key element is to revise the scope of the EIR. This goes some way in addressing the root causes of forum shopping. The EIR is limited to collective insolvency proceedings, which entail the partial or total divestment of a debtor and the appointment of a liquidator based on the traditional view to insolvency. It does not cover those national procedures which provide for the restructuring of a company at a pre-insolvency stage ('pre-insolvency proceedings'), or proceedings which leave the

---

50 The recast Regulation, para.1 of Article 3.
51 The recast Regulation, Preamble sub-paragraph 30.
52 The recast Regulation, para.1 of Article 3.
53 The recast Regulation, para.1 of Article 4.

existing management in place ('hybrid proceedings').[54] However, such proceedings have recently been introduced in many Member States to increase the chances of successful restructuring of businesses, for instance, the *Conciliation* proceedings, the SFA and the *Sauvegarde Accélérée* in French law, and the Protective Shield proceedings under German law. As a consequence, parties may seek to achieve restructuring through insolvency procedures in another member state, which can tackle more effectively the holding-out problem caused by dissenting creditors, as long as the desired procedures are included in the scope of the EIR and therefore their cross-border recognition is ensured. It is accepted that EIR's narrow scope does not sufficiently reflect current EU priorities and national practices in promoting the rescue of companies in difficulties.[55]

Article 1 of the recast Regulation makes an express reference to proceedings for the adjustment of debts and the purpose of rescue or reorganisation in order to also include those proceedings, which enable the debtor to find an arrangement with its creditors at a pre-insolvency stage.[56] The current definition of 'insolvency proceedings' is amended to

---

[54] The 'pre-insolvency proceedings' was defined as 'quasi-collective proceedings under the supervision of a court or an administrative authority which give a debtor in financial difficulties the opportunity to restructure at a pre-insolvency stage and to avoid the commencement of insolvency proceedings in the traditional sense'. The 'hybrid proceedings' are defined as 'proceedings in which the debtor retains some control over its assets and affairs albeit subject to the control or supervision by a court or an insolvency practitioner'. See Commission's *Report on the Application of Council Regulation (EC) No. 1346/2000 of 29 May 2000 on Insolvency Proceedings*, section 2: Scope of the Regulation.

[55] *Proposal for a Regulation of the European Parliament and of the Council amending Council Regulations (EC) No. 1346/2000 on Insolvency Proceedings*, 2.

[56] Para.1 of Article 1 of the recast Regulation states:

> 'This Regulation shall apply to public collective proceedings, including interim proceedings, which are based on a law relating to insolvency and in which, for the purpose of rescue, adjustment of debt, reorganization or liquidation,
>
> (a) the debtor is totally or partially divested of his assets and an insolvency practitioner is appointed,
> (b) the assets and affairs of the debtor are subject to control or supervision by a court or
> (c) a temporary stay of individual enforcement proceedings is granted by a court or by operation of law in order to allow for negotiations between the debtor and his creditors, provided that the proceedings in which the stay is granted provide for suitable measures to protect the general body of creditors, and, where no agreement is reached, are preliminary to one of the proceedings referred to under points (a) or (b).

include proceedings which do not involve a liquidator but in which the assets and affairs of the debtor are subject to control or supervision by a court. This would allow proceedings where the debtor remains in possession without a liquidator being appointed, to benefit from the EU-wide recognition of the effects of insolvency procedures covered by the Regulation. It is worth noting that the term 'control' in this context includes situations where the court only intervenes on appeal by a creditor or another interested party.[57]

It also extends to procedures which grant a temporary moratorium with creditors provided that such procedures are not detrimental to the general body of creditors or are merely the preliminary part of other covered procedures under this Regulation where no agreement on a restructuring plan can be reached. It should be noted that insolvency proceedings that are confidential, whether accompanied by a moratorium of individual enforcement or not, are excluded because their contractual and confidential nature would make it difficult to recognise their effects on a EU-wide basis, as a court or creditor located in another Member State would not know that such proceedings are pending.[58] As a result, proceedings such as the French *Conciliation* and *Mandate ad hoc* would not be included.

Although the Regulation does not and cannot harmonise substantive law between EU Member States, it should be noted that the reform to the EIR was adopted in parallel with the European Commission Recommendation that contains detailed provisions seeking to harmonise insolvencies and restructurings throughout the EU ('the Recommendation')[59] and is already based on the Commission Communication on A New Approach to Business Failure and Insolvency of 12 December 2012.[60]

Where the proceedings referred to in this paragraph may be commenced in situations where there is only a likelihood of insolvency, their purpose must be to avoid the debtor's insolvency or the cessation of his business activities.'

57 The recast Regulation, Preamble sub-paragraph 10.

58 The recast Regulation, Preamble sub-paragraph 13. This, however, does not prevent such a procedure from being subsequently covered by the scope of the Regulation from the moment it becomes public.

59 *Commission Recommendation of 12 March 2014 on a New Approach to Business Failure and Insolvency* (COM(2014) 1500 final) <http://ec.europa.eu/justice/civil/files/c_2014_1500_en.pdf> accessed 30 January 2016.

60 *The Commission Communication on A New Approach to Business Failure and Insolvency of 12 December 2012* (COM(2012) 742 final) <http://eur-lex.europa.eu/legal-content/EN/TXT/PDF/?uri=CELEX:52012DC0742&from=en> accessed 30 January 2016. It highlights certain areas where differences between domestic insolvency laws may hamper the establishment of an efficient internal market.

The objective of the Recommendation is to encourage greater coherence between the national insolvency frameworks in order to reduce divergences and inefficiencies which hamper the early restructuring of viable companies in financial difficulties, and thereby to lower the cost of restructuring for both debtors and creditors.[61] The Commission, in the Recommendation, set out a series of common principles for national insolvency procedures in order to shift the focus away from liquidation towards encouraging viable businesses to restructure at an early stage to prevent insolvency.[62] Although the European Commission's Recommendation on harmonisation does not have any legal force and is not binding on Member States, it does have a political weight in encouraging Member States to prepare legislation to address the issues identified. Yet it seems unlikely that current divergences among national insolvency laws in the EU will be overcome in the near future.

Future Outlook

To ban abusive and non-genuine COMI migration, the recast Regulation expands its scope to include more national insolvency proceedings with more room and flexibility for pre-insolvency restructuring, and imposes a mandatory three-month time limit for the admissibility of forum shopping. Although these measures will have a drastic impact on preventing abusive and fraudulent forum shopping, the Regulation leaves the door open for bona fide COMI migration, which is arguably in line with the

---

[61] The Commission Recommendation, 3.

[62] The Commission asks Member States to:

(1) facilitate the restructuring of businesses in financial difficulties at an early stage, before starting formal insolvency proceedings, and without lengthy or costly procedures to help limit recourse to liquidation;
(2) allow debtors to restructure their business without needing to formally open court proceedings;
(3) give businesses in financial difficulties the possibility to request a temporary stay of up to four months (renewable up to a maximum of 12 months) to adopt a restructuring plan before creditors can launch enforcement proceedings against them;
(4) facilitate the process for adopting a restructuring plan, keeping in mind the interests of both debtors and creditors, with a view to increasing the chances of rescuing viable businesses;
(5) reduce the negative effects of a bankruptcy on entrepreneurs' future chances of launching a business, in particular by discharging their debts within a maximum of three years.

foundational freedoms under the EC Treaty.[63] It is also a very reasonable approach to adopt. Given that companies are increasingly becoming more globalised, we can expect more insolvency forum shopping in the future.

In addition, it is arguable that COMI-shifting at the European level has changed, to some extent, the landscape of insolvency practice in a rather positive direction. As explained in Chapter 7, many EU Member States have started to change their national laws to incorporate more quasi-formal restructuring strategies to lower the cost of restructuring for both debtors and creditors. This competition between jurisdictions may encourage countries to improve their insolvency and restructuring laws to enable them to deal with more cases and to avoid COMI being moved to a more favourable jurisdiction.[64] This could probably be seen as a positive thing in the sense that like it or not, its popularity has to some extent motivated an advanced level of harmonisation of substantive national insolvency law at European level.

The tendency of insolvency law reforms at the national level means that more rescue-friendly proceedings are increasingly becoming available in other (than the UK) EU Member States. This, coupled with the recent EIR reform raising the bar for dishonest insolvency forum shopping, will have an important impact on diminishing the desire of achieving a business rescue through a UK pre-pack administration for its effectiveness in reducing the holdout problem. Nevertheless, it will take a couple of years for the recast Regulation to come into effect, and there is still a long way to go down the road of legislative changes and harmonisation of substantive national insolvency laws. But one thing is clear: the interaction of national insolvency laws through COMI-shifting ought to build on a healthy level of competition between domestic laws, while legislators should steer towards building a more attractive and dynamic insolvency and restructuring regime. This would spread the benefits of the UK approach to company restructurings to a wider number of EU companies, and not just those willing to engage in COMI-shifting.

---

[63] On a thorough analysis of the validity of the COMI approach of the EIR under the fundamental freedoms of the EC Treaty, see WG Ringe, 'Forum Shopping under the EU Insolvency Regulation' (2008) 9 *European Business Organization Law Review* 579.

[64] This can be evidenced by the 2012 reform of the Germany's Insolvency Code, where the German government justified important changes to its insolvency law, in particular, permitting debt for equity swaps, by referring to COMI-shifting out of Germany such as the *Schefenacker* case.

CONCLUSION

Companies in trouble are increasingly seeking to take advantage of the possibility of shifting COMI in order to avail themselves of the full range of restructuring and insolvency options of a jurisdiction like the UK. This chapter has examined the legality of COMI-shifting under the EU Insolvency Regulation, illustrated with the *Hellas II* case. It has also analysed the reasons for the popularity of the pre-pack administrations in this context. For foreign companies there is an incentive to move their COMI to the UK to take advantage of the administration process with its speed of appointment of the administrator and the ability to effectuate a pre-packed business sale. In other jurisdictions, comparable processes involve significantly greater court and/or creditor consultation, which may derail prospects of achieving a consensual deal.

Whether this trend is a good or bad thing can be judged from different perspectives. At micro-level, forum shopping increases competition between different jurisdictions and allows companies to reap the rewards of more efficient and responsive insolvency regimes. Also, the author largely agrees with a test that would deem COMI-shifting and forum arbitrage that gives rise to a different distribution scheme with the intention of benefiting certain stakeholders at the expense of others as an abuse of procedure. At the same time, applying a comprehensive test to prevent suspicious COMI-shifting would involve considerable cost and uncertainty given the considerable divergence between the national insolvency laws and policy. The EIR is currently undergoing reform to introduce further measures to control abusive and non-genuine COMI migration and prevent dishonest forum shopping, including the expended scope and a mandatory three-month time limit.

At the macro-level, COMI-migration can be seen as a manifestation of competition of insolvency laws throughout Europe. This competition between jurisdictions may encourage countries to improve their insolvency and restructuring laws to avoid their national companies moving their COMI to another jurisdiction in order to raise the likelihood of achieving a consensual corporate rescue deal. The popularity of pre-packs calls, to some extent, for an advanced level of harmonisation of substantive national insolvency law and deeper integration at European level, thereby more evenly spreading the efficiency gains of the pre-pack approach.

With the advent of more rescue-friendly proceedings increasingly being made available in other Member States and the raised bar for COMI-shifting in the recast EIR, one may expect that forum shopping by companies wishing to avail themselves of the UK pre-packs will gradually lose its attractiveness. Nevertheless, EIR reforms will take more than two years to come into effect and implementation of other legislative changes into substantive national insolvency laws will probably take even longer. Thus, provision of a more even European playing field for forum shopping through harmonisation is still a long way off.

PART V

Conclusion

9. Conclusion

SUMMARY OF FINDINGS AND CRITICAL REFLECTIONS

The most important development in contemporary insolvency law and practice is a marked shift in insolvency culture, with a greater emphasis placed on company rescue and going-concern value preservation. In line with this shift towards a rescue culture is the rise of the pre-pack approach to conduct corporate rescue, arguably rendering insolvency proceedings more cost-effective. As a result, the pre-pack approach plays an increasingly important role in corporate rescue. In the main it offers the clear benefit that it allows a clear pre-arranged exit and therefore it streamlines the process and makes it faster and more flexible. At the same time, the pre-pack approach to corporate rescue is fraught with controversy. While the goals of speed and transaction-cost economisation may be achieved under the current framework, the democratic aspect, representativeness in the decision-making and procedural inclusiveness, is often aggravated.

Accordingly, the true challenge is in devising a diagnostic mechanism to permit pre-packs that are beneficial, while discouraging their opportunistic use. But the ongoing theoretical debate has yet to come with any agreed working standard to measure trade-offs between different goals. The first obstacle is that the process itself presents inherent uncertainty regarding realisable value and ongoing commercial viability and trade-offs have to be judged in particular contexts and cannot be pre-ordained according to a fixed set of rules.

The absence of precise benchmarks means that the task of deciding how the multiple objectives should be weighed and traded against each other is largely left to the legitimate decision-maker(s) who enjoy considerable discretion. Who should be assigned to perform this most important duty? Different jurisdictions take different approaches, and behind the different approaches to regulation may lie different cultural attitudes toward debt forgiveness, corporate financing practice and different political and economic considerations. However, the fundamental questions underpinning corporate rescue are the same:

(1) Who is the more capable decision-maker to determine the best outcome of a rescue process, given that most corporate rescue scenarios demand creativity, skill, judgment, anticipation and taking into consideration the uncertainty of the impact?
(2) If the decision-maker has to be afforded considerable discretionary powers with regard to commercial decision-making so that decisions can be made in a timely manner, is there a workable check on the exercise of those powers, without impending the flexibility of the process, so as to ensure that that right decisions are made?

In an attempt to address these questions and provide some answers, this book has examined the challenges brought by the pre-pack way of rescue from a comparative perspective and has discussed in depth the different approaches in dealing with its opportunistic use. The preceding chapters have offered a critical analysis of the law and practice of pre-packaged insolvency arrangements in the UK, the USA and in key EU jurisdictions. In this context the different strands of analysis have explored the strengths and weakness of pre-packaged arrangements in the respective jurisdictions from a comparative perspective. The book has also examined the latest UK proposals for reform of the applicable framework, as the problem of business sales to connected parties is more acute in the UK. One thing that comparative analysis highlights is that pre-pack rescue mechanisms reflect the legal, political and cultural context of the countries that have developed them. At the same time existing arrangements are increasingly put under pressure from fast-changing corporate finance markets and competition. So any new approaches to pre-pack regulation must have regard for the legal traditions and institutional constrains to achieve what is necessary and appropriate.

The pre-pack approach is frequently employed in business rescue through going-concern sales, exemplified by the UK pre-pack sales in administration and the US s 363(b) pre-plan sales under Chapter 11. The efficacy of the accelerated sales path through a formal procedure is often questioned, as it entails an increased risk of erroneous undervaluation caused by fast sales (fire sales). The need for speed often leaves non-participating creditors with very little opportunity to evaluate the case, and the short timeframe limits the ability of potential investors to gather information and bid, and more critically, the short timeframe works as a defensive strategy by limiting the ability of general creditors to react.

Arguably, the UK pre-pack administration is surrounded by considerable controversy due to the frequency of the phenomenon of business sales to connected parties. Lack of impartial monitoring in the UK law of pre-packs creates a risk that pre-formal negotiations are carried out in a self-serving manner by insiders. UK law places its full faith in a neutral decision-making body, namely, the administrator. In seeking measures to lessen the controversy, primary emphasis therefore has been placed on the accountability of the insolvency practitioners involved in the process, with heightened standards of disclosure designed to protect creditors from opportunistic behaviour.

This alone, however, cannot adequately address the conflict of interest issues that may be present in connected sales for two reasons: (1) because the assumption that the administrator will fulfil a neutral decision-making function becomes questionable when it comes to the delicate matter of business sales to connected parties. (2) heightened ex post disclosure requirements may effectively facilitate a creditor challenge against pre-packaged arrangements, but they do not address the underlying problem of asymmetric information ex ante in the decision-making during the pre-packing stage, which is at the root of potential managerial opportunism, although the latter is often the driving force behind the sale. Lessening the controversy necessitates establishing a level playing field at the pre-packing stage with appropriate sanitising measures to cleanse the taint of questionable connected pre-pack sales and adequately check and curtail questionable business sale arrangements.

US bankruptcy law has premised its governance structure on a regulatory system that attracts much intervention from the bankruptcy courts. Because of the existence of the judicial approval mechanism under Chapter 11, the US pre-packaged Chapter 11 regulates the pre-formal stage by imposing additional restraints on pre-petition solicitation and voting through information disclosure requirements and giving interested parties the chance to be heard prior to its implementation. This warrants creditors having a place at the negotiation table and therefore performing a certain supervisory role. By replicating the conditions of arm's length bargaining to ensure that the reorganisation plan is 'fairly' bargained in the pre-pack route, it liberates the courts from engaging in substantively evaluating the economics of business transactions.

But this is not the case for the s 363(b) pre-plan sales in Chapter 11 where requisite procedural protections, especially those accompanied in the plan confirmation process, may be bypassed or summarily discarded. In the absence of a negotiated resolution between the debtor and the affected creditors, the bankruptcy courts are left to stand astride complex valuation disputes, as a decision of a bankruptcy court approving a sale becomes the last sanitising measure before its completion. This, however, not only runs counter to the judicial trend of moving away from substantive review of the business merits of particular transactions, but may also assign to the courts an uncomfortable role, which is different from its traditional role of ensuring that the legislative standards that have been laid down are fully compliant in the negotiation and decision-making process. This begs the old question – are courts really better placed and well-enough equipped to tackle the issues and meet the challenge involved in matters of commercial judgment?

The book also examined three key European civil law jurisdictions (France, Germany and the Netherlands) on their deployment of a pre-pack approach in introducing new and/or improved procedures that may promote and achieve better possibilities for company rescue. In all three countries, the courts play an important role in substituting or retaining most of the safeguard mechanisms built to protect the procedural fairness under a standard insolvency procedure. It is done by introducing a monitor at the stage of private pre-formal negotiations. Thus the speed element of pre-packaged arrangements remains but the process becomes subject to the same set of requirements as non-pre-packed arrangements. A common procedural safeguard appearing in the continental pre-pack approaches is to place a neutral and well-informed party to serve as a proxy for creditors in the course of the pre-pack negotiations. This does not just mean that there is procedural judicial scrutiny from the outset, but also that there is some court-coordinated control keeping the balance of competing interests throughout the process. This mechanism ensures adequate monitoring of decision-making and some respects of existing safeguards and legal constraints.

Furthermore, the book also examined the use of pre-packs in the context of cross-border insolvency forum shopping, which has increased in popularity in recent years. This is not incidental because many distressed companies have been pushed to effect business sales as a result of a mixture of difficult trade conditions during the recent financial turmoil and ensuing economic slowdown as well as fraught relations with creditor classes. These conditions included: an inability to obtain new bank loans to refinance existing debt; a lack of liquidity; and a lack of investors willing to offer fresh capital.

Since comparable processes in other jurisdictions might have involved significantly greater court and/or creditor consultation, which could have derailed the prospects of reaching a consensual deal, the UK administration procedure attracted attention for its swift appointment of administrators and its ability to effectuate a pre-packed business sale. More importantly the recent increase in insolvency forum shopping and COMI migration has had two repercussions: (1) it highlighted the (in)ability of continental European jurisdictions to minimise the holdout problem and the (in)flexibility of coping with the commercial requirement of swift action and (2) this trend has to some extent motivated an increased harmonisation of activity of substantive national insolvency law at the European level. Arguably, EU legislators have an important role to play in ensuring that interaction between national insolvency laws through COMI-shifting inspires a healthy level of competition (as opposed to a 'race to the bottom') among national insolvency law-makers within Europe.

SUGGESTIONS FOR IMPROVING UK PRE-PACKS

The UK takes a discretionary approach with regard to insolvency decision-making, as the law places a significant amount of faith in the expertise and experience of the insolvency practitioners, giving them a key role in governing insolvency proceedings. Nevertheless, the conventional balance of control between the board of directors and an appointed administrator could be reversed in the context of pre-pack sales. This is especially true in connected pre-pack sales. The risk of administrators favouring better placed creditors or managers involved in the sale is not theoretical. This finding inevitably casts questions on the effectiveness and legitimacy of the pre-pack administrations being used in achieving sensitive business sales where the business is sold back to the existing management.

In seeking credible and impartial monitoring of pre-pack administrations in the UK, further steps must be taken. Proposals have been made to add additional safeguards to the process by allowing the invocation of verification by an independent (successive or second) insolvency practitioner, or by requiring the approval of the court or of creditors. A practical constraint in placing such controls in rescue proceedings is that it would likely increase the cost of the procedure. This may happen directly by means of additional professional fees and procedural expenses as well as indirectly, as any delay and uncertainty will run the risk of losing the support of other players or creating a considerable detriment to the value of the business.

In ensuring a level playing field at the pre-packing stage with appropriate sanitising measures to cleanse the taint of questionable connected pre-pack sales and adequately check and frustrate questionable business sale arrangements, it is worth considering heightening monitoring through the use of three independent routes.

The first recommendation refers to strengthening the quality of the procedure for the appointment of administrators to minimise the concern over the insolvency practitioners' self-serving alliance with any insiders involved in the transaction in connected pre-packs. It is, thus, worth considering whether to impose some restrictions on the directors' or/and the company's power to appoint an insolvency practitioner as administrator via the out-of-court route when the proposed arrangement involves a sale of the business to a connected party. What is required is to mandate that in the absence of a QFC holder, the directors and/or the company may only make an out-of-court appointment where there is no objection from major creditors, either HMRC or other unsecured creditors who are owed a considerable amount of credit by the company concerned. This proposal would avoid the need for judicial intervention at the outset, and it would assist in ensuring that the process is more transparent to the larger creditors, at least, by virtue of the compulsory consultation.

The second proposed measure refers to an improvement of accountability and augmenting the quality of relevant decision-making. This may be achieved by requiring administrators to provide a 'sensitivity analysis' or something similar in their report. The 'sensitivity analysis' will illustrate to stakeholders in the case of connected pre-pack sales not only the relevant projections or appraisals underpinning such key decisions as the timing of the sale and any relevant substantial agreement, e.g. the necessity of entering into a binding/lock-up agreement with a particular purchaser, but also the impact of changes in major assumptions on which such projections or appraisals are based, for example, the likelihood of securing any new financing or the possibility of finding any other bidders. In composing those alternative scenarios in their 'sensitivity analysis', administrators would illustrate the rationales of how they make judgements and form strategies to the best of their abilities in a situation involving a significant change in the ongoing commercial viability. Such a 'sensitivity analysis' would allow creditors to gain additional insight into the various factors contributing to the final disposal of the business and assets of the company and enable them to comprehend the complexity of the commercial reality.

The third recommendation refers to strengthening the system of sanctioning insolvency practitioners over unprofessional, improper or unethical behaviour. A review of the administrator's decision-making process can be triggered by filing complaints against individual insolvency practitioners. A new single gateway through which complaints are directed in the first instance is already in place in order to make procedures for handling the complaints of insolvency practitioners more straightforward and efficient. Yet the framework could be further strengthened. One of the proposals set out in the 2014 Consultation on Strengthening the Regulatory Regime of the Insolvency Profession is to enhance the powers of the Insolvency Service as the oversight regulator dealing with misconduct and abuse. It was proposed to grant the Insolvency Service (acting on behalf of the Secretary of State) a power to directly sanction an insolvency practitioner on public interest grounds, or to apply to the court directly to sanction a practitioner, but principal responsibility for dealing with poor behaviour by IPs would remain with the RPBs. What is suggested here though is that this power should be more extensive and used more widely and not just in exceptional circumstances where the reputation of the profession and the insolvency regime is involved as the original proposal suggests.

Corporate rescue is a challenging process both in legal and economic terms. It is surrounded by inherent uncertainty regarding realisable value and the fairness of the solution for different stakeholders, Therefore, the successful conclusion of rescue proceedings demands creativity, skill, judgment and integrity. The popularity of the pre-pack approach in corporate rescue has risen on the back of the assertion that the capacity of a full-blown insolvency procedure in capturing going-concern value in ailing businesses, either by rescuing the company or by selling the business as a going concern, is limited due to its built-in devices for procedural inclusiveness and decision-making democracy. The pre-pack approach is widely viewed as a pragmatic way to introduce the required speed in business sales. Thus, its reputation must be safeguarded. The critical analysis undertaken by this book in a comparative context has shown that there is both the need and the room for improvement. Implementation of the recommendations presented above could go a long way towards redressing the accepted weakness of the current framework for pre-pack administrations in the UK. It will further enhance the quality of the process and its reputation without prejudicing its distinct advantages in terms of procedural speed and business efficiency.

Index